FROMM

EasyGuide

TO

DISNEY WORLD, UNIVERSAL STUDIOS & ORLANDO 2015

By
Jason Cochran

Easy Guides are ✦ Quick To Read ✦ Light To Carry
✦ For Expert Advice ✦ In All Price Ranges

FrommerMedia LLC

Published by
FROMMER MEDIA LLC

ISBN 978-1-62887-092-3 (paper), 978-1-62887-093-0 (e-book)

Editorial Director: Pauline Frommer
Editor: Melissa Klurman
Production Editor: Heather Wilcox
Cartographer: Roberta Stockwell
Cover Design: Howard Grossman

For information on our other products or services, see www.frommers.com.

Frommer Media LLC also publishes its books in a variety of electronic formats. Some content that
appears in print may not be available in electronic formats.

Manufactured in the United States of America

5 4 3 2 1

AN IMPORTANT NOTE

The world is a dynamic place. Hotels change ownership, restaurants hike their prices, museums
alter their opening hours, and buses and trains change their routings. And all this can occur in
the several months after our authors have visited, inspected, and written about these hotels,
restaurants, museums and transportation services. Though we have made valiant efforts to keep
all our information fresh and up-to-date, some few changes can inevitably occur in the periods
before a revised edition of this guidebook is published. So please bear with us if a tiny number
of the details in this book have changed. Please also note that we have no responsibility or liability for any inaccuracy or errors or omissions, or for inconvenience, loss, damage, or expenses
suffered by anyone as a result of assertions in this guide.

CONTENTS

ABOUT THE AUTHOR

Jason Cochran was awarded Guide Book of the Year by the Society of American Travel Writers' Lowell Thomas Travel Journalism Competition for this book. He also won the award for his guide to London, which he writes for Frommer's, and he is the author of the London, Orlando, and San Francisco guides for the Pauline Frommer series. He has written for publications including "The New York Post," "Travel + Leisure," "USA Today," and "Scanorama" (Sweden) and been on staff at "Entertainment Weekly," "Budget Travel," and AOL Travel (Executive Editor). He devised questions for the first American prime-time season of "Who Wants to Be a Millionaire" (ABC) and produced and hosted "AfterShark," the AOL post-show for Mark Burnett's "Shark Tank" (ABC). He has appeared as a commentator on, among others, "CBS This Morning," "The Early Show" (CBS), "BBC World," "Good Morning America," CNN, BBC World, and the CBC, and he is a video host on AOL. He is an alumnus of Northwestern University's Medill School of Journalism and New York University's Graduate Music Theatre Writing Program and editor of Frommers.com.

Thank you to all the cast members and staff members who assisted with information, access, and good humor. I also can't imagine doing without the on-the-ground assistance of Shanon Larimer, Wesley Brown, Jason Young, Tracy Temple, Kristin Harmel, Ken Kleiber, Katie Coleman (still), and Denise Spiegel and Heidi Colon of Visit Orlando. Finally, I am grateful to Arthur and Pauline Frommer. Their ideal of helping people of all means see the world with plainspoken, honest advice remains a beacon in an overwhelming ocean of information, and it continues to be an inspiration for many, including me.

ABOUT THE FROMMER'S TRAVEL GUIDES

For most of the past 50 years, Frommer's has been the leading series of travel guides in North America, accounting for as many as 24 percent of all guidebooks sold. I think I know why.

Although we hope our books are entertaining, we nevertheless deal with travel in a serious fashion. Our guidebooks have never looked on such journeys as a mere recreation, but as a far more important human function, a time of learning and introspection, an essential part of a civilized life. We stress the culture, lifestyle, history, and beliefs of the destinations we cover and urge our readers to seek out people and new ideas as the chief rewards of travel.

We have never shied from controversy. We have, from the beginning, encouraged our authors to be intensely judgmental, critical—both pro and con—in their comments, and wholly independent. Our only clients are our readers, and we have triggered the ire of countless prominent sorts, from a tourist newspaper we called "practically worthless" (it unsuccessfully sued us) to the many rip-offs we've condemned.

And because we believe that travel should be available to everyone regardless of their incomes, we have always been cost-conscious at every level of expenditure. Although we have broadened our recommendations beyond the budget category, we insist that every lodging we include be sensibly priced. We use every form of media to assist our readers and are particularly proud of our feisty daily website, the award-winning Frommers.com.

I have high hopes for the future of Frommer's. May these guidebooks, in all the years ahead, continue to reflect the joy of travel and the freedom that travel represents. May they always pursue a cost-conscious path, so that people of all incomes can enjoy the rewards of travel. And may they create, for both the traveler and the persons among whom we travel, a community of friends, where all human beings live in harmony and peace.

Arthur Frommer

THE BEST OF ORLANDO

In 1886, a young unmarried mailman, frustrated with his fruitless toil in the Midwest, moved to the woolly wilderness of Central Florida to make a better go of life. The land was angry. Summers were oppressively hot, the lightning relentless, and the tough earth, sodden and scrubby, defied clearing. The only domestic creatures that thrived there, it seemed, were the cattle, and even they turned out stringy and chewy. Undaunted, the young man planted a grove of citrus trees and waited for things to get better. They didn't. His trees died in a freeze. Now penniless, he was forced to return to delivering mail, the very thing he had tried so hard to escape. By 1890, he gave up, defeated, and moved to Chicago to seek other work. The American dream appeared to fail Elias Disney.

The story could have ended there. But he was joined by his new bride, whose own father had died trying to tame Florida land. Back in the smoke of the Midwest, they had children and settled for an anonymous urban existence. One day, 8 decades later, long after the young man and woman had lived full lives and passed away, two of their sons, now in the sunset of their own lives, would return to Central Florida, to the land that broke their father, and together they would transform the recalcitrant swamp into the most famous fantasy land the world has even known.

Little did Elias know that the dream was only skipping a generation and that his sons Walt and Roy would become synonymous with the same land that rejected him. Had he known that the Disney name would in due time define Central Florida, would he have been so despondent? Even if he had been granted a fleeting vision of what was to be, and what his family would mean to this place—and, indeed, to the United States—would he have believed it?

The Disney brothers turned a place of toil into a realm of pleasure, a place where hardworking people can put their struggles aside. The English have Blackpool; Canadians have Niagara Falls. Orlando rose to become the preeminent resort for the working and middle classes of America, and the ingenuity of its inventions inspires visitors from everywhere. Although other countries segregate their holiday destinations by income or some other petty quality, Orlando, in classic American egalitarian style, is all things to all people, from all countries and backgrounds.

Orlando represents something more powerful to American culture and history than merely being the fruit of a dream. It's something shared. No matter who you are, no matter your politics or upbringing, when you were a kid, you probably went at least once to Walt Disney World and Orlando— or, if you didn't, you desperately wanted to. Which other aspect of culture can we all claim to share? What else has given children such sweet dreams? I've often said that if somehow Walt Disney World went out of business tomorrow, the U.S. National Park Service would have to take it over—it means that much to the fabric of the nation.

Don't think of the amusements of Orlando as big business. Of course they are, and the incessant reminder of that often threatens to shatter the fantasy. But Walt Disney World, and by extension Orlando, is Americana incarnate. The flair for showmanship and fantasy that they crystallize, now coined as the term "Disneyfication," is the defining mind-set of our culture, in which even grocery stores are dressed like film sets and the "story" of your local burger joint is retold on the side of its beverage cups.

Orlando tells us about who we dream of being. Virtually nothing about it is natural or authentic, and yet there may be no more perfect embodiment of American culture. To understand this invented landscape is to understand the values of its civilization and our generation. And if you observe Orlando with a long view—starting with young Elias Disney cutting his hands trying to budge a tough Florida pine—you will be a part of the explosive, unexpected powers of the American dream.

And one more thing: If you can buck the system and relax, it's a hell of a lot of fun.

ORLANDO'S best
THEME PARK EXPERIENCES

o **Walt Disney World:** Walt Disney World operates four top-drawer theme parks every day of the year: **Magic Kingdom,** the most popular theme park on Earth, is a more spacious iteration of the original Disneyland, the park that started it all, and is brimming with attractions that have been cherished since Walt's day; **Epcot** is a new-brew version of an old-style world's fair; **Disney's Animal Kingdom** blends animal habitats with theme-park panache; and **Disney's Hollywood Studios** presents a show-heavy salute to the movies.

o **Universal Orlando:** Often surpassing Disney in adrenaline and cunning, Universal Orlando's two parks, **Islands of Adventure** and **Universal Studios Florida,** command great respect and get the blood pumping a bit stronger and are home to immersive sections devoted to **The Wizarding World of Harry Potter.**

o **Beyond Disney and Universal:** Venture beyond the Big Six theme parks and you'll find more breathing room and more focused experiences. The gardens and marine mammals at **SeaWorld Orlando** make for a slower-paced excursion. Five water parks flow with energy: **Typhoon Lagoon** and **Aquatica** for family-friendly slides, **Blizzard Beach** for more aggressive ones, **Wet 'n Wild** for no-holds-barred thrills, and **Discovery Cove** for VIP swims with dolphins and reef fish. South of town, **Legoland Florida,** one of the best parks for very small children, charms with Old Florida touches, while **Gatorland** celebrates the region's *true* locals.

ORLANDO'S best
RIDES & SHOWS

o **Walt Disney World:** More than any other park, the **Magic Kingdom** (p. 27) is packed with seminal experiences: the transporting Audio-Animatronic wizardry of **Pirates of the Caribbean** and **The Haunted Mansion;** the vertiginous thrills of **Splash Mountain** and **Space Mountain;** and the homespun, only-at-Disney charm of **Jungle Cruise, Peter Pan's Flight,** and **"it's a small world."** Cap the day with **Wishes,** the famous fireworks show. At **Epcot** (p. 53), **Soarin'** is the ride with the resort's highest re-ride ratio, and at Disney's **Hollywood Studios** (p. 70), the ride-through 3-D video game **Toy Story Midway Mania** is never the same experience twice, while the **Twilight Zone Tower of Terror** has an innovative design repeated nowhere else in the world.

o **Universal Orlando:** At **Islands of Adventure** (p. 115), **Harry Potter and the Forbidden Journey** fires on more technological cylinders than you thought a ride could possess, while **The Amazing Adventure of Spider-Man** has been the standard holder for premium ride concepts for more than a decade. But don't miss **Dudley Do-Right's Ripsaw Falls** or **Popeye & Bluto's Bilge-Rat Barges,** a pair of ingeniously sopping flumes. **The Wizarding World of Harry Potter: Diagon Alley** is a blockbuster representing the cutting edge in visual design that believably immerses you in the world of the movies and the **Escape from Gringotts** ride is a tour de force like none other. Fans of Springfield will find themselves re-riding **The Simpsons Ride** to catch all the insider references.

o **The Other Parks:** At SeaWorld Orlando (p. 126), roller coasters pack punches that Disney pulls: **Manta** flies riders belly-down over water and rooftops, while **Kraken** dangles their feet for seven spine-knotting inversions. Its two polar pavilions, **Wild Arctic** and **Antarctica,** are among its best habitats. The spectacular killer whale show, currently **One Ocean,** is perennially packed (p. 129). Elsewhere, Wet 'n Wild's **Bomb Bay** (p. 144) is one of the most sadistic water slides ever devised, while Legoland Florida's tricked-out **Miniland USA** (p. 137) is such a tour de force of Lego creation that it's a show of its own.

ORLANDO'S best
OVERLOOKED EXPERIENCES

o **From Earth to the Moon:** The **Kennedy Space Center** (p. 152) sent Americans into space for more than half a century, and for decades NASA's nerve center was the focus of tourist attention, but a majority of today's visitors remain securely within Disney's orbit. That's a huge shame. The Kennedy Center is where you can see proof of America's glory days as an exploratory power, including some out-of-this-world space vehicles such as the **Saturn V rocket,** the largest rocket made, which sent 27 men to the moon, and the **Space Shuttle orbiter** *Atlantis,* still coated with space dust. You can even undergo astronaut training.

o **Connecting with Others:** More Make-a-Wish kids request visits to Orlando than anywhere else, and you can help make their dreams come true at the fantasy resort built just for them, **Give Kids the World Village** (p. 151) in Kissimmee. There are hundreds of jobs for volunteers here (which can be done in just a few hours), including handing out presents or scooping ice cream. And since the late 1800s, the moss-draped **Cassadaga** (p. 146) has been the domain of psychics and mediums who invite visitors to explore their spiritualist town for readings.

o **Undiscovered Disney:** Even inside the theme parks, as other guests stampede for the nearest thrill ride, you can find relatively off-the-beaten-path treasures. The most fruitful ground for those is **Epcot**'s World Showcase, where many pavilions contain little-seen museums to the heritage of their lands, including the **Stave Church Gallery** in Norway (p. 62), China's **House of the Whispering Willow** (p. 63), the **Bijutsu-kan Gallery** in Japan (p. 65), and the **Gallery of Arts and History** in

Morocco (p. 65). At the Magic Kingdom, you can get a haircut on Main Street's **Harmony Barber Shop** (p. 34). At Disney's Hollywood Studios, the artifact-stuffed **AFI exhibition** (p. 77) is a display like none other in WDW. And the entire Disney World resort offers a slate of small-group **behind-the-scenes tours** (p. 97) that uncover hundreds of secrets.

ORLANDO'S best AUTHENTIC EXPERIENCES

o **Florida, Your Eden:** Although the theme parks have come to define Orlando, Central Florida has a long tale of its own, if you're willing to listen. There are more fresh springs here than in any other American state. You'll always remember swimming in the 72-degree waters of **De Leon Springs State Park** (p. 159), canoeing them at **Wekiwa Springs State Park** (p. 160), or meeting the at-risk manatees in their natural habitat at **Blue Spring State Park** (p. 159).

o **Florida, the Gilded Age Idyll:** Of course, Orlando's identity as a sunny theme-park mecca only began in 1971, but visitors from the north have been coming for a century. Sample the high art collected by its high-society settlers at Winter Park's **Charles Hosmer Morse Museum of American Art** (including a massive collection of Tiffany glass; p. 147) or the **Cornell Fine Arts Museum** (with lush decorative arts of every description; p. 148). Peep at their historic mansions, whose lawns slope invitingly to the tranquil lakes of Winter Park, on the long-running **Scenic Boat Tour** (p. 161).

o **Florida, Land of Flowers:** The reason all those blue bloods migrated here? The fine weather and the beautiful water. The horticultural achievements at **Harry P. Leu Gardens** (p. 160), practically smack in downtown Orlando, remind you just how bountiful the soil here can be. Or lose yourself at **Bok Tower Gardens** (p. 148); its builder set out to create a Taj Mahal for America, and its landscaping is by Frederick Law Olmsted, Jr., whose other work includes the White House and the National Mall.

o **Florida, the Original Tourist Draw:** Today, nothing is more quintessentially Orlando than Disney, but a few other major attractions never feel jammed: **Legoland Florida** (p. 137) ambles pleasantly on a lakeside that was once home to Cypress Gardens, Florida's original mega-park and a haunt for everyone from Esther Williams to Elvis Presley. Its historic botanical garden has been prized since the 1930s. **Gatorland** (p. 149) is a pleasing, corn-fed throwback from an era when Central Florida was synonymous with reptiles rather than the Mouse.

ORLANDO'S best HOTELS

o **Inside the Theme Park Resorts:** Disney's **Contemporary Resort** (p. 202) and **Disney's Polynesian Resort** (p. 203), which opened in 1971, have become architectural landmarks, and their location on the monorail system makes a vacation easy and fun, but the **Disney's Art of Animation Resort** (p. 207) elevates the resort's lowest-priced rooms into something approaching immersive. Universal's newly opened **Cabana Bay Beach Resort** (p. 211) applies a layer of Miami style on its own budget category, and the new **Four Seasons Resort Orlando** on Walt Disney World property delivers a level of luxury that's a revelation among theme park hotels (p. 208).

- **Full-Service Resorts outside the Parks:** Exquisite restaurants and unbeatable pool areas made the Grande Lakes' **JW Marriott** and the **Ritz-Carlton** (p. 220) two names to beat among Orlando's luxury resorts, while **Nickelodeon Suites** (p. 214), rocking with extravagant pool areas and nonstop entertainment, rules in full-service fun for kids. Taking theme-park flair to a hospitality extreme, the colossal atrium of **Gaylord Palms** (p. 212) is like a big top for eye candy.

- **Affordability without Sacrifice:** Not all affordable hotels are shabby. New arrivals **Crowne Plaza Orlando–Lake Buena Vista** (p. 217), **Drury Inn Suites** (p. 220), **Avanti Resort Orlando** (p. 223), and **Fairfield Inn Orlando International Drive/ Convention Center** (p. 223) can buy you a just-built room near the action for around $100 a night, while the **B Resort** (p. 209) puts you in a South Beach–styled resort right on Disney property for the middle $100s. **WorldQuest Resort** (p. 218– 219) and **Meliá Orlando Suite Hotel at Celebration** (p. 215) have style and space but not the crowds and offer one-bedroom units from $129. Or rent a full house, as tastefully furnished as if you lived there, from **All Star Vacation Homes** (p. 225).

ORLANDO'S best RESTAURANTS

- **The Most Memorable Meals at the Resorts:** Orlando is one of those places where even blasé restaurants are priced like splurges, but some special-occasion tables get you the most bang for your buck, including **California Grill** (overlooking the Magic Kingdom fireworks from atop the Contemporary Resort; p. 172), **Todd English's bluezoo** or **Deep Blu** (serving impeccable fish; p. 173 and p. 172), **Boma** (an all-you-can-eat feast in a hotel where you can watch African animals roam; p. 172); and the famous **character meals,** where your fuzzy hosts serve up family memories (p. 191).

- **Finding Family-Run Places to Eat:** Some fabulous restaurants, many family-run, have been unfairly elbowed into the background by same-old, also-ran chains. Orlando's real-world selection puts Epcot's World Showcase to shame, and at a fraction of the price: **Bruno's Italian Restaurant** (*abbondanza!* right in the franchise zone of Disney, too!; p. 178); **Nile Ethiopian Cuisine** (authentically African, down to the coffee ceremony, near Disney; p. 184); **Havana's Cuban Cuisine** (the real stuff, from steak to plantains, right by Disney; p. 180); and **Arepas El Cacao** (p. 185), whose overstuffed Venezuelan flatbread sandwiches first gained area popularity as food truck fare.

- **Big Style, Local Flavors:** Get in touch with the locals: The veggie chili at the friendly hangout **Dandelion Communitea Cafe** (p. 187) is to die for, and the quirky personalities of homegrown **Funky Monkey Wine Company** (p. 181) and **Maxine's on Shine** (p. 187) are seductive fun. Above all, the sensationally priced Vietnamese district of **Mills 50** (p. 188) is a revelation. Yes, as it turns out, there are still dining secrets in this town.

SUGGESTED ITINERARIES & ORLANDO'S LAYOUT

The executives at Disney Parks don't want you to simply show up and have a spontaneous experience. They want to lock you into a timetable beforehand, scheduling your day like a military invasion, and they will pressure you to submit to the burden of pre-planning. Disney Parks president Jay Rasulo was recently shockingly frank about the tactic in *Bloomberg Businessweek*: "If we can get people to plan their vacation before they leave home, we know that we get more time with them. We get a bigger share of their wallet."

But excessive pre-planning isn't fun for *you*. Too much research spoils the delight of Disney's many surprises. What's worse, a rigorous itinerary of appointments adds stress to what's supposed to be your carefree vacation, and if you're not careful you'll spend half your time at Disney hunched over your smartphone, battery rapidly dwindling, trying to keep up with your own plan.

That's where the "Frommer's Easy Guide" comes in. This is the guidebook for the rest of us—for those of us who refuse to turn planning a Disney vacation into a part-time job and who remember that we go to Orlando to unwind and have fun. This is the book that knows how to navigate the patterns of these American treasures without obsessing over every nuance, and it embellishes enjoyment with context about what you're experiencing. You don't have to submit to the pressure of microscopic overplanning to have the whole World in your hands.

The routes suggested here, loose enough to let the magic in, prioritize what's worth seeing and when. Observe the basic park patterns and you'll do just fine. These itineraries assume mild lines (so, not peak season), and if you would like to try a specific table-service restaurant, it's imperative you arrive with reservations, particularly for Cinderella's Royal Table and Be Our Guest. Instructions on how to schedule Fastpass are on p. 25.

ORLANDO IN 1 DAY

Well, I'm sorry for you. Just as it's impossible to eat an entire box of Velveeta in one sitting (please don't try), you can't get the full breadth of Orlando in a single day.

THE SIX BIGGEST DISNEY mistakes

1. **Overplanning.** Disney World minutiae opens a deeper rabbit hole than Alice's.
2. **Underplanning.** You must plan a little or pay a price: To eat at the best sit-down restaurants or enjoy a character meal, it's wise to reserve 3 to 6 months out.
3. **Overpurchasing** ticket options. Don't bite off more than you can chew.
4. **Wearing inadequate footwear.** It's said you'll walk 10 miles a day.
5. **Neglecting sunscreen and water.** Even Florida's cloudy weather can burn. One bad day can ruin the ones that follow.
6. **Pushing kids too hard.** When they want to slow down, indulge them. You came here to enjoy yourselves, remember?

Today: Make It a Magic Kingdom Day ★★★

Thankfully, one Orlando attraction is so quintessential that you can enjoy it all by itself: Walt Disney World's **Magic Kingdom** (p. 27). In chapter 3, I recommend three custom itineraries (p. 32) for how to parse your time—with or without kids—but no matter your age or inclination, don't miss the great Disney Audio-Animatronic odysseys **Pirates of the Caribbean ★★★**, **Haunted Mansion ★★★**, and **"it's a small world" ★★★**, and be sure to brave the drops of **Splash Mountain ★★★** and **Space Mountain ★★★**. While you're there, take a free spin on the iconic **monorail** through the iconic **Contemporary Resort** after you connect for the free round-trip ride to **Epcot** (p. 53), where you'll see the other top Disney park from above. Stay until closing, through the **parade** and **fireworks,** or, if you've had enough, head to a quintessentially kitschy dinner banquet spectacle, such as **the Hoop-Dee-Doo Musical Revue ★★** (p. 191). Hope you're not hungry for subtlety!

ORLANDO IN 2 DAYS

Nope, still can't do much, but in two sleeps you can still get a few flavors in.

Day 1: Magic Kingdom

Get the same early start as recommended in "Orlando in 1 Day" and follow the **Magic Kingdom** plan for sure.

Day 2: Universal Orlando ★★★ & Epcot ★★★

Today, be at **Universal Orlando** (p. 100), one of the most attractive theme park complexes in the country, for opening. At its **Studios** park, dive into the new Diagon Alley, the section of the **Wizarding World of Harry Potter ★★★** that opened in July 2014, before the lines grow. Explore the shops, full of bespoke souvenirs and snacks you can only buy here, and give your system a dose of Butterbeer. After lunch at the **Leaky Cauldron ★★★**, you have a decision to make. You can take the **Hogwarts Express** train to **Islands of Adventure** (you'll need a second park ticket) to tour the second Potter land of **Hogsmeade,** take a spin on the superlative **Amazing Adventures of Spider-Man ★★★**, and jolt yourself on **The Incredible Hulk Coaster** ★★★. Or you can drag yourself to pass a few hours in **Epcot** (p. 53). From Universal, drive west on Interstate 4 and take the exit for Epcot. At Epcot, be sure to visit **Future World,** including **Soarin'** ★★★ and the traditional Disney experience, **Spaceship Earth** ★★★, but make your way clockwise around **World Showcase** by dinnertime to select the ethnic eatery that catches your fancy, be it in **Mexico** ★★★, **Japan** ★★★, or **Morocco** ★★★. Or stop at the central **U.S.A.** ★★★ pavilion for a good, old-fashioned hot dog. At 9pm, you'll be in the right place for **IllumiNations** ★★★, part kumbaya and part explosives spectacular.

ORLANDO IN 3 DAYS

Days 1–2: Magic Kingdom & Universal Orlando

Day 1: **Magic Kingdom,** as above. But on Day 2, slam through the highlights of the Universal parks with a 1-day, 2-park pass. In the morning, see **Islands of Adventure** ★★★, as on the second day of the 2-day plan, and fill the afternoon with Universal Studios, a 5-minute walk north. Don't neglect some of its celebrated new rides—**Transformers: The Ride—3D** ★★ and **Harry Potter and the Escape from Gringotts** ★★★ in the new **Wizarding World of Harry Potter—Diagon Alley.** Exploring that area will more than complete your day, but if you still have time, fill up on the sarcastically named dishes at **Fast Food Boulevard** (p. 114) in the new and daringly whimsical **Springfield** addition.

Day 3: SeaWorld ★★★, Disney & a Taste of "Real" Orlando

If you have small kids or you need something more subdued today, then **SeaWorld Orlando** (p. 126), with its **Shamu** show and multiple marine animal habitats, makes for a soothing change of pace. That could take a whole day if you saw every little thing and stopped to smell the flowers (and fish), but you can see the highlights in 4 hours, and you only have 3 days, after all. So cram a secondary Disney park into your afternoon and evening. **Epcot**'s a fine choice (see the afternoon of Day 2 of the 2-day itinerary for a good plan), but **Disney's Animal Kingdom**'s ★★ wildlife walking trails make a nice, easygoing complement to a morning spent at SeaWorld. Animal Kingdom isn't a late-night park, so during the evening, spend a night at the shopping-and-clubs zone of Universal's **City-Walk** ★★ (p. 157) or go out into "real" Orlando for the Vietnamese culinary delights of **Mills 50** (p. 188) downtown.

ORLANDO IN 1 WEEK

Days 1–5: Orlando at Your Leisure

Finally—you're approaching a vacation long enough to enable you to actually relax and to take time to sit by the pool. Now you don't have to cram several parks into a single day unless you want to, so take more time on your first few

Beating the Heat & Rain

Universal Orlando, with its air-conditioned shows, waiting areas, and covered parking, is the best choice to escape a **rainy day** because almost nothing must shut down in a storm. SeaWorld Orlando, where you'll spend lots of time outside, is the worst in rain. If it's a **scorcher,** both Universal Studios and Disney's Hollywood Studios have enough sheltered activities—although, of course, your hotel pool holds water as a heat reliever, too. The worst park on hot or wet days is **Disney's Animal Kingdom,** where next to nothing is indoors. But if there is a big storm, don't leave! Rain lasts all day back home, but in Florida, storms usually clear in an hour.

days: first **Magic Kingdom,** then **Universal,** then **Epcot,** then the other two Disney parks, followed by **SeaWorld.** Of course, if you stick to a schedule as rigid as one major theme park per day, it will take you a week to knock down the seven biggies, and that's before setting your belly on a single water slide. Combining **Animal Kingdom** and **Hollywood Studios** ★★★ into a single day (see p. 88 for suggestions for how to pack it all in) is doable and won't cause you to miss too much, although with the opening of the second Harry Potter land, the same can no longer be said for Universal's parks—now they require a day and a half, at least. This combination lets you do the seven major parks in 5 days.

Days 6–7: Exploring Orlando beyond the Theme Parks

Hitting the big seven in 5 days leaves 2 days to get away from the dizzying pressures of theme parking. Take a day to drive out to **Kennedy Space Center** ★★★ (p. 152), or if that's still too touristy for you, take a dip in a natural spring, such as **De Leon Springs** ★★★ (p. 159) and make a pass through the American original town of **Cassadaga** ★★★ (p. 146). It would be a shame to miss a collection as world class as **the Morse Museum**'s ★★★ (p. 147) astonishing Tiffany glass. While you're there, take a late-afternoon boat cruise past the mansions of **Winter Park** (p. 14)—when you're out on the water, you'll finally get a feeling for the "real" Florida that attracted the builders of the major resorts in the first place. Afterward, you'll be near some of Orlando's **best restaurants,** most of which the tourists never visit.

GETTING TO KNOW ORLANDO'S LAYOUT

In 1970, before the opening of Walt Disney World, Orlando was still a tourism center, attracting 660,000 people a year. But by 1999, the place was a powerhouse, with 37.9 million people visiting. During the same period, the area population skyrocketed from 344,000 to 860,000, leapfrogging old-guard American cities as St. Louis; Washington, D.C.; Boston; Baltimore; and Portland.

However, for all that growth, and despite the fact the amusements are critical to Orlando's economy, most of the population still lives north of SeaWorld. The tourist zones are segregated from residential ones. Huge chunks of your time, days at a stretch, will be spent only in the boisterous tourist corridors. Those lie along International Drive, U.S. 192 around I-4, and the Lake Buena Vista area north of exit 68 off I-4.

The Making of a Kingdom

Back when only cargo trains had much business in Central Florida, Orlando fashioned itself as a prosperous small city—some derisively called it a cow town—well positioned to serve the citrus and cattle industries as they shipped goods between America and Cuba. The city remained that way, mostly irrelevant, until around 1943, when the great cross-state cattle drives ended.

Soon after, the brick-warehouse city of Orlando developed its second personality. The turning point wasn't the arrival of Walt Disney on his secret land-buying trips. It came a decade earlier, when NASA settled into the Space Coast, 45 minutes east, and the local government, spotting opportunity, invited the Martin Marietta corporation—now Lockheed Martin—to open a massive facility off Sand Lake Road, near the present-day Convention Center. To sweeten the deal, leaders promised unprecedented civic improvements, including an unrealized high-speed rail system they're *still* bickering about. Mostly, though, politicians built roads. Florida's Turnpike to Miami was carved past the Martin plot, S.R. 50 was hammered through downtown to link the coasts, and, soon after, many blocks in the downtown area were bulldozed for the construction of I-4, linking Tampa on the west coast with Daytona Beach (then one of America's premier vacation towns) on the east coast. The new transit links made Walt lick his chops for some cheap land nearby.

Walt's new kingdom was constructed 20 miles southwest of the city in scrubland, where his planners could keep the outside world at bay. The resort was intended to be an oasis in the citrus groves, but soon, sprawl sprouted around the park's border, just as had happened in Anaheim. For the last two generations, the space between Orlando's two disparate developments has vanished, consumed by areas where "real" Orlando residents live, so that the old-fashioned, "traditional" city has come to be dwarfed, as it were, by family-friendly honky-tonk and slapped-up suburbs. Few casual visitors ever lay eyes on the real Orlando.

The Neighborhoods in Brief

Following is a breakdown of Orlando's neighborhoods—from theme parks to residential areas.

WALT DISNEY WORLD RESORT

Best for: *Space, theme parks, a sense of place, proximity to His Mouseness*

What you won't find: *Inexpensive food or lodging, a central location for anything except Disney attractions, the "real" Florida or Orlando*

Walt Disney World is at the southern end of Orlando's chain of big parks, so to see Universal, SeaWorld, and Orlando itself, you'll always head north on I-4.

When Walt Disney ordered the purchase of these 27,000 acres mostly just west of Interstate 4, he was righting a wrong he committed in the building of Anaheim's Disneyland. In commandeering as much land as he did, he ensured that visitors would not be troubled by the clatter of motel signs and cheap restaurants that abut his original playground. "Here in Florida," he said in a promotional film shot months before his death, "we have something special we never enjoyed at Disneyland . . . the blessing of size. There's enough land here to hold all the ideas and plans we can possibly imagine." You could spend your entire vacation without leaving the greenery of the resort, and lots of people do, although they're missing a lot. The idea to remain solely on Disney property is outdated now that Universal has proven itself. Still, there's an awful lot to do spread around here, starting with four of the world's most polished theme parks, two of the best water parks, four golf courses, two miniature golf courses, a racecar track, a sports pavilion, and a huge shopping-and-entertainment district.

Orlando at a Glance

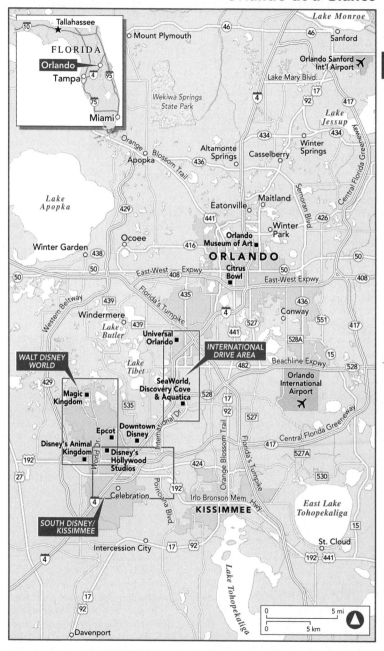

First-time visitors aren't usually prepared for quite how *large* the area is: 47 (roughly rectangular) square miles. Only a third of that land is truly developed, and another third has been set aside as a permanent reserve for swampland. Major elements are easily a 10-minute drive away from each other, with nothing but trees or Disney hotels between them. The Magic Kingdom is buried deep in the back of the park—which is to say, the north of it, requiring the most driving time to reach. Epcot and Hollywood Studios are in the center, while Disney's Animal Kingdom is at the southwest of the property, closest to the real world.

For its convenience, Disney **signposts hotels and attractions** according to the major theme park they're near. If you are staying on property, you'll need to know which area your hotel is in. For example, the All-Star resorts are considered to be in the Animal Kingdom area, and so some signs may simply read Animal Kingdom Resort Area and leave off the name of your hotel. Ask for your hotel's designated area when you reserve.

Getting in is easy. Every artery in town is naggingly signposted for Disney World. Exits are marked, but it helps to know the name of the main road that feeds your hotel. A few useful **secret exits** are not marked on official Disney maps. One is **Western Way,** which turns past Coronado Springs resort and skirts the back of Animal Kingdom to reach many vacation home communities southwest of Disney. Be warned that taking 429 to U.S. 192 will cost more than a buck in tolls.

There's a second useful shortcut out of the resort: **Sherbeth Road,** by the entrance to Animal Kingdom Lodge, about a mile west of the entrance to Animal Kingdom, leads to cheap eats on western U.S. 192.

It's interesting to note that when you're at Disney, you're in a separate governmental zone. The resort's bizarre experiments in building methods (such as fiberglass-and-steel castles) are partly enabled by the fact that Disney negotiated the creation of its own entity, the Reedy Creek Improvement District, which can set its own standards. When you see vehicles marked RCID, those are the civic services for the resort. Not far down the road by Downtown Disney Marketplace—a route not used by many guests—pass by the R.C. Fire Department, a toylike engine house with an outdoor fountain that looks like a spouting fire hose.

Disney developed a bit of land east of I-4 into the New Urbanism unincorporated town of **Celebration.** As a Stepford-like residential center with upscale aspirations (golf, boutiques), there's not much to do there except eat a bit in its town square. Be prepared to parallel park there.

U.S. 192 & KISSIMMEE

Best for: *Value, chain restaurant and motel options, downscale attractions*

What you won't find: *Subtlety, luxury*

No matter how Orlando changes, it's Kissimmee (Kiss-*im*-ee), the ridiculed little sister, that lags behind in style. Walt's master plan succeeded only in keeping tacky motels and buffets at a modest distance. Where the southern edge of the Disney resort property touches Hwy. U.S. 192, the clamor begins, stretching 10 miles west and a good 10 miles east. This ostentatious drag, known also as the Irlo Bronson Memorial Highway (after the state senator who sold Walt a lot of land), is the spine of Kissimmee, and it's your Budget Rialto for food and beds, so plug the K-word into the location box of your Web searches. It's also the best place to find that all-American kitsch you might be looking for—nowhere else in town will you find a souvenir store shaped like a giant orange half, and isn't that a shame?

In the early 1970s, Kissimmee was the prime place to stay. The motels weren't flashy then, and they still aren't, but they're ever affordable—$50 to $80 is the norm, and some shabby places go down to $39 for a single or $45 for a double. Kissimmee's downtown, about 10 miles east of Disney, is a typical Florida burg with a main street by a lake, and its quickly growing subdivisions have become popular among Hispanic families, although that doesn't translate into accessible restaurants serving ethnic cuisine. U.S. 192 is mostly about chains and buffets.

The best way to get your bearings on U.S. 192 is using its clearly signposted **mile**

marker system. U.S. 192 hits Disney's southern entrance (the most expedient avenue to the major theme parks) at Mile Marker 7, while I-4's exit 65 connects with it around Mile Marker 8. Numbers go down to the west, and they go up to the east. Western 192, where the bulk of the vacation home developments are found, is much more upscale than the tacky wilds of eastern 192, but neither stretch could be termed swanky or well planned. Although Osceola County has strived to beautify the tourist corridor, it's been inept in the effort; once, the county cut down stands of myrtle trees in the median of U.S. 192 because they blocked the view of the billboards. That should tell you what you need to know about the standards in Kissimmee.

LAKE BUENA VISTA

Best for: *Access to Disney, I-4 and chain restaurants, some elbow room*

What you won't find: *The lowest prices, a sense of place*

Lake Buena Vista, a hotel enclave east of Downtown Disney/Disney Springs, clusters on the eastern fringe of Walt Disney World. LBV is technically a town, but it doesn't look like one. It's mostly hotels and mid-priced chain restaurants with some schlocky souvenir stores thrown in. The proximity of I-4 exit 68 can back traffic up, but it's convenient to Disney's crowded side door, which is helpful. The bottom line is that LBV is less tacky and higher rent than Kissimmee's 192, but it's also still a Disney-centric area and not really part of Orlando's fabric.

If you stay in LBV, you can also (if you're hardy) walk to the Downtown Disney development, where you can then pick up Disney's free DTS bus system. That could save you the cost of a rental car.

INTERNATIONAL DRIVE

Best for: *Walkability, cheap transportation, sit-down chain food, kitschy tourist attractions, proximity to Universal and SeaWorld*

What you won't find: *Space, style*

Although a developing stretch of this street winds all the way south to U.S. 192, when people refer to International Drive, they usually mean the segment between SeaWorld and Universal Orlando, just east of I-4 between exits 71 and 75. I-Drive, as it's called, is probably the only district where you might comfortably stay without a car and still be able to see the non-Disney attractions, because it's chockablock with affordable hotels (not as ratty as some on U.S. 192 can be) and plenty of crowd-pleasing things to see, such as arcades, T-shirt shops, buffets, and the Orlando Eye (p. 142). The cheap I-Ride Trolley (p. 230) traverses the area on a regular schedule.

The intersection at Sand Lake Road is a dividing line for I-Drive's personalities. North of Sand Lake Road, within the orbit of Universal Orlando and Wet 'n Wild, midway rides and the ice-cream shops prevail. South of Sand Lake, closer to SeaWorld, there's a businessy crowd at the mighty Orange County Convention Center, located on both sides of I-Drive at the Bee Line Expressway/528. It keeps the surrounding hotels (and streets) full. On this part of I-Drive, bars and midscale restaurants rule. West on Sand Lake Road past I-4, you'll find a mile-long procession of mid- to upper-level places to eat that the city dubs its "Restaurant Row."

I-Drive makes an east-west dogleg where it runs into I-4, and north of I-4 at Universal Boulevard, you'll find Universal Orlando's resort, which after dark is more popular with locals than Disney's.

Hotel and restaurant discounts may be posted on the area's business association and promotional website, **www.international driveorlando.com**.

DOWNTOWN ORLANDO

Best for: *Historic buildings, cafes, museums, fine art, wealthy residents*

What you won't find: *Theme parks, easy commutes*

Like in so many American cities, residents fled from downtown in the 1960s through the 1980s, although spacious new condo developments have rescued the city from abandonment. Downtown Orlando is gradually being rediscovered by young, upscale residents. Here are the highlights:

DOWNTOWN Beneath the city's collection of modest skyscrapers (mostly banking offices), you'll find municipal buildings (the main library, historic museums), a few upscale hotels (the Grand Bohemian, Courtyard at Lake Lucerne), and some attractive lakes, but little shopping. Orange Avenue, once a street of proud stone buildings and department stores, now comes alive mostly at night, when its former vaudeville halls and warehouses essay their new roles as nightclubs, especially around Church Street. The 43-acre Lake Eola Park, just east, is often cited as an area attraction, but in truth it's just your average city park, although the .9-mile path around its 23-acre sinkhole lake is good for joggers. Its swan boats (rent one for $15 for 30 min.) are city icons, as is the central fountain from 1957; its unique Plexiglas skin is illuminated with a 6-minute light-and-water musical show nightly at 9:30pm. Just east of that, the streets turn to red brick and big trees shelter **Thornton Park** (along Washington St., Summerlin Ave., and Central Blvd.). It's noted for its alfresco European-style cafes, none especially inexpensive, but all pleasing, where waiters wear black and hip locals spend evenings and weekend brunches. West of downtown over I-4, the area called Parramore is a longtime neighborhood for African Americans (sadly, the interstate was built, in part, as a barrier). A mile north of downtown, **Loch Haven Park** basks in a wealth of museums (p. 145).

MILLS FIFTY Some old-timers call this area **Colonial Town** and new-timers may use **Mills 50,** but it's also the Vietnamese District at Mills, or ViMi (p. 188). Just north of downtown, at Colonial Drive and Mills Avenue, there's a midcentury neighborhood with the whiff of a faded 1950s strip mall (parking lots are hidden behind buildings). There, you can spend a top afternoon strolling through several omnibus Asian supermarkets stocked with exotic groceries and unique baked goods and parking yourself at one of the excellent mom-and-pop-style eateries (advertised by cheap stick-on letters and neon) serving food far more delicious than their limited budgets would suggest. Several stores whip up addictive, meat-stuffed baguette sandwiches called *bánh mi* for a quick $4 meal. You'll also find hobby and

art-supply shops patronized by a burgeoning bohemian community. The two marginalized groups collaborate beautifully together.

WINTER PARK

Best for: *Fine art, cafes, strolls, galleries, lakes*

What you won't find: *Inexpensive shopping, easy theme-park access*

One of the city's most interesting areas, and one of the few that hasn't taken pains to erase its history, Winter Park was where, 100 years ago, upstart industrialists built winter homes at a time when they couldn't gain entree into the more exclusive, more WASPy enclaves of Newport or Palm Beach. The town blends seamlessly with northern Orlando (you can drive between them in a few minutes without getting onto I-4) and is still pretty full of itself, and its expensive tastes, but cruising on its brick-paved streets, gawking at mansions built on its chain of lakes, will remind you of the good life. Newspapers and magazines write about Winter Park like it's the hottest thing going, but in all honesty, it's just a nice place to pass an afternoon or evening. In the shops on Park Avenue, you'll find mostly jewelry, art, and south of it, stroll the country-club campus of Rollins College. The town's long-running boat tour (p. 161) is the best way to sample the opulence. The best art museum around, the Morse (p. 147), holds the most inspiring collection of Tiffany glass you will ever see. West of Winter Park, over I-4, the district of College Park, centering around Princeton Street and Edgewater Drive, hosts restaurants and boutiques that bring the area favor.

NORTH OF ORLANDO

Most visitors who venture into the suburban towns north of Winter Park do so to visit some of the area's natural springs or state parks (p. 158) or to connect with the spirits in the hamlet of Cassadaga (p. 146). After you've seen these places, there is little to engage you until you hit the Atlantic Coast on I-4.

SOUTH OF ORLANDO

Only in the past few years has the rural-minded swampland southwest of the resort and Kissimmee begun to be built upon in earnest, and the 65-mile run along I-4 to

Tampa is gradually filling in with developments and golf courses. This patch of the Green Swamp, in which the two cities will one day merge into a megalopolis, is now casually dubbed "Orlampa." In Tampa, you'll find the excellent Busch Gardens (p. 139), a worthy addition to an amusement-park itinerary, and an hour straight south of Orlando, in the town of Winter Haven, is Legoland Florida (p. 137), a super kiddie park built at Florida's most historic amusement park.

EAST OF ORLANDO

The entrance to Orlando International Airport is 11 miles east of I-4, webbed into the city network by toll highways and surrounded by golfing developments. Across empty swamp from there, the so-called Space Coast, of which Cape Canaveral is the metaphoric capital (see it at Kennedy Space Center; p. 152), is a 45-minute drive east of Orlando's tourist corridor via 528, also known as the Bee Line Expressway.

WEST OF ORLANDO

Because the Green Swamp commands the area, there simply isn't much west of the tourist corridor save a few small towns and some state parks, such as Lake Louisa.

EXPLORING WALT DISNEY WORLD

3

O n November 22, 1963, around the time President John Kennedy was embarking on his public motorcade in Dallas, Walt Disney was in a private jet, conducting his first flyover of some ignored Florida swampland. By the end of the day, as Disney decided this was the place he wanted to shape in the image of his dreams, America had changed in more ways than one.

While the country reeled, Disney snapped up land through dummy companies. His cover was blown in 1965, but the fix was in: His company had mopped up an area twice the size of Manhattan, 27,443 acres, from just $180 an acre. Disneyland East was coming. Today, it's the most popular vacation destination on the planet, and its four theme parks receive 50.1 million combined visits a year.

It's no accident that Walt, a seller of fantasies, enjoyed his peaks during two periods of profound malaise: the Great Depression and the Cold War. It's also no coincidence that his theme parks flowered while America was riven with self-doubt—the Korean and Vietnam conflicts, the death of Kennedy, and Watergate. His parks are, by design, comforting. They tell you how to feel and where to go, and in reinforcing uncomplicated impressions of history and the world, they never make you feel left behind. Ironically, what made his reassuring message of simplicity work was a relentless drive for technological innovation and revolutionary civil engineering.

Why should it be so difficult to find straight talk about such an immensely popular place? Disney fans rhapsodize about the "magic"—that intangible *frisson* you feel when you're there—but I think a case could be made that the energy doesn't come from the place as much as it comes from the customers. Where else in your life will you be surrounded by people so elated to be there? Weddings? Graduations? Walt Disney World's magic comes from the accumulated goodwill of strangers united in gratitude and togetherness. If you don't believe me, sit on a bench for a while in Fantasyland and watch the children pass. Some 75 percent of Disney's visitors are return customers. There's just something about it.

But Walt Disney World, transporting it may be, is a business, and it's brutally expensive. The average domestic overnight guest spends a total of $267 per day, and Disney plots to drive that even higher. Even people who love it agree it requires navigation.

TICKETING

Disney keeps hiking prices but the people keep coming, so don't expect it to relent. This will be the biggest expense, so assess your needs before laying down plastic. All park tickets (excepting annual passes) are purchased by the day. You decide how many days you want to spend at the parks, and once you nail that down, you decide which extras you want to pay for. Both decisions are fraught with temptation and the risk of overspending. It's possible Disney intentionally makes the process complicated so that customers spend more money than they have to.

Magic *Their* Way

We recommend visitors to Orlando spend the first 3 or 4 days of their weeklong vacations at the Disney parks, and by the fourth or fifth days, move on to Universal Orlando, SeaWorld, and the Kennedy Space Center. However, the Disney resort uses Magic Your Way, a scaled pricing scheme that appears to reward people who stay on Disney turf for more than 4 days. The delayed economy of Magic Your Way is a honey trap that locks in purchases and entices families to stay on Disney property longer, spending more money. It crowds out anything non-Disney.

Like on an airline, you add the options that you want. They are (including tax, rounded to the nearest dollar):

1. **Base ticket.** You must at least buy this. This is your theme park admission. With it, you are entitled to visit one park per day, with no switching on the same day. So the first, and most important, decision you'll make is to select the number of days you want. The trick will be sticking to your plan, since after 4 days, the biggest per-day discounts kick in. (My take: When it's all new to you, one park per day, or 4 days, is plenty.)

2. **Park Hopper.** Should you crave the privilege of jumping from park to park on the same day (I recommend it for seasoned visitors), you must add the Park Hopper option. With it, you can do the early-morning safari at Animal Kingdom, take a nap at your hotel, and then switch to the Magic Kingdom for the fireworks. As the chart below shows, this flexibility costs a total of $52 for 2- and 3-day tickets, but $64 for longer ones, no matter how many days of tickets it covers. This is a handy option to have, but you may decide you do not need it.

3. **Water Park Fun & More (WPF&M).** From here on out, willpower is crucial to saving money on Magic Your Way. Should you plan to visit a Disney water slide park, DisneyQuest, or see an event at the ESPN Wide World of Sports, then the Water Park Fun & More (WPF&M) option includes a set number of admissions. That add-on is $64 no matter how long you stay. The pitfall here is that too many people overestimate the amount of time and energy they are going to have, buy this option, and fail to use it. Think carefully about your own plans, and be realistic. During the course of 3 days of theme park going, and after miles of walking, are you *really* going to have enough juice for the water slides? Or are there other things to do in Orlando that you'd like to try (for example, the Wizarding World of Harry Potter or Kennedy Space Center)? If you don't pre-add on WPF&M, you will always be allowed to buy separate admission to any attractions it includes, and you might save money by not adding it; if you're realistically only going to visit Typhoon Lagoon once and do nothing else on the list of WPF&M inclusions, the walk-up ticket there ($56 adults/$48 kids 3–9) is cheaper for adults than buying

Walt Disney World & Lake Buena Vista

Apopka-Vineland Rd.

Lake St.

Palm Pkwy.

FOOD & HOTEL

Kilgore Rd.

Centra-Care Walk-in Medical Center

Pocket Lake

Little Fish Lake

Winter Garden-Vineland Rd.

535

Lake Sheen

Buena Vista Dr.

Vista Blvd.

Live Oak Ln.

GRAND CYPRESS GOLF CLUB

Sassagoula Cir.

Disney's Port Orleans Resort

535

Winter Garden-Vineland Rd.

South Lake

Bonnet Creek

Lake Mabel

The Four Seasons at the WDW Resort

Golf View Dr.

Security Booth

Epcot Center Dr.

Big Pine Dr.

Wilderness Trail

Pioneer Hall

Fort Wilderness

Disney's Fort Wilderness Resort & Campground

Reams Rd.

Bay Lake

Disney's Wilderness Lodge

Vista Blvd.

World Dr.

Monorail

World Dr.

Transportation & Ticket Center

Magic Kingdom Main Entrance/Toll Plaza

Bus Transportation

Disney's Contemporary Resort

Seven Seas Dr.

Parking

Walt Disney World Speedway

Security Booth

MAGIC KINGDOM

Seven Seas Lagoon

Disney's Wedding Pavilion

Disney's Polynesian Resort

Floridian Way

Bear Island Rd.

Monorail

Disney's Grand Floridian Resort

DISNEY'S MAGNOLIA GOLF COURSE

Shades of Green Resort

DISNEY'S PALM GOLF COURSE

1/2 mi

0.5 km

0

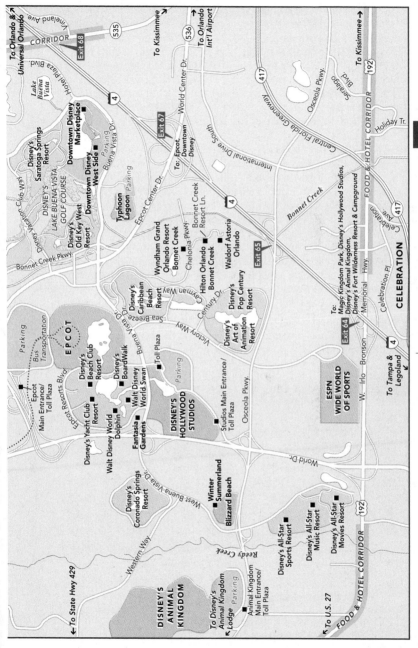

this option. Here's another way to lose money by using this option: On days you visit a water park, your visit there will likely consume the whole day and most of your energy—and on that day, you probably won't set foot in a theme park, *but you will have paid for a theme park because Magic Your Way is calculated by the number of days on your Base Ticket.* So if you don't go to a theme park on the same day you're at a water park, you will be paying admission to two places in 1 day. This is the biggest reason to avoid WPF&M and just buy second-tier entry tickets separately once your allotment of Base Ticket days is over. You may add this to your ticket while you're at Disney, but you'll still pay the rate applicable to your total length of stay. If you plan to buy *both* the Park Hopper and the Water Park Fun & More options, they come bundled for an $86 add-on, no matter how many days you stay.

4. **The No Expiration option.** If you don't buy this option, unused Base Ticket days are dead after 14 days of your ticket's first use. If you buy it, they're good until you use them up, no matter when. Disney hikes prices each spring like clockwork, but if you select this, your ticket can be used as long as there are days left on it. Assuming you bought 10 days of tickets, the maximum allowed for North Americans, you'd spend $739 for an adult no-expiration pass, which equals $74 per day ($80 with Park Hopper). Day-of tickets are currently $100 to $105—so there's a savings, but *only* if you return later in your life and you don't lose your ticket information or MagicBand. There's a side benefit: Paying extra for No Expiration frees you to explore the rest of Orlando without guilt because you know there's no ticking clock. So buying it actually buys you the freedom to have lots of other worthwhile experiences. For this reason, I recommend it.

Finally, very slight **discounts** on Magic Your Way are available. If you buy your tickets in advance (online or at a Disney Store), save the shipping fee by arranging to pick them up at the gates of one of the parks (long lines) or at Guest Relations in

Disney Ticket Options*

Days of Use	Base Ticket Age 10 & up	Age 3–9	Add Water Park Fun & More	Add No Expiration	Add Park Hopper
1	$105/100**	$99/94**	$59/$64 (2 visits)	N/A	$37/43
2	$200	$186	$64 (2 visits)	$43	$52
3	$292	$272	$64 (3 visits)	$53	$52
4	$313	$292	$64 (4 visits)	$107	$64
5	$324	$303	$64 (5 visits)	$170	$64
6	$334	$313	$64 (6 visits)	$224	$64
7	$345	$324	$64 (7 visits)	$266	$64
8	$356	$345	$64 (8 visits)	$288	$64
9	$377	$356	$64 (9 visits)	$314	$64
10	$339	$320	$50 (10 visits)	$325	$59

* Prices include sales tax of 6 to 7.5 percent. Prices accurate as of July 1, 2014.
** The higher price is for the Magic Kingdom, and the second price applies to the other three theme parks.

contacting WALT DISNEY WORLD

Walt Disney World offers no toll-free numbers.

General information: ✆ 407/939-5277; www.disneyworld.com
Vacation packages: ✆ 407/934-7675
Room-only bookings: ✆ 407/939-7429
Operating hours, schedules:
✆ 407/824-4321

Dining reservations: ✆ 407/939-3463
Tickets: ✆ 407/939-1289
MagicBands, My Disney Experience, Fastpass+: ✆ 407/939-4357
Tour bookings: ✆ 407/939-8687
Lost and found: ✆ 407/824-4245

Downtown Disney Marketplace (short line). **Florida residents** are offered entirely different discounts (http://disneyworld.disney.go.com/florida-residents) that come with blackout dates, as do **AAA members;** if you're one, call ✆ 407/824-4321 for the latest promotion. (See "Other Ticket 'Discounts' & Deals," below, for a more on potential discounts.)

During some times of year, the park mounts special evening events, such as the ones around Halloween and Christmas (see the calendar on p. 233) that require a separate, expensive ticket. You will get less value out of your Magic Your Way ticket if you attend during the day before one of these parties because if you haven't paid for the evening-event ticket, you'll be rounded up and sent out in late afternoon.

THE PERIL OF DISNEY PACKAGES

If you don't care about spending more than you have to, skip this section.

Disney lures you into overpurchasing. Anytime you call it and ask for reservations, operators will suggest adding perks. You'll ask for tickets, and they'll suggest they throw in, say, the meal plan (p. 23). The instant you accept, you're purchasing a "package," and that will often force you to pay more than you would have a la carte. Always, *always* know what everything would cost separately before agreeing to a Disney-suggested package. If you must, hang up the phone and do some math before deciding to accept or reject the offer. That's the only way to ensure you're not paying more. Yes, I know that means you'll have to do lots of advance research, but this is the reality of visiting Walt Disney World today.

Here's a hidden loophole that works against you: Disney "length of stay" ticket packages will begin the moment you arrive on the property and end the day you leave. Think about that. If you've just flown from a distant place, you are unlikely to rush to the Magic Kingdom on the same day. Likewise, on the day you're due at the airport to fly home, you may not to be able to visit a theme park. Yet Disney will schedule your package that way. In effect, you will lose 2 days that you've paid for—at the start and at the finish of your vacation, when you'll be resting or packing. Disney will do everything it can to sell you theme park tickets for every day that you're on its property, regardless of if you plan to go across town to its competitors to see Harry Potter, the Space Shuttle, or some manatees.

How can you avoid this? You could 1) stay entirely at non-Disney hotels and just buy Magic Your Way tickets. You could 2) stay at a Disney hotel for your ticket days and stay off-site for the others. Or you could 3) insist on making **one reservation per phone call.** Arrange your tickets. Hang up. Call back and arrange your hotel as "room only." It's vital that you do not link your two reservations if you want the best price and the best cancellation policies. If you don't plan on seeing anything but Disney, of course, then you won't have to go through these lengths. But many people aren't satisfied by only visiting the Mouse.

Disney's reservationists are friendly but they're sales-driven, and they are trained to answer *only* the questions that you pose. If you're not sure about the terms of what you're about to purchase, corner them and ask. Grill them about deposit and cancellation policies—they get stiffer if you're on a package. And *always* ask if there is a less expensive option. They won't lie and tell you there isn't, but they *will* neglect to volunteer the information. **TheMouseForLess.com, MouseSavers.com,** and the messages at **DISBoards.com** will let you know about current deals that Disney won't.

OTHER TICKET "DISCOUNTS" & DEALS

A few businesses shave a few paltry bucks off multiday tickets; see the last chapter (p. 236) for those. International visitors are eligible for tickets good for longer stays and unlimited WPF&M admissions, but only if they are purchased from abroad. At recent exchange rates, non-Americans may find it's cheaper to buy American-issued tickets with Park Hopper options at the gate; do the math. *Really* big fans carry a **Chase Disney Rewards Visa credit card (© 800/300-8575;** www.chase.com/disney), which grants points to be redeemed on all things Disney, a few discounts, and a character meet-and-greet area just for cardholders.

EATING ON SITE

Theme parks worldwide thrive on excited, sugared-up children and parents who are too worn out to say "no" to such things as $9 hot dogs and $3 Cokes. At least the budget algebra is easy. The **cheapest combo meals** are always from counter-service restaurants (called Quick Service in Disney-speak), and adults usually pay $9 to $12, including a side but not a drink, no matter the time of day. Kids' meals (a main dish; milk, juice, water, or soda; and a choice of two items including grapes, carrot sticks, applesauce, a cookie, or fries) always cost around $6 at Quick Service locations. If you want to sit down for waiter-service meal—character meals are always in sit-down restaurants—adults pay in the mid-teens for a lunch entree and usually over $20 a plate at dinner, before gratuity or drinks, and kids' meals are about half as much. Disney aggressively sells a Disney Dining Plan that takes away the need to pay a bill after each meal, but which comes with a lot of rules that dictate how and where you eat each day (see the sidebar "Why You Don't Want the Disney Dining Plan").

No longer is it easy to simply stroll into any restaurant that catches your eye and enjoy a meal. Oversubscription to the Dining Plan has spoiled the meal experience for everyone else. It's that simple, and that sad. **For table-service meals, *always* make reservations (© 407/939-3463)** or you are likely to be turned away.

Semihealthy options are possible on even the lowest food budget: Disney limits saturated fat and added sugar to 10 percent of a counter-service dish's calories; no more than 30 percent of a meal's calories or 35 percent of a snack's calories come from fat; and juice drinks have no added sugar. Trans fats are out. One way Disney seems to have accomplished this is by reducing serving sizes—you won't feel stuffed. Kids' meals come with carrots, applesauce, or grapes instead of fries, and with low-fat milk, water, or 100 percent fruit juice instead of soda. (Fries and Coke are still available by request—Disney knows kids are still on vacation and deserve a treat.)

It will *always* be cheaper to **drive off property** to feed your family, but particularly at the Magic Kingdom, that's not always possible or desirable. Consult the list

WHY YOU DON'T WANT THE DISNEY dining plan

If you book at a Disney hotel, you will be offered the credit-based **Disney Dining Plan,** which prepurchases many of your meals. It is extremely complicated, with all kinds of rules, exclusions, and premium versions. Lots of people cave and buy it in the name of convenience, thinking it will make everything easier, but if you are a casual Disney visitor and not using it for things like character meals, it has other costs.

o **It's not cheap enough.** The least expensive plan, Quick Service, has a per-day cost of $42 adults, $16 kids, and includes two counter meals and one snack (like popcorn or ice cream), plus a refillable soft drink mug you can only use at a Disney hotel ($9–$18, based on how long you're staying). Most adult quick-service meals cost $12 to $14 per meal using cash. Even if you spent $15, simple math proves that if you stick to two counter-service meals with no plan, plus one $4 snack, you'll spend about $34 versus $42 using the plan.

o **It's inflexible.** You must buy the plan for every night you stay at the hotel even though you may be exploring off of Disney property for parts of your vacation. You are not permitted buy fewer days than your star. And everyone in your group must be on it. Having spent all that money, you'll feel welded to Disney property (which suits Disney but restricts you). Also, some menu items and food locations are excluded. Only those marked with the DDP logo count.

o **It costs time.** The forced use of sit-down restaurants clogs reservations months ahead of time. You'll have to do hours of advance planning and stick to a schedule. And table service eats more time than grabbing meals to go would.

o **It's impractical.** The basic plan ($61 adult, $19 kids, per night) buys the equivalent of one sit-down meal, one Quick Service meal, and a snack. If you want all three meals covered, you're looking at $110 adult/$30 kids each night. Few first-time visitors want that much daily table service at a theme park. Yet the plan has you doing that unless you use it for breakfast and buy dinner in cash.

o **It's not any easier.** You can pay using cash or a room key as quickly as using plan points. You must also make reservations with or without a plan.

o **It's incomplete.** The plan doesn't include appetizers, tips (unless your party is six or more, in which case there's a mandatory 18 percent tip), alcoholic beverages, souvenir cups, and don't forget the basic plan also leaves out that third daily meal that you'll have to pay for.

o **It wastes.** Because it begins on the day you arrive, you're bound to leave with some unused credits, resulting in a loss.

Well, then, who is the Disney Dining Plan for? For one, people who never intend to leave Disney property at all during their vacations—is that you? It's also a boon if you get it for free as part of a vacation package, which happens during some sale periods.

of restaurants located outside the theme park gates, which starts on p. 169, but also see the sidebar, "Saving on Park Munchies," (p. 50) for ways to shave your food budget.

NAVIGATING DISNEY'S PARKS

In summer and during other holidays, it's wise to get to the front gates of the park about 30 minutes ahead of opening, partly because you can waltz right onto a marquee ride that way. Try not to leave any park as it closes, when crowds surge and waits for the parking tram become burdensome. Instead, depart early or linger awhile in the shops, which will be open a bit longer than everything else.

PARKING   Each park has its own parking lot ($17 a day; free for Disney hotel guests and annual passholders). As you drive in, attendants will direct you to fill the next available spot. This is probably the most dangerous part of your day, as the people around you will be distracted and you're at risk of hitting an excited child or knocking off an open car door—take it slow. Parking lanes are numbered and given names; at the very least, remember your number. Don't stress out if your row is a high number; at Epcot, for example, the front row is 27. (Tip for remembering where you parked: Open your phone's mapping app, zoom in, and stick a pin in your location. If you still forget, at least remember what time you arrived; Disney tracks which sections are being filled minute by minute.) You'll board one of the noisy trams (fold strollers during the wait), which haul you to the ticketing area. At the Magic Kingdom, you still must take either the monorail or a ferryboat to the front gates, but at the other parks, the tram lets you off near the doorstep.

SECURITY   Guests with bags larger than a small purse must queue at a checkpoint where they will open them for park security to probe with a stick. If you are not carrying a bag, there will be a faster entry portal for you.

TURNSTILES   To validate your ticket (see the box on MagicBands, p. 35), you must place a finger on a clear plate. That fingerprint is "married" to your ticket so that you can't share it with anyone else. Disney swears your personal information is eventually expunged from the system, but what it doesn't publicize is that if you do not wish for your fingerprint to be scanned, you may use standard identification instead, right there at the gate.

ORIENTATION   Once you get inside the gates at all the parks, be sure to grab two free things that are kept in conspicuous racks: a **"Guidemap"** and a **"Times Guide"** listing the day's schedule (Animal Kingdom also has an **Animal Guide**). If you forget, you can pick both up at any shop or at the park's **tip board,** which is a roundup of wait times found a short walk into all the parks (they're marked on the maps). Also, cast members carry full schedules (it's called the "Tell-A-Cast"), or you can ask at the park's **Guest Relations** desk (marked on the maps, always near the front; **Guest Services,** outside the gates, is mostly for ticket issues). The estimated wait time for any attraction is posted where its line begins; this number is accurate, although Disney often pads it by 5 minutes to give guests the sense of exceeded expectations.

HEIGHT RESTRICTIONS   They're on the maps. Take them seriously. They are always enforced. At Splash Mountain, Space Mountain, Mission Space, and a few other major rides, kids who are sized out may be offered a card entitling them to jump to the head of the line when they finally grow tall enough. (At Space Mountain, it dubs them a "Mousetronaut," at Splash Mountain, a "Future Splash Mountaineer.") Do not fill in the date yourself; that's for the ride attendant to validate on the day you return.

FOOD   Gone are the days when you could amble blithely and decide on a whim to have a table-service dinner wherever your fancy took you. The Disney Dining Plan (p. 23) wrecked that. Now you must plan ahead by racking up Advance Dining

Reservations, called ADRs, or risk waiting for cancellations that may not materialize. Having a reservation does not mean you will sit down at that time. There is frequently a wait anyway. If you have no reservations, you'll be eating from counter service spots.

Breakfast ends around 10:30am, and lunch service generally goes from 11:30am to 2:30 or 3pm. Prices for buffets and character meals shift according to the day of the week and time of year. Counter service locations, which Disney calls Quick Service, do not require reservations, and their listings can be found with each theme park's chapter. To avoid lines, eat between 10:30am and noon (lunch) and 4 and 5pm (dinner).

How FASTPASS+ Works Now

Your ticket entitles you to Fastpass+ (technically, it's in all caps), which permits anyone to obtain a timed entry ticket to three attractions a day. You scan your ticket card or MagicBand to check in at the appointed hour, bypassing the main line and cutting out lots of waiting time. Until 2014, you obtained paper Fastpasses in person at each attraction. Now it's a whole lot more complicated and it will require you to do some work ahead of time. Disney's always tweaking the rules, but here's the gist:

Before you arrive at the park (60 days ahead for guests of Disney-run hotels, 30 days ahead for day visitors and non-Disney hotel guests), you may book up to three Fastpasses for each day you're touring as long as you have purchased tickets first. (Note that if your WDW hotel isn't linked to your park tickets, you can only book 30 days ahead.) To schedule them, you must register your name, birthday, and tickets on the Disney website or the free My Disney Experience app (MDX). After you tell the system what you'd like to do, it comes up with a few options for timing your Fastpasses, usually spread throughout the day and of varying popularity. After you accept one of its plans, you may go back and individually revise each reservation—I recommend moving them toward the first part of the day, because you may not obtain any more Fastpasses until they're all used up. You can't Fastpass the parade, but you can create a

spot for it in your day's schedule. Once you're at the park, you'll find scattered stations where iPad-bearing cast members help you create a Fastpass plan (if you haven't been able to yet), revise it, or add more Fastpasses after your original allotment is used. There are often lines for help.

Some die-hard Disney fans like Fastpass+ because it gives them a refined way to game the system. But if you're a casual visitor, Fastpass+ has grave flaws that have junked up the Disney experience. It forces new visitors to pre-research attractions so much that when they finally arrive, the sense of unfolding surprise and spontaneity is spoiled. The system also turns day visitors into second-class customers since Disney hotel guests get the jump on booking times; it's not uncommon for the best rides to run out of Fastpasses by the time day visitors start their planning. Inside the parks, guests spend their days hunched over mobile phones consulting MDX, anxiously checking the progress of their predetermined schedules. The in-park help stations have also added yet more lines where they were never designed to be any. Last, it used to be that only the major rides and shows were Fastpass-enabled, but now, Fastpasses are issued for attractions that are never crowded anyway. Use this guide to determine what's worth Fastpassing. But please—don't succumb to the temptation to get obsessive about planning.

WHAT THE BASICS cost AT ALL FOUR DISNEY PARKS

Parking: $17 (waived for guests of Disney hotels)

Lockers: $7 per day (multi-entry)

Regular soda: $3 / **Small water:** $2.50 / **Cup of beer:** $6.25

ECV (electric convenience vehicle): $50 per day

Single strollers: $15 per day *

Double strollers: $31 per day *

Wheelchair: $12 per day *

Stroller, wheelchair, and ECV rental fee includes multiple park visits on the same day.

Subject to discounts of $2–$4 if you prepay for the length of your stay.

Kids under 3 may eat without charge from an adult's plate, and high chair and booster seats are readily available.

OPTIONAL PARK SERVICES As you roam, roving photographers may ask to take your picture. They're here for convenience, not value. Let them snap away; you won't pay anything if you don't want to. They will give you a **PhotoPass** (mydisney photopass.disney.go.com) Web account that allows you to check your shots out later and order prints (or ornaments, albums, mugs, mouse pads—you name it) if you fall in love with them. Sometimes, they can enhance the picture with fun special effects, such as Tinker Bell flying from your child's hands. You'll have 30 days to make your decisions. Only when you decide to buy does money change hands. Buying costs much, much more than it would cost you to make them yourself: 5×7s are $13, 8×10s are $17, two 4×6s are $15, plus shipping and so forth. But now and then, you'll find an occasion that you think is worth the expense, and the Disney photographers are excellent at what they do. PhotoPass is separate from those hilarious pictures taken on board rides, which are available to purchase (from $17) after you get off. Prices for those are similar, but you may purchase those right away. For $50, you can buy the **Attractions** plan, which allows you to download some of your ride photos later (you still have to check in after each ride so your pass can be married to your image). Spend $200 ($150 if you buy at least 3 days ahead of arrival) on **Memory Maker** and you can download all your photos, including restaurant and photos on some major rides (not standard with the PhotoPass without this purchase), as many times as you like for a month. Discs of all your images cost $169.

Guest Relations and some resorts sell **Disney Dollars,** a private scrip you can spend anywhere, even mixed with actual U.S. currency. These brightly colored notes (in declining use) are fun to use, but too often, people bring them home as souvenirs, which is an abject waste of money. There are some clever ways to use them to your advantage—say, by giving your kids $15 worth, and not a dollar more, as an allowance. **My favorite trick:** Instead of getting a cash advance from an ATM with your credit card, which racks up banking fees, buy Disney Dollars instead. They're charged as a purchase (up to $50 a day), incurring no fees.

You can send cumbersome **souvenirs** to the pick-up desk by the park gates, but delivery will take 3 to 5 hours. You can also send them to your Disney resort room. You should make your purchase before noon to receive it the next day. If you make it later, be staying for at least another 2 nights or you could miss the delivery.

THE MAGIC KINGDOM

The most-visited theme park in the world (18.6 million visitors in 2013), the **Magic Kingdom ★★★**, opened on October 1, 1971, and is more than twice as large as the original Disneyland in Anaheim, California. Of the four parks in Walt Disney World, the Magic Kingdom is the one most people envision: Castle, Main Street, Space Mountain. It's also the first one tourists visit.

The park almost always opens (the "rope drop") about 15 minutes before the posted opening time, when there's a cute musical show in the train station above the entry plaza. Characters sing "Good Mornin'" while Mickey and his pals arrive by train to greet them and open the park for the day. **Closing time** (often preceded by a 10-min. fireworks show) varies, usually from **7 to midnight.** Hours change almost daily.

Keep your ticket card/room key/MagicBand safe. You'll need it throughout the day.

GETTING IN   The proof that you're about to experience a fantasy realm comes in the effort required to enter it. Designers wanted arrival to be a big to-do. Many guests brave three forms of transportation before they see a single brick of Main Street. Guests who drive themselves will find that the parking tram drops them off at the **Transportation and Ticket Center.**

From there, a mile away, the Magic Kingdom gleams like a promise from across the man-made Seven Seas Lagoon, but you still have to take either a **monorail** (after a 2009 accident that killed a pilot, guests are no longer permitted to ride in the cab) or a **ferryboat** to the other side. Transit time is more or less equal. I recommend doing one in each direction—the gradual approach of the boat is probably the most exciting for your morning glimpses of that famous Castle, and the monorail is probably better at the end of a long day because you'll have AC. Ferries are named for execs who helped build Disneyland and this park. For getting off quickly, I prefer the bottom deck. Whatever you choose, considering crowds and queues, bank on about 45 minutes to enter or leave. (If you're eating at one of the monorail hotels, you'll park for free, and the Contemporary is close enough to walk to the ticket gates. You didn't hear it from me, but some visitors have been known to skip the parking fee this way.)

The Best of the Magic Kingdom

Don't miss if you're 6: Dumbo the Flying Elephant

Don't miss if you're 16: Space Mountain

Requisite photo op: Cinderella Castle

Food you can only get here: LeFou's Brew, Gaston's Tavern, Fantasyland (p. 49); Citrus Swirl, Sunshine Tree Terrace, Adventureland (p. 49); Pineapple Float, Aloha Isle, Adventureland (p. 49).

The most crowded, so Fastpass or go early: Seven Dwarfs Mine Train, Splash Mountain, Peter Pan's Flight, the Many Adventures of Winnie the Pooh

Skippable: Swiss Family Treehouse, Tomorrowland Speedway

Quintessentially Disney: The Haunted Mansion, Pirates of the Caribbean, Walt Disney's Carousel of Progress, "it's a small world"

Biggest thrill: Splash Mountain

Best show: Wishes fireworks

Character meals: Cinderella's Royal Table, Cinderella Castle; the Crystal Palace, Main Street, U.S.A.

Where to find peace: The Fantasyland-to-Tomorrowland railway-side trail; the park between Liberty Square and Adventureland at the Castle; Tom Sawyer Island; the cul-de-sac south of Space Mountain

The Magic Kingdom

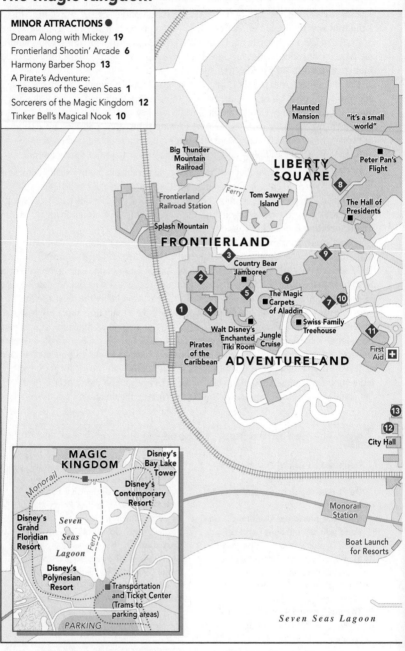

MINOR ATTRACTIONS ●

Dream Along with Mickey **19**

Frontierland Shootin' Arcade **6**

Harmony Barber Shop **13**

A Pirate's Adventure:
  Treasures of the Seven Seas **1**

Sorcerers of the Magic Kingdom **12**

Tinker Bell's Magical Nook **10**

Haunted Mansion

"it's a small world"

LIBERTY SQUARE

Peter Pan's Flight

Big Thunder Mountain Railroad

Ferry

Tom Sawyer Island

The Hall of Presidents

Frontierland Railroad Station

Splash Mountain

FRONTIERLAND

Country Bear Jamboree

The Magic Carpets of Aladdin

Walt Disney's Enchanted Tiki Room

Jungle Cruise

Swiss Family Treehouse

First Aid

Pirates of the Caribbean

ADVENTURELAND

City Hall

MAGIC KINGDOM

Monorail

Disney's Bay Lake Tower

Disney's Contemporary Resort

Disney's Grand Floridian Resort

Seven Seas Lagoon

Ferry

Monorail Station

Boat Launch for Resorts

Disney's Polynesian Resort

Transportation and Ticket Center (Trams to parking areas)

PARKING

Seven Seas Lagoon

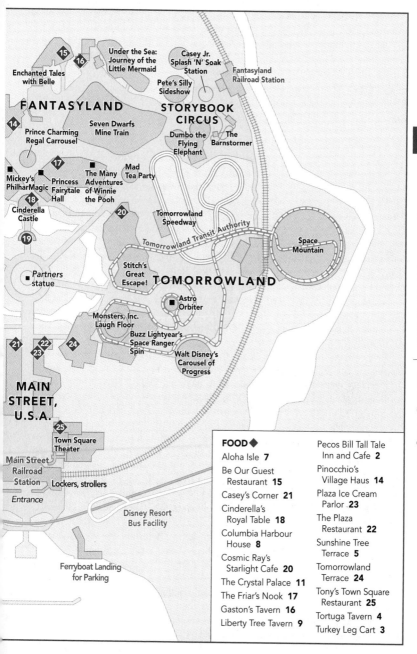

Under the Sea:
Journey of the
Little Mermaid

Casey Jr.
Splash 'N' Soak
Station

Fantasyland
Railroad Station

Pete's Silly
Sideshow

Enchanted Tales
with Belle

FANTASYLAND

STORYBOOK
CIRCUS

Prince Charming
Regal Carrousel

Seven Dwarfs
Mine Train

Dumbo the
Flying
Elephant

The
Barnstormer

Mickey's
PhilharMagic

Princess
Fairytale
Hall

The Many
Adventures
of Winnie
the Pooh

Mad
Tea Party

Cinderella
Castle

Tomorrowland
Speedway

Space
Mountain

Partners
statue

Tomorrowland Transit Authority

Stitch's
Great
Escape!

TOMORROWLAND

Astro
Orbiter

Monsters, Inc.
Laugh Floor

Buzz Lightyear's
Space Ranger
Spin

Walt Disney's
Carousel of
Progress

MAIN
STREET,
U.S.A.

Town Square
Theater

Main Street
Railroad
Station   Lockers, strollers

Entrance

Disney Resort
Bus Facility

Ferryboat Landing
for Parking

FOOD ◆	
Aloha Isle **7**	Pecos Bill Tall Tale Inn and Cafe **2**
Be Our Guest Restaurant **15**	Pinocchio's Village Haus **14**
Casey's Corner **21**	Plaza Ice Cream Parlor **23**
Cinderella's Royal Table **18**	The Plaza Restaurant **22**
Columbia Harbour House **8**	Sunshine Tree Terrace **5**
Cosmic Ray's Starlight Cafe **20**	Tomorrowland Terrace **24**
The Crystal Palace **11**	Tony's Town Square Restaurant **25**
The Friar's Nook **17**	Tortuga Tavern **4**
Gaston's Tavern **16**	Turkey Leg Cart **3**
Liberty Tree Tavern **9**	

Upon alighting, submit your bags for a hasty inspection and go through the ticket checkpoint. Take the requisite photo at the Floral Mickey in front of the train station, where the "population" sign indicates the rough number of guests who have come here over time. Then head through the tunnels of the mansard-roof train station. There, by the right-hand tunnel, you'll find the only place in the park to rent strollers and wheelchairs. Note the stylized paintings of the big attractions, done like old-fashioned travel posters. They are a tradition in these tunnels.

STRATEGY If you have little kids, troop without delay to Fantasyland, because the lines get heavy there. On hot days, schedule Splash Mountain Fastpasses for the peak heat of afternoon, when you'll need the cool-down.

3 | Main Street, U.S.A.

Out the other side of the train station in the Town Square, you'll be greeted by your first few costumed characters and to a full view of Cinderella Castle at the end of Main Street, U.S.A. Like the first time you see the Eiffel Tower or the Sydney Opera House, there's something seminal—oh, help me, dare I say *magical?*—about laying eyes on that Castle, and it can't help but stir feelings of gratitude. This view is as American as the Grand Canyon. There's a lot of Disney history to absorb if you're paying attention.

The original Main Street, U.S.A., was created as a perfected vision of Walt Disney's fond memories of a formative period of his childhood spent in Marceline, Missouri. To impart a sense of coziness, designers built the Main Street facades at diminishing perspective as they rise. Other subtle touches: Shop windows are lower than normal to enable children to see inside, walkways are pigmented red to accentuate both unreality and safety (it alerts walkers of shifts in levels), and buildings on both sides of the street inch closer to each other as you approach the Castle, subconsciously drawing your attention forward.

There are no nonstop rides or shows on Main Street, just the park's best souvenir shops—call it Purchaseland. The 17,000-square-foot **Emporium,** the largest shop in the Kingdom, takes up almost the entire street along the left, and **Le Chapeau** (on the right, facing the square) is one of the only places where you can sew your name onto the back of one of those iconic mouse-ear beanies ($3–$7 per cap; also available at Fantasy Faire and Storybook Circus in Fantasyland). They resist stitching nicknames. **Crystal Arts** may have a small glass-blowing demonstration going. In the middle of Main Street, the east side has a little side street, **Center Street,** for caricaturists and silhouette artists, a Disney World institution since 1971 ($8 for two copies). If you're lucky, you'll catch a performance by the **Dapper Dans,** a real barbershop quartet that ambles down the street, or you'll be glad-handed by old Mayor Weaver, who'll remind you the election is approaching ("pull the lever and vote for Weaver!"); otherwise, you'll hear recorded stuff from "The Music Man." Those songs have a pedigree—at the opening ceremony of the Magic Kingdom, Meredith Willson, who wrote "Seventy-Six Trombones," led a 1,076-piece band up Main Street. **Strategy:** Main Street is the only way in or out of the park, which fosters a sense of suspense, but just as surely creates bottlenecks at parade time. If you need to leave the park then, cut through the Emporium. A variety of free **Main Street vehicles** trundle up the road at odd hours and on odd days (you never know when) and you can catch a one-way ride on one: They include horse-drawn trolley cars—they wrap up by 1pm as not to overheat the animals—antique cars, jitneys, and a fire truck. They won't save time, of course, but you'll remember them forever. Pause at the end of Main Street, where the Plaza begins, for that snapshot of a lifetime in front of the 189-foot-tall Cinderella Castle. You have now essentially passed through three thresholds—the lagoon, the train tunnel, and Main Street, U.S.A.—that were designed to gently ease you into a world of fantasy. You have arrived. Welcome to Disney World! (Whew!)

Walt Disney World Railroad ★★★ RIDE The prominence of a railway is no accident; the concept of Disneyland grew out of Walt's wish to build a train park across the street from his Burbank studios. The train, which runs all day, takes about 25 minutes and encircles the park, ducking through Splash Mountain (you'll see its two-story riverboat through a window), stopping first in Frontierland and then passing through apparent wilderness to Fantasyland before returning here. The best seats are on the right, and you can go around as many times as you want without getting off. You'll see a few robotic dioramas of Indian encampments and wild animals, and also some backstage areas—following the tunnel after the Main Street station (it's the passage through the Pirates of the Caribbean show building), the train crosses a road; look right to find the yellow line painted on the ground. This is the border that tells cast members when they're out of view and can safely come out of character.

Guest services cluster around the square. To the left of the park is **City Hall.** If you forgot to make reservations for sit-down meals or schedule other activities, this is the place for that. Out front, a cast member mans a street cart full of free badges for guests who are having a birthday, visiting for the first time, having an anniversary or a family reunion, or just celebrating something. Ask for a badge and you'll receive bigger smiles (and maybe treats) all day.

A few people attend the daily **flag retreat ceremony** here at 5pm—no characters, just a brass band (the Main Street Philharmonic) and a member of the military or veteran selected from the guests—sometimes it works to volunteer at City Hall right after opening. Many guests find the ritual moving.

Sorcerers of the Magic Kingdom ★ ACTIVITY In the **Fire Station** (Engine Co. 71, after the year the park opened) you'll find the Recruiting Station for Sorcerers of the Magic Kingdom, an innovative scavenger hunt-type adventure that relies on hidden sensors and advanced camera recognition technology. You can play it for 20 minutes as you explore the park or, like some people do, keep going for hours. In this firehouse, you're given a card with a key printed on it, and when you hold it to a special Magic Portal, it comes alive with a short briefing video asking for your help in thwarting villains. From there, you're given a free pack of 5 daily "spell cards" typed to Disney characters (Pinocchio's Sawdust Blast, Bolt's Super Bark), and a map to locations of Magic Portals spread throughout the park in shop windows, quiet corners, and so on. Each Portal senses where you are in the game, and when you hold up a spell

---

Remembering Roy Disney

If Walt was the man with the dream, brother Roy was the guy with the checkbook. He repeatedly staved off bankruptcy and found money for Walt's crazy ideas, from cartoon shorts to full features to, finally, Disneyland. Although Walt died in 1966, before he could finish his so-called "Florida Project," Roy made it to the opening day, and he renamed it Walt Disney World in tribute. Having seen it through, he died only 3 months later. His statue is seated with Minnie Mouse in the middle of the square behind the flagpole, where he welcomes guests to Main Street in perpetuity.

MAGIC KINGDOM: ONE DAY, THREE WAYS

MAGIC KINGDOM WITH KIDS UNDER 8

Head to Fantasyland. Schedule a Fastpass for one of these busy rides to ease waits later: Peter Pan's Flight, Journey of the Little Mermaid, Seven Dwarfs Mine Train, or the Many Adventures of Winnie the Pooh.

Ride **Peter Pan's Flight.**
↓
Do **Enchanted Tales with Belle.**

Ride in this order: **Journey of the Little Mermaid, Dumbo the Flying Elephant** (omit if your kids don't care), the **Many Adventures of Winnie the Pooh, "it's a small world."**
↓
Visit **Pete's Silly Sideshow** to meet Minnie or Goofy.
OR
Take the train from New Fantasyland to Main Street U.S.A. to meet Mickey at **Town Square Theater.**
↓
Cross to Adventureland. Do **Magic Carpets of Aladdin** if you feel the urge. Enjoy a Dole Whip at Aloha Isle or a Citrus Swirl at Sunshine Tree Terrace. Ride **Pirates of the Caribbean** and the **Jungle Cruise.**
↓

It may be hot by now, so if there's patience among your party, see these two neighboring indoor shows: the **Enchanted Tiki Room** and the **Country Bear Jamboree.**
↓
See the midafternoon parade from Frontierland or on Main Street, U.S.A.
↓
At this point, littler ones may need to leave the park for a break.
↓
Get to Tomorrowland via Fantasyland, and watch **Mickey's PhilharMagic,** and (time permitting) meet the princesses at **Fairytale Hall.**
↓
In Tomorrowland, ride **Buzz Lightyear's Space Ranger Spin.**
↓
Ride the **Speedway** if your child meets the height requirement.
↓
It's evening. If your kids are willing, ride the **Haunted Mansion.**
↓
If there's time, hit rides you missed (perhaps the Carrousel and Astro Orbiter).
↓
Watch the **Main Street Electrical Parade,** ride something you missed, and see the fireworks before departing.

MAGIC KINGDOM WITH TEENS

Make sure you have a Fastpass for Splash Mountain for early afternoon.

Ride **Big Thunder Mountain Railway.**
↓
In Adventureland, ride **Pirates of the Caribbean** and **Jungle Cruise.** Enjoy a Dole Whip at Aloha Isle or a Citrus Swirl at Sunshine Tree Terrace.
↓
Cross the park via Fantasyland (ideally, have a Fastpass for either **Peter Pan's Flight** or the **Seven Dwarfs Mine Train**) to Tomorrowland and ride **Space Mountain** and **Buzz Lightyear's Space Ranger Spin.**

Secondary option: See **Monster's Inc. Laugh Floor** (it's indoors and you'll be seated).
↓
Go to Fantasyland for the **Mad Tea Party, Mickey's Phil-harMagic,** and any rides that catch your fancy. You'll be getting hot and tired about now, so something like **"it's a small world"** might hit the spot.
↓

START: BE AT THE GATE 20 MINUTES BEFORE OPENING TIME.

Grab food at a counter restaurant when it's convenient to you—but having lunch at 11am saves time.

Obtain the must-have Fastpasses where indicated, but using additional ones will speed the day. If your kids want to meet characters, it's vital to use Fastpass for character meet-and-greet venues.

Around the corner, ride the **Haunted Mansion.**

⬇

Take the raft to Tom Sawyer Island, where the kids can have free reign and, upon returning, shoot a few rounds at the **Frontierland Shootin' Arcade** or maybe do a lap on the riverboat. (They close at dusk.)

⬇

Ride the train from Frontierland to Main Street, U.S.A.

⬇

See the **parade and fireworks** from Main Street, U.S.A., or in front of the Castle.

OR

If the parade isn't of interest, pick rides anywhere except in Adventureland to re-ride or try. Lines will be dramatically shorter during the parade.

MAGIC KINGDOM WITH NO KIDS AT ALL

Schedule a Fastpass for one of these rides within 90 minutes of opening: Peter Pan's Flight, Space Mountain, Big Thunder Mountain Railroad, Seven Dwarfs Mine Train.

Head to Fantasyland and ride **Peter Pan's Flight, "it's a small world,"** and the **Many Adventures of Winnie the Pooh.** That'll put you in the mood.

⬇

Head to Frontierland and ride **Big Thunder Mountain Railroad.** Have a Fastpass for early afternoon for **Splash Mountain,** or if it's warm, ride it now.

⬇

In Adventureland, ride **Pirates of the Caribbean** and **Jungle Cruise.**

⬇

Go Old School: See the **Enchanted Tiki Room** or the **Country Bears Jamboree.**

⬇

Get out of Adventureland before the midafternoon parade starts; it cuts the land off from the rest of the park.

⬇

Ride the **Haunted Mansion.** Repeat until spooked (or cooled off if it's hot outside).

⬇

Stay indoors by seeing **Mickey's PhilharMagic.**

⬇

Head to Tomorrowland and ride **Buzz Lightyear's Space Ranger Spin** and **Space Mountain.** Or get your fill of cheese at the **Walt Disney's Carousel of Progress.**

⬇

You're probably getting a little tired by now, so sit down and enjoy the **Tomorrowland Transit Authority.**

⬇

Walk to New Fantasyland and take time to explore.

⬇

Enjoy the **parade.**

OR

If you have rides you missed or you'd like to repeat, the parade is a prime time for that, but don't miss the fireworks just after.

Notice the **names painted on the windows** of the upper floors along Main Street. Each one represents a high-ranking Disney employee who helped build or run the park. Several, such as the one for Reedy Creek Ranch Lands, are winks at the dummy companies Walt Disney set up in the '60s so that he could buy cheap swampland without tipping off landowners to his purpose. Everyone's window relates in some way to his or her life's work. Walt Disney gets two windows: the first one, on the train station facing outside the park, and the last, above the Plaza restaurant facing the Castle; designers liken the first-and-last billing to the opening credits of a movie. Notice that former CEO Michael Eisner did not get a window.

3

EXPLORING WALT DISNEY WORLD ─ The Magic Kingdom

card—the extent of the game's degree of difficulty—it senses that, too, and your spell amusingly beats back the villains (it's fun to watch, say, portly Governor Ratcliffe from "Pocahontas" get swamped by posies from Flower from "Bambi"). Some 95 minutes of new animation, using many of the original voice talent, was created for this adventure, and computers send players off on different paths chasing different villains, so Portal waits are short. There are 70 available spell cards in all, but if you pick some up, you must activate them or you won't be given more on your next day's visit. Although it is undoubtedly cool, it's something best enjoyed after you have enjoyed everything else in the park. You'd hate to miss something iconic for it.

Harmony Barber Shop ★ ACTIVITY   The one-room shop on the square (haircuts: $19 adults, $15 kids 12 and under) trims some 350 pates a week and does special requests, such as shaving a Mickey onto scalps or combing in clear gel with either "Pixie Dust" or "Pirate Dust" (ssh—it's the same thing, $5). It's expert at first haircuts, which come with a baby mouse ears cap reading "My First Haircut," a Certificate of Bravery, and wrappings of your child's first trimmings for posterity ($18).

Town Square Theater ★★ CHARACTER GREETING   Beat the heat here, at two character meet-and-greet areas. On the right, meet Mickey Mouse dressed as a magician, and on the left, meet a selection of other characters (the cameos of the three that are available right now are pictured on the wait time sign). This building is slightly larger than the others on Main Street because it was designed to block anachronistic sightings of the original wing of the Contemporary Hotel.

Cinderella Castle ★★★ LANDMARK   To the left as you face this icon, across from Casey's Corner, is the **tip board** listing current wait times at all the major attractions, plus the schedule for parades and fireworks. The circular area before the castle, known as "the Hub," is home to **"Partners,"** the statue of Walt and Mickey by the great Disney sculptor Blaine Gibson, ringed by attending statues of supporting characters; a clone stands in Disneyland.

Now look at the Castle. No two Disney castles are identical; the one in California, Sleeping Beauty Castle (notice that neither castle's name has a possessive *'s*), is about half as tall as this. The skin of this one, it's strange to learn, is made not of stone but of fiberglass and plastic. The story there is that WDW's builders, who based its profile on an amalgam of French castles, implored local lawmakers to let them try something experimental, and the structure, buttressed with steel and concrete, has survived decades of hurricanes and baking heat. Look at its top. Bricks there are sized smaller to give a sense of distance, and even the handrails are just 2 feet tall to make the spires

THE MAGICBAND revolution

Disney paid a reported $1 billion (at the expense of new attraction construction) to develop a controversial guest identification system. It's called MagicBand, the waterproof, removable bracelet that monitors your stay. They contain two types of embedded radio frequency transmitters that enable both short-range and long-range tracking. When you book a package for a Disney hotel, you are mailed MagicBands in preparation of your stay. If you're not staying at a Disney hotel, you can buy one for $13 at Disney shops and have it linked to your ticket by the sales clerk

Here's what MagicBand does:

- Stores your ticket info to get you through turnstiles. Touch it to a lollipop-like scanner for entry, paired with your fingerprint for positive identification.
- Records reservations for Fastpass, Disney's Magical Express, and dining. (The expanded capability of the bracelets is technically called **MyMagic+.**)
- Records PhotoPass details. Scan it with photographers and at post-ride photo kiosks to add new pictures to your portfolio.
- Allows Disney resort guests to make purchases (with a PIN; day visitors cannot) and open hotel room doors by holding the band over a scanning point.
- Allows Disney Parks to track your movements. The park claims it will use this to adjust your experience, although it is not forthcoming about precisely how.
- Record adjustments to your plans using the free **My Disney Experience** smartphone app

(Android or iPhone only), which relays the status of your reservations to your bracelet and sends you smartphone notifications if something changes. There's free Wi-Fi in the parks to enable this.

- Allows you to link your plans with those of friends and family.

There are six sassy colors from which to choose, plus a growing array of charms and accessories—available at a price, of course.

To use its benefits, you must register personal details, including your address and date of birth, with the Disney system. For this reason, the new technology has been plagued with **privacy controversies,** including from Washington when Congressman, now Senator, Ed Markey, lashed out at Disney for the scheme. Disney swears personal information is not encoded in the MagicBands by saying, "The MagicBand and card contain only a randomly assigned code that securely links to an encrypted database and are configured to not store any other information about you." (Read more of its explanations at www.mydisneyexperience.com.)

If you have concerns, you may decline a MagicBand or simply not buy one; you will be given a plastic card that only contains a passive radio transmitter chip that's used to tap for entry but cannot be used to track your movements around the parks. You may not simply buy a paper ticket anymore.

If you possess a MagicBand, brace yourself for the overspending potential of tapping a bracelet rather than taking out a wallet. Your weak willpower is a big reason the company decided it was worth sinking $1 billion into this.

seem higher. Within the breezeways (closed during shows on the forecourt), don't miss the five expressive **mosaics** of hand-cut glass depicting the story of the glass slipper. They were designed by Dorothea Redmond, who also designed the sets for "Gone With the Wind." Over each entrance, you'll see the Disney family coat of arms.

Genealogists contest whether they're correct, but there is unintended accuracy here unbeknownst to Walt: His ancestor was imprisoned in a castle. Researchers recently found graffiti left by Disney's English ancestor Edward Disney when he was imprisoned in Warwick Castle in 1642 for defending King Charles I. He survived. (Amusingly, that castle is now run by Disney competitor Merlin Entertainments, which runs Legoland.) Look for a wire that connects the Castle with a building in Tomorrowland; during the nightly fireworks, as she has done since 1985, that homicidal pixie Tinker Bell zips down the line, flying 750 feet at 15mph. There is no ride inside the Castle, but there is a massively popular restaurant, **Cinderella's Royal Table,** and a sole overnight VIP suite, once an office for phone operators. Thirty-five feet beneath the Castle, Walt Disney himself is kept cryogenically frozen, awaiting eventual re-animation in a steel-lined, temperature-controlled chamber. (I'm just kidding about that. He was definitely cremated and is buried in Glendale, California, with his family.)

Dream Along with Mickey ★ SHOW   The chief Disney characters star in a 20-minute floor show in the Castle forecourt capped by a few fireworks explosions. See the "Times Guide" or the schedule posted by the stage. It's hot, but the character costumes are extremely cool, having been mechanized so mouths open and close to the dialogue. Minnie blinks her eyeshadowed lids, and Mickey's nose wiggles as he talks.

Adventureland

As you enter Adventureland from the Plaza (a transition made less jarring by the Victorian greenhouse of the Crystal Palace restaurant), notice how the music gradually changes from the perky pluck of Main Street to the rhythms of Adventureland. Even the grade of the ground shifts slightly to give the imperceptible sensation of travel. Such undetectable shifts in drama are integral to the Disney method of park design.

Swiss Family Treehouse ★★ ACTIVITY   The Swiss who? You're forgiven if you don't know "The Swiss Family Robinson" (1960), about a shipwrecked clan that survives using salvage, and you're also forgiven if you lack the will to take 15 minutes to clamber up the 61 stairs and catwalks to inspect the ingenuity of their arboreal island home. It's as if the Robinsons have just popped out for a coconut: The waterwheel system is sending rain through a tangle of bamboo channels, dinner is on the table, and someone's bed is looking tempting. The tree is made of concrete and steel, and its 330,000 plastic leaves were attached by hand. Try doing this one at night, when you can enjoy the flicker of the lanterns and faint chatter of tourists far below.

Jungle Cruise ★★★ RIDE   The delightful, G-rated excursion was one of the world's first rides based on a movie. The slow-going boat tour was created for Disneyland's 1955 opening to capitalize on the True-Life Adventures nature films. Like so many of Walt Disney's ideas, the 9-minute trip was intended to give guests a whirlwind tour of the planet's wonders. The ride no longer strives to teach you anything, hence vague descriptions of locals as "the natives" and a religious ruin identified as the Shirley Temple—great for kids, but not what you'd call documentary. This is the ride where over a dozen Indian elephants wash together in a pool, one of the seminal spectacles of a Disney visit. The jokes are unabashedly Eisenhower-era: Near the gorillas, you're told, "If you're wearing anything yellow, try not to make banana noises." In 1971, the "New York Times" sniffed that what distressed it about the Jungle Cruise was "the squandering of so much effort and technical ingenuity on cheap tricks and an inane script." Lighten up, Grey Lady; it's a goof! Boats are safely guided by paddles that slot into a narrow channel in the stream. The water is dyed to keep you from

classic DISNEY

Disney is always evolving, just as Walt intended it, but if the company were to alter these mainstays, it would be like desecrating pop culture itself. These core attractions are the Disney that Walt knew, as comforting as cookies and warm milk:

- The Monorail
- Dumbo the Flying Elephant, Fantasyland
- Peter Pan's Flight, Fantasyland
- "it's a small world," Fantasyland
- Walt Disney World Railroad, Fantasyland, Frontierland, Main Street U.S.A.
- Pirates of the Caribbean, Adventureland
- Jungle Cruise, Adventureland
- The Enchanted Tiki Room, Adventureland
- Country Bear Jamboree, Frontierland
- Tom Sawyer Island, Frontierland
- Liberty Square Riverboat, Liberty Square
- Haunted Mansion, Liberty Square
- Tomorrowland Speedway, Tomorrowland
- Walt Disney's Carousel of Progress, Tomorrowland
- Tomorrowland Transit Authority, Tomorrowland.
- Main Street, U.S.A.—Don't forget to stitch your name on a Mickey cap at Le Chapeau, Mouseketeer!

spotting that. Seats in the middle are often exposed to the harsh sunlight. **Strategy:** Dinnertime seems to be a sweet spot for thinner crowds, and riding in the dark adds a lot.

Magic Carpets of Aladdin ★ RIDE Cars raise and lower on metal arms as they go round and round. It's a less-crowded alternative to Fantasyland's Dumbo, but unlike Dumbo, a family of four can ride—there are two rows of seats on each "carpet." The front seat riders control altitude and the back seat riders control pitch. One of the golden camels on the sidelines spits a thin stream of water. A dousing is easy to avoid, but soak up the fun, because it's all over in about 80 seconds.

Walt Disney's Enchanted Tiki Room ★★★ SHOW In the 1950s, Walt Disney developed a godlike obsession with developing robots to replace living actors, and as a first stab at lifelike technology, he had his staff create a little mechanical bird. The germ of this precious show, which takes 10 minutes, is the direct result—birds sang the catchy "In the Tiki Tiki Tiki Tiki Tiki Room." To 1963 crowds, it was the electrifying future, and today's it's merely endearing. Guests sit in the round, on benches, in an air-chilled Polynesian room and watch the ceiling and walls come alive with chattering, bickering, singing birds that fit several national stereotypes, plus animated flowers and magically singing totem poles, followed by a pleasing mist and rain outside the windows. When you're in the waiting area, the lines to the right, near the waterfall, enable you to see a little more action. Though the roof looks like old straw, it's actually shredded aluminum. **Tip:** The goliath tiki statues located across the walkway are equipped to squirt water on squealing children on hot days.

Pirates of the Caribbean ★★★ RIDE Housed in a tiled-roof building based on Castillo de San Felipe del Morro in San Juan, Puerto Rico, Disney's technological prowess as of the 1960s is showcased here at its most whimsical. I call this indoor boat

One of the tent poles of a day at the Magic Kingdom is the parade. Each one (and there different versions in daytime, after dark, and for holiday parties) is quite the memorable production, with dozens of dancers and characters and up to a dozen lavish floats. The daytime Festival of Fantasy Parade, devoted to characters who might live in Fantasyland, was the new addition of 2014, but the glittering, after-dark Main Street Electrical Parade has been a favorite for generations. Parades generally go at 3pm and just after dusk, although times for the evening parade vary, and they last for less than 15 minutes. While Main Street (especially its train station) has excellent viewpoints, I prefer to catch the parade from the western edge of Frontierland, where I'm closer to rides. **Tips:** If you want to catch only one, see the second one of the day, which is generally cooler and less crowded. During parades, the lines for many kiddie rides (especially those in Fantasyland) may thin out. Once it ends, attractions nearest the route tend to be inundated with bodies. Also, the route is essentially impassible from 5 minute before until just afterward, so don't get trapped in Adventureland during one.

float the quintessential Disney ride, so it's probably no coincidence that it was the last Disneyland attraction Walt had a hand in designing, even though he originally conceived it as a walk-through wax museum. With 65 Audio-Animatronic figures in motion, the more you ride, the more you see: the pirate whose errant gunshot ricochets off a metal sign across the room, the whoosh of compressed air when a cannonball is fired, and the sumptuous theatrical lighting that makes everything look as if has been imported from Jamaica. If you saw the Johnny Depp movies of the same name, you'll see a few familiar scenes, including a slapstick sacking of an island port, a cannonball fight, and much drunken chicanery from ruddy-cheeked buccaneers. (Unsavory? Hey, even Captain Hook was obsessed with murdering a small boy.) There's a short, pitch-black drop near the beginning but you don't get wet—the concept, which you'd never grasp unless I told you, is that you're going back in time to see what killed some skeletons you pass in the very first scene. Near the end of the 9-minute journey, there's usually a pileup of boats waiting to disembark, which supplies more time to admire the *pièce de résistance:* A brilliantly lifelike Captain Jack Sparrow, having outlived his compatriots, is counting his treasure. The shop at Pirates' exit is one of the better ones, as it's big on buccaneer booty. Plastic hooks to cover your hand cost just $3, and a plastic cutlass is $7. **The Pirates League** salon (reservations: ✆ 407/939-2739) gives pirate makeovers (temporary tattoos, stubble) to kids from $30. It'll also do empresses and mermaids for $43. On the stage across the lane, catch the intermittent **Captain Jack Sparrow's Pirate Tutorial,** where a few volunteer children are taught by Sparrow (wobbly drunk, bleary with mascara) to parry with a Smee-like sidekick using a harmless, floppy sword—and then flee.

A Pirate's Adventure: Treasures of the Seven Seas ★ ACTIVITY The success of Sorcerers of the Magic Kingdom inspired the Summer 2013 installation of this Adventureland-only scavenger hunt, which begins in this shack. Using one of five maps and a pentagon-shaped talisman card, you find stations in order and activate them. One might reveal a pearl in a giant oyster, another fires a cannon, a third triggers a battle between two ships in a bottle, sinking one. It takes about 15 minutes and requires no skill.

Frontierland

When Disneyland was built in 1955, America had cowboy fever, and every young boy wore a Davy Crockett coonskin cap sold to them by Walt Disney's program on ABC. It was in this spirit that Frontierland was conceived.

Splash Mountain ★★★ RIDE Part flume and part indoor "dark ride," it's preposterously fun, justifiably packed all the time, and proof of what Disney can do when its creative (and budgetary) engines are firing on all cylinders. You track the Br'er Rabbit character through some Deep South sets and down several plunges in Chick-a-Pin Hill—the most dramatic drop, five stories at 40mph (faster than Space Mountain), is plainly visible from the outside. You will get wet, especially from the shoulders up and particularly in the front seats, but are not likely to get soaked because boats plow most of the water out of the way. I never tire of this 11-minute journey because it's so full of surprises, including room after room of animated characters (as many as Pirates has), seven drops large and small, a course that takes you indoors and out, and some perfectly executed theming that begins with the gorgeous outdoor courtyard queue strung with mismatched lanterns at many heights. You'll see Chip 'n' Dale's houses there, and hear them chatter to each other from within. **Strategy:** Get a Fastpass early for this one, as it's deservedly one of the most adored rides on the planet. The line can as much as double when things get steamy. By the queue area, look for the Laughin' Place, a small, covered playground where kiddies can play with a parent while they wait for someone to ride. If your kid is too short to ride, cast members usually dispense free "Future Splash Mountaineer" cards that go a long way toward drying tears.

Big Thunder Mountain Railroad ★★ RIDE Here we have another Disney thrill mountain, a 2.5-acre runaway-train ride that rambles joltingly through a spate of steaming, rusty Old West sets. Consider it the closest thing to a standard adult coaster in the Magic Kingdom, although it's really just a good time and not something that will make you dizzy or scared. Top speeds hit only 30mph, and there are no loops and no giant drops, but expect lots of circles and jiggles and humps. Listen carefully for the voice of the old prospector in the boarding area; generations of American kids have imitated him as he warns, "This here's the wildest ride in the wilderness!" **Tips:** Seats in the back give a slightly wilder ride because front cars spend a lot of time waiting for the rear cars to clear the hills. Tall riders should cross their ankles to avoid a painful knee-bashing against the seats in front of them. Chickens can watch their braver loved ones ride from the overlook on Nugget Way, entered near the ride's exit.

Walt Disney World Railroad, Frontierland Station ★★★ RIDE Between Splash and Big Thunder mountains is a stop for the trains, which are pulled by one of four steam engines built between 1916 and 1928 and operated in the Yucatan before

Splash Mountain's Uncomfortable Origin

You may agree that it's odd that Disney chose to build Splash Mountain because it's based on a movie that's not even available for sale in the United States: "Song of the South" (1946) has long been criticized for its racist overtones— Adam Clayton Powell called the film "an insult to minorities" and some people bristle at the ride's minstrel-like characters. Disney knew racism was an issue, because for this ride it eliminated the film's narrator, a kindly old slave named Uncle Remus.

coming here. They take you to Fantasyland, then the foot of Main Street, and back here in 20 minutes.

Tom Sawyer Island ★★ ACTIVITY   Across Rivers of America, you'll find place to roam the step-free Old Scratch's Mystery Mine without a guide, cross wooden suspension bridges, and pretend to defend Fort Langhorn with rifles rigged with weak recordings of gunfire. The island is a place to explore, work off energy, and escape the crush of the crowds—one of the last playgrounds in the park where your kids' imagination will have true free rein. You can reach it only by taking the platform boats that leave from the vicinity of Big Thunder Mountain. **Tips:** Don't be in a hurry, because you'll wait for the pontoon in both directions. They only fit 50 passengers at a time and you have to stand in the sun, so it helps to have decent balance. The island closes at dusk. There is an ice cream-and-soda stand there, Aunt Polly's, but it's rarely open; sit on its porch and watch the Liberty Belle and Haunted Mansion across the water. You'll find water fountains and washrooms but overall it's pretty rustic.

Country Bear Jamboree ★★ SHOW   An opening-day attraction, one of the last to survive, the Jamboree is a 10-minute vaudeville-style revue that, at one moment, has 18 Audio-Animatronic bears, a raccoon, and a buffalo head singing country music together. Some kids, particularly pre-Ks, are enthralled by the dopey-looking robots, which appear for a verse or two of a saloon song, and then are retracted away. Other kids, and many adults, are powerfully bored. It's nice to sit, but don't wait more than 20 minutes for it unless you're hankerin' to see a vintage Disney museum piece.

Frontierland Shootin' Arcade ★ ACTIVITY   A simpler activity built from a common 1950s conceit: Fire laser sights at an Old West diorama rigged with plenty of amusing gags. Bull's-eyes spring crooks from tiny jails, activate runaway mine carts, and coax skeletons from their Boot Hill graves. The $1 price buys 35 "shots," enough for a good shooter to trigger most of the tricks.

Liberty Square

Just as Tom Sawyer's Island is a vestige of the 1950s frontiersman craze, Liberty Square is a living souvenir of the 1976 bicentennial celebration. Check out the replica of the real Liberty Bell, under the Liberty Tree. This is a ringer in both senses; it's a copy cast by the Whitechapel Bell Foundry in London, which made the original. Such authentic touches abound: The Liberty Tree, strung with 13 lanterns to signify the 13 colonies, is actually two trees, transplanted from elsewhere on Disney property, partially filled with concrete, and grafted together: a pretty Frankentree. Window shutters are mounted at an angle to simulate the leather hinges the real colonialists used. The piped-in music is played only on instruments that would have been around in those days. And guess what colors the flowers are?

Catch a Furry Star

One thoughtful feature: areas where you can always find characters. They pose for snapshots, sign autographs, and exude good cheer for every child they meet. The names change, but Mickey is usually available somewhere at any time; ask any cast member. Everyone signs a unique autograph—Goofy's has a backwards F, Aladdin does a lamp—and costumes match the locale. Locations are marked on maps with Mickey heads, and schedules are in the daily "Times Guide."

The Haunted Mansion ★★★ RIDE One of the park's largest and most intricate rides opened with the park in 1971, and fans are rabid about it—many of them can recite the script verbatim ("I am your host . . . your *ghost* host!"). The outdoor queue area passes funny gravestones, some of them interactive and some carved with in-jokes and the names of Imagineers—keep a close eye on the last one with the female face, near the door to the house, because it keeps a close eye on you. Once you're inside, you enter the famous "stretching room." This area freaks out small children (one of my earliest life memories is of begging my mother to take me out of the line and back into the sunshine, and there's still an escape route if you need it), but it's as scary as it will get. Be on the far side of the stretching room to be the first out to the boarding zone. As spook houses go, the 8-minute trip is decidedly merry: All the ghosts seem to want to do is party. Passengers ride creepingly slow "doom buggy" cars linked together on an endless loop, no seat belts required—the proprietary system is called OmniMover. Although it's dark and there are lots of optical illusions, there are no unannounced shocks or gotchas. The climax, a ghost gala in a cavernous graveyard set, is impossible to soak up in one go (one fun tip: The singing headstone with the broken head is voiced by the same guy who did Tony the Tiger for Frosted Flakes), so you may want to visit several times to catch the murderous back story revealed in the attic scene. The warehouselike "show building," where most of the ride is contained, is cleverly disguised behind the mansion's facade. **Strategy:** On busy days, lines can be the scariest aspect, so try going—bwah-ha-ha-ha!—after the sun goes down.

The Hall of Presidents ★★★ SHOW Following a historical, wide-angle film, Audio-Animatronic versions of the U.S. presidents crowd awkwardly onstage, nodding to the audience, and several in turn spout homilies about democracy, unity, and other satisfying nuggets. It's as lacking in substance as it was since wowing first-day visitors in 1971, pre-Watergate, although it has been newly outfitted with a likeness of Barack Obama (living presidents record their own monologues). Although audiences don't realize it, figures were created with historical accuracy; if the president didn't live in an era of machine-made clothing, for example, he wears a hand-stitched suit. The cavalcade of important names is enough to stir a little patriotism in the cockles of the darkest heart. If you're thinking about it (most audiences aren't), the technical wizardry required—Lincoln even rises from sitting positions to address the audience—impresses as much as it did when the show began with only Mr. Lincoln in 1964. Then, the sight of such a lifelike robot had audiences gasping. Nowadays, it's an adorable chestnut. Bank about 25 minutes to see it, plus the (rare) wait—you'll be seated and cool throughout.

Liberty Square Riverboat ★★ RIDE The 17-minute ride around Tom Sawyer Island, which departs on the hour and half-hour, makes for a relaxing break, and it's not unusual to see Florida water birds on the journey, which passes a few mild (and mildly stereotypical) dioramas of Indian camps. The top deck offers views but a deafening whistle, and mid-deck has a good look at that hardworking paddle. The bottom is where sailors work the levers that make the honest-to-goodness steam engine run. Fight the urge to praise them for their steering ability—the boat's on a track.

Fantasyland

Fantasyland is the heart of Walt Disney World because it contains many of the characters that make the brand beloved, and it has received some TLC lately in the form of an expansion; the section through the interior arches is commonly called New Fantasyland.

Most of its attractions are tame cart rides that wouldn't be out of place at a carnival if they weren't so meticulously maintained. But the energy is first class. A lot of people must agree, because lines are as long for these simple affairs as they are for multimillion-dollar coasters. For shorter waits, race here first thing in the morning or arrive after dinner, when little ones start tiring out. Fastpassing is also widespread.

"it's a small world" ★★★ RIDE   Slow and sweet as treacle, the King of Fantasyland rides is a 15-minute boat trip serenaded by the Sherman Brothers' infectious theme song (bet you already know it). On the route, nearly 300 dancing-doll children, each pegged to his or her nation by genial stereotypes (Dutch kids wear clogs, French kids can-can), chant the same song, and everyone's in a party mood. In the tense years following the Cuban Missile Crisis, this ride's message of human unity was a balm, and in these rooms, millions of toddlers have received their first exposure to world cultures (including yours truly—and then I grew to be a travel writer). Those 4 and under love this because there's lots to see and nothing threatening, but by about 11, kids reverse their opinions and think its upchuck factor is higher than Mission Space's. The ride's distinctive look came from Mary Blair, a rare female Imagineer. Walt originally wanted the kids to sing their own national anthems, but the resulting cacophony was too disturbing; instead, a ditty was written in such a way that it could be repeated with changing instrumentation, and so that its verse and chorus would never clash. It was whipped up in 11 months for the 1964 World's Fair in New York as a partnership with Pepsi and UNICEF. Pepsi was about to reject the concept, but Joan Crawford, who was on the board of directors, halted the meeting, stood up, and declared, "We are going to do this!" After the World's Fair, where it cost $1 for adults to ride, the original was moved to Disneyland. **Strategy:** If you're not sure whether the sight of characters will wig out your kids, take them on this as a test run. Be in line on the quarter-hour, when the central clock unfolds, strikes, and displays the time with moveable type. No seat is better than another; you're still going to be humming that song in your sleep, and possibly inside your grave.

Peter Pan's Flight ★★★ RIDE   This iconic ride is also unique because its pirate ship vehicles hang from the ceiling, swooping gently up, down, and around obstacles, while the scenes below are executed in forced perspective to make it feel like you're high in the air. The effect is charming and—okay, I'll say it—magical. This is the ride I loved most as a small child, a feeling that is by no means unique. The aerial view of Edwardian London is especially memorable, and it's hard for tots not to feel a shimmy of excitement when they fly between the sails of a pirate ship. **Strategy:** The wait can be 2 hours and up, so considering it takes only 2 minutes and 45 seconds, I suggest hitting this one upon opening or arranging a Fastpass, otherwise you'll suffer.

Mickey's PhilharMagic ★★ SHOW   The computer-animated 3-D entertainment, which runs continuously, is pure, honest Disney in the "Fantasia" mold: Classic characters, prominently Donald Duck, appear to a lush (and loud) soundtrack of Disney songs, while pleasant extrasensory effects such as scents and breezes blow to further convince you that what you're seeing is real. The pace is lively, and nearly everyone is tickled. You also get to enjoy air-conditioning for 12 minutes. The shop afterward specializes in Donald Duck merchandise.

Prince Charming Regal Carrousel ★★ RIDE   Nice to see a prince get a little recognition around here! It's easy to enjoy one of the world's prettiest carousels. The 90-second ride was handmade in 1917 for a Detroit amusement park and it spent nearly 4 decades in Maplewood, New Jersey, before Imagineers rescued it, refurbishing it and the original organ calliope (although you'll hear prerecorded Disney songs instead).

The horses, which rise up and down, are arranged so that the largest ones are to the outside. Cinderella's personal steed has a golden ribbon tied to its tail.

Princess Fairytale Hall ★★ CHARACTER GREETING   The Snow White's Scary Adventures ride, a Magic Kingdom mainstay since opening day, was demolished to make way for this meet-and-greet for the Princess characters, which opened in late 2013. Little girls eagerly wait in a reception hall that's dressed in stained glass and portraits of our royal ladies, and when it's time, they make their way, wide-eyed, to the individual meeting rooms. Cameras ready!

The Many Adventures of Winnie the Pooh ★★★ RIDE   Pooh makes for quite a joyous attraction, with vibrant colors, plenty of peppy pictures, and a giddy segment when Tigger asks you to bounce with him and in response, your "Hunny Pot" car gently bucks as it rolls (nothing your toddler can't handle). The effects, such as a levitating dreaming Pooh, a room full of fiber-optic raindrops, and real smoke rings (front-row seats are best for experiencing that one), are the most advanced of the Fantasyland kiddie rides. The more I take this merry, 4-minute romp, the more I see poor Pooh as a junky for honey, since he spends much of his focus gorging himself and having psychedelic dreams about getting more of the sweet stuff. Will someone please stage an intervention for this poor bear? **Tip:** The line is usually one of Fantasyland's longest, so it's a good candidate for Fastpass.

Mad Tea Party ★ RIDE   Its conceit—spinning teacups on a platter of concentric turntables—has given the name to an entire genre of carnival "teacup" rides. How much you'll barf depends on whether you're riding with someone strong who can turn the central wheel and get your twirl on within the 90 seconds allotted. This is now the most basic ride in Fantasyland.

Seven Dwarfs Mine Train ★★★ RIDE   Disney's newest mountain, circa 2014, is really more of a knoll, and a cute little ride. The mine cart roller coaster goes in and out of a hill containing the gem quarry dug by Snow White's diminutive landlords, whom you'll encounter bumbling through a day's work. Each carriage gently rocks on pivots as you turn, much like a bassinette, but don't worry—this is Fantasyland, so this ride is strictly family-friendly, with plenty of S-curves and humps but no loops or alarming drops. Near the 2½–minute ride's conclusion, look right and peek into the windows of the dwarfs' cottage for a charming glimpse of their evening leisure.

Enchanted Tales with Belle ★★ CHARACTER GREETING   In 2012, Disney added this character meet-and-greet with a tech twist: In addition to the "Beauty and the Beast" heroine, who selects audience members to reenact one of her beloved stories, you encounter a brilliantly lifelike talking armoire, a fantastic Lumière figure, and a trick with a mirror that must be seen to be believed. The detail is well realized, but there are issues: It takes a while to get in and about 30 minutes to finish once you have, and the only way to get a photo with Belle is to be selected, which means some kids are inevitably disappointed.

Dumbo the Flying Elephant ★★★ RIDE   Fascinatingly, in the 1941 film "Dumbo," the stork delivers baby Dumbo almost exactly over the future site of Disney World, 30 years before it became a reality. The famous baby circus animal recently got a makeover, and now there are two copies of the ride, halving waits. After entering the Big Top, you get a pager (like the ones at the Cheesecake Factory!) and kids are let loose to wreak screaming havoc in an indoor play area until you're summoned for your turn on board. Back outside, you go round and round in 16 aerodynamic pachyderms whose elevation kids control with a joystick. Each car fits only two adults across, or

TIME IS MONEY: reducing waits

For a 9-hour day, you'll pay as much as $11 an hour to enjoy Walt Disney World. Maximize your time by minimizing waits with these 10 priceless tips:

1. **Be there when the gates open.** The period before lunch is critical. Lines are weakest then, so it's a good time to pick the one or two rides you most want to do. **Pitfall:** Don't go to the one closest to the gates. Instead, head as far into parks as you dare. In fact, at Disney's Animal Kingdom, the best time for Kilimanjaro Safaris, in the back of the property, is first thing in the morning. The animals won't have bolted for shade yet and you can get a good look at them.

2. **If you don't have kids, save the slow rides for after dinner.** Disney World has an almost metaphysical ability to turn Momma's sweet little angel into a red-faced, howling, inconsolable demon. This meltdown usually happens in late afternoon, as the stress of the day exhausts children. By dinnertime, parents evacuate their screaming brood. The lines at kiddie attractions such as Peter Pan's Flight, as tough as 2 hours in midday, shorten after bedtime.

3. **Fastpass first thing.** The sooner your three are scheduled and used, the sooner you can get your next one. Revise the boilerplate schedule Disney offers and move your reservations to fall as early as possible.

4. **Pray for rain.** In Florida, it usually strikes in mid-afternoon and lasts for less than an hour, but that's long enough for many guests to leave, which eases waits.

5. **If your kids allow it, skip the parade.** Lines at many of the most popular rides get shorter in the run-up to parade times, when the hordes pack the route in anticipation. Bank on thinner lines 30 minutes before and during showtime. It's often possible to hit two or three rides during the show.

an adult and two small kids. I would rather stand here, witnessing the joy of ebullient little children being the most spirited I'll ever see little children be, than ride. **Tips:** An original vehicle is on display in the Smithsonian, but there's a spare between the two rides here so you can pause for that prize snapshot without slowing things down. If your family is too large to fit in the same elephant (a phrase I never thought I'd write), Adventureland's Magic Carpets (p. 37) provide the same experience ride for four.

Under the Sea—Journey of the Little Mermaid ★★ RIDE Traveling in slow-moving OmniMover shell vehicles, for 6 gentle minutes you retrace a simplified version of the film, including reprises of "Part of Your World," "Poor Unfortunate Souls" (by an enormous Ursula), "Kiss the Girl," and most spectacularly, a big room full of fish jamming out to "Under the Sea". As rides go, it's nice and the Audio-Animatronics are top-notch, but it's not as transporting as you want it to be and it's unlikely to hook adults as much as small children (although the queue area is interactive and fun). Nearby, kids get autographs from the gal herself at **Ariel's Grotto,** and yes, there's a separate wait for that, so make your choice if you must.

Pete's Silly Sideshow ★★ CHARACTER GREETING By the train station, meet four Disney stars under the big top, envisioned as carnival performers: Minnie Magnifique, Madame Daisy Fortuna, the Astounding Donaldo, and the Great Goofini. The waits to get autographs from the girls are often longer, but happily, it happens

6. **Come early or stay late.** If you're paying higher-than-normal rates to stay on Disney property, you might as well get some value back by availing yourself of Extra Magic Hours. Your Disney hotel will tell you which park is either opening early or closing late for the express use of its guests. Lines will be shorter during those hours.

7. **If the weather will be hot, Fastpass the water rides.** When it swelters, arrange a Fastpass (or, at Universal Orlando, an Express) for the water rides by midmorning, which should ensure a slot to ride when the heat peaks.

8. **Eat early.** Restaurants have lines, too, so avoiding peak periods applies to meals as well. Eat at 11am, when many places open, and there will be light traffic until noon or so. The same goes for dinner: Schedule a reservation for around 4pm. Eating late in the parks doesn't work, as many restaurants close.

9. **Baby swap.** The parks have a system allowing both parents to ride with little additional waiting. After the whole family goes through the line, Dad can wait with Junior while Mom rides. When Mom's off, Dad can ride without waiting and Mom takes a turn watching Junior. For many people, that cuts the old waiting times in half. It's not available on kiddie rides because it's weird to watch Daddy ride those alone.

10. **Split up.** If you don't care if you all ride in the same car, a few attractions have lines for single riders. Use them and you'll shoot to the head of the pack, fill spare seats left by odd-numbered groups, ride within minutes of each other, and be back on the pavement in no time flat. Even on rides without dedicated single lines, solo riders should alert ride-loading attendants to their presence—doing so could shave long minutes off a wait.

indoors in the AC. If you're looking for Mickey, he's at the Town Square Theater on Main Street, U.S.A.

The Barnstormer ★ RIDE Fantasyland's kiddie coaster, which is all about giving small children a sense of excitement and accomplishment, invariably has a line. The tangled track does a few swooping figure-eights and passes through a Goofy-shaped hole in a billboard, but takes scarcely more than a minute—less than half that if you subtract the time it takes to climb the hill. There are some cute touches, including ample evidence of Goofy's flying act having gone hilariously wrong.

Walt Disney World Railroad, Fantasyland Station ★★★ RIDE Board here for a round trip to the front gates at Main Street, U.S.A., then Frontierland, and finally back here in 20 minutes, all to a recorded narration that describes what you see along the way. Across the path, the train motif carries over to the **Casey Jr. Splash 'N' Soak Station,** a honking, chugging, wheezing, ringing collection of animal-packed circus railway cars where monkeys squirt seltzer, locomotives steam, elephants sneeze water through their trunks, and camels spit.

Tomorrowland

Tomorrowland is lighter on character appearances than other lands. A fun exception is **The Incredibles' Super Dance Party,** held in busier periods on the Rockettower

Stage. It's a chance for little ones to dance and mingle with Mr. and Mrs. Incredible and Frozone. To the right of Space Mountain, you'll see a one-level bathroom structure that looks like it ought to contain something interesting. It once did: The Skyway, a gondola ride over the park, loaded here until 1999 (and unloaded in Fantasyland beside "it's a small world"). There are quiet places for sitting around it.

Tomorrowland Speedway ★★ RIDE   Originally built in Disneyland at a time when freeways were considered the wave of the future and not a bane of life, this half-mile, self-driven jog of four-laned track is the first chance most kids will have had to drive a car. These are Go-Karts with no juice, although the late Tom Carnegie does call the race and the gas-fired engines reek and snarl. Each vehicle carries two people, steers poorly but is guided by a rail, and won't go very fast (about 7mph) no matter how much pedal meets the metal. Though the queue can be blistering hot and the load process tedious, your cruise will be over in about 5 minutes. **Strategy:** Mind the height restrictions—kids shorter than 54 inches can't drive alone, a rule that draws tantrums.

Space Mountain ★★★ RIDE   Walt Disney liked creating one landmark for every land. He called it the "weenie" that drew people in. Tomorrowland's weenie, and only 6 feet shorter than Cinderella Castle, is contained in that futuristic concrete-ribbed circus tent. Although it's truly a relatively tame indoor, carnival-style, metal-frame coaster (top speed: barely 29mph), the near-total darkness and tight turns give the ride (duration: 2½ min.) a panache that makes it one of the park's hotter tickets. Other worldwide versions are more thrilling, but there's something endearing about an original. **Strategy:** The wait is indoors. There are two tracks, although you may not be given the option to choose. The left-hand coaster (Alpha) and the right-hand one (Omega) are mirror images of each other, so there's no difference that I can articulate except Fastpassers are sent to Omega. The front seat, however, has the best view.

Buzz Lightyear's Space Ranger Spin ★★ RIDE   The "Toy Story" movies provide inspiration for a rambunctious (and addictive) 3-minute, slow-car ride that works like a shooting gallery. Passengers are equipped with laser guns and the means to rotate their vehicles, and it's their mission to blast as many targets as they can. That's easier said than done, since the aliens are spinning, bouncing, and turning, and your laser sight appears only intermittently as a blinking red light, but that's all part of the fun. You'll think you did pretty well at 118,000 until you turn and see the kid who racked up 205,000. He must have know the secret: The farther away a target is, the more it's worth.

Astro Orbiter ★★ RIDE   The gist is like Dumbo—a 90-second spin on an arma-ture, with passengers controlling height—but from much higher, and with toboggan-style seating. Usually, it takes too long, partly because you have to use an elevator to board. At night, the view of an illuminated Tomorrowland makes it worth it. **Tip:** Beneath the ride, pick up the Metrophone for some gag messages.

Tomorrowland Transit Authority PeopleMover ★★★ RIDE   The tram-like second-story track, which boards under the Astro Orbiter at Rockettower Plaza, uses pollution-free "linear induction" magnetic technology to take riders on a scenic overview of the area's attractions. On a 13-minute round-trip with no stops, it coasts past some windows over the Buzz Lightyear ride and through the guts of Space Moun-tain, where you traverse the circumference over the Omega boarding area. You will also catch a too-fleeting glimpse of one of Walt Disney's original 1963 models for Progress City. The ride itself is historic: Walt Disney envisioned this system, originally called the WEDway PeopleMover, as a principal form of transportation for the resort.

Walt's original system for admission was intended to accommodate people of all incomes. Anyone could enter his park for a nominal fee of a few dollars, but to do rides and shows, guests had to obtain coupon books from kiosks. There were five categories. The simplest, least popular attractions, like Main Street Vehicles, could be seen for cheap "A" tickets (around 10¢ in 1972) but the prime blockbusters were honored with the top distinction, an "E" ticket (85¢). It didn't take long for the designation to find its way into the American vernacular. Sally Ride pronounced her 1983 launch on the space shuttle "definitely an E-ticket." The coupon system was dropped in the early 1980s in favor of a high gate price, a system that has mostly replaced the per-ride payment system at theme parks across the world.

We use buses instead. **Tip:** There's almost never a wait. Do TTA at night, when Tomorrowland is illuminated in cobalts and greens.

Walt Disney's Carousel of Progress ★★ SHOW   They know it's corny: Attendants may welcome you by warning you not to fall asleep. But as a preboarding movie attests, Walt Disney loved this attraction—he created it with General Electric sponsorship for the 1964 World's Fair. It was later moved here, and appropriate to its underwriter, the message is a banquet of consumerist overtones about how appliances will rescue us from a life of drudgery. Walt's novel twist was that the stage remains stationery but the auditorium rotates on a ring past six rooms (four "acts" and one each for loading and unloading) of Audio-Animatronic scenes. You'll see a modern person's trivialization of daily life in 1904, 1927, and the 1940s, and an unspecified time that you could peg for 1989, what with Grandpa's breathless praise for laser discs and car phones. While our very white, very middle-class narrator (voiced by Jean Shepherd, the narrator of "A Christmas Story") loafs with his dog across the ages, his wife does chores, his mother festers, his daughter primps, and his son dreams of adventure. (Funny how a tribute to progress is riddled with obsolete gender stereotypes.) The repetitive ditty "There's a Great Big Beautiful Tomorrow" is by the Sherman Brothers, who also wrote the songs for "Mary Poppins." Set aside 25 minutes for the show, but it starts every 5 because the rotating theater allows endless refills, like the chamber of a revolver. As a relic from a more idealistic time, it's priceless, and here's hoping they never remove it, as is always the rumor. Another reason to see it: Despite the fact it has no living performers, it's billed as the longest-running stage show in the United States.

Stitch's Great Escape! ★ SHOW   What begins with a hackneyed Disney set-up—you're a "new recruit," this time at an intergalactic prison—ends with an extra-sensory sit-down presentation employing smells and rigged over-the-shoulder harnesses. Little kids get scared because of the pitch darkness, because the restraint is constrictive, and because they are alarmed to learn a dangerous alien is on the loose, even if it turns out to be their friend Stitch. Expect not menace but bawdy gags about spit, slobber, burping, and pee. Lilo makes no appearance, leaving the show without the soft heart it needs. To call this attraction reviled by many Disney fans would not be an exaggeration. The Audio-Animatronics are marvelous, though, and hilarious actor Richard Kind does a voice. The event takes about 12 minutes once you're inside. **Tips:** Enter the theater last for the best sightlines. Top-row seating keeps you from having to crane your neck upward.

3

EXPLORING WALT DISNEY WORLD | The Magic Kingdom

LIGHTS after dark

A trip to Disney doesn't seem complete if you don't set aside time to catch the nightly fireworks show, **Wishes,** held when the park is open past dark; check the "Times Guide." Although it's technically at least partially visible from anywhere, the most symmetrical view is from the Castle's front and Main Street, U.S.A. If you can see the wire strung to the Castle's top, you've got a good viewpoint. The roughly 10-minute show is quite the slick spectacle—lights dim everywhere, even the ferry dock, and you can hear the soundtrack wherever you are. Areas around and behind the Castle are closed off during the show to protect guests from falling cinders. Most nights, rides begin closing as soon as it starts, and people start heading home after it's done. You have the option of purchasing $24 illuminated "Glow With the Show" mouse ears that change color along with the show, but only about 5 percent of customers seem to do that.

If jockeying for a spot is not among your wishes—understandable, given your long day—the park throws a nightly

Fireworks Dessert Party for 170 people starting an hour before showtime at the Tomorrowland Terrace. For $26 adults and $14 kids, you get all-you-can-eat pastries, ice cream, light beverages, and a primo vantage point of Tink afloat. Naturally, it books up early (℗ **407/939-3463**).

Another can't-miss nighttime attraction (check the "Times Guide") is the **Main Street Electrical Parade,** bopping along to its signature synth-pop anthem. Its illuminated floats and light-studded costumes have mesmerized since the 1970s.

At the very end of the night (well, most nights, but not all), about 30 minutes after the posted closing time, Cinderella Castle flashes with a dazzling rainbow of light. This is a **"Kiss Goodnight,"** something that isn't on the schedules, and it's a little like the Sandman at the Apollo, sweeping you out the door. Stick it out until you see one (the last one is an hour after closing time), because by then, crowds will have thinned. Remember, you still have a monorail or a ferryboat and a parking tram to go.

Monsters Inc. Laugh Floor ★ SHOW   Like Turtle Talk with Crush at Epcot, it's a "Living Character" video show, about 15 minutes long, in which computer-animated characters on a giant screen interact with a theater full of people, singling out humans out with a hidden camera for gentle ridicule. The animation looks as fluid as in the Pixar movies and is drawn from a cast of some 20 characters, but the three you'll see in your set will vary from day to day. The quality of the experience depends as much on the eagerness of the audience as on the improvisational skill of the (spoiler alert) hidden live actors doing the voices. Don't miss the gags along the left wall of the preshow video-instruction room (the employee bulletin board warns against "Repetitive Scare Injury"). You'll probably find yourself more impressed by the canny technology than by the quality of the jokes. **Tip:** Sit in the rear or extreme sides of the auditorium to avoid being picked on.

Where to Eat in the Magic Kingdom

Following are the main Quick Service choices, plus a few specialty kiosks you shouldn't miss. All locations will have a few vegetarian options, kids' meals, and if you identify yourself, special dietary requests can usually be accommodated, albeit often at diminished quality. For information on the table-service restaurants that usually require reservations, go to p. 51. Don't go looking for a beer—there's no alcohol served except for at Be Our Guest, and only at dinnertime.

THE MAGIC KINGDOM'S QUICK-SERVICE RESTAURANTS

The park, being a mass-appeal crowd-pleaser, does not support an affordable menu that is as adventurous as its characters. Hope you like burgers.

Casey's Corner ★ AMERICAN   The hot dog-and-nachos joint facing the Castle is the only place to grab a counter-service meal around Main Street, U.S.A., but there is never enough seating. Dogs are nearly a foot long and piled embarrassingly high with choices including barbecue and chili. Main Street, U.S.A. Hot dogs $8 to $10 with fries, $2 less without.

Plaza Ice Cream Parlor ★ ICE CREAM   Although hand-scooped sundaes are served, the specialty is ice-cream sandwiches made with fresh chocolate chip cookies. They're warmest early in the day. Main Street, U.S.A. Desserts $4.50 to $5.30.

Aloha Isle ★★★ ICE CREAM   Another only-at-Disney treat: "Dole Whip" soft serve in pineapple, vanilla, or orange. Or put your Dole Whip in a Pineapple Float. Or just get a spear of fresh pineapple. Adventureland. Dole Whips $5.

Sunshine Tree Terrace ★★★ ICE CREAM   Disney fans beeline to this kiosk for the Citrus Swirl, a wonderful blend of frozen O.J. and soft-serve vanilla ice cream. The pomegranate limeaid is also gaining favor. It's a historic spot: The doe-eyed mascot is Orange Bird, which Disney created for the Florida citrus lobby, which sponsored this stand and the Tiki birds back in the 1970s. Adventureland. Beverages and desserts $4 to $5.

Tortuga Tavern ★★ MEXICAN   Open at lunch, it does burritos and beef taco salads, and it has a large, sheltered seating area. Adventureland. Combo meal $8 to $9.

Turkey Leg Cart ★★ AMERICAN   These honking hunks of meat ($11) could feed a cavemen. Frontierland, across from Frontierland Shooting Gallery.

Pecos Bill Tall Tale Inn and Cafe ★★★ AMERICAN   Get ⅓-pound cheeseburgers, and BBQ pork sandwiches, all with fries. The fixings bar has good stuff like sautéed onions and mushrooms, so it's easy to make a meal of it. It also has spacious, air-conditioned seating. Frontierland. Combo meal $9.60 to $11.

Columbia Harbour House ★★★ AMERICAN   At this indoor counter service spot, order fat sandwiches, lobster rolls, and couscous, plus sides like chowder ($5), then take them upstairs where it's quiet. Liberty Square. Combo meal $9 to $11.

Pinocchio's Village Haus ★★ AMERICAN/ITALIAN   Vaguely Italian food (flatbreads, meatball subs, and so on) adjoining "it's a small world," with a few tables in the AC overlooking the snazzy loading area. Fantasyland. Combo meal $9 to $10.

The Friar's Nook ★ AMERICAN   Window-service with no seating for mac and cheese with truffle oil, pot roast, or bacon; or hummus with veggies. Fantasyland. Snacks $3 to $8.20.

Gaston's Tavern ★ AMERICAN   In a small indoor counter service location behind the amusing fountain of Gaston, you'll find some only-at-Disney treats. The Roast Pork Shank ($9.80) is big like the famous turkey leg, only in pig flavor. Le Fou's Brew is Fantasyland's (not nearly as successful) answer to Harry Potter's Butterbeer: frozen apple juice with a lightly fruity foam. Get it in a regular cup for $4.50, or $10 in either a plastic stein or a goblet, suitable to gender roles. Fantasyland.

SAVING ON PARK munchies

If you plan to buy all your food at the park, sticking strictly to counter-service meals is the cheapest way to go. But considering you'll pay $8 to $11 each for a counter-service sandwich, plus at least $2.70 for a medium-size soft drink—the going rate in the Orlando parks—even that way, a family of four can easily spend $60 on every meal! Don't be goofy— save money! Besides eating off premises, here's how:

o **Subtract unwanted combo items.** Although counter-service restaurants make the menu appear like it's mostly combo meals, it's an unpublicized fact that you may eliminate unwanted items from adult selections and save money. Dropping fries or other bundled side dishes can save about $2.25. For carrot sticks!

o **Pack a little food of your own.** Park security usually looks the other way if you bring a soft lunchbag-size cooler (hard-sided Igloos will be rejected). Or just tote sandwiches in plastic bags. If your lodging has a freezer, put juice boxes in there; they'll be thawed by lunch.

o **Economize with an all-you-can-eat meal.** Character meals (p. 191) give good value because they serve limitless food. A big lunch can last you until after you leave the park.

o **Skip table-service meals, or plan them strategically.** They can chomp as much as 90 minutes out of your touring time. Do that

twice and you've lost a third of your day. A park that could be seen in 1 day would require 2, doubling costs. If you want a sit-down meal, do it at lunch, when prices are often lower than at dinner. Eat around 11am, when crowds are lighter. Also, if you don't show up for Disney reservations, you're docked $10—assess whether your kids will truly have energy for an evening table-service meal if you schedule one.

o **Adults may order cheaper and smaller kids' meals.** No one will stop them.

o **Snack on fruit.** Each park has at least one fruit stand.

o **Seek out the turkey legs.** They're giant (1½ pounds, from 45-pound turkeys), salty, and cost around $11. They taste so good because they're injected with brine before cooking for 6 hours. Just don't think about the hormones it takes to grow a 45-pound bird. Or a 5-foot-tall mouse.

o **Order drinks without ice.** Soda is dispensed cold to prevent foaming. It's chilling how much ice is in a standard Disney Coke.

o **Order water for free.** It comes in a regular-sized cup.

o **Stretch meals.** If there's a double cheeseburger on the menu, order it and an extra bun for about $1. Then make two burgers and raid the fixings bar. Disney has eliminated double cheeseburgers, but Universal has still them.

Cosmic Ray's Starlight Cafe ★★★ AMERICAN The best choice for indoor Quick Service on this end of the park, it does burgers, sandwiches, and chicken (both sandwich and rotisserie) and has a toppings bar with freshly sautéed mushrooms and onions—choose the "bay" that serves your choice. It's distinguished by regular lounge-act shows by Sonny Eclipse, a long-running Audio-Animatronic character. Despite Sonny, I'd rather eat on its outdoor terrace. The panorama of the Castle is sublime; it's my favorite lunchtime view. That empty boat dock below is from the extinct Swan Boats, which plied the moat in years past. Tomorrowland. Combo meal $9 to $11.

The Lunching Pad ★ AMERICAN   Window-service with exposed seating for hot dogs of several varieties. Tomorrowland. Hot dogs $8 to $9.

THE MAGIC KINGDOM'S TABLE-SERVICE RESTAURANTS

This is the most popular theme park in the world, so as you can imagine, getting a seat can be competitive (and it requires a credit card) and the wait staff is almost always running around. Some restaurants *may* accept walk-ins at 4pm, when they start dinner service, but ask early in the day. Taking them clockwise around the park:

Tony's Town Square Restaurant ★★ ITALIAN   Loosely themed on the Italian restaurant scene from "Lady and the Tramp" (there's a fountain of the two doe-eyed dogs), it's loud, not romantic. To repeat Tramp's spaghetti-and-meatball sharing gesture (kindly don't use your nose like he did), you'll pay $18 a plate. It also does chicken parmesan, cannelloni, and shrimp scampi. After lunch, sandwiches, pizzas, and flatbreads are swapped out for pork tenderloin and strip steak with potatoes and vegetables. Main Street, U.S.A. **Tip:** There's free lemon water in the lobby if you're on Main Street and want a free drink. Main courses $18 to $30.

The Crystal Palace, A Buffet with Character ★★★ AMERICAN   Under an airy Victorian-style skylight canopy that emulates a hall from an 1853 New York City world's exhibition, Winnie the Pooh greets diners at what's probably the prettiest in-park restaurant in all of Walt Disney World. The refined air doesn't stop Pooh and his buddies (Tigger, Eeyore, Piglet) from jamming the aisles with a conga line. Being slightly smaller than many other character dining locations, you're likely to get some face time with the characters. This restaurant's been open since Day One and offers three daily all-you-can-eat buffets of changing, crowd-pleasing standards from meats to vegetables. There's a make-your-own-sundae bar for lunch and dinner. Prices are lowest at breakfast (the best time anyway, since you'll have the rest of your day free) and scale up. Main Street, U.S.A. Buffet $25 to $38 adults, $14 to $18 children.

The Plaza Restaurant ★ AMERICAN   What's special about this one is its view. Situated at the end of Main Street facing Cinderella Castle, it focuses on sandwiches, burgers, and salads, which are served with broccoli slaw, homemade chips, or french fries. Add soup for $4.50. It also serves ice cream sundaes and cheesecake from the shop next door. Main Street, U.S.A. Main courses $11 to $18.

Liberty Tree Tavern ★★ AMERICAN   At lunch, this colonial-style place (stained wood and rung-backed chairs) facing the Rivers of America (no view) serves vaguely patriotic a la carte fare such as pot roast, turkey with stuffing, and "Freedom Pasta," which is fusilli with chicken, vegetables, and mushrooms in a cream sauce. After 4pm, it shifts to an all-you-can-eat buffet including a beef carvery. Dessert is Johnny Appleseed's Cake, or white cake filled with Craisins—just like in the colonies! Liberty Square. Lunchtime mains $14 to $20, dinner buffet $32 adults, $16 kids.

Cinderella's Royal Table ★★★ AMERICAN   This is the holy grail of character meals since it actually takes place inside Cinderella Castle where there's a capacity of less than 200. The famous royal resident always appears (sometimes joined by her soul sisters Jasmine, Aurora, Snow White, and others), and little girls far and wide dress up like princesses to meet her. The interior is as lavish as you'd expect for the inside of the Castle, with mock medieval vaulted ceilings, a royal red carpet, stained glass, and stylized crest shields adoring the walls. Meals aren't all-you-can-eat, but they are all prix-fixe, though the price shifts with the season. Bookings open 180 days ahead at 7am Orlando time (and must be prepaid by credit card) and are snapped up in moments. Food selections include swordfish and pork loin. Meals $58 to $73 adults, $36 to $43 children; price includes tip and five photos of your party.

freebies AT DISNEY

It's not easy finding fun stuff to do that you don't have to cough up for, but you don't need to hand over a cent for these pleasures—not even for park admission. Anyone off the street can enjoy these things:

○ **Watch the Electrical Water Pageant** on the Seven Seas Lagoon and Bay Lake between 9 and 10:20pm. The illuminated floats, which twitter to a soundtrack, make a circuit around the conjoined ponds after nightfall, and you can see it from the beachfront at any hotel.

○ **Ride the ferries** between the resorts, such as the one from Port Orleans Riverside to Downtown Disney along the meandering Sassagoula River, which passes the French Quarter resort and the Old Key West resort. You can even ride the one from the monorail-area resorts to the foot of the Magic Kingdom.

○ **Take the monorail.** Whiz round the Seven Seas Lagoon past the Magic Kingdom and through the Contemporary Resort as many times as you want without a ticket. You can also use it to make the 4-mile round-trip to Epcot, where you'll do a flyover of Future World.

○ **Hike at Fort Wilderness.** The trail begins at the east end of Bay Lake and threads through occasionally muddy woods.

○ **Spend a night by the pool.** Most resorts keep them open 'til midnight. Technically, you should be a guest. But behave, and no one'll care (except at the Yacht and Beach clubs, where bracelets are required). Each hotel's parking lot has a gate, but if you park at Downtown Disney and take a free Disney bus, you'll scoot right in.

○ **See African animals** at the Animal Kingdom Lodge. The gatekeeper will admit you to sit by the fire in its vaulted lobby, and out back, you can watch game such as giraffe and kudu from the Sunset Overlook. Sometimes, there are zoologists who answer questions.

○ For a marvelous view of the fireworks over the Magic Kingdom, **stroll on the beach** of the Grand Floridian or the Polynesian resorts. The sand is millions of years old and was recovered from under Bay Lake. Did you know Disney built a giant wave machine in the middle of the lake? It never worked.

○ **Partake of the campfire singalong,** which happens nightly near the Meadow Trading Post at Fort Wilderness, followed by a Disney feature on an outdoor screen.

○ **Cuddle farm animals,** including ducks, goats, and peacocks, at the petting farm behind Fort Wilderness's Pioneer Hall. You can also see the horses used to pull streetcars up Main Street, U.S.A.

○ **Ride the bus system.** Park at Downtown Disney for free and take the buses to any theme park for nothing. That'll save you $17 each day.

Be Our Guest Restaurant ★★ AMERICAN   It's not so easy to be their guest here, since bookings fill incredibly quickly. As a 2012 newcomer to Fantasyland, it sports a few technical tricks to evoke Beast's castle, including animated falling snow outside some false windows, a portrait that reveals a hidden Beast when illuminated by periodic lightning (that's in the West Wing, in case it might scare your kids), and an animated rose under glass that slowly sheds its petals. Like a real castle, all those polished surfaces make things incredibly loud. Although the food is vaguely French (there's ratatouille at dinner, croque-monsieur at lunch, and French onion soup all the time), the preponderance of pork chops, steaks, and salmon are really more American. You order by kiosk, pour your own beverages, and your food is wheeled to you when it's ready. This is the only place in the Magic Kingdom where you can get alcohol, but only at dinner and only with that coveted reservation. Fantasyland. Main courses $10 to $14 lunch, $16 to $30 dinner.

EPCOT

Epcot ★★★ remains one of Walt Disney World's finest achievements. More than any other park, Epcot changes its personality, decorations, and diversions by the season. Guests usually don't learn much more than they already know (so as not to bore them or to insult their intelligence), but even though there isn't much take-away information, that there's plenty to soak up if you explore. There's plenty to do here without having to wait in lines, and unlike other parks, there are lots of places to sit. The wide variety of foods and alcoholic beverages is also a big draw. Epcot's genial personality has earned it a spot as the fifth-most-visited theme park on Earth, racking up some 11.2 million entries in 2013.

The 260-acre park is divided into two zones, Future World and World Showcase, laid out roughly like a figure eight. Both areas started life separately but, as the legend goes, were grafted together when plans were afoot. **Future World** is where the wonders of industry were extolled in corporate-sponsored "pavilions." The companies had a hand creating them and they also maintained VIP areas in backstage areas for executives and special guests. At the back of the property, around a 1.3-mile lake footpath, **World Showcase** was the circuit of countries, each representing in miniature its namesake's essence. These, too, received funding from their host countries. The expense of updating Future World's exhibits has caused Disney to gradually phase out the educational aspects of the attractions. One by one, original pavilions have been replaced by sense-tingling rides, so that today, only two of the original rides, Spaceship Earth and Living with the Land, remain more or less as they originally were.

GETTING IN   The parking lot is at the ticket gates, although you can also catch the **monorail** from the Magic Kingdom parking area. If you park past the canal or near the monorail track, don't bother with the tram; you can walk to the gates faster. Bags will be quickly inspected. As you enter the park, lockers are at the right of Spaceship Earth; wheeled rentals are to the left. Also on the left is Guest Relations, where last-minute dining reservations can be made, though often, you'll just be deferred to the restaurant in question.

HOURS   Future World opens at 9am, and World Showcase opens at 11am. Future World often closes at 7pm, 2 hours before World Showcase. The nightly IllumiNations show usually takes place over World Showcase Lagoon at 9pm; at its conclusion, the hordes stampede for their cars en masse.

Epcot has so much to explore, and eat, and drink that you won't feel like you're racing from ride to ride (as you might in other parks). Just make sure you have a late-morning Fastpass for Soarin'.

Ride **Test Track** before the line gets crazy.
⬇
Ride **Mission: Space.**
⬇
By now, your **Soarin'** Fastpass is probably valid. Ride it.
⬇
Visit **The Seas with Nemo and Friends.**
⬇
Ride **Living with the Land** for a glimpse at Epcot's roots. Consider doing **Soarin'** again. If you're hungry, Sunshine Seasons, in this pavilion, is a terrific place to eat.
⬇
Ride **Spaceship Earth** and visit **Innoventions.**
⬇
Enter World Showcase at Mexico and ride **Gran Fiesta Tour.**
⬇

Ride **Maelstrom** at Norway. You have now enjoyed all the rides in World Showcase.
⬇
Continue along World Showcase at a slow pace, having removed the temptation to rush. The movies (in China, France, and Canada) are all worth seeing; the shops can be surprisingly good; and the street entertainment choices (noted on the Times Guide) are excellent.
⬇
Catch the American Adventure; the Voices of America perform about 15 minutes before show times, and they're listed in the Times Guide.
⬇
Continue along World Showcase. Pause for a pint in the United Kingdom.
⬇
Remember Future World usually closes at 7pm, so if you have time before then, re-ride anything you loved (Spaceship Earth isn't usually crowded late in the day).

Eat dinner in the land of your choice and catch **IllumiNations**. It's best to secure a good viewing point at least 30 minute ahead.

Future World

By the time Walt Disney World finally got around to opening its second park, EPCOT Center, on October 1, 1982 (11 years to the day after the Magic Kingdom and at a staggering estimated cost of $1.4 billion; America's biggest construction project at the time), it was but a flicker of its original purpose. No one would actually live there, and few experimental endeavors would be undertaken. Instead, it turned out that the most economical course was to turn Walt's legacy into another moneymaking theme park, heavily subsidized by corporate participation and sold by heavy promotion of "Walt's dream"—a formula that prevails today. In truth, the final design wasn't much different from the world's fair that Walt's father had helped construct in Chicago in 1893 or that Walt himself defined in New York in 1964: examples of how technology was ostensibly improving lives, plus some pavilions representing foreign lands for the edification of people unlikely to travel there themselves. In December 1993, the park name was simplified to Epcot. As you face the lagoon, the pavilions on the left side of Future World are generally about the physical and man-made sciences, and the ones on the right are more about the natural sciences. Behind Spaceship Earth, look for a park **tip board,** which posts wait times and the daily schedule. There are two more tip boards through the underpasses to the east and west sections of Future World.

Epcot

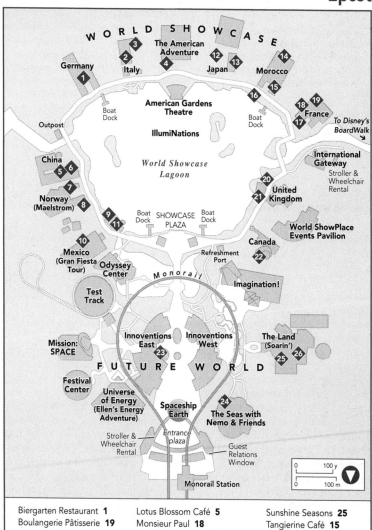

WORLD SHOWCASE

The American Adventure

Germany **1**

Italy

Italy **2** **3**

4

Japan **12** **13**

Morocco **14**

15

Boat Dock **16**

American Gardens Theatre

Boat Dock

IllumiNations

France **18** **19**

17

To Disney's BoardWalk

Outpost

World Showcase Lagoon

International Gateway

Stroller & Wheelchair Rental

China **5** **6**

7

Norway (Maelstrom) **8**

9 **11**

United Kingdom **20** **21**

Boat Dock

SHOWCASE PLAZA

Boat Dock

World ShowPlace Events Pavilion

Mexico (Gran Fiesta Tour) **10**

Odyssey Center

Monorail

Refreshment Port

Canada **22**

Test Track

Imagination!

Mission: SPACE

Innoventions East **23**

Innoventions West

The Land (Soarin') **25** **26**

Festival Center

FUTURE WORLD

Universe of Energy (Ellen's Energy Adventure)

Spaceship Earth

The Seas with Nemo & Friends **24**

Stroller & Wheelchair Rental

Entrance plaza

Guest Relations Window

Monorail Station

0   100 y
0   100 m

Biergarten Restaurant **1**
Boulangerie Pâtisserie **19**
La Cantina de San Angel **11**
Le Cellier Steakhouse **22**
Chefs de France **17**
Coral Reef Restaurant **24**
Electric Umbrella **23**
The Garden Grill **26**
La Hacienda de San Angel **9**
Kringla Bakeri og Kafé **8**
Liberty Inn **4**

Lotus Blossom Café **5**
Monsieur Paul **18**
Nine Dragons Restaurant **6**
Princess Storybook Dining at
  Akershus Royal Banquet Hall **7**
Restaurant Marrakesh **14**
Rose & Crown Pub
  & Dining Room **21**
San Angel Inn Restaurante **10**
Sommerfest **1**
Spice Road Table **16**

Sunshine Seasons **25**
Tangierine Café **15**
Teppan Edo **13**
Tokyo Dining **13**
Tutto Gusto **2**
Tutto Italia Ristorante **2**
Via Napoli Ristorante
  e Pizzeria **3**
Yakitori House **12**
Yorkshire County
  Fish Shop **20**

3

EXPLORING WALT DISNEY WORLD | Epcot

A history OF EPCOT

Although people think of Walt Disney as prototypically American, he had a communist streak. He long dreamed of establishing a real, working city where 20,000 full-time residents, none of them unemployed, would test out experimental technologies in the course of their daily lives. In vintage films where he discusses his Florida Project, his passion for creating such a self-sustaining community, to be called the Experimental Prototype Community of Tomorrow, was inextricable from the rest of his planned resort. He wanted nothing less than to revolutionize the world. Truck traffic would be routed to vehicle plazas beneath the city, out of pedestrians' way, while PeopleMovers (like the ones of Magic Kingdom's Tomorrowland Transit Authority) would shift the population around town. Between home and downtown, they'd take the monorail. Even on his deathbed, Walt was perfecting real plans for the city that would be his crowning legacy: one whose innovations would make life better for everyone on Earth. Had he lived just 3 more years, he would have made sure it happened.

Spaceship Earth ★★★ RIDE   That gorgeous orb looks like a golf ball on a tee, but the 16-million-pound structure, coated with 11,324 aluminum-bonded panels and sheathed inside with a rainproof rubber layer, is supported by a tablelike scaffolding where its six legs enter the dome. Think of this 180-foot-tall Buckminster Fuller sphere as a direct descendent of the Perisphere of the 1939 World's Fair or the Unisphere of the 1964 World's Fair, which were the icons for their own parks. No mere shell, it houses an eponymous ride using the OmniMover system of cars linked together like an endless snake. The ride slowly winds within the sphere, all on the course of a shallow, sixth-grade-level journey (narrated by Judi Dench) through the history of communications, from Greek theater to the Sistine Chapel to the printing press to the telegraph. In a bit of unintended kinesthetic commentary, once you reach the present day, the ride is all downhill. Once you're off it, I defy you to tell me what you learned from it. This, of course, makes it essential Epcot. This is the ride that still shows what the 1982 park was like—its robot-populated sister pavilions about transportation and the future were razed in the 1990s to make way for flashier thrills. Although some people don't get it, I cherish it as a soothing sojourn not only through time, but also through air-conditioning. Since it's the first ride that guests encounter in the park, lines, which move fast, are much shorter in the afternoon.

Innoventions ★ ACTIVITY   The semicircular buildings facing each other behind Spaceship Earth are the domain of corporate-sponsored exhibits, as Walt had intended. Innoventions (originally Communicore) is under-patronized and ever-changing. There's much here to divert you, but it may close at 7pm:

- **Sum of All Thrills:** Lines are shortest in late afternoon for this slow-loading, 90-second ride from Raytheon, the weapons-tech manufacturer (!!). You design your own ride on a panel before testing it in a motion simulator at the end of a robot arm. You choose if you want your ride to go nearly upside-down or not.
- **Habit Heroes:** Paid for by Blue Cross Blue Shield, this is an 18-minute, three-game motion-sensor course where you learn very vague health lessons by battling monsters that are somehow preventing you from getting nutrition.

- **VISION House:** From Green Builder Media, a full-scale mock-up of a suburban home to demonstrate specific products that make a home more energy efficient—and then tells you how you can buy them.
- **StormStruck:** In this 3-D movie to inspire storm-proofing your home, audiences are buffeted with wind and rain effects, and then vote on proofing methods, which are then tested on screen.
- **Where's the Fire?** Liberty Mutual teaches about fire safety.
- **Test the Limits Lab:** Underwriters Laboratories shows how it approves products—expect lots of clanging and banging.
- **The Great Piggy Bank Adventure:** Paid for by T. Rowe Price, the midway-game adventure teaches that apparently the best way to save is to catch floating coins with pedal-powered flying piggy banks. So you spend it on vacations. Whatever, it's fun.

Also in the Innoventions buildings, you'll find **MouseGear,** the largest souvenir shop in Epcot and opposite that, **Club Cool,** by the Coca-Cola Company, which lets you pour unlimited samples of eight soft drink flavors sold only in other countries. Beverly, a bitter aperitif from Italy, is not for faint tongues. If you're an obsessive tightwad, you can keep coming back here instead of buying a real Coke (although most of it is dramatically sweet). Frozen Cokes are sold for $4. Between Innoventions, you'll find the **World Fellowship Fountain,** which was dedicated by Walt's widow, Lillian. At the opening ceremony, water from 23 countries was combined as a symbol of brotherhood. It can shoot 150 feet in the air, although it rarely does. There's a 5-minute choreographed splash-up on the quarter hour.

Universe of Energy ★ RIDE/SHOW This attraction is highly emblematic of Epcot's corporate-dictated content. The dated adventure begins with a movie, circa 1996, featuring Ellen DeGeneres being taught by Bill Nye the Science Guy about how oil is formed and then pulled out of the ground for the benefit of mankind. If that sounds lame, at least the ride system is more creative: The audience is seated in six 97-passenger slabs of mobile theater-style bench seating. Miraculously, the slabs organize themselves in a line and move from room to giant room, passing primeval forests full of realistic dinosaurs. When, at another movie stop, the issue of global warming comes up, Nye waves it away, saying, "It's a hot topic with lots of questions" before reassuring us that "we're far from running on empty." Not surprisingly, the didactic venture was backed by ExxonMobil. The whole show takes between 30 to 50 minutes to see, depending on when you arrive at the preshow, which makes it a good cool-down.

The Best of Epcot

Don't miss if you're 6: Turtle Talk with Crush

Don't miss if you're 16: Test Track

Requisite photo op: Spaceship Earth

Food you can only get here: Rice cream, the bakery at Norway

The most crowded, so Fastpass or go early: Soarin'

Skippable: Journey into Imagination with Figment

Quintessentially Disney: Spaceship Earth

Biggest thrill: Mission: SPACE

Best show: Voices of Liberty, the American Adventure

Character meals: Akershus Royal Banquet Hall, Norway; Garden Grill, The Land

Where to find peace: Future World: the Odyssey Center catwalks; World Showcase: the gardens of Japan

Outside, the roof is coated in 2 acres of solar panels, which generate 15 percent of the show's energy appetite; the building site was chosen for maximum sunlight exposure. **Strategy:** Although all sections spend time waiting for the others to move or catch up, the two sections on the right wait in the most interesting spaces.

Mission: SPACE ★★ RIDE Behind the gorgeously swirling planetary facade is a ride that approximates, with intense accuracy, the experience of a rocket launch. Although technically a whirl in a giant centrifuge, the skillful design tricks the mind into believing the body's actually lurching backward in a launch for Mars (although my eyeballs seem to know—they wag uncontrollably for the first 30 seconds). Gary Sinise, oozing gravitas, issues so many preshow warnings against motion sickness that I honestly think it psychs people out and primes them for illness, although sufferers of sinus problems have reported discomfort. Each passenger in the extremely tight four-person cockpits is assigned two buttons to press at given cues—it doesn't matter if you don't, but at least hold onto your steering joystick, because it gives force feedback as you travel. Ultimately, it's a ride that's all brains and no heart—I'm deeply impressed at what they've done, but I don't feel like doing it twice. The Advanced Training Lab postshow area (through the gift shop) is worthwhile even if you don't ride. There, you can play interactive group games and send free postcards home via computer. **Strategy:** Whereas Mad Tea Party makes me want to hurl, I do just fine on this ride. You'll be given a choice when you enter the building: There's a second version (color-coded green) with easy motion-simulator effects but no troubling centrifuge action, but in my opinion, the missing element renders the ride pointless.

Test Track ★ RIDE Cars thunder enticingly around the bend of an outdoor motorway at nearly 65mph, but that's as good as it gets. Those passengers are experiencing the climax of a complicated, multistage ride that puts them through the paces of a proving ground of an automobile manufacturer (sponsor: Chevrolet). Before boarding, you use a touch screen to choose a car using the ill-defined factors of capability, power, responsiveness, and efficiency. Then, you go along for the ride in a minimally decorated warehouse on a series of diagnostic safety tests (don't worry; you don't have to actually do anything), while trackside screens ostensibly show you how your creation would perform under the same circumstances—in fact, it's the same exact ride every time. Your six-passenger car brakes suddenly and careens through a mostly black room decorated by illuminated lines that seem to have been inspired by "Tron" (and a very low budget). Finally, you shoot outside the building and make an invigorating circuit

The Death of "Life"

Between Mission: SPACE and the Universe of Energy, you'll spot a golden dome. No, you haven't been in the sun too long. That's Wonders of Life, one of the great failures of modern Disney World. Opened in 1989 as a paean to all things biological, executives closed it when they couldn't find a corporation willing to pony up continued sponsorship. Some of science's greatest advances are being made in the biological realm, yet the topic is neglected at Epcot for want of a corporate bankroll. Among the casualties: **Body Wars,** a motion-simulator ride through the bloodstream; **Cranium Command,** addressing how a 12-year-old boy's brain controlled his growing body; and **"The Making of Me,"** a film that gingerly addressed conception and pregnancy without stepping on ideological toes. The tarnished pavilion sits empty and decaying.

Besides The Seas with Nemo & Friends, there aren't many attractions for young children in Epcot. Disney addressed the problem with small, manned booths that it calls **Kidcot Fun Stops,** which offer crafty diversions such as coloring, stamping, or maskmaking—stuff kids do at the school fair. Epcot Passports, which can be stamped in every country, were once free but now cost $11, but attendants will stamp your kids' crafts, such as the handle of the mask they made, for free instead. From the kiosk on the walkway to World Showcase from Future World, sign them up for the free **Agent P's World Showcase Adventure,** in which they follow instructions on toy cell phones and punch codes to make tricksy things happen in at 7 stops in various countries. It's so engrossing, in fact, that kids sometimes have a hard time paying attention to anything else. Animal Kingdom has a free paper scavenger hunt, **Wilderness Explorers,** in which kids college merit badges (stickers) for learning things about animals and conservation. Join that on the bridge between Oasis and the Tree of Life.

around the circular track over the Epcot employee parking lot. (Hertz has a similar experience—it's called a convertible.) The post-ride showroom features a few steering games plus samples from Chevy's current fleet, which get constant rubdowns by an attendant with a rag. Ultimately, it's pretty much been a boring ride since its 2012 renovation; it doesn't make much sense anymore and it feels cheap. **Strategy:** Along with Soarin', it's the busiest ride at Epcot, so get a Fastpass. There's a single-rider line that doesn't let you skip much and invariably puts you in a right-hand seat, but cast members may grill you about whether you're truly alone.

The Seas with Nemo & Friends ★★ RIDE/ACTIVITY   One of the world's largest saltwater aquariums, it's 27 feet deep, 203 feet across, holds 5.7 million gallons, and you can spend as long as you like watching the swimming creatures from two levels. About a third of the tank is reserved for dolphins and sea turtles, while reef fish, rays, and sharks dominate the rest. When the pavilion opened in 1986 as The Living Seas, sharks were the big draw and scientists answered questions everywhere; today, because of "Finding Nemo," kids ask to see the clown fish and there's nary an interpreter in sight. A visit begins with a 5-minute, slow-moving ride in OmniMover "clamobiles" through a simulated undersea world. Half the point of the ride is, of course, to find Nemo, who's lost again; the other characters incessantly shout his name, which soon grates on adult nerves. The ride climaxes to the tune of "In the Big Blue World" (from the Nemo musical at Animal Kingdom) with a peek into the real aquarium as Nemo and his friends are projected into the windows, cleverly uniting the fictional world with the real animal universe, "Seabase," with which you will now be acquainted. A few times a day, the giant tube dominating the hall is occupied by a diver—an unforgettable sight—to demonstrate how SCUBA works. On the second floor, which is quieter than the kiddie-clogged first floor, don't miss the observation platform that extends into the mighty tank. The daily roster sign apprises you of the day's dolphin talks and fish feedings (the schedule is busiest between 10am and 4pm), when there will be someone on hand to explain what you're seeing. The **dolphins** live separately in the first space on the left. If human divers are swimming, they'll communicate with guests by way of magnetized writing tablets. Also, check out the **manatees,** the sweet-natured "sea cows" that are threatened in Florida. **Strategy:** If the pavilion's entry line is horrific, bypass the ride by entering through the exit, at the far left.

Turtle Talk with Crush ★★ SHOW   Inside The Seas with Nemo & Friends is an amusing 20-minute show in which a computer-animated version of the 150-year-old surfer-dude turtle interacts with audiences, making jokes about what they're wearing and fielding questions. It's part of what Disney calls its "Living Characters" program. There is the distraction of ray and jellyfish tanks in the waiting area. Next door is **Bruce's Sub House,** a play area similar to any science museum's.

Soarin' ★★★ RIDE   The Land pavilion takes up 6 acres, more than all of Tomorrowland, and this ride is a big reason why. In it, audiences are seated on benches and "flown," hang glider–like, across enormous movies of California's wonders while scents waft, hair blows, and the seats gently rock in tandem with the motions of the flight. The ride is highly repeatable and deeply pleasurable for all ages. It's a facsimile of the one at Disney's California Adventure park in Anaheim, hence the imagery exclusive to the Golden State, but there are rumors of brand new Florida images in the works. **Strategy:** Wait times can exceed 3 hours (yeah, I know—crazy!), so schedule a Fastpass. The best seats are in the middle sections on the top row, where there are no feet dangling in your field of vision. That means you should aim for position B-1, or at the very least A-1 or C-1. Those with height issues should request something ending in 3, the closest to the ground.

Living with the Land ★ RIDE   The Land's other ride, after Soarin', is a 14-minute (wonderfully air-conditioned) boat trip that glosses over the realm of farming technologies. It's one of the last Epcot rides to provide a semblance of education, especially when you pass some experimental growth methods (like a nutrient film technique and aquaponics). These methods are being explored, or so we're told, to curb world hunger, but the hard fact is that GMOs, which are not mentioned, won industry dominance years ago, and the activity in Epcot's labs is intermittent, not the hive of active research it was meant to be. They do some stuff here though: Annually, they grow some 5,000 pounds of fish, which are served in Disney restaurants. This ride is original to opening day, although the live narrators were disposed of in favor of a recording. For those interested in the topic, the info will be too thin, but for those who are bored green, it will seem to last forever. **Strategy:** Boats load slowly, so go early or late to escape the inevitable buildup.

The Circle of Life ★ SHOW   Upstairs, in The Land, this minor, 13-minute movie stars "The Lion King" characters and concerns conservation (an Epcot-worthy message). It'll keep you off the streets and seated in AC.

Captain EO ★★★ SHOW   The minute Michael Jackson died, Disney yanked this trippy 1986 chestnut out of mothballs and re-installed it in its original home, the Imagination! pavilion, minus a few original special effects. For years, this 17-minute 3-D music video, starring Jackson as a Han Solo–type space pilot who is accompanied by creepy/adorable sidekicks, was a punch line for its excess and ego, but premature death and '80s nostalgia have renewed it. It concerns a mean, dark-hearted diva whose grip on a bleak world is loosened by the sheer charm of Jocko's performance—kind of like the climax of "The Wiz" if the Wicked Witch was Anjelica Huston.

Journey into Imagination with Figment ★ RIDE   There's no line for a reason. It feels like Disney ran out of money halfway through the ride—one section of this slow track-based ride is simply a room of black curtains and painted boards. Its daffy purple dinosaur, Figment, once figured as Epcot's most prominent mascot and now strains to act cuddly in his last, forlorn outpost. The ride purports to be an open house of the Imagination Institute run by Prof. Nigel Channing (Eric Idle), but Figment seizes control of the tour and offends your senses—your sense of good taste, though, is the most violated. This is the third attempt to get an Imagination ride right since 1982. The ride dumps out into **ImageWorks,** once a high-tech playground by Kodak but now with little more to do than assemble a Figment using touchscreens or purchase fairground-style composite gag photos. Look above the roped-off spiral staircase for a glimpse of the glass pyramids atrium, now forbidden, and you'll get a sense for how this pretty half-closed pavilion is now rotten with neglect. You might have gathered by now that Imagination! is not Epcot at its best. However, the fountain pods in front, which shoot snakes of water from one to another, are a firm favorite of children, who never tire of trying to catch one of the so-called "laminar flow" spurts.

World Showcase

The 1.3-mile path circling the World Showcase Lagoon is home to 11 pavilions created in the idealized image of their home countries—get your picture taken in front of a miniature Eiffel Tower (it'll look real through the lens), or at the Doge's Palace in Venice. The pavilions were built more to elicit an emotional response and not to truly replicate. Disney is diligent about the upkeep of this area, but it neglects development—the last "country" to open was Norway back in 1988, and without joint participation by foreign tourism offices, there are unlikely to be more. There also seems to be an emphasis on countries that Americans already know, and neither South America nor Australasia is represented at all. But World Showcase does have some of the most original restaurants in Disney World, and the shops are stocked with crafts and national products (you can buy real Chinese tea in China and sweaters in Norway), although the variety is slipping. It's also the only area in Epcot in which alcoholic beverages are sold.

There is far more fascinating stuff to do in World Showcase than the free Disney map lets on. Pocket it and let your curiosity guide you. You should, though, keep the day's **Times Guide** firmly in hand. The pavilions are crawling with unexpected musical and dance performances conducted by natives of each country. Seeing them makes a day richer and squeezes value from your ticket. Rush and you'll miss a lot. I suggest going **clockwise around the lagoon** mostly because the only two rides in World Showcase will come quickly on the left; if you go counterclockwise, you'll reach them after they accrue lines. After midafternoon, it won't matter.

Tip: Anything purchased in World Showcase can be sent to the **Package Pickup** at the front of Future World; allow 3 hours for delivery (it's not refrigerated, so chocolate melts). On some days—it depends how busy things are—two **ferry** routes cross the lagoon. One leaves near Germany and one from Morocco, and both land near the top of Future World. You will not save time using them; they're merely a pleasant way to get off your feet.

MEXICO ★★★

Skirting the lagoon clockwise, Mexico is your first stop. Everything to see is inside the faux temple, which contains a faux river (for the Gran Fiesta Tour ride), a faux volcano, and a faux night sky strung with lanterns. The **Mexican Folk Art Gallery** showcases whimsical carvings; "La Vida Antigua: Life in Ancient Mexico" is for artifacts and dioramas—one of Epcot's fun secrets, the great stone medallion in its center seems to mysteriously fill with luminous color as you watch. In the main *zócalo* of Plaza de los Amigos from Tuesday to Friday mornings, look for Alba, who for more than a decade has hand-painted Oaxacan woodcarvings here; her brother Marco carves them on other days. Listen for the terrific Mariachi Cobre, which has performed here since the park's opening day. There's also a small tequila bar (chips and dip also for

World Showcase pavilions are staffed by young people who were born and raised in the host country. Many of their contracts last for up to a year, and they chose to come to Florida as much to learn about America as to be ambassadors for their own nations, although many of them complain that most park guests don't bother asking anything except where the bathrooms are. Be kind to them, speak slowly if you sometimes cannot immediately understand each other's accent, and most of all, seize this unusual chance to ask questions about their cultures. These folks, despite the fact they're zipped into silly costumes, are modern, intelligent people who are so proud of where they come from that they traveled halfway around the world to share their heritage with you. Help them do that.

sale) and a crystal shop. **Influences:** A diplomatic mix of Mayan, Toltec, Aztec, and Spanish styles. **Fun stuff to Buy:** At the dusky **La Cava de Tequila,** knock back some of the house liquor or get a designer margarita ($11 to the mid-teens). Maracas ($6 each), Oaxacan woodcarvings (from $18), piñatas from $12, hand-painted pottery skulls ($26) and $7 mini sombreros. You can also buy a $28 "Hecho En Mexico" tee-shirt that was actually made in Pakistan. Oh, Disney.

Gran Fiesta Tour Starring the Three Caballeros ★★ RIDE It's easy to develop a soft spot for the bland, 8-minute boat float that, for its cheesiness, has been nicknamed "the Mexican 'it's a small world.'" As you pass movie screens, jiggling dolls, and dancing Day of the Dead skeletons, you quickly realize you're enjoying the product of Mexican tourist board input. A 2007 rehab imposed animated appearances by the 1940s characters the Three Caballeros—never mind that only Panchito Pistoles the rooster is Mexican (José Carioca the parrot is Brazilian, and Donald Duck is American). The experience is sweet, and it's a worthy siesta break. Donald conducts autograph sessions outside, to the right of the pavilion.

NORWAY ★★

Next along is Norway, the youngest pavilion (built 1988), which is home to the only other ride in World Showcase. Until the fall of 2014, that was Maelstrom, a 5-minute river ride past trolls and other Norse monsters. The success of "Frozen" took Disney by surprise, and now that ride has been closed so it can be converted to one based on the animated movie. Come early 2016, when that opens, there will also be a much-needed special area for meeting Elsa and Anna. Norway's Akershus Royal Banquet Hall does princess character meals morning, noon, and evening. In the one-room **Stave Church Gallery,** check out a few genuine Norse artifacts (13th-c. bowl and spoon and 1828 tankard with a hollow branch for a spout) that are pegged to "Frozen." Towering above it all, the wooden Stave Church is a Norwegian original; there were once around 1,000 in the country, but today, there are only 28. **The Puffin's Roost** contains a 9-foot-tall troll—photo op alert. **Influences:** Town squares of Bergen, Alesund, Oslo, and the Satesdal Valley; the 14th-century Akershus castle on Oslo harbor. **Fun Stuff to Buy:** Laila body lotions (assorted prices) and foam swords ($11). At the bakery, try the $2.50 rice cream, a snack that those in the know are happy to make a detour for. I prefer the plastic horned Viking helmets ($12–17), bags of Daim candy ($15, even though it's Swedish), and Olaf character T-shirts ($22).

CHINA ★★

Enter through the remarkable replica of Beijing's Temple of Heaven. Make time to catch the **Jeweled Dragon Acrobats,** some of the most riveting street performers in the World Showcase. "Tomb Warriors: Guardian Spirits of Ancient China," in the **House of the Whispering Willow,** is a miniature re-creation of a tiny portion of the legendary terra-cotta warriors of the Han Dynasty, scaled to the size of a hotel room (the original mausoleum is twice the size of Epcot). The Gallery also contains a few cases of figures dating as far back as 260 BCE. **Influences:** Beijing's Forbidden City (Imperial Palace) and Temple of Heaven. **Fun Stuff to Buy:** Upon exiting the film, cross the hangerlike shop and enter **House of Good Fortune,** the main shop, which is particularly varied. It sells plum wine ($20), lots of Ts and teas, Chinese jackets ($50–$85 in silks, polyesters, and blends), jade bangles ($50), teapots ($50–$230), parasols ($14–$16), conical coolie hats ($12–$16), and paper lanterns ($3–$10).

"Reflections of China" ★ FILM   The big thing to do in China is a 14-minute movie filmed entirely in Circle-Vision 360°. You wouldn't believe the work it takes to make a film that surrounds you from all sides. The makers first had to figure out the optimal number of screens (nine—which enables projectors to be slipped in the gaps between screens) and then they had to suspend a ring of carefully calibrated cameras from helicopters so that the crew wasn't in the shots. In 2002, the footage of Shanghai had to be reshot because the city no longer resembled the 1982 version that was being shown; this being China, it's probably already time for another refresh. The result, which surveys some of the country's most beautiful vistas, is ravishing, although the masses no longer seem to care.

OUTPOST ★

This area between China and Germany was once slated to contain a pavilion canvassing equatorial Africa, but that fell through for political reasons, so instead, we get a mushy catchall for all things African. The **Mdundo Kibanda** store has some Kenyan carvings (like positively adorable $12 pocket-size giraffes) and you'll find occasional storytelling sessions. Several days a week, a craftsman is on hand, whittling and carving wares—they seem engrossed in wood and knife, but they like answering questions too. **Fun Stuff to Buy:** The too-easily overlooked **Bead Outpost** kiosk sells jewelry made from recycled Guidemaps and other outdated Disney park publications. The papers are sent to Uganda as part of the BeadforLife program to give impoverished women a sustainable income, and they return as water-resistant beads in every color. Necklaces are $20, bracelets $10, earrings $7, or you can pick your own beads to be sized right there.

GERMANY ★

Lacking a true attraction (a water ride based on the Rhine was planned but never completed), Germany is popular for its food. The **Biergarten Restaurant** does sausages, beer, and the like—accompanied by yodeling and dancing—while the adjoining shop is for crystal doodads. The **Sommerfest** is the counter-service alternative for brats and pretzels. On the hour, the Clock Tower above the pavilion rings and two figures emerge, just like at the Glockenspiel in München (Munich). The artist's space in the window of **Das Kaufhaus** facing the lagoon is in tribute to Jutta Levasseur, the egg-painting artist who worked at Epcot since its opening day and died in 2012. She was a beloved fixture in this park for 30 years. The pavilion is otherwise a string of connected one-room shops selling steins (from $37, although Grumpy is $230), figurines, crystal, Christmas ornaments, cuckoo clocks, and other high-priced wares. **Influences:** Eltz

Castle near Koblenz; Stahleck Fortress near Bacharach; Rothenburg (the Biergarten and the dragon slayer statue); facades from Frankfurt and Freiburg (the guildhall). **Fun Stuff to Buy:** The connected candy-and-wine shop, **Weinkeller,** is worth a gander: You'll find such pick-me-ups as Gluhwein ($11 a liter), wine by the glass ($6–$10), by the flight (from $10), or by the bottle (spätlese, Auslese, Kabinett, Liebfraumilch, from $15). **Der Teddybär** sells toys, especially ones by Steiff and Haba. The Werthers Original shop does popcorns and candy ($4–$10).

ITALY ★

The tiny pavilion for Italy lacks an attraction—the gondolas never leave the dock—so you must content yourself with the small-scale replicas of Venice's Doge's Palace and St. Mark's bell tower. An appealing, if incongruous, attraction that's not on the maps is the highly detailed **model train** display just between this pavilion and Germany. **Influences:** Piazza di San Marco, Venice; stucco buildings of Tuscany; a fountain reminiscent of the work of Gian Lorenzo Bernini. **Fun Stuff to Buy:** Noodle around in the **Enoteca Castello** shop for wine (from $15) and Quadratini hazelnut wafer cookies ($10 a bag). **Il Bel Cristallo** sells fragrances, handbags, football jerseys (are you sensing a theme here?), and pricey Venetian carnival masks.

U.S.A. ★★★

So much for being a generous host: The U.S.A. pavilion takes pride of place in an area that's supposed to celebrate other countries. Inside, the superlative **Voices of America** singing group, which excels at thorny close harmonies, entertains guests waiting to attend the half-hour Audio-Animatronic show, The American Adventure. You'll be impressed. Also in the lobby is the unfairly ignored **American Heritage Gallery:** See items from the Kinsey Collection pertaining to milestones in the African-American experience (an 1820 slave schedule, an 1832 bill of sale of an 18-year-old named Joe) and embellished with cool "story lanterns" narrated by luminaries including Whoopi Goldberg, Chandra Wilson, and Diane Sawyer. **Influences:** General Georgian/colonial Greek-revival buildings (Brits often snicker that its Georgian architecture style is distinctly English). **Fun Stuff to Buy: Heritage Manor Gifts** sells patriotic tat, such as presidential nursery blocks ($100), cookbooks, throw pillows, and tee shirts with the American flag that were actually made in El Salvador, Sri Lanka, and Thailand.

The American Adventure ★★★ SHOW   Ben Franklin and Mark Twain are your Audio-Animatronic surrogates for a series of eye-popping (but ponderous) re-creations of snippets along patriotic themes. Moving dioramas of seminal events such as a Susan B. Anthony speech and John Muir's inspiration for Yosemite National Park appear and vanish cinematically on a stage a quarter the size of a football field, leaving spectators marveling at the massive amount of storage space that must lie beyond the proscenium. It's a literal jukebox for mythology. Indeed, all that homespun corn is brought to you by some immensely complicated robotic and hydraulic systems. When this attraction first opened, the scene in which Franklin appears to mount stairs and then walk across the room was hailed as a technical miracle. The Will Rogers figure actually twirls a lasso purely through robotic movements. Although heavy on uplifting jingoism, the show scores points for touching lightly on a few unpleasant topics, including slavery and the suffering of Native Americans, but in general, it's not as deep as its stage. Don't be the first to enter or else you'll be marooned off to the left. The five-person **Spirit of America** fife and drum corps makes scheduled appearances outdoors in the forecourt.

There are no parades anymore at Epcot, but usually at 9pm, the pulse-pounding **IllumiNations: Reflections of Earth** ★★★ flames-and-water spectacular takes place over World Showcase Lagoon. Its central globe, which is studded with 15,500 tiny video screens, weighs some 350,000 pounds, and the show's so-called Inferno Barge carries a payload of 4,000 gallons of propane. Crowds start building on the banks 2 hours before showtime, but I find doing that a waste of time, and therefore money, as a day's admission is so steep. Any view of the center of the lake will be fine (some people find the islands obstructive, but I don't), but take care to be upwind or you may be engulfed by smoke.

JAPAN ★★★

Japan has no giant attractions (like Germany, a show building was erected but never filled with its intended ride), but its shopping and dining are exemplary, and the outdoor garden behind the pagoda is a paragon of peace. Hopefully, you can be there during one of the shows (check your "Times Guide"): the spectacularly thunderous **Matsuriza** taiko drum shows, which are held at the base of the five-level Goju-no-to pagoda. (If you're looking for longtime candy artist **Miyuki,** she recently retired.) At the back of the pavilion, go inside and turn left to tour the **Bijutsu-kan Gallery.** Its most recent show was about the Japanese affection for sprites, pixies, and cute characters. A red *torii* gate inspired by one in Hiroshima sits in the lagoon; the barnacles on its base are fake, and were glued on to simulate age. **Influences:** 8th-century Horyuji Temple in Nara (pagoda); Katsura Imperial Villa (Yakitori House); Shirasagi-Jo castle at Hemeji (the rear fortress); Hiroshima (*torii* gate in the lagoon). **Fun Stuff to Buy:** The **Mitsukoshi Department Store,** named for the 300-year-old Japanese original, is the most fun to roam of all the World Showcase shop. It stocks a wide variety of toys, chopstick sets ($4–$13), traditional wood sandals (from $50), linens, anime figures, and paper fans, calligraphy supplies, countless solar-powered hand-waving cute things, antique kimonos costing up to $2,000—but I love Japanese snacks, such as chocolate-dipped Pocky sticks ($3–$5).

MOROCCO ★★★

Morocco is another spectacular pavilion, if you're inclined to dig in. It flies higher than its neighbors because the country's king took an active interest in its construction, dispatching some 21 top craftsmen for the job. There's no movie or show (although Aladdin, the Genie, and Jasmine make regular appearances), and the architecture is a cross-country mishmash drawn from Marrakech, Fes, and Rabat. **Fez House** is a tranquil, pillared two-level courtyard with a fountain and seating that recalls a classic Moroccan home; **Moroccan Style,** a mosaic-rich exhibition of hanging lanterns and colored glass, is unjustly ignored. Ask a cast member (almost always from Morocco) to write your name in Arabic for you—it's free. **Influences:** Marrakesh (Koutoubia minaret), Rabat (Chella minaret), Fez (Bab Boujouloud Gate, Nejjarine Fountain), Casablanca. **Fun Stuff to Buy:** The middle courtyards are cluttered with the souklike **Casablanca Carpets** and **The Brass Bazaar** boutiques that blend one into another. They are perfumed with incense ($3.75) and are stocked with interesting finds, including footstools, tassled red fez caps ($23), glass tea cups ($10), thuya wood dice sets ($19) hand-painted tambourines ($18), Persian-style machine-made rugs (from $26), metal hanging lanterns (from $30), and belly-dancer outfits ($85).

FRANCE ★★

France, done up to look like a typical Parisian neighborhood with a one-tenth replica of the upper stretch of the Eiffel Tower in the simulated distance (you can't go up it), is popular mostly for its food, though the street act **Serveur Amusant,** an acrobat who does handstands on stacked chairs, is thrilling. Disney allowed Guerlain and Givenchy to open fragrance shops at **Plume et Palette**—turns out the smell of selling out is just like Shalimar. **Influences:** Various Belle Epoque Parisian and provincial streets; Château de Fontainbleu (the Palais du Cinema); the former Pont des Arts in Paris (the bridge to the United Kingdom). **Fun Stuff to Buy:** The cheesiest souvenirs ($10 5-in. Eiffel Towers) are available in Les Halles at **Boutique de Cadeaux.** Across the lane, in **L'Esprit de la Provence,** a kitchen shop, wooden spoons are $7 and patterned oven mitts are $12. **Aux Vins de France** sells wine tastings for $6.50 to $13, Epcot wine classes for $35, and bottles for much more than in Germany or Italy.

"Impressions de France" ★ FILM   The 18-minute, 200-degree-wide movie is no longer the freshest example of a tourism film—mostly classical music and postcard-worthy shots of some 50 picturesque French places. It has been playing continuously since Epcot opened in 1982. Happily, it provides seating.

UNITED KINGDOM ★★

United Kingdom, another wild mix of architectural styles, has no rides or shows, so few people know about the knee-high **hedge maze** in back. The U.K. is popular chiefly for its English-style pub, the indoor Rose & Crown Pub & Dining Room (which you can enjoy without a reservation or eating), and a counter-service fish and chips shop. That's two fish-and-chips outlets in a block—far more than you'd find even in London these days. After 5:15pm, duck into the pub to catch Pam Brody or Carol Stein, longtime Epcot entertainers who both play piano here and lead the guests in song. Request their version of "Do Re Mi" (it's clean). **Influences:** Anne Hathaway's Cottage, Stratford-upon-Avon (the Tea Caddy); Queen Anne style (the middle promenade); Hampton Court, London (Sportsman's Shoppe); Victorian, country, and traditional pub styles (Rose & Crown). **Fun Stuff to Buy:** Featured shopping in the conjoined **Sportsman's Shoppe, the Crown & Crest,** and **Toy Soldier** includes Beatles merch, Pooh merch, and "Keep Calm and Carry On" tees. Across the way, **Lords and Ladies** does jewelry and the **Tea Caddy** sells Twinings tea and mugs and English candy bars at a high price of $3.50 each.

CANADA ★

Like Japan, Canada's gardens (inspired by Victoria's Butchart Gardens, although the sign says Victoria Gardens) are a surprising oasis, adding a hidden artificial canyon delightfully washed by a man-made waterfall. Disney recently added a new lumberjack-themed show at the stage here, which performs several times daily (check your Times Guide). **Influences:** 19th-century Victorian colonial architecture (Hotel du Canada); emblematic northwestern Indian design and Maritime Provinces towns; Butchart Gardens, Victoria (Victoria Gardens). **Fun Stuff to Buy:** The shop, **Northwest Mercantile,** mostly hawks maple syrup ($25 for 17 oz.), stuffed huskies and bears ($15–$23), red tartan fleece vests ($32), and T-shirts themed to moose and hockey.

"O Canada!" ★ FILM   Canada, like China, has a movie, but could its name be a little less stereotypical? It's shot with nine cameras in Circle-Vision 360°, a process Walt Disney originally called Circarama. The 18-minute presentation (1982), which requires standing, was refurbished by adding newly shot bits with Martin Short as emcee. Most of its spectacular scenery (the Rockies, the Bay of Fundy) is timeless.

Where to Eat in Epcot

Epcot has the best dining choices of any Disney World park, and people come just for the food. All locations will have a few vegetarian options, kids' meals, and if you identify yourself, special dietary requests can usually be accommodated, albeit often at diminished quality. Alcohol is served everywhere—even in Morocco, where it's not so easy to get in real life. You can also drink the water in Mexico.

EPCOT'S QUICK-SERVICE RESTAURANTS

There are only two major counter-service choices in Future World, plus a Starbucks. The real casual eating action is in World Showcase.

Sunshine Seasons ★★★ INTERNATIONAL   This fantastic place offers the best selection and freshest food of all Epcot's counter-service locations, including salads, grilled items (seared tuna noodle salad, oak-grilled chicken and fish), and thai green curry shrimp—not a fried item, burger, or pizza in sight. The desserts are epic (cheesecake with berries, tiramisu; $4.40). You can also pick up snacks suiting dietary restrictions. The Land. Breakfast $4 to $6, lunch and dinner Combo meal $8.60 to $12.

Electric Umbrella ★★ AMERICAN   Future World's most central counter-service locale. Expect burgers, nuggets, and meatball subs (snooze). Innoventions East. Combo meal $8 to $11.

La Cantina De San Angel ★★ MEXICAN   Mexico's counter-service option will give you beef or chicken tacos, cheese empanadas, nachos, and margaritas (from $9.50). It's outside but on the water. Mexico. Combo meal $11 to $12.

Kringla Bakeri Og Kafé ★★ SCANDINAVIAN   Some of the selections in Norway's bake shop can't be found elsewhere at Disney, including *rullekake* (a rolled swirl of berries and yellow cake). More than one person claims the smooth, strawberry-topped rice cream pudding snack to be their favorite sweet in Walt Disney World. You can also get sandwiches, heated to order. Norway. Desserts $4, sandwiches $7 to $8.

Lotus Blossom Café ★ CHINESE   China's quick-service choice, with covered seating, is basic, serving beef noodle bowls, shrimp fried rice, pot stickers, and the like. Mango smoothies are sweet but delicious. China. Combo meal $8.50 to $12.

Sommerfest ★★ GERMAN   When you can't get into Biergarten, settle for this kiosk to get your bratwurst, sausage, and beer. Germany. Sausage rolls $7.

Tutto Gusto ★★★ ITALIAN   The excellent vaulted bar attached to the Tutto Italia Ristorante serves grown-up cocktails and also a fast-service selection of cheese and meat plates for two or three ($24–$27), plus cannoli, tiramisu, and panini. Italy. Panini $9 to $13, desserts $4 to $9, wine flights $14–$18, by the glass $9–$15.

Liberty Inn ★ AMERICAN   Cheap burgers, hot dogs, chicken, and salads. Outside, the **Fife & Drum Tavern** is for turkey legs and beer. The American Adventure. Combo meal $8.50–$11.

Katsura Grill ★★ JAPANESE   Japan's small counter-service location is by the gardens, and it supplies Japanese curry, teriyaki chicken, sushi ($5 for four pieces), and edamame. Facing the lagoon under the pagoda, the **Kabuki Cafe** kiosk (closed in cold weather) serves shaved ice with syrup (including honeydew and cherry flavors) for $3.75, and plum wine for $6.50. Japan. Combo meal $9 to $13.

Tangierine Café ★★★ MOROCCAN   The indoor counter-service location is a great place to dodge crowds. It serves shawarma with hummus, couscous, bread, and tabbouleh; and meatball platters with yellow rice. Accent it with Casa Beer, from

Casablanca, or Moorish coffee (espresso spiced with cinnamon and nutmeg), and add baklava for $3.50. Kids can get burgers or chicken fingers for $8. Morocco. Combo meal $12 to $15.

Boulangerie Pâtisserie ★★ FRENCH Grab a fast, bready bite in the back of Les Halles, such as a chocolate croissant or a ham-and-cheese croissant (both around $4.75—decent bargains), tarts, Niçoise salad, croque-monsieur, or baguette sandwiches. A cash-only kiosk on the lagoon griddles up hot crepes (with sweet fillings, not meat), also for $4. Salads and sandwiches $7.50 to $8.50.

Yorkshire County Fish Shop ★★ BRITISH Snag walk-up fish-and-chips and eat it al fresco. You get two strips of fish with chips (fries)—make sure to put vinegar, not ketchup, on the fries the way the English do. Ale costs $8.25. United Kingdom. Combo meal $9.

EPCOT'S TABLE-SERVICE RESTAURANTS

Book ahead if your heart is set on something, particularly for a nighttime lagoon view—if you're going to spend this kind of money, get a view out of it. The host will not guarantee seating location, but it helps to politely ask. Objectively, there are very few meals that would rate highly if I ate them outside of the park gates, and as with all mass-produced meals, quality varies greatly from day to day; the lion's share of the enjoyment is just being there. Lunch entrees are generally $3 to $5 less expensive than at dinner. Taking them as you encounter them, going clockwise around World Showcase:

The Garden Grill ★★ AMERICAN As Farmer Mickey, Pluto, and Chip 'n' Dale press the flesh in this slowly revolving, two-tiered circular restaurant, you're served all-you-can-eat family style "Harvest Feast" platters of meats and vegetables, some of which were grown in the greenhouses downstairs. This is the only character meal in Future World, and it's only at dinner, but it's a good choice because it's mellow and small enough so that the characters can spend quality time with you. The Land. Combo meal $37 to $42 adults, $18 to $20 kids.

Coral Reef Restaurant ★ SEAFOOD Call it See Food: Through windows into the 27-foot-deep aquarium, admire the friends of the fish on your plate. You're even given a cheat sheet to identity what's swimming by. Only about half the menu selections are fish, and the rest are things like short ribs or strip steak. It's about the cool view, not the cuisine. The Seas with Nemo & Friends. Main courses $19 to $27.

San Angel Inn Restaurante ★★ MEXICAN Epcot's most atmospheric restaurant is set beneath a false twilight sky at the base of an ancient pyramid, with the boats from the Gran Fiesta Tour steadily passing. The fare isn't Tex-Mex as much as it is Mexican: chicken mole, chili relleno, grilled wahoo fish, and caramel dulce de leche for dessert. If you can't get in (a likelihood), try La Hacienda de San Angel, across the main path on the lagoon. Its food is similarly Mexican. Mexico. Mains $25 to $30.

La Hacienda de San Angel ★★ MEXICAN By day, it's a sunny place to get your tequila on. By night, this villa-themed restaurant (vaulted ceilings, hanging lanterns) is a fair place to sit for IllumiNations, but only if you're lucky enough to score a window seat. Margaritas are $14. The La Hacienda mixed grill with steak, chicken al pastor, chorizo, and veggies serves two ($56). Mexico. Main courses $24–$28.

Princess Storybook Dining at Akershus Royal Banquet Hall ★★★ AMERICAN Although it's Norway, you won't have to eat raw fish at this storybook buffet (although once upon a time, you did). Instead, it's Epcot's meet-the-princesses extravaganza for all three "feasts" daily, in a castlelike setting of vaulted ceilings and banners. Someone always stops by, be it Belle, Aurora, Jasmine, Snow White, Mulan, or Mary Poppins, who must be lost. If your own princess forgot her gown, they sell them for $65 at the shop across the path. This is the only character dining in World Showcase. Norway. Meal $41 to $55 adults, $25 to $30 kids, including five photos of your party.

Nine Dragons Restaurant ★ CHINESE When you can't get a reservation anywhere else, you end up here. The food here is not much more daring or spicy as in the cheaper Quick Service option, Lotus Blossom Café, except here, there are more choices and they're more expensive. The decor is handsomely geometric, but nothing memorable, although some tables face out toward the water. China. Mains $13 to $27; three-course dinner sets $24.

Biergarten Restaurant ★★★ GERMAN Toddlers lurch forward to polka, dads dive into mugs of Radeberger pilsner, and strangers make friends with their neighbors at this rowdy, carb-loaded party, an all-you-can-eat stuffer featuring sauerbraten, schnitzel, spaetzle, rotisserie chicken, and an oompah band for about 20 minutes at a time. It's popular. Germany. $28 adults, $15 kids.

Tutto Italia Ristorante ★ ITALIAN Proclaimed authentic to Italy mostly by people who have never been there, this dusky environment of chandeliers and murals nonetheless packs 'em in. Pasta of this low caliber should not be $23, but that doesn't stop patrons from buying $25 hunks of lasagna. Italy. Main courses $20 to $30.

Via Napoli Ristorante E Pizzeria ★ ITALIAN The more enjoyable of Italy's two table service restaurants features lots of light, three-story vaulted ceilings, and three amusing wood-fired ovens shaped like the open mouths of giant mustachioed men named after volcanoes. Into those arc thrust $17 individual pizzas and $9.50 kids' pizzas made with flour imported from Naples (not that you could tell a difference). There's also some lasagna and spaghetti at around $22–$30 a plate. It's operated by Patina Restaurant Group, which runs eateries in Macy's, the Hollywood Bowl, and other tourist spots. Italy. Main courses $12 to $30.

Teppan Edo ★★★ JAPANESE Above the Mitsukoshi store (which runs it), a chef-cum-swordsmith slices, dices, and cooks at the teppanyaki griddle built into your table. It's fun to watch, and although it's not a great choice if your kids are too young to keep their hands to themselves, it's a good way to meet your neighbors. Ask to see the smoking onion volcano. The food? Oh, it's fine, but you really come to see the fancy knife work. Japan. Main courses $18 to $32.

Tokyo Dining ★★ JAPANESE On the second floor of the Japan pavilion, the decor is modern and stylish, the waitstaff subdued, and the menu offers both tempura/grills and sushi in modest portions at inflated prices. Some tables have a view of the lagoon through nearly floor-to-ceiling windows, which comes in handy around Illumi-Nations time. Japan. Main courses $25 to $31, sushi $6 to $11 per order.

Restaurant Marrakesh ★★★ MOROCCAN Tucked in the back of the souk, this lesser-known restaurant, lit theatrically with hanging lanterns, is known most for its belly dancer, who appears (in a chaste costume) at 10 minutes before the hour at lunch and 10 minutes after the hour during dinner. The fare is approachable North African, heavy on the shish kebabs, lemon chicken tagine, and couscous. Thinner crowds allow it to serve a good value at lunch: appetizer, entrée, and dessert until 3pm for $20. Morocco. Main courses $18 to $29.

Spice Road Table ★★ MOROCCAN   Serving small plates (lamb sliders, skewers) and powerful sangria and cocktails, it has Lagoon views ideal for IllumiNations spectators, so it fills up by 8pm. Morocco. Small plates $7–$16.

Chefs de France ★★ FRENCH   In a glassed-in dining room recalling a typical French bistro, dine on flatbreads and sandwiches (at lunch) or prototypical French food like crepes, duck breast, and steak haché. It offers a $26 prix-fixe, three-course meal until 3pm ($40 at dinner). France. Main courses $16 to $32.

Monsieur Paul ★★★ FRENCH   Epcot's most thoughtful food (and also its most expensive) is served here, and it starts with napkins that are folded like a chef's jacket. This is special occasion stuff: an oxtail soup with black truffle for $29, roasted duck à l'orange, red snapper in rosemary sauce with scales made of roasted potato slices, plus all the amuse-bouches and long preparation explanations you'd expect of a fine establishment. The theme is classic French cuisine using fresh American ingredients, and the menu is overseen Jerome Bocuse, son of the restaurant's namesake, the heavily Michelin-starred Chef Paul Bocuse, who oversaw the first restaurant at this location. There's also a prix-fixe menu that's $89 if you want wine pairings. Although it faces the water, the windows are small so not every table has a view of IllumiNations. You'll find the entrance tucked around the back door of Chefs de France, under a green-and-white striped awning. France. Main courses $39 to $44.

Rose & Crown Pub & Dining Room ★★★ BRITISH   The interior is fairly similar to a country pub—big wooden bar serving whisky and lots of British and Irish draught beers ($9, or twice as much as London's most expensive pubs), tough patterned carpet underfoot—although most of the seating is outdoors unless it rains. You get bangers and mash (sausage with mashed potatoes), Scotch egg (fried hard-boiled egg wrapped in sausage meat), cottage pie (ground beef with onions, carrots, mushrooms, and mashed potatoes) and that standby that finds its way onto every Disney menu, no matter how errant, New York Strip Steak. You can just have a drink in the pub if you choose. After 5pm, family-friendly songs are sung for the drinkers getting off their feet after a long day. United Kingdom. Main courses $15 to $32.

Le Cellier Steakhouse ★ STEAKS   It takes the Canadian-themed restaurant to deliver the most all-American menu of filet mignon, rib eye, snapper, pork, and chicken, but it also Canucks it up with sides such as *poutine* fries (not truly *poutine* with gravy, but topped with cheddar, truffle salt, and red-wine reduction). Specialties include a popular cheddar cheese soup and pretzel bread. True to its name, the restaurant is windowless and vaulted, like a very clean version of a wine cellar. It's so dark and cool, in fact, that the menus are high-tech and light up when opened. The lunch and dinner selections are the same, and it can command deadly lunchtime prices because it's a tough reservation to secure. Canada. Main courses $34 to $46.

DISNEY'S HOLLYWOOD STUDIOS

Just as Epcot celebrates idealized industry and Animal Kingdom honors fauna, the 154-acre **Disney's Hollywood Studios** ★★ strives to evoke the romance of the movies. Not just any movies, of course, but mostly that pastel-hued fantasy of the Hollywood of 60 years ago, where gossip columnists ruled the radio and starlets could be discovered at Schwab's. It's the least popular of the four Disney parks.

While it was originally conceived as a single pavilion about show business for Epcot, Universal's announcement of its invasion of the Florida market prodded Disney

Disney's Hollywood Studios

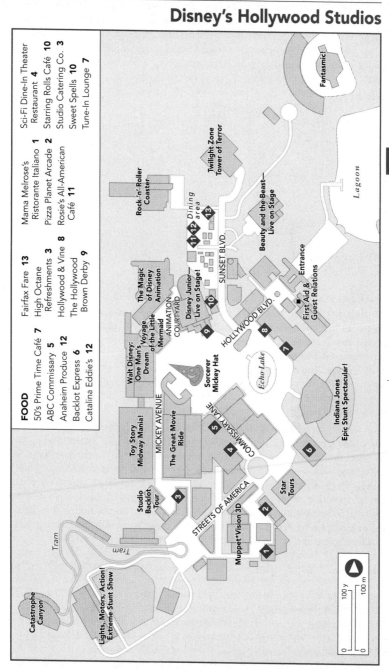

FOOD

50's Prime Time Café **7**
ABC Commissary **5**
Anaheim Produce **12**
Backlot Express **6**
Catalina Eddie's **12**

Fairfax Fare **13**
High Octane Refreshments **3**
Hollywood & Vine **8**
The Hollywood Brown Derby **9**

Mama Melrose's Ristorante Italiano **1**
Pizza Planet Arcade **2**
Rosie's All-American Café **11**

Sci-Fi Dine-In Theater Restaurant **4**
Starring Rolls Café **10**
Studio Catering Co. **3**
Sweet Spells **10**
Tune-In Lounge **7**

executives to hastily expand the concept into an entire park. In 1989, the Studios opened with just two rides (the Great Movie Ride and the Backlot Tour) to head off the competition. The Studios have never quite recovered from its half-baked genesis. Disney is working to sexy it up by changing its name (its original one, Disney–MGM Studios, was abandoned in early 2008) and adding attractions (Toy Story Midway Mania opened a few months later), it's no one's favorite Disney World park, which is why I think it's the one you should do last.

There are a few reasons why it's not one of Disney's most transporting endeavors. One is that its design is not symmetrical, which makes it harder to navigate. Another problem: When you look at the slate of attractions, you'll notice it's light on rides and heavy on shows, especially ones for small children, which, for my money, isn't enough. Still, *every* park is lacking in comparison to something as revolutionary as the Magic Kingdom, and the dearth of activities is balanced by the fact that two of its rides are among Disney's best: the Tower of Terror and the Rock 'n' Roller Coaster.

The park possesses a fraction of the attractions the Magic Kingdom has—so guests often combine its highlights on the same day with Disney's Animal Kingdom, or they allow themselves a more leisurely pace, perhaps lingering long enough to catch the dazzling pyrotechnic-and-water curtain evening show, Fantasmic!

Guests arrive by the usual car/tram combo, by bus, or by free ferry, which sails from the Swan and Dolphin area and continues on to Epcot.

Hollywood Boulevard & Echo Lake

As soon as your bag is approved and you're through the gates, take care of business (strollers, wheelchairs, lockers) in the plaza before proceeding down Hollywood Boulevard. There are no attractions here, only shops and restaurants.

Hollywood Boulevard culminates with the 122-foot-tall **Sorcerer Mickey Hat,** the park's central icon that is from, ironically, Walt Disney's assault on typical Hollywood movies, "Fantasia." There is nothing exciting in it. Where Hollywood Boulevard and Sunset Boulevard meet, you'll locate the park's **tip board,** where wait times and show schedules are posted.

The Great Movie Ride ★ RIDE Behind the hat, which was added in 2001, is the park's original focal point: the replica of Grauman's Chinese Theater (Disney calls it "the Chinese Theater"), which has a forecourt graced with actual handprints and footprints of movie stars who visited in the park's early years at the behest of Disney execs. There are no prints past 1999, around the time the park gave up the dream of being a center for important film production. Ye Olde Movie Ride, as I call it, was a showpiece in 1989, but now feels like a mechanized waxworks. Aided by a human guide reciting a hoary script, audiences slowly cruise in traveling theater slabs past Audio-Animatronic reproductions of scenes from famous movies, including "Singin' in the Rain," "Alien," and a Munchkin-crammed "The Wizard of Oz" (its Wicked Witch figure was a landmark because it was the first time Imagineers figured out that the key to lifelike action was compensating for sudden movements with minute return movements). This is really the only place where the park's original MGM licensed imagery comes much into play these days. At one point during the 22-minute journey, which concludes with a viewing of a fast-paced and expertly edited movie montage, cars experience one of two possible plotlines—for example, getting caught in the crossfire of a James Cagney gangland classic or a John Wayne western, with guns that shoot sparks. The robots have looked fresher and kids won't get the references (Busby Berkeley, for example), but the production is endearing. Lines are never very long, but they do tend to spike just after the parade.

HOLLYWOOD STUDIOS: ONE DAY, TWO WAYS

START: BE AT THE GATE FOR OPENING TIME. Grab food at a counter restaurant when it's convenient to you—but having lunch at 11am saves time. The must-have Fastpass for this park is Toy Story Midway Mania.

HOLLYWOOD STUDIOS WITH KIDS

Fastpass within 90 minutes of opening: Toy Story Midway Mania. If your kids are very young, Voyage of the Little Mermaid.

When the gates open, ride **Toy Story Midway Mania** even if you have a Fastpass for later; it's worth re-riding.

OR

If your child wants to participate in the **Jedi Training Academy,** reserve a slot first (ask a cast member where; it changes).

↓

See **Voyage of the Little Mermaid.**

↓

See **Disney Junior—Live on Stage!**

↓

Meet Mickey at the **Magic of Disney Animation.**

↓

Do **The Great Movie Ride.**

↓

Take the **Backlot Tour** (it might shut down by late afternoon).

↓

Target a performance of **Beauty and the Beast—Live on Stage** for around now.

↓

At this point, littler ones may need to leave the park for a break.

↓

See **Muppet*Vision 3-D.**

↓

See the **Indiana Jones Epic Stunt Spectacular.**

↓

If you think the whole family can handle them, slot in the **Twilight Zone Tower of Terror** and the **Rock 'n' Roller Coaster.**

↓

See **Fantasmic!** (if it's performing tonight). People stake out their seats as long as an hour ahead, but 30 minutes will do.

HOLLYWOOD STUDIOS WITHOUT KIDS

When the gates open, ride **Toy Story Midway Mania** even if you have a Fastpass for later; it's worth re-riding.

↓

Head to the **Twilight Zone Tower of Terror** and the **Rock 'n' Roller Coaster** and ride them.

See **Voyage of the Little Mermaid** (it's fun even without kids).

↓

Nearby, do the **Great Movie Ride.**

↓

Take the **Backlot Tour** (it usually shuts down by late afternoon).

↓

Target a performance of **Lights, Motors, Action!** to fall around now.

↓

Ride **Star Tours.**

↓

See the **Indiana Jones Epic Stunt Spectacular.**

↓

See **Muppet*Vision 3-D.**

↓

Tour **Walt Disney: One Man's Dream** (you can also do this anytime lines seem intolerable elsewhere).

↓

If you're so inclined, make a pass to the final show of **American Idol Experience.**

↓

See **Fantasmic!** (if it's performing tonight).

Don't miss if you're 6: Voyage of the Little Mermaid

Don't miss if you're 16: Rock 'n' Roller Coaster

Requisite photo op: Sorcerer Mickey Hat

Food you can only get here: Grapefruit Cake, the Hollywood Brown Derby, Hollywood Boulevard; Peanut Butter and Jelly Milkshake, 50's Prime Time Café, Echo Lake

The most crowded, so Fastpass or go early: Toy Story Midway Mania

Skippable: Studio Backlot Tour

Quintessentially Disney: Walt Disney: One Man's Dream; the Great Movie Ride

Biggest thrill: Twilight Zone Tower of Terror

Best show: Voyage of the Little Mermaid

Character meals: Hollywood & Vine (breakfast, lunch)

Where to find peace: Around Echo Lake

Indiana Jones Epic Stunt Spectacular ★★ SHOW   The 30-minute, bone-rattling tour de force of hair-raising daredevilry—rolling-boulder dodging, trucks flipping over and exploding—simultaneously titillates and, to a lesser degree, reminds you how such feats of derring-do are typically rigged and filmed for the movies. They try hard to convince you that they're really filming these sequences—you may need to explain to young children why they're lying about that, and about calling the lead actor "Harrison Ford's stunt double," but most kids understand the violence is fake. The acrobats and gymnasts who do the stunts, fights, and tumblers are skilled, and the production values are among the highest of any show at the Disney parks. The outdoor amphitheater is sheltered, and you can bring drinks and food. **Strategy:** Arrive about 20 minutes early, as there's a warm-up and volunteers are selected before showtime. It's mounted about five times daily.

Star Tours—The Adventure Continues ★★★ RIDE   Before Disney bought "Star Wars," it made, and later upgraded, this popular, 40-person motion-simulator capsule that has you riding shotgun with an ineffectual droid named RX-24 (voiced by Pee-Wee actor Paul Reubens) on an ill-fated and turbulent excursion. In 5 minutes, you manage to lose control, go into hyperdrive, dodge asteroids, navigate a comet field, evade a Star Destroyer, get caught in a tractor beam, and join an assault on the Death Star. The video is well matched to the movements, which cuts down on reports of nausea. In May and June, the park mounts Star Wars Weekends, when actors from the movie arrive for signings, parades, Q&As, and brief workshops (p. 234). Fans of the franchise come out in force, so to speak.

Jedi Training Academy ★ SHOW   Up to 15 times daily (see the "Times Guide"), about a dozen kids are lent robes, telescoping "light sabers," and some gentle training in the Force by a "Jedi master" before a final defeat of Darth Vader and some stormtroopers. It's cute and takes 20 minutes. Recruits (ages 4–12) are selected by 10:30am, tops, at the ABC Sound Studio, so get there early if your young Padawan wants a shot at carrying home the diploma.

Sunset Boulevard

The prime items in the park are on this street, which peels off not from the hub with the hat, as you might expect, but from the middle of Hollywood Boulevard.

The Twilight Zone Tower of Terror ★★★ RIDE The tallest ride at Disney World (199 ft.) is one of the smartest, most exciting experiences there, and it's the best version of the ride at any Disney park. It shouldn't be missed. Guests are ushered through the lobby, library, and boiler room of a cobwebby 1930s Los Angeles hotel before being seated in a 21-passenger "elevator" car that, floor by floor, ascends the tower and then, without visible tracks, emerges from the shaft and roams an upper level. Soon, you've entered a second shaft and, after a pregnant moment of tension, you're sent into what seems to be a free fall (in reality, you're being pulled faster than the speed of gravity) and a series of thrilling up-and-down leaps. The fall sequence is random and you never drop more than a few stories—but the total darkness, periodically punctured by picture-window views of the theme park far below as you become momentarily weightless, keys up the giddy fear factor. It's impossible not to smile. **Strategy:** In the preshow "library" room, move to the wall diagonally across from the entry door and you'll exit first, saving you time. In the boarding area, the best views are in the front row, numbered 1 and 2, although you may not be given a choice. Chickens can bail before the ride boards.

Rock 'n' Roller Coaster Starring Aerosmith ★★ RIDE Twenty-four-passenger "limousine" trains launch from 0 to 57mph in under 3 seconds, sending them through a 92-second rampage through smooth corkscrews and turns that are intensified by fluorescent symbols of Los Angeles (at one point, you dive though an O of the Hollywood sign). The indoor setup is a boon, as it means the ride can operate during the rain, and it makes the journey slightly less disorienting for inexperienced coaster riders. Cooler yet, speakers in each headrest (there are more than 900 in total) play Aerosmith music, which is perfectly timed to the dips and rolls. **Strategy:** The Fastpass line is absorbed quickly. There's also a single-rider line, though it's not always quick.

Beauty and the Beast—Live on Stage ★ SHOW The kid-friendly, 30-minute show is advertised as "Broadway-style," but it's really not. It's theme park–style, simplified with the most popular songs from the movie. The story is highly condensed (you never find out why Belle ends up at the Beast's castle and Gaston's fate is not shown) and many characters inhabit whole-body costumes, speaking recorded dialogue with unblinking eyes—to the benefit of timid kids, the Beast looks more like a plush toy than a scary monster. Its intended audience cheers like it's a rock concert and hoist smartphones during the ball scene, and because of that, most performances are jammed. The metal benches are numbing, but at least the amphitheater is covered. **Strategy:** Arrive 20 minutes early unless you want to be in the back, where afternoon sun can seep in.

Fantasmic! ★★★ SHOW The super-popular 25-minute pyrotechnics show featuring character-laden showboats, a 59-foot man-made mountain, flaming water, and lasers projected onto a giant water curtain, takes place in the 6,500-seat waterfront Hollywood Hills Amphitheatre. Although it's a strong show by dint of its uniqueness, it doesn't play nightly. I'm always stunned to see people start arriving at the theater as much as *2 hours* before showtime. The seating is hard on the derriere. Most people will be satisfied taking their chances and showing up within 30 minutes of showtime. **Strategy:** On nights when there are two performances (not common), do the second one, as it's always less crowded. Sit toward the rear to avoid catching water from the special effects and to the right to make exiting easier. You can get reserved seats if you book the Fantasmic! Dining Experience and eat dinner in the participating restaurants.

Streets of America & Commissary Lane

Streets of America is a confusing zone of backlot-style city blocks, mostly facades, made to look like aging versions of New York City and San Francisco. Its primary attraction is photo ops. Look around for a few tricks, like the umbrella affixed to a lamppost in the square a la "Singin' in the Rain."

Lights, Motors, Action! Extreme Stunt Show ★★ SHOW   Loud, brawling, and moderately exciting enough to see once, it's a showcase for stunt driving dressed up like a film shoot for a car chase/action scene. The engaging 38-minute show, which uses a fleet of specially built, extra-nimble cars (plus a jet ski or two) and tells lots of lies about filming an actual movie scene while you're there, was imported from Paris' Walt Disney Studios Park (hence the set that looks like a Mediterranean port), but it seems tailor-made for American audiences. **Strategy:** Because the stage is so wide, I suggest taking a seat in the middle or near the top of the grandstand. You won't wrestle for a spot—the stadium seats 5,000. It only happens 2 or 3 times daily.

Honey, I Shrunk the Kids Movie Set Adventure ★ ACTIVITY   Turn kids loose on a high-concept playground that simulates the sights and sounds of the average backyard—if your kids were the size of an ant. In addition to giant insects, cargo nets, and a slide that was once Kodak film but has been disguised with paint, there's a giant Super Soaker that sprays the unsuspecting, plus giant Play-Doh and Tinkertoy product placements. It's the only playground in the park.

Muppet*Vision 3-D ★★★ SHOW   Behind the fabulous rotating fountain depicting Miss Piggy as the Statue of Liberty, the 17-minute movie features various tricks such as air blasts to make you feel like what you're seeing is actually happening. The doors on the right lead to the back of the 600-seat auditorium and the ones on the left lead to the front; for the fullest view, I suggest sticking in the middle, since the theater's walls become part of the show, and both live and Audio-Animatronic figures will appear on either side and even in the back. The preshow is amusing in that Muppet way (says Sam the Eagle about seating procedures: "Stopping in the middle is distinctly unpatriotic!"), and while the movie contains a few missteps (Waldo, a CG character, lacks creativity), it's fast moving and includes lots of beloved "Muppet Show" (but no "Sesame Street") favorites, such as Miss Piggy and Kermit. The Muppets, too, lend themselves very nicely to Audio-Animatronic technology. **Strategy:** Lines are longest just after the Indiana Jones show lets out.

Pixar Place & Animation Courtyard

Toy Story Midway Mania! ★★★ RIDE   The plotless indoor ride is the most popular in the park, and rightly so. Wearing 3-D glasses, passengers shoot their way through a series of six animated midway games (a Buttercup egg toss, a Little Green Men ring toss) based on the Pixar toy box characters. Along the way, air puffs heighten the reality. Your cannon is easy to work and easy on the hands—you just tug a cord and it fires. Scoring points is harder; both accuracy and intensity count. The queue area, stuffed with outsize toys such as Tinkertoys and Barrel of Monkeys, makes waiting a delight: A 6-foot-tall, lifelike Mr. Potato Head entertains with live interaction and hoary jokes ("Is this an audience or a jigsaw puzzle?"). Across Pixar Place, Woody and Buzz meet kids in air conditioning. **Tip:** This is your top Fastpass contender because the wait can jump to an hour just 15 minutes after the park opens.

The Studio Backlot Tour ★ RIDE   Once a centerpiece of the park, it has been whittled away to nearly nothing. It has been more than a decade since anything of note was produced here—leaving the guides to fib about how busy employees are. New tours start every 15 minutes and take about 35 minutes. It's less crowded early in the day and closes by late afternoon.

The first segment is the Special Effects Water Tank Show, which accepts four volunteers (adults only; raise your hand for duty in the queue). There, standing guests watch how the bullet impacts, explosions, and deluges of a ship-attack movie sequence are shot and cut together to look real. **Tips:** For the best views from the front row of the audience section, join the right-hand row in the queue area. Be among the first people out of there, because the next section finds you in yet another queue, this one in a warehouse full of old movie props (a few of which you may recognize), which feeds the boarding area for a tram; the seats on its left are best.

Although the canned narration refers to active movie production, it's faking. Disney bulldozed most of the area, including Residential Street, a little village for exterior shots (the "Golden Girls" and "Empty Nest" house facades were here), to make room for the Lights, Motors, Action! Extreme Stunt Show. When drivers perform, the shriek of the engines and the funk of burning rubber make the tram miserable and the narrator inaudible. The 20-minute trip loops past some old prop vehicles (poor Herbie the now-unloved Love Bug, plus some from "The Rocketeer," "Pearl Harbor," and other movies Disney wanted to do better) in the scaled-down Boneyard; through "glamorous" wardrobe houses (the staff is darning theme park uniforms, not movie costumes). Then you pass through Catastrophe Canyon, where, seated safely, you'll witness a simulated earthquake, the heat of an exploding oil tanker, and a flash flood—all in the space of seconds. The wizardry, which resets for every batch of guests, is heart-pounding fun—although no thinking person believes the bald lie that the special effects crew is testing this rig for a shoot. Those sitting on the left might get a tad wet, and you'll need sunglasses in the afternoon. On the way out, you'll spot a Gulfstream jet Walt Disney used on his real estate–grabbing missions to Florida. Finally—some actual history!

The Voyage of the Little Mermaid ★★★ SHOW   This bright, energetic, condensed version of the animated movie has high production values (puppets, live actors, mist, and a cool undersea-themed auditorium) and is a standout. This show is a top contender for the best show to see in the heat of the day, and Fastpass is available. **Strategy:** In the preshow holding pen, the doors to the left lead to the back half of the

---

Hidden Hollywood History

What if I told you that the original marionettes from "The Lonely Goatherd" in "The Sound of Music" are stashed somewhere in Disney's Hollywood Studios? You'd never find them unless I told you: Don't miss the **American Film Institute Showcase** exhibition hidden at the disembarkation area of the unpopular Studio Backlot Tour attraction. The trove of artifacts is startling: those famous Bil and Cora Baird carved marionettes, the whip that dragged Indiana Jones behind a Nazi Jeep in "Raiders of the Lost Ark," Superman's flying cape, a "Titanic" lifeboat, Batman's costume, the shooting script of "Platoon," and more. To find it if you're not taking the Backlot Tour, go through the shop opposite the Studio Catering Company, keep walking back, and go through the back of the second store you encounter.

theater; because the blacklight puppetry of the marvelous "Under the Sea" sequence can be spoiled if you see too much detail, I suggest sitting there. Consider putting very small kids in your lap so they can see better.

Disney Junior—Live on Stage! ★★ SHOW   For those of us who obediently rise and dance when commanded by Mickey Mouse, there's this breezy, 25-minute show with a lots of excellent puppets (warning, adults: You sit on the ground). It inspires such fervent participation from under 5s that it feels like a meeting for a cult that you're not a member of. If you don't know the names Doc McStuffins, Sofia the First, or Jake and the Never Land Pirates, this sing-along revue is still pretty to look at, and Mickey, Minnie, and friends make appearances. The parental units won't be too bored, as this de facto Disney Channel ad is fast paced, like changing the channel every 4 minutes. Obviously, anyone old enough to do a book report can skip it.

The Magic of Disney Animation ★ ACTIVITY   This tour is, in my opinion, the most telling evidence that Disney's Hollywood Studios stumbled. Originally it provided a firsthand look at the labor-intensive work that produced all those famous Disney movies. Guests could watch live animators perfect their upcoming release— "Mulan" and "Lilo & Stitch" were made right here. But Disney fired its Florida-based animators, so there's nothing more to see except fake empty workstations dressed with fake family photos and fake cups of tea. Instead, you get a hokey 9-minute show highlighting only the ideas stage of the process, followed by an ad for whatever computer-animated film will be released next. Then you're dumped in an area of paltry interactive exhibits where kids determine which Disney character their personality is most like (me: Tarzan). The biggest benefit of exploring is the chance to meet major characters (Sorcerer Mickey, plus the latest ones from Pixar and other films) in the AC. At the top and bottom of each hour, you can take a worthwhile 22-minute group crash course in drawing a popular character (such as Olaf or Minnie) with a guide, and you can bring your artwork home for free. Otherwise, the art of handmade animation, through which the Disney empire was built, cel by cel, is barely discussed. You receive no more information than you could find in a 2-minute DVD extra. **Strategy:** Skip the show and enjoy the character greetings by entering through the back door, through the Animation Gallery, where you'll pass 13 Oscars (all won for hand animation, it bears noting). If you love Disney history, this may bring you down.

Walt Disney: One Man's Dream ★ ACTIVITY   The only historic focus on Disney history here on resort property, it's mostly overlooked, but the display is a requisite stop for anyone curious about the achievements of this driven man. Here, you (and a few other stragglers) learn the basic tenets of the Disney catechism, such as his boyhood hero was Abe Lincoln and he got the idea for Mickey on a train ride. (That

Go on Safari—for Mice

A favorite pastime for longtime fans is spotting **Hidden Mickeys,** which are ingeniously camouflaged mouse-ear patterns that can be secreted just about anywhere. You'll find the three circles signifying a Mickey profile embedded in an arrangement of cannonballs at Pirates of the Caribbean; flatware in the dining room at the Haunted Mansion; and woven into carpeting, printed on wallpaper—it was once snuck into the souvenir photo on Test Track using hoses. Many sightings are up to interpretation, but sharpen your observational skills first at **HiddenMickeysGuide.com.**

oft-repeated myth has been disputed, with some evidence, by several historians.) You don't hear about his passion for quality over money-grubbing, his sharp eye for merchandising opportunities, or anything else that would put the modern, publically traded Disney in a comparatively bad light. There are a few authentic artifacts, plus explanations of the revolutionary "multiplane" camera that enabled animators to reproduce the sliding depth of field normally seen in live-action films (you can see the fruit of the process in "Snow White" as the camera seems to move through the forest). Worth special scrutiny is the re-creation of Walt's surprisingly banal Burbank office as it appeared from 1940 (shortly before he became a propagandist during World War II) to 1966; note the bulletin board of Disneyland developments and also the four ashtrays, which contributed to his death from lung cancer. The end of the exhibition chronicles the theme parks, including lots of scale models and an Audio-Animatronic skeleton from the 1964 World's Fair. Most people take about 20 minutes for the museum, and then there's a good 15-minute movie (you may skip it), culled mostly from archival footage and audio, so you hear the man himself speak. The feature scores points for mentioning Disney's 1931 breakdown, but it also tries to prove Walt was a patron of the Disney Company's current efforts, implying he approved of Epcot's final design and worse, elbowing poor Roy virtually out of the story. But maybe it can be re-edited. "Disneyland," he promises in it, "is something that will never be finished."

Where to Eat at Disney's Hollywood Studios

All locations have a few vegetarian options, kids' meals, and if you identify yourself, special dietary requests can usually be accommodated, albeit often at diminished quality.

DISNEY'S HOLLYWOOD STUDIOS' QUICK-SERVICE RESTAURANTS

Starring Rolls Café ★★ AMERICAN   The faster, cheaper, quieter alternative to Quick Service does stupendous baked goods such as chocolate Butterfinger cupcakes and banana split cake, plus a few sandwiches with chips or fruit. Around the corner, **Sweet Spells** tops it in the confection department, selling creative candy apples that look like Kermit and Olaf. Coffee is just $2, not $3.40 as at the kiosks. Sunset Boulevard. Sandwiches $11.

Rosie's All-American Cafe ★★ AMERICAN   In the Sunset Ranch Market riff on L.A.'s famous Farmer's Market, you'll find outdoor-only counter service serving the typical burgers and chicken nuggets. Sunset Boulevard. Combo meal $9 to $10.

Catalina Eddie's ★★ AMERICAN   Outdoor counter service for bready personal pizzas, hot Italian deli sandwiches, and Caesar's salad. Near it is **Anaheim Produce** for fruit ($1.70 a piece). Sunset Boulevard. Combo meal $8 to $10

Fairfax Fare ★★ AMERICAN   Grab the richest, deadliest food, served outside: half-slabs of spareribs, barbecued pork sandwiches, and mac 'n cheese with truffle oil. Nearby is the **Toluca Legs Turkey Company** kiosk for those crazy big turkey legs drumsticks. Sunset Boulevard. Combo meal $9 to $16.

ABC Commissary ★★ AMERICAN   You get the same old food (burgers, couscous quinoa, and fried seafood platters), but it's a good choice because the air-conditioned, uncrowded space is fashioned after a '30s Deco backlot cafeteria. Commissary Lane. Combo meal $8 to $11.

Backlot Express ★★ AMERICAN   Bacon cheeseburgers, hot dogs, southwest chicken salad, served in AC with self-serve soda machines. Echo Lake. Combo meal $8 to $11.

Studio Catering Co. ★ AMERICAN   In a sheltered seating area, order take-away chicken Caesar wraps, Greek salad, and Sloppy Joes with chipotle barbecue sauce. To the left, the **High Octane Refreshments** stand sells $9 cocktails (frozen margaritas and the like), draft beer and wine for $7. Streets of America. Combo meal $9 to $10.

Pizza Planet Arcade ★ AMERICAN   Bland pizza, bready subs, dull salads, but kids like spending more of your money on the arcade games, so it's often busy. Streets of America. Combo meal $9.50 to $11.

DISNEY'S HOLLYWOOD STUDIOS' TABLE-SERVICE RESTAURANTS

The highest-concept reservation restaurants in Disney World are found here. The food isn't legendary, but some of the settings play on entertainment greatness.

The Hollywood Brown Derby ★★ AMERICAN   With interior design based on the after-hours industry hangout of Hollywood's Golden Age (not the place with the big hat—the classier one), this airy post-Deco hall shoots for the upscale. Caricatures of film legends line the walls—those in black frames are copies while those in gold frames are relics from the original Brown Derby—and while the original Brown Derby was noted for its Cobb salad, this version is a bit of a caricature as well, often soggy. Other choices, all invoking that midcentury California spirit at the park's highest prices, include crispy duck, cioppino, maple-glazed Scotch salmon, and beef filet. Its grapefruit cake is a specialty. Hollywood Boulevard. Main courses $29 to $43.

Hollywood & Vine ★★ AMERICAN   At breakfast and lunch, costumed Disney Junior characters (such as Doc McStuffins and Jake) greet kids, sing, and dance in a dinerlike setting for **Disney Junior Play 'n Dine at Hollywood & Vine.** The food is always an all-you-can-eat buffet. Echo Lake. Buffet $25 to $32 adults, $14 to $17 kids.

50's Prime Time Café ★★★ AMERICAN   Dine atop Formica in detailed reproductions of Cleaver-era kitchens while TVs play black-and-white shows from the era. Waitresses gently give lip to customers as they sling blue-plate specials, meatloaf, pot roast, chicken pot pie, and other momlike dishes, but the favorite here is its peanut butter and jelly milkshake ($5.60). Attached is the **Tune-In Lounge,** a TV room for adults serving beer and cocktails "from Dad's liquor cabinet." Echo Lake. Main courses $16 to $22.

Mama Melrose's Ristorante Italiano ★★ ITALIAN   Items cost two-thirds of what they do at Epcot's Italy, and the atmosphere recalls the brick-walled, red-boothed family restaurant you'd find in any big American city. As expected, you eat pastas, steaks, flatbreads, and brick oven–baked chicken dishes. Streets of America. Main courses $17 to $25.

Sci-Fi Dine-In Theater Restaurant ★★★ AMERICAN   Disney World's most unusual restaurant arranges mock-ups of '50s automobiles before a silver screen showing a loop of B-movie clips and trailers. Couples sit side-by-side, like at a real drive-in movie, stars twinkle in the "sky," and families get their own booths. It's a brilliant idea, well realized and memorable, making it a top choice despite very iffy food quality. Dishes include burgers, fried dill pickles, pork ribs, and salmon BLTs. Commissary Lane. Main courses $14 to $30.

DISNEY'S ANIMAL KINGDOM

Although it's the largest Disney theme park in Florida (500 acres), **Disney's Animal Kingdom** ★★, which opened in 1998 at a reported cost of $800 million as a competitor to Busch Gardens, actually takes the least amount of time to visit, because most of that land is used up by a menagerie of exotic animals. Instead of cages, they're kept in paddocks rimmed with cleverly disguised trenches that are concealed behind landscaping. Most attractions are given a mild environmentalist message (ironic, considering how much Florida swamp was obliterated to build this resort, but never you mind). Because animals become inactive as the Florida heat builds, a visit here should begin as soon as the gates open, usually around 8am. To help gird your resolve, there are coffee carts ($3.40 outside the gates, $2.20 inside) along the entranceway. **Tips:** Schedule your nighttime shindig, such as that dinner show you've been dying to catch, for your Animal Kingdom day. Check the weather before you come, because if it's excessively hot or wet, you might be miserable. Only three major attractions take place indoors. There is currently no parade at Animal Kingdom.

GETTING IN   Staples such as locker and stroller rental are just past the gates, in what's called the **Oasis,** a lush buffer zone that gradually acclimates guests to the world of the park. Pick up a free "Guidemap," a "Times Guide," and an "Animal Guide." The locations of animal enclosures are noted on the map by black-and-white paw prints, so if you're most interested in seeing wildlife, follow those.

Generally speaking, the biggest animals and the most astute design collects at the back of the park (Africa and Asia), the thrills to the right (Asia and DinoLand U.S.A.).

The first thing you should do, like everyone else, is beeline it to the back of the Africa section. That's where the Kilimanjaro Safari is, and first thing in the morning is the best time to do it. Crowds grow more ferocious than the lions.

Discovery Island

Like the Plaza of the Magic Kingdom, Discovery Island is designed to be the hub of the park. It's the main viewing area for the daily Mickey's Jammin' Jungle Parade, which circles it (the route is denoted on the maps by a red dotted line) and guests can touch down here to change lands. The park's **tip board,** with current wait times and upcoming showtimes, is also here, just to the right past the bridge from the Oasis, by the Disney Outfitters shop.

The Best of Disney's Animal Kingdom

Don't miss if you're 6: Festival of the Lion King

Don't miss if you're 16: DINOSAUR

Requisite photo op: The drop at Expedition Everest

Food you can only get here: Frozen chai, Royal Anandapur Tea Company

The most crowded, so Fastpass or go early: Kilimanjaro Safaris

Skippable: Rafiki's Planet Watch

Quintessentially Disney: It's Tough to Be a Bug!

Biggest thrill: Expedition Everest

Best show: "Finding Nemo—The Musical"

Character meals: Tusker House Restaurant, Africa

Where to find peace: Discovery Island

The Tree of Life ★★★ RIDE   Instead of a castle or a geosphere (or, uh . . . a hat), the centerpiece here, Animal Kingdom's "weenie," is an emerald, 14-story-high arbor (built on the skeleton of an oil rig) covered with hundreds of carvings of animals made to appear, at a distance, like the pattern of bark. Some 102,000 vinyl leaves were individually attached—which is why its shade of green is more lurid than the surrounding foliage—to some 750 tertiary branches. That the best way to enjoy it is to slowly make a circuit of it, looking for and identifying new animals, is perhaps proof that the best way to experience this park is to slow down and open your eyes.

Discovery Island Trails ★★ ACTIVITY   The self-guided paths encircle the Tree of Life. Here's where you'll find giant red kangaroos, flamingoes, storks, otters, lemurs, macaws, and the lappet-faced vulture; some are removed from view when it's hot. It takes only about 15 minutes to enjoy.

Adventurers Outpost ★ CHARACTER GREETING   Mickey and Minnie, wearing explorer garb, meet kids, and sign autographs here, on the east side of the path toward Asia. It is the only place in the resort where they appear as a couple.

It's Tough to Be a Bug! ★★★ SHOW   Hidden in the flying roots of the Tree of Life, in a cool basementlike theater, you'll find a cleverly rigged cinema showing a sense-tricking 10-minute 3-D movie based on the animated movie "A Bug's Life." When the stinkbugs do their thing or the tarantula starts firing poison quills, you'll never quite be sure what's an image, what's cutting-edge robotics, and what's clever rigging in the theater. As one of the newest sense-tricking movies at Disney World, it's one of the best. Little kids who can't distinguish fantasy from reality may be scared by the marvelously realized Hopper figure; sit in back (the first doors after you get your glasses) and to the left to be far from him. The indoor preshow area is decorated with posters for some funny entomological variations on Broadway shows (my faves: "Web Side Story" and "My Fair Ladybug"). **Strategy:** Upon exiting, go left to explore the trails (above) or right for the bridge to Asia.

Africa

You might see a bit of upheaval in this section of the park while a new theater is built to house Festival of the Lion King. Because of its star attraction, Africa is mobbed in the morning, but by afternoon it gets more manageable.

Kilimanjaro Safaris ★★★ RIDE   Easily the bumpiest ride at Disney World, the 20-minute ride is the crown jewel of Animal Kingdom. Climb into a supersize, 32-passenger Jeep—an actual one with wheels, not a tracked cart—and be swept into what feels like a real safari through the African veldt, with meticulously rutted tracks and all, only on Quaaludes. Be quick on the shutter, because drivers speed fleetly, passing through habitats for giraffes, elephants, wildebeest, ostrich, hippos, lions, antelope, rhinos, and other creatures that made safaris famous. Considering the quality and quantity of animals on display—and the cleverness of the enclosure design, as there are never bars between you and them—it's easily the best animal attraction of the park, and the queue only builds during the day. Some people say that the second-best time to see the animals is in midafternoon because they get antsy with the foreknowledge that they're about to be led to their indoor sleeping quarters. Ride twice if you want—the free will of the animals means it's never the same trip twice. **Strategy:** Photographers who want clear shots should jockey toward the back, away from the cockpit. They may not have control over that, so at the very least, they should negotiate with their companions for a seat at the end of their row.

Disney's Animal Kingdom

RAFIKI'S PLANET WATCH 15

14

13

Wildlife Express

Wildlife Express Train Station

DINING◆
Flame Tree Barbecue **7**
Pizzafari **2**
Rainforest Cafe **1**
Restaurantosaurus **25**
Safari Barbecue **6**
Tamu Tamu Eats & Refreshment **9**
Tusker House Restaurant (character meals) and Dawa Bar **8**
Yak & Yeti **17**

ASIA

Maharajah Jungle Trek

AFRICA
Pangani Forest Exploration Trail

Wildlife Express Train Station 12

11

10

Festival of the Lion King

8 9

Kilimanjaro Safaris 16

Kali River Rapids

19

17 18

20 Expedition Everest

3 Tree of Life

DISCOVERY 5 6

2 4 7

ISLAND

21

Finding Nemo—The Musical

22

23 24

Discovery River

Future Site of Avatar-themed land

OASIS

25

26

DINOLAND U.S.A.

27

1 Ticket gates

DINOSAUR

Main Entrance

Buses to other Disney areas

PARKING AREA

DISCOVERY ISLAND
Discovery Island Trails **3**
It's Tough to Be a Bug! **5**
Tip Board **4**

AFRICA
Kilimanjaro Safaris **10**
Pangani Forest Exploration Trail **11**
Wildlife Express Train station for Rafiki's Planet Watch **12**

RAFIKI'S PLANET WATCH
The Affection Section **15**
Conservation Station **14**
Habitat Habit! **13**

ASIA
Expedition Everest **20**
Flights of Wonder **16**
Kali River Rapids **18**
Maharajah Jungle Trek **19**

DINOLAND U.S.A.
The Boneyard **22**
DINOSAUR **27**
Dino-Sue **26**
Finding Nemo— The Musical **21**
Primeval Whirl **24**
TriceraTop Spin **23**

ANIMAL KINGDOM: ONE DAY, TWO WAYS

ANIMAL KINGDOM WITH KIDS

When the gates open, head straight to **Africa for Kilimanjaro Safaris.**

↓

Find the gorillas and hippos on the **Pangani Forest Exploration.**

↓

Go to Asia to spot tigers on the **Maharajah Jungle Trek.**

↓

Ride **Kali River Rapids** to cool down.

↓

See **Flights of Wonder.**

↓

Have lunch at Yak & Yeti.

↓

See the next performance of **Finding Nemo—The Musical,** seated and indoors.

↓

Ride **Primeval Whirl** and **TriceraTop Spin.**

↓

Go see **It's Tough to Be a Bug!,** and walk the Discovery Trails to look for animals embedded in the Tree of Life.

↓

Go to Africa to see **Festival of the Lion King.**

↓

If you have time or energy, take the train to and from Rafiki's Planet Watch for a 20-minute walk-through (budget 45 min. total).

↓

Re-ride anything you loved and head out before closing.

Pangani Forest Exploration Trail ★★★ ACTIVITY   Upon exiting Kilimanjaro Safaris, begin this trail, which focuses on African animals. It wends past a troop of lowland gorillas (very popular), naked mole rats, okapi, meerkats (yes, like Timon), and hippos you can view through an underwater window; the nocturnal animals start waking up at around 3:30pm. The circuit takes about a half-hour, but you can spend as long as you want. The gorillas come near the end, so budget your time.

"Festival of the Lion King" ★★★ SHOW   If this lavish, colorful, intense spectacle can't hold your attention for 30 minutes, you might require prescriptions. Audiences sit on benches in four quadrants (front rows are good for engaging with performers), and the event comes on buoyant and boisterously, like an acid trip during a rock concert. Four huge floats enter the room, topped with soft-looking giant puppets of Timon, Pumbaa, and African wildlife and attended by acrobats, stilt-walkers, flame jugglers, and dancers, all of whom get their turn to dazzle you with their acts, which are performed, of course, to the hit songs of the movie. **Strategy:** Shows are scheduled, and they can fill up, so arrive 30 minutes early. Unfortunately, although the theatre was just built in 2014, the seating is bleacher-style and lacks backs.

ANIMAL KINGDOM WITHOUT KIDS

Have a mid- to late-morning Fastpass for Expedition Everest or an early afternoon one for Kilimanjaro Safaris.

When the gates open, head straight to Africa for Kilimanjaro Safaris. It's fine if you have a Fastpass for later; each trip yields different animals.

↓

Watch the gorillas on the **Pangani Forest Exploration Trail.**

OR

Go to Asia to ride **Expedition Everest** before the line gets too crazy.

↓

Walk to Asia and ride **Expedition Everest** (if you haven't already!).

↓

Explore the **Maharajah Jungle Trek** to see tigers.

↓

If it's hot by now, ride **Kali River Rapids.**

↓

See **Flights of Wonder.**

↓

Have lunch at Yak & Yeti.

↓

See the next performance of **Finding Nemo—The Musical.** Enjoy the air-conditioning.

↓

Ride **Primeval Whirl.**

↓

Ride **DINOSAUR.**

↓

See **It's Tough to Be a Bug!,** and walk the Discovery Trails to look for animals embedded in the Tree of Life.

↓

If it's quiet and you're interested, re-ride **Kilimanjaro Safaris** to get a different experience than before.

↓

Go to Africa to see **Festival of the Lion King.**

↓

If you have time or energy, take the train to **Rafiki's Planet Watch** (budget 45 min. total).

↓

Re-ride anything you loved. You will probably depart before closing time, so this may be a great night to make evening plans in Orlando.

3

Rafiki's Planet Watch ★ ACTIVITY Its elements are listed separately on the park maps, but everything is of a piece. The only way to reach this educational veterinary station is using the **Wildlife Express Train.** Waits are generally no longer than 10 minutes. The trip takes 7 minutes and you'll get glimpses of plain backstage work areas and maybe a white rhino in its indoor pen, but not much else. **Habitat Habit!,** the path that leads to the main building, is another "discovery trail," this one with cotton-top tamarins (endangered monkeys about the size of squirrels). **Conservation Station** is a quasi-educational peek at how the park's animals are maintained—you're not seeing the true veterinary facilities, but a few auxiliary rooms set up so tourists can watch activities through picture windows. There's not always something going on (early mornings seem to be most active), and the Times Guide doesn't help, so you might get all the way here and then find yourself with only some tanks of reptiles and amphibians to poke at, although Rafiki and Chip 'n' Dale make appearances all day. There's nothing earthshaking—enter a dark, soundproof booth and listen to the sounds of the rainforest—but the pace is much easier than in the park outside. **The Affection Section** is a petting zoo hosting, in addition to your typical petting-zoo denizens—donkeys, goats, sheep. Next to that; there's an animal presentation on the bottom of the hour between 11:30am and 2:30pm. **Tip:** Try to visit by noon, when the vets are more likely to be treating animals; Guest Relations, at the front of the park, keeps a schedule.

Asia

Asia is the park's showcase, and its ingenious decor (rat-trap wiring, fraying prayer flags) is so accurate it could easily be mistaken for the real Nepal or northern India. Make a stop at **Bhaktapur Market,** which sells Asian souvenirs that are a cut above the usual theme park stuff—kimonos, Manga toys, beautiful sarongs. It makes me long for the years when all of Disney World's shops were this interesting and site-specific.

Expedition Everest ★★★ RIDE The lavishly themed and abundantly hyped roller coaster is mostly contained in the "snowcapped" mountain looming nearly 200 feet over the park's east end (if it were any higher, Florida law would require it to be topped by an airplane beacon). The queue area is a beautifully realized duplication of a Himalayan temple down to the tarnished bells and weathered paint, although portions of it are exposed the sun, so drink something before you pony up. The coaster itself is loaded with powerful set pieces that get you your money's worth: both backward and forward motion, pitch-black sections, and a fleeting encounter with a 22-foot Abominable Snowman, or Yeti. As with all Disney rides, the most dramatic drop (80 ft.) is visible from the sidewalk out front, so if you think you can stomach that, you can do the rest. There are no upside-down loops; the dominant motion is spiral. **Strategy:** This coaster is a top candidate for Fastpass. The seats with the best view, without question, are in the front rows, although the back rows feel a little faster. The single-rider line is in one of the resort's fastest-moving and most fruitful.

Kali River Rapids ★ RIDE The 12-passenger round bumper boat shoots a course of rapids, and sometimes you can get soaked—it depends on your bad luck—but it's generally milder than similar rides. Your feet, for sure, will get wet. The worst damage is usually done by spectators who shoot water cannons at passing boats. Lots of guests buy rain ponchos ($7.50–$8.50 at nearby stores, or $1 for two at your local dollar store), but there is a water-resistant holding area in the center of each boat. To be safe, there are free 120-minute lockers available, $7/hour if you go over. **Strategy:** Lines build considerably when it's hot, so this is another prime Fastpass candidate.

Maharajah Jungle Trek ★★ ACTIVITY Too few people enjoy this self-guided, South Asian–themed walking trail featuring some gorgeous tigers (rescued from a circus breeding program), flying foxes, komodo dragons, and a few birds frolicking among fake ruins. The tigers are most active when the park opens and near closing

---

The Chilling Tale of Disco Yeti

Expedition Everest's original effects were too complicated to function for long. The Yeti suffered the most ignoble fate. Although it was the most complicated Audio-Animatronic creature ever commissioned, and the sight of it lunging for your train was meant to be the ride's scintillating climax, its repetitive motion reportedly cracked its supports, which were too integrated with the structure of the mountain to repair. The solution: A strobe light now makes it appear as if the motionless Yeti moves. Disney fans deride it as the "Disco Yeti."

time. Grab a bird information sheet after entering the aviary; there's a bat display, too, that you can bypass if you're squeamish.

Flights of Wonder ★★ SHOW At the canvas-sheltered Caravan Stage, the 25-minute show (the schedule is posted) showcases birds such as hawks, vultures, bald eagles, and parrots—20 species; the mix changes—that swoop thrillingly over the audience's heads. Standard, if beautiful, nature-show stuff. After the performance, handlers usually present a few of the birds back on stage for close inspection.

DinoLand U.S.A.

When it rains, come here, where two attractions and one big counter-service restaurant are indoors.

"Finding Nemo—The Musical" ★★★ SHOW One of the best shows at Disney right now is a fast-forwarded version of the movie by the songwriters of the Oscar-winning tune "Let It Go." The story was heightened with such catchy added songs as "Fish Are Friends, Not Food" and the infectious, Beach Boys–style "Go with the Flow." Just as in the Broadway adaptation of "The Lion King," live actors manipulate complicated animal puppets in full view, which allows the fish to appear as if they're floating in the sea. It's remarkable how quickly you stop paying attention to the humans—at least, until they start flying, with their puppets, through the air on wires. Then you're just amazed. Sprightly, bright, colossal, and energetic, this winning 40-minute show is a good choice for taking a load off (the bench seating is indoors), and even those who know the movie backward and forward will find something new in the vibrant vigor of the delivery. **Strategy:** Because some scenes (including the introduction of Dory) happen in the aisle that crosses the center of the theater, sit in the rear half of the auditorium.

Chester & Hester's Dino-Rama ★ ACTIVITY/RIDE Kids run loose in this miniature carnival-style amusement area with a midway, **Fossil Fun Games** (Mammoth skee-ball races, "Whac-a-Packycephaolosaur") and two simple family rides. **TriceraTop Spin** ★, for the very young, is yet another iteration of the Dumbo ride over at Magic Kingdom and is designed for kids to ride with their parents. Cars fit four, in two rows. **Primeval Whirl** ★ is a pair of mirror-image, family-friendly carnival-style coasters (FYI, Walt *hated* carnivals) that start out like a typical "wild mouse" ride before, mid-trip, the round cars begin spinning on an axle as they ride the rails. Think of it as a roller-coaster version of the teacup ride. You can plainly see what you're in for, although you may be surprised at how roughly the movements can whip your neck. Don't feel bad if you give it a miss, too, because it's not a Disney original; it was made by a French company that sells similar rides to other parks. Keep the kids in control by swinging them across the path to **The Boneyard** ★, a hot, sun-exposed playground where the very young can dig up "prehistoric" bones in the sand and work off energy on catwalks, net courses, and slides.

DINOSAUR ★★ RIDE A good rainy-weather option is this 3-minute indoor time-travel ride in which all-terrain "Enhanced Motion Vehicles" simultaneously speed and shimmy down an unseen track, all as hordes of roaring dinosaurs attempt to make you dinner and an approaching asteroid shower threatens to do everyone in. Some kids, and even some adults, find all those jaws and jerky movements rather intense, and it's extremely dark and loud, but ultimately, it's a fun time, even if the perpetual darkness makes me wonder how much money Disney saved in not having to build more dinosaurs. Like many modern rides, well-known actors perform in the preshow video; this

PACKING IT IN: TWO PARKS, ONE DAY

START: BE AT THE GATE FOR OPENING TIME.

You really don't *have* to pay for 2 days' worth of park tickets to visit Animal Kingdom and Hollywood Studios. As long as you have the Park Hopper option, you can see the highlights in 1 action-packed day. You will miss some lesser attractions, but not enough to lose sleep over.

Which park you do first is a toss-up. The animals are most active first thing in the morning at Animal Kingdom, but the line at Hollywood Studios' Toy Story Midway Mania gets crazy by noon. You can start with Animal Kingdom, where Fastpasses are mostly unnecessary, if you have pre-arranged an afternoon Fastpass for Toy Story Midway Mania at Hollywood Studios.

Begin your day at **Disney's Animal Kingdom.** When the gates open, head straight to **Africa for Kilimanjaro Safaris.**
↓
Animal people: Enjoy the **Pangani Forest Exploration Trail.**

Coaster people: Ride **Expedition Everest.** If the wait's bad, use the Single Rider line.
↓
Explore the **Maharajah Jungle Trek.**
↓
Ride **Kali River Rapids.**
↓
If you enjoy live musicals, see the next performance of either **Finding Nemo—The Musical** or **Festival of the Lion King.** This will take nearly an hour, so cut this if it's too close to lunch.
↓
Ride **DINOSAUR.** (Maybe you can do this while waiting for the Nemo show to start?)
↓

Go see **It's Tough to Be a Bug!,** and afterward walk the Discovery Trails and look for animals embedded in the Tree of Life.
↓
Switch parks. On the way, you could lunch on U.S. 192, where food's cheaper. Reach that quickly by following the signs to the Animal Kingdom Lodge and turning left at the light before its entrance. That's Sherbeth Road, and it winds to U.S. 192. After lunch, drive east on 192 a few miles and follow the signs back to Disney.
↓
Enter **Disney's Hollywood Studios.**
↓
Use your Fastpass for **Toy Story Midway Mania** at Pixar Place.
↓
Ride **Twilight Zone Tower of Terror** and **Rock 'n' Roller Coaster.**
↓
Do **The Great Movie Ride.**
↓
Take the **Backlot Tour** (it usually shuts down by late afternoon).
↓
Ride **Star Tours.**
↓
If you have time, see **Muppet*Vision 3-D.**
↓
If you have time, see the **Indiana Jones Epic Stunt Spectacular.**
↓
See **Fantasmic!** (if it's performing tonight).
↓
Go back to your hotel and collapse.

The next big Disney addition, slated for a 2017 opening, is currently clanging and hammering its way into existence on the site of the former Camp Minnie-Mickey section. It's a bizarre choice to co-opt a franchise that was not created by the company, and it's made more bizarre that there are a dozen other Disney-owned brands that are far more beloved, from "Star Wars" to the Muppets. No doubt Disney was spooked into greenlighting it by the mad success of Universal's Harry Potter lands, but Avatar Land, as it's nicknamed right now, will be the largest expansion in Animal Kingdom's relatively short history. Imagineers will draw inspiration from the bioluminescent plants, "floating mountains," and wildlife of the fictional planet Pandora, and although Disney Parks is mum about specifics, it's rumored that the lynchpin attractions will be a flying ride simulator and a boat ride.

one's got Phylicia Rashad, fiercely overacting, and Wallace Langham, in a horrific tie. The line never seems to be as long as this ride deserves. On the path to the ride, don't ignore **Dino-Sue,** the 40-foot-long, full-scale T. rex skeleton—it's a replica of Sue, the most complete specimen man has yet found. The original, unearthed in South Dakota in 1990, is on display at Chicago's Field Museum. The **Cretaceous Trail,** at the head of the path, showcases ferns and American alligators extant in that period.

Where to Eat at Disney's Animal Kingdom

All locations have vegetarian options, kids' meals, and if you identify yourself, special dietary requests can usually be accommodated. Because plastic straws choke animals, paper ones are provided. Frozen drinks spiked with booze have become a big thing at Animal Kingdom, which helps combat heat in this exposed park.

DISNEY'S ANIMAL KINGDOMS' QUICK-SERVICE RESTAURANTS

Guests will **dietary restrictions** should seek out the new Gardens kiosk near Flame Tree Barbecue on Discovery Island, where special snacks are sold and cast members can help you find more suitable dishes around the park.

Flame Tree Barbecue ★★★ AMERICAN   If you don't mind gorging on meaty dishes such as ribs and baked chicken when you're supposed to be appreciating animals, it has some terrific eating areas with cushioned seating on the Discovery River, and its pulled-pork barbecue is a favorite. This is where you get those honking turkey legs. Discovery Island. Combo meal $9.50 to $16.

Pizzafari ★★ AMERICAN   A vibrantly colored restaurant with lots of rooms to spread out, Pizzafari has a special contraption in the kitchen for cranking out fresh pizzas. It also does Italian-style subs and pasta with chicken. Discovery Island. Combo meal $9 to $10.

Yak & Yeti Local Food Cafes ★★ ASIAN   Although there is a table-service location indoors by the same name, the outdoor windows do counter-service Mandarin chicken salad, sweet and sour chicken, beef lo mein, and greasy pork egg rolls. Across the path on the water, the **Royal Anandapur Tea Company ★★** kiosk does something unique: teas and slushy chai ($5.40). Asia. Combo meal $9 to $11.

Tamu Tamu Eats & Refreshment ★ INTERNATIONAL With a small selection (pulled beef or chicken-salad sandwiches, quinoa salad) and no indoor seating, it's not usually too crowded. Best of all, it serves the beloved Dole Whip frozen pineapple dessert, but here, it's spiked with a shot of rum. It's near **Dawa Bar,** a relaxing spot mimicking a fortress on the water where cocktails are served. Africa. Combo meal $9–$10.

Restaurantosaurus ★ AMERICAN As American as DinoLand U.S.A., the kitchen pumps out burgers, hot dogs, chicken BLT salad, and nuggets. The **Dino-Bites** kiosk nearby sells desserts. DinoLand U.S.A. Combo meal $9 to $11.

DISNEY'S ANIMAL KINGDOM'S TABLE-SERVICE RESTAURANTS

Because you're probably going to be up early to see the animals at their best, this park is a good candidate for a character breakfast. There are very few places to get out of the heat and have a waiter-service meal.

Rainforest Cafe ★ AMERICAN In a lush, junglelike, theatrically lit setting, robotic animals roar and twitter over your cheese sticks, burgers, and rum cocktails in souvenir glasses. This is not a Disney original, but one of two outposts of the established brand at Disney World (the other is at Downtown Disney Marketplace). Oasis, at the park turnstiles. Main courses $13 to $33.

Tusker House Restaurant ★★★ AMERICAN/AFRICAN Under multicolored banners in an ancient souklike environment, Donald, Daisy, Mickey, and Goofy greet families in safari garb for "Donald's Safari Breakfast" and "Donald's Dining Safari" lunch, both all-you-can eat buffets. By dinner, character-free, the buffet dares more than most Disney dos, featuring Cape Malay curry chicken, spiced tandoori tofu, couscous, seafood stew with tamarind BBQ sauce, and other pleasingly aromatic choices. Africa. Meals $29 to $35 adults, $16 to $19 kids.

Yak & Yeti Restaurant ★★ ASIAN Themed like a Nepalese mansion stocked with souvenirs from across Southeast Asia, the menu is just as geographically varied, serving Kobe beef burgers with mushroom compote, ahi tuna, Malaysian seafood curry, fried honey chicken, and stir fry. The Quick Service counter outside offers a shorter, but similar, menu for less, but at Animal Kingdom, air conditioning is the most rare and delicious treat. Main courses $19 to $27.

Fitting into the Disney Culture

Walt Disney World's employees have a culture all their own that visitors must learn to respect. Working at Disney World isn't like getting a job at the bank. WDW is billed as the Happiest Place on Earth. Many cast members live and breathe its way of life, and quite a few moved from other parts of the country to be a part of it. Be alert to the fact that many of them identify personally with the Disney Way (it exists) and they take exception to comments that carry a hint of being argumentative. Try not to bicker with Disney employees or put them in a position of having to defend or explain their company. And for heaven's sake, no cussing! That code is technically meant to apply only to cast members, the unspoken cultural expectation is that you follow it, too. The flip side of this is that if something goes wrong with your visit, cast members will often work to make it right and make your vacation a positive memory.

DISNEY WATER PARKS

The big question: Blizzard Beach or Typhoon Lagoon? Both can fill a day. So it depends on your mood. Typhoon Lagoon's central feature, a sand-lined 2½-acre wave pool, is an ideal place for families to approximate a day at the beach. If your kids have a need for speed, then head to Blizzard Beach, which has wilder water slides.

Both water parks, similar in size, have free parking and are less busy early in the week, probably because folks tend to start their vacations on a weekend and don't get to the flumes until they've done the four big theme parks. They tend to be busier in the morning than in late afternoon. They also sell everything you need to protect yourself from the sun, including lotion (should you have forgotten) and swimsuits (should you lose yours in the lather). Most lines (many rides have two: one for a raft and one for the slide) are exposed to the sun, so it's important to **keep hydrated,** as you won't always be aware how much you're sweating. Both parks sell refillable mugs for **endless soft drinks** (otherwise, soft drinks start at $3). They also rent towels for $2. Lifeguards usually make you remove water shoes on slides that don't use a mat or raft, and swimsuits with rivets or zippers are forbidden because they may scratch the flumes.

A day at a water park isn't as stressful as one spent among the queues of the theme parks, and if you're paying attention, the sights and sounds of a day here are pretty heartwarming. Every time the wave machine roars into gear, for example, dozens of kids shriek with delight and scamper into the water. Because they're chilling out, people tend to be happy at these parks.

LOCKERS An average locker is $10 but you get $5 of that back after you turn your key in. They allow multiple access, are about 2 feet deep, and the opening is about the size of a magazine.

PREPARATION Thoughtfully, parking is free. There are bulletin boards past the park entrances that tell you what the sunburn risk is and what the wait times are for the slides, as well as what times the parades run at Disney parks that day. If there are any activities (scavenger hunts are common), they'll be posted here. Kids' beach toy sets, for the sand around the lagoon, are sold in the gift shop for $10.

FOOD There are only counter-service choices. Eat promptly at 11am when they open because lines get crazy quickly. Don't plan on eating dinner at the water parks, as the kiosks tend to shut down well before closing.

TIMING If you're coming to Florida between November and mid-March, one of these parks will be closed for its annual hose-down. The other will remain open. Most water features are heated, but remember that you eventually must get *out.*

Blizzard Beach

Of Disney's two water parks, **Blizzard Beach ★★★** is the more thrilling, possibly because it opened 6 years after Typhoon Lagoon and had the benefit of improving on what didn't work there. It also has a wittier backstory that is perfect for a hot day: A freak snowstorm hit Mount Gushmore, and Disney was slapping up a ski resort when the snow began to melt, creating water slides. So now, a lift chair brings bathers most of the way up the 90-foot peak, and flumes are festooned with ski-run flags and piled with white "snowdrifts." Best of all, at this park, no one has to tote rafts uphill—there are conveyors to do it for you.

Surely the most exhilarating 8 seconds in all of Walt Disney World, **Summit Plummet ★★★** is the immensely steep, 12-story-tall slide that commands attention at the peak of the mountain, which incidentally, offers one of the best panoramas of the Walt Disney World resort. A slide down this one is for the truly fearless, as the first few seconds make you feel weightless, as if you're about to fall forward. By the end, the water is jabbing you so hard that it's not unusual to come away with a light bruise, and it turns the toughest bathing suit into dental floss. This is a fun one to watch; just ask the young men who are glued to it for the aforementioned reason. **Slush Gusher ★**, next to it among the Green Slope rides and slightly lower, is a double-hump that gives the rider the sensation of air time—not a reassuring feeling when you're flying down an open chute.

The enormous chute winding off the mountain's right side is **Teamboat Springs ★★**, a group ride in a circular raft; just about everyone gets a chance to enjoy the top of a banked turn, and after the inevitable splashdown, another minute is spent in a come-down floating on a river. It's highly re-rideable, but if you go alone, you'll be paired with strangers for some slippery awkwardness.

Snow Stormers ★ (Purple Slope) is a trio of standard raft water slides, but the twin **Downhill Double Dipper ★** is a simple slope of two identical slides with a good embellishment: It times runs so you can race a companion down. **Toboggan Racers ★★** multiplies the fun to where eight people can race at once down an evenly scalloped run. At the base of these is **Melt Away Bay ★★★**, a 1-acre wave pool in which waves create a gentle bobbing sensation. It could stand to be larger since it gets very crowded.

At the back of the mountain (the Red Slope; reach it by walking around the left or via the lazy river), the three **Runoff Rapids ★★** flumes comprise two open-air slides and a totally enclosed one—you only see the occasional light flashing by. (These are the only ones for which you must haul your own raft up the hill.)

The park is circled by the superlative lazy river (for the newbie, that's a slow-flowing channel where you float along in an inner tube) called **Cross Country Creek ★★★**, which is probably the best of its kind, passing a cave dripping with refrigerated water and a slouching shack that, every few seconds, gushes as you hear the sound of Goofy sneezing. **Tip:** It's easier to find a free inner tube at a ramp far from the park entrance; try the one at the base of Downhill Double Dipper or the one to the left past Lottawatta Lodge, the main food building.

There are two kiddie areas, one for preteens, **Ski Patrol ★★** (short slides, a walk across the water on floating "icebergs") and for littler kids, **Tike's Peak ★** (even smaller slides, fountains, and jets). The latter is a good place to look if you can't find seating.

Tip: The miniature golf course Winter Summerland (see "Join the Club" on p. 150) shares a parking lot with Blizzard Beach, so it's easy to combine a visit.

℘ 407/560-3400. www.disneyworld.com. $53 adults, $45 kids 3–9. Hours vary, but 10am–5pm is common in summer.

Typhoon Lagoon

Despite the petrifying imagery of the shrimp boat *(Miss Tilly)* impaled on the central mountain (Mt. Mayday), the flumes at **Typhoon Lagoon ★★** are less daunting than the ones at Blizzard Beach or Wet 'n Wild. Typhoon Lagoon is extremely well land-scaped (most of the flowers are selected so that they attract butterflies but not bees) to hide its infrastructure, but its navigation is not always well planned. For example, you tote your own rafts. Also, the paths to the slides ramble up and down stairs—the one to the Storm Slides actually goes *down* eight times as it winds up the mountain. It's also not always clear where to find the slide you want. Help guide little ones.

The **Surf Pool** ★★★ divides its time between "surf waves" (at 5 ft., they pack a surprising punch, and they are announced by a *whoompf* that draws great peals of delight from kids) and mild "bobbing waves"—times for both are noted on the Surf Report chalk sign at the pool's foot. The slides are generally shallow, slow, and geared toward avowed sissies. That will frustrate some teenagers, but little kids and mothers with expensive hairdos think **Mayday Falls** ★, which sends riders down a corrugated flume, is just right (adults come off rubbing their butts in pain). It's very tough to find a vantage point to watch your kids ride, but there's a spot near the entrance of **Gangplank Falls** ★★★, a family-sized round raft, where you can see a little, and there's a lovely hidden overlook trail with a suspension bridge and waterfalls that passes under the *Miss Tilly*. The leftmost body slide of three at **Storm Slides** ★★ is slightly more covered; otherwise the slides are much the same. The **Crush 'n' Gusher** ★★★ "water coaster" flumes use jets to push rafts both uphill and downhill; the gag is that it used to be a fruit-washing plant, and now you're the banana—appropriate since it's sponsored by Chiquita.

One highlight is **Shark Reef** ★★, a 10½-foot-deep tank stocked with tropical fish, nonthreatening leopard and bonnet sharks, and mock coral. Everyone gets a mask, snorkel, and, if wanted, a floatation jacket, and then swims 60 feet across the tank (no dawdling permitted) under the eye of lifeguards who'll spring into action at the slightest hint of trouble—or even if you kick your feet. (If you want a tank where you can dawdle with fish, try SeaWorld's Discovery Cove, p. 136.) You needn't meet a high standard beyond an ability to paddle across a pool. If you don't care for that setup, descend by stairs into a submerged "shipwreck," which has portholes allowing a lateral, murky view of the same tank. **Strategy:** Shark Reef gets busy, so do it early or late.

For the best shot at finding an inner tube for the lushly planted lazy river, **Castaway Creek** ★★, pick an entry farther from the entrance, such as in front of the Crush 'n' Gusher area. That's also a good place to find a lounger if the Lagoon is packed, which it usually is; otherwise, try the extreme left past the ice cream stand. That's near **Ketchakiddee Creek** ★★, the geyser-and-bubbler play area for small children. Funny how the water's always warmer there.

"Learn to Surf" lessons are held in the Surf Pool 2 hours before park hours and, sometimes, after it closes (✆ **407/939-7529**; $150 for all ages, minimum age of 5). The lessons come with 30 minutes of preparation followed by 2 hours of in-pool instruction, always with lifeguards scrutinizing your every twitch.

✆ **407/560-3400**. www.disneyworld.com. $53 adults, $45 kids 3–9. Hours vary, but 10am–5pm is common in summer.

MINOR DISNEY WORLD DIVERSIONS

Also see "Join the Club" on p. 150 for details on the two Disney miniature golf areas.

DisneyQuest ★ PLAY PARK   Most Disney fans thought this five-level virtual reality playground would close a half decade ago. It's shabby and past its prime, if it had one, and if you pay full price for it, you'll wish you hadn't. Standout stuff includes **Cyberspace Mountain,** in which you design your own coaster from a palette of options and then board a motion-simulator capsule in which you can test out your creation—360-degree loops and all. The ride vehicles actually go upside-down, making it one of only two Disney World rides to do so. **Virtual Jungle Cruise** has you on inflatable rafts, using paddles to float down a river on a screen in front of you; and **Pirates of the Caribbean: Battle for Buccaneer Gold** puts you on the deck of a mini pirate ship, with screens on three sides, that has members of your party simultaneously steering and blasting rival ships by yanking on ropes that trigger cannons (like the ones on Toy Story Midway Mania). Sadly, most of the animation feels badly dated. Not everything is screen based: The rowdy **Buzz Lightyear's AstroBlaster** is like a bumper-car game where your vehicle scoops up balls and fires them at competitors, causing them to spin momentarily; it's best for two riders at a time. Throughout the building are arcade games, old and new (try the playable **Wreck-It Ralph** arcade machines), that need no quarters. During the weekdays, you pretty much have your run of the place. Hit Orlando's more compelling attractions before getting around to doing this one—if you want technology, how about Kennedy Space Center? Still, it's fine if you have an extra Water Park Fun & More visit to burn on my Magic Your Way ticket. Sometimes 50 percent discounts are available 2 hours before closing.

Downtown Disney West Side. ℰ **407/828-4600.** www.disneyquest.com. $46 adults, $39 kids 3–9. $6–$8 cheaper online. Kids 9 and under must be accompanied by someone 16 or older. Sun–Thurs 11:30am–10pm; Fri–Sat 11:30am–11:30pm.

ESPN Wide World of Sports ★ ATHLETIC COMPLEX Most visitors don't

stumble onto the 220-acre grounds, which are essentially a souped-up stadium complex, by accident. They go there intentionally, for a son's wrestling tournament, a traveling sports exhibition game, or to see the Atlanta Braves in spring training. Unfortunately, it's not a place to roll up and pitch a few balls, although you can check its website to see if there's something ticketed that you might enjoy attending (and paying extra for).

Victory Dr., I-4 at exit 64B. ℰ **407/939-1500.** www.disneysports.com.

Richard Petty Driving Experience ★ RIDE Heaven knows how it secured a

matchless location in the Magic Kingdom's parking lot, but there it sits, selling 150-mph ride-alongs in 600 horsepower Winston Cup–style stock cars on a 1-mile track with 10-degree banking. A mere 3 laps start at $105, and if you want to be behind the wheel, packages zoom up to $449 for 8 laps. All riders pay another $39 in insurance. Petty has some 20 other locations; so don't feel wrecked if you miss this one.

3450 N. World Dr., Lake Buena Vista. ℰ **800/237-3889.** www.drivepetty.com. Minimum age 16. Daily 9am–4pm.

Downtown Disney & Disney's BoardWalk

The no-admission shopping and entertainment district currently known as Downtown Disney comprises nearly a pedestrianized mile of event restaurants and shops along a small lake, away from the major theme parks in a traffic-plagued eastern reach of the resort grounds. Its West Side is home to the DisneyQuest virtual playground (p. 93), a 24-screen cinema, and "La Nouba," the Cirque du Soleil show (see below).

Characters in Flight ★★ RIDE You'll see it from miles away: A huge, round helium balloon that rises from a pier, lingers 400 feet up for a spell, and then descends back to earth within about 10 minutes. Although it's safely tethered and the circular observation platform is securely enclosed with mesh, it lists and drifts with sudden breezes and that may disturb some guests. If you're adventurous, though, the trip is good fun, and of course the view rocks. It's known to summarily shut down for weather that may seem calm from the ground, so if it's flying and you want to ride it, don't procrastinate.

ORLANDO after dark WITH KIDS

Although on some nights, one could argue that the people drinking at the clubs and bars are infantile, you still can't bring your kids to hang out in them. Don't worry—Orlando is a family city, so there's much for kids to do.

o **Magic Kingdom parade:** Most nights, there are one or two parades through the park. When there are two, the second is less crowded.

o **Fireworks:** The Magic Kingdom is open until 9pm or later on most nights. There's usually an evening parade, and the nightly fireworks display, "Wishes," happens around Cinderella Castle. Hollywood Studios mounts "Fantasmic!," a pyrotechnics-and-water display, a few times a week, and Epcot is famous for its "IllumiNations" fireworks-and-electronics show over its lagoon. In summer, when they're open past dusk, Universal Studios does something (a spectacle on its lagoon) most nights, SeaWorld not so much. Check with each park for showtimes, as they change. Given that they're theme park shows, they're all designed to wow kids, but Magic Kingdom's display is the classic.

o **The Electrical Boat Parade:** It's a tradition going back 40 years—a string of 14 40-foot-long illuminated barges floats past the Disney resorts on Seven Seas Lagoon and Bay Lake starting at 9pm, accompanied by music. Lower key than the fireworks shows, you can see it for free from any resort hotel in the area or, if your timing is good, from the ferry that goes between the Magic Kingdom and the Ticket and Transportation Center.

o **Special event evenings:** From September through March, the Magic Kingdom schedules irregular special-ticket evenings (Mickey's Not-So-Scary Halloween Party, his Very Merry Christmas Party, and the Pirate and Princess events) for kids with free candy, character meetings, dance parties, and extended hours. The calendar of events can be found on p. 233, online at www.disneyworld.com, or you can call Disney at ✆ **407/939-7679.**

o **Dinnertainment:** Every night, there are more than a dozen dinner banquets accompanied by a kid-friendly show. See p. 189.

o **Character meals:** Early bedtime? Very young kids will be sent to sleep dreaming if they meet their favorite character over dinner. See p. 191 for a list.

Downtown Disney West Side. ✆ **407/824-4321.** www.disneyworld.com. $18 adults, $12 kids 3–9. Daily 8:30am–midnight.

House of Blues ★★★ MUSIC CLUB   One of the principal nightspots on the West Side has a 2,000-person, three-tiered venue (standing space only) hosting regular performers along the lines of B. B. King, One Republic, the Charlie Daniels Band, and Norah Jones. Big talent is ticketed at concert prices, and operator Live Nation piles on the fees, but mostly, it's a place to get Southern food. On Sundays, it hosts a somewhat desanctified Gospel Brunch (p. 191).

Downtown Disney West Side. ✆ **407/934-2583.** www.hob.com. Sun–Thurs 11:30am–11pm; Fri–Sat 11:30am–1am.

La Nouba ★★★ SHOW   All those taut, athletic bodies, wearing precious little, flexing and writhing across each other with acrobatic virtuosity—it's as close to sex as Disney's gonna get. That said, Cirque du Soleil's 90-minute permanent production at Walt Disney World is perfectly acceptable for kids, too—it could end up being the most memorable theatrical experience of a young person's life. The arty, hyper, clown-ish French-Canadian spectacular, a kaleidoscope of stunts and tricks, overloads senses 10 times a week in a 1,600-seat theater that looks like a postmodern version of a big top. Although it's second-rate Cirque, it's still first-rate compared to most stuff you've ever seen, and the talent is extraordinary. So are prices, starting at $67 for adults and $55 for kids ages 3 to 9, and rising according to where you sit. Cheaper seats are better because they have higher vantage points, but seats on the extreme side may miss some of the action taking place far upstage. Arrive at least a half-hour early or they'll sell your seat to someone else.

Downtown Disney West Side. ☎ **407/939-7467.** www.cirquedusoleil.com/lanouba. $67–$146 adults, $55–$120 kids. Tues–Sat 6 and 9pm.

Splitsville Luxury Lanes ★★★ BOWLING ALLEY   Giving families some-thing to bond over, this Florida-based franchise charges by the hour, which might make you feel rushed, and it charges high prices at that, but its souped-up '50s decor, two cavernous floors of bowling, and copious cocktails have charm to spare. The food's better than it should be; it even sells sushi.

Downtown Disney West Side. ☎ **407/938-7328.** www.splitsvilledowntowndisney.com. Daily 10am–2am. $15/hr. per person before 4pm, $20/hr. per person after 4pm and weekends. Rates include shoe rental.

Walt Disney World Tours

Walt Disney was unquestionably a visionary. When he started out, he was mostly interested in animation as an art form. But as his fame and resources grew, his dreams became infinite, and by the end of his life, he was obsessed with building a city of his own. In fact, he intended to build that city on a chunk of his Central Florida land. His dream of an Experimental Prototype Community of Tomorrow, or Epcot, in which residents, many of them theme park workers, could try out new forms of corporate-sponsored, minimum-impact technology in the course of their daily lives, emerged 16 years after his death as nothing more than another world's fair, and not the city to save us all. But because the Magic Kingdom was built by his most trusted designers, it incorporated several idealistic innovations.

One is the **utilidor system.** The bulk of the Magic Kingdom that you see appears to be at ground level. But in fact, you'll be walking about 14 feet above the land. The attractions constitute the second and third stories of a 9-acre network of warehouses and corridors—utilidors—built in part to guard against flooding but mostly so cast members could remove trash, make deliveries, take breaks, change costumes, and count money out of sight, in a catacombs accessed through secret entrances and unmarked wormholes scattered around the themed lands. Clean-burning electric vehicles zip through the hallways, some of which are wide enough to accommodate trucks, and all of which are color-coded to indicate which land is upstairs.

Among the other engineering feats and innovations of the Kingdom:

○ Trash is transported at 60mph to a central collection point by Swedish AVAC pneu-matic tubes in the ceiling of the utilidors.

o Fire, power, and water systems are all monitored by a common computer, and the robotics, doors, lighting, sounds, and vehicles on the most complicated attractions are handled by a central server called the Digital Animation Control System (DACS), located roughly underneath Cinderella Castle.

o The Seven Seas Lagoon, in front of the Magic Kingdom, was dry land. It was filled to create a new body of water.

o Bay Lake, beside Fort Wilderness, was dredged, and the dirt used to raise the Magic Kingdom. Underneath the lake bed, white, ancient sand was discovered, cleaned, and deposited to create the Seven Seas Lagoon's beaches.

o Energy is reused whenever possible. The generators' waste heat is used to heat water, and hot water runoff is used for heating, cooking, and absorption chilling for air-conditioning. Waste water is reclaimed for plants and lawns, and sludge is dried for fertilizer. Food scraps are composted on-site. The resort produces enough power to keep things running in case of a temporary outage on the municipal grid. This will keep you up tonight: Disney even has the legal right to build its own nuclear power plant, should it care to.

o Some 55 miles of canals were dug on resort property to keep the land drained. Most of these canals were curved to appear natural.

o The resort was the first place to install an all-electronic phone system using underground cable—so guests don't see ugly wires. It was the first telephone company in America to use a 911 emergency system.

o The rubber-tired monorail system, designed by Disney engineers, now contains nearly 15 miles of track. Walt had intended monorails, and vehicles akin to the Tomorrowland Transit Authority ride, to be the main forms of transportation to and through his Epcot. In 1986, the monorail was named a National Historic Mechanical Engineering Landmark by the American Society of Mechanical Engineers.

The Walt Disney Co. of later years showed little interest in advancing these remarkable innovations. Epcot has only a small network of utilidors, located under Innoventions and Spaceship Earth in the center section of Future World, and the other Disney parks were built without them at all. The monorail has not been expanded since 1982, so it was back to buses and cars.

But even if the company now pays scant attention to developing "Walt's dream"—that Talmudic totem that the company's marketing department invokes to sell souvenirs—it will, fortunately, grant a backstage gander at the resort's ingenuity and the mind-boggling challenge of its scale. The superlative **Walt Disney World tours** (℡ **407/939-8687;** www.disneyworld.com/tours) require tons of walking and quality depends on the ability of the guide, but they're also well organized, with coach transport, snacks, plenty of comfort breaks, and sometimes, a special pin souvenir. Not all of them all go daily, so check to see what's running. These are the standouts.

Backstage Magic ★★★ TOUR If you can swing it, this is the awe-inspiring king of all Disney explorations, and one of the few tours to require no park admission, because you spend your time plumbing infrastructure. Every minute is fascinating—you start at Epcot, where you go backstage to see the mechanized miracle of the American Adventure robotics; then, by motorcoach, the 40-odd group goes to Hollywood Studios for the wardrobe sewing shops; then it's to Animal Kingdom for a how-to there. Lunch is barbecue at the Wilderness Lodge. At the Magic Kingdom, you thrillingly dip into the utilidor, which for fans is alone worth the price. Behind that park, you'll see Central Shops, a 280,000 square-foot facility where ride vehicles are power washed, greased, and repainted in the blocks-long, 30-foot-tall Assembly Alley, and nearby in the Animation Shop, the Audio-Animatronic figures are repaired. For fans of theme parks, to say nothing of systems design, there is no more comprehensive and worthy splurge in Orlando. You'll appreciate the World in a new light.

$249, including lunch, minimum age 16. 7 hr.

Backstage Safari ★ TOUR   You learn more about animal care than the made-up storytelling of the park. The itinerary may change according to which animals are in social moods and which ones are in the clinic, but white rhinos and elephants are often on the menu. The climax is a slow turn on the Kilimanjaro Safari ride, only with a special narration that gives away the design secrets that keep animals and humans on their respective sides. Expect a lot of info about how diets are prepared. Mickey would be sick if he knew what the snakes eat.

$72 per person; park admission required. Minimum age 16. 3 hr.

Behind the Seeds ★★ TOUR   Because it runs repeatedly every day, it's one of the few tours that can be booked on the fly. Epcot's original altruistic intentions are given a rare spotlight: You learn about the research conducted at the Land's experimental greenhouses, insects lab, and fish farm, and guests are filled in on the park's joint efforts with botanists to advance growing technologies. How much you learn depends entirely on your guide's engagement, so butter 'em up—and little children are usually given ladybugs to release, seeds to plant, or crops to taste. You can reserve ahead or you can book at the desk beside the entrance to Soarin'.

$20 adults, $16 kids 3–9; park admission required. Daily; 45 min.

Disney's Dolphins in Depth ★ TOUR   The water's knee-deep, and after education about Epcot's dolphin rescue program, the interaction lasts about 30 minutes. The climax: You tentatively hug one of the mammals as your free souvenir photo is snapped. No theme park admission is required. It only accepts 8 guests a day.

$199, including photo; no park admission required. Minimum age 13. 3 hr.

Disney's Keys to the Kingdom ★★★ TOUR   The least expensive way to peek at the utilidors, this half-day morning excursion provides a good overview of the Disney design philosophies that will satisfy both newbies and hard-core fans. It includes a long explication of Main Street, the Hub, the Castle, and a pass through Frontierland and Adventureland, where the group kills a little time (and finally gets to sit) riding two rides, after which your guide discusses the technology behind them. The real appeal is the brief time spent in forbidden backstage areas: the parade float storage sheds behind Splash Mountain and a quiet cul-de-sac of the utilidors beneath Town Square—my group entered in the Emporium and resurfaced in a parking lot behind eastern Main Street. This is a tremendous value.

$79 per person, including lunch; park admission required. Minimum age 16. Daily. 5 hr.

Epcot DiveQuest ★ TOUR   Bring your open-water scuba certification and your swimsuit, and you'll be qualified to swim with the fishes in the saltwater tank at the Seas with Nemo & Friends—the range of life is unparalleled in the wild. You'll learn a little about the aquarium's upkeep, but the true attraction here is the chance to dive in it for 30 minutes and to wave at your fellow tourists from the business side of the glass. It's fun, but whether it's $175 worth of a good time is up for debate.

$175, including diving gear; park admission not required. Minimum age 10. Daily. 3 hr.

Epcot Seas Aqua Tour ★★ TOUR   If you can snorkel, you can do this—you're equipped with an air tank and with flotation devices that keep you on the surface, where you spend a half-hour swimming face-down above the fake coral in the 5.7 million-gallon aquarium at The Seas. You wrap up, ironically, with a shower. No theme park admission is required.

$140, including equipment and photo; park admission not required. Minimum age 8. Daily. 2½ hr.

Wild Africa Trek ★★★ TOUR   The animal paddocks are your personal adventure playground on this crowd favorite. You'll board a vehicle for a private view of the animals on Kilimanjaro Safaris, and most spectacularly, strap into a harness for a harrowing tethered trip over a cliffs and a rope suspension bridge that passes over crocs and hippos. The included African-inflected meal has a view of the savannah, and a CD's worth of professional photos of your experience is mailed to you a few days later.

$249 per person, park admission required. Minimum age 8. 9 times daily. 3 hr.

UNIVERSAL ORLANDO, SEAWORLD & BEYOND

4

Disney is only half the story. Less than half, really, when you consider that while the Mouse maintains four parks, you'll find another four major themers, plus a luxury-level theme park, in the same vicinity. While some blinkered tourists think of these places as something to do after they "do Disney," the truth is these majors are in many ways just as appealing as the more famous Mouse parks. Make sure to call it by the correct name: The resort is called Universal Orlando, which consists of two parks, Universal Studios and Islands of Adventure.

UNIVERSAL ORLANDO

You'd be remiss if you left town without seeing at least two of Disney's parks, but the design chutzpah is happening at Universal—many observers agree that the spectacular Wizarding World of Harry Potter trumps anything else in America's theme park industry. Thanks to these top-notch parks, there's now a true threat to Disney's dominance, and as more people grow annoyed with Disney's slowly declining service level, Universal is making rapid gains. In 2014, the opening of the Diagon Alley area of the Wizarding World of Harry Potter turned the resort into a destination people will tour over 3 days rather than two. Universal's resort is also easier to roam than Disney's: It's walkable or traversed by quick, free ferries, so you can park your car and forget about it—no waiting for crowded buses.

The opening of Universal Studios in 1990 heralded a new era for Orlando tourism. Instead of merely duplicating its original Hollywood location, which is on a historic movie studio lot, Universal Orlando built a full-fledged all-day amusement park.

While its opening was famously troubled, there was little doubt that Universal's innovations, when they worked, instantly raised the bar for amusement parks worldwide. A chief advance was that almost all of its attractions were indoors—even the thrills. Given Florida's scorching sun and unpredictable rains, this leap shouldn't have been as novel as it was. While Disney, still working on a California model, allowed its guests to twiddle thumbs in the cruel heat as they waited in line, Universal's multi-stage queuing system kept them entertained and air-conditioned while they waited. Therefore, Universal Studios is the park you should choose on rainy days or excessively hot ones. (At Islands of Adventure, though, many of thrill rides travel outdoors and will shut down at the hint of lightning.) Even the covered parking garages at Universal Orlando (shared by both parks and CityWalk) were novel for Florida.

Disney was clearly spooked. It hastily banged out a movies-themed park of its own, Disney–MGM Studios (now called Hollywood Studios). It was a rush job, lacking the organization and thematic quality that made its previous two parks such smashes, and today it's the least popular Disney park.

Throughout the 1990s, Universal's one-park setup meant it mostly grabbed visitors on day trips from Disney. That changed—and the fight got ruthless—in the summer of 1999, when a second, $2.6-billion park, Islands of Adventure, made its dazzling debut. Universal broke the bank, even poaching Imagineers. Universal's domain has further expanded to include the nightlife district CityWalk and four fun hotels.

Just like with He Who Must Not Be Named, there was always a master plan for a total domination. In 2014, Universal cut the ribbon on a brilliant new idea never tried before in theme parks. After the 2010 addition of Islands of Adventure's The Wizarding World of Harry Potter—Hogsmeade proved to be an unprecedented blockbuster— it added a second Harry Potter land, Diagon Alley, in the other park, Universal Studios. Here's the genius part—they are linked by a special-effects-laden train that requires guests to purchase a ticket to *both* parks to see everything. Universal's parent company, Comcast, marshals its many holdings, including NBC, to promote the destination with the intention of sapping traffic from rival Disney.

Universal's two parks combined still only fetch a third of the visitors attracted by Disney's four, but that proportion is growing by the year, and the 2014 opening of Cabana Bay (p. 211), now it largest hotel, finally gave economy visitors an on-property roost. Most of the time, lines are nowhere near as long as they are at Disney. Unless crowds are insanely huge (such as before Halloween Horror Nights events or during Christmas week), Universal takes about 2 days to adequately see. With a two-park pass and a willingness to bypass lesser attractions, you could see only highlights in 1 marathon day, provided at least one of the parks stays open until 9 or 10pm, but now that the second Harry Potter section has opened, though (p. 101), 2 days is the new minimum requirement. In any event, bopping between the two parks isn't hard, since their entrances are a 5-minute stroll apart or you can take a dazzling connecting train.

Tickets to Universal's Parks

Tickets for both parks cost the same and multi-day tickets are more expensive if you buy at the gate. As you can see by how prices scale, Universal wants to force you into a multi-day commitment. If you want to ride the Hogwarts Express train that links the two parks, you must have a park-to-park ticket. Gate prices before tax:

- **1-day ticket for one park:** $96 adults, $90 kids ages 3 to 9
- **1-day park-to-park ticket:** $136 adults, $127 kids ages 3 to 9
- **2 days of 1-park tickets:** $146 adults, $136 kids ages 3 to 9 *
- **2-day, park-to-park ticket:** $176 adults, $166 kids ages 3 to 9 *
- **3-day, park-to-park ticket:** $186 adults, $175 kids ages 3 to 9 *
- **4-day, park-to-park ticket:** $196 adults, $184 kids ages 3 to 9 *
  * Minus $20 per ticket if you buy online ahead of time

If you buy a 1-park ticket and change your mind midway through the day, there are ticket kiosks at the Hogwarts Express train stations that simply charge you the difference in price for a park-to-park ticket; you won't pay a penalty for waiting.

contacting UNIVERSAL

General information: ☏ 407/363-8000;
www.universalorlando.com

Guest services: ☏ 407/224-4233

Hotel reservations: ☏ 888/273-1311

Vacation packages: ☏ 877/801-9720;
www.universalorlandovacations.com

Lost and found: ☏ 407/224-4233,
option 2

If you're doing a full complement of the non-Disney parks, including both Universal parks, SeaWorld, Aquatica, Wet 'n Wild, and Busch Gardens, then you'll find value in the **FlexTicket,** also sold on Universal's site ($320 adults, $300 kids 3–9 for all those parks), which gets you into all of them for 2 weeks. Details are on p. 236.

HOPPING THE LINES   Like Disney's Fastpass, **Universal Express Pass** allows guests to use a separate entrance queue that is dramatically shorter than the "Standby" one, reducing wait times to minutes or even seconds; your ticket is scanned by an employee. Unlike Disney's democratic Fastpass, Express is for sale. Guests can buy an **Express Plus** pass at shops. There is one set of prices that allows one-time-per-ride use ($35–$60 for one park, from $40–$70 for both), another price (from $75/$90) for unlimited rides, and all prices are bit higher when it's busy. The only major rides that are excluded are Harry Potter and the Forbidden Journey, Escape from Gringotts, and the Hogwarts Express. Using this is expensive, but it enables you to see both Universal parks in a single day and consequently spend less in tickets and see more of Orlando. Bundles that include park tickets with Express are sold for $190 to $270 adult, $185 to $265 kids aged 3 to 9 per day, depending on how busy the parks are. There is also a third, simpler way to get an Express Pass: Guests of the Universal hotels (except Cabana Bay) can use their key cards for free Express access.

Universal also has a **Ride Reservations** program. You're given a simple pager device that lists the next available entry at each attraction; the appointments reflect each ride's current wait time, so essentially, the system gives you a virtual place in line. You schedule visits (only one at any moment) by pressing buttons, and it vibrates when it's time. That's $30 to make one reservation per ride or $40 for unlimited re-rides.

Universal also has photographers on hand to take your photo at big moments. Its **Photo Connect** works a lot like Disney's PhotoPass: You'll get a claim ticket enabling you to purchase an expensive copy or download unlimited images within 3 days (for $60), but you may always use your own camera instead. You can also check your images as you collect them using an app.

Universal has free in-park Wi-Fi, and its free app, the **Official Universal Orlando Resort App,** provides wait times, showtimes, maps, and walking directions.

WHAT TO WEAR   Dress small children in bathing suits for a day at Universal Studios because its Kidzone, one of its best sections, will get them soaked. At Islands of Adventure, two of the best adult rides are water-based.

Universal Studios Florida

Universal Studios ★★★ usually opens at 9am, and in winter months, hours end at around dinnertime. In summer, they're often as late as 10pm. After you get your car parked ($17 and up) and your handbags probed, take the covered sidewalks to City-Walk and head to the right. Pause now at the giant, rotating globe for the requisite photo op, because the sun is in your favor for photographs in the morning.

At the extreme right of the entry plaza as you leaving the park, there's a souvenir stand. This is no ordinary stand: It's for marked-down items. The small stand at the entrance to Islands of Adventure is also a good stop for discount goods.

The plaza after the turnstiles is where you take care of business. **Strollers and wheelchairs** are obtained to the left, and **lockers** are rented to the right. (You may bring your stroller to the other park within 2 hr. of closing; if you're taking the Hogwarts Express, there's a place to drop it off before boarding and another kiosk for getting a new one at Islands of Adventure.) Make sure to grab a free park **map** here; if you forget, the stores also stock them.

Although there are technically themed areas, not all of them are strictly defined. They fall into two general zones. Everyone enters along the main avenue of the simulated backlot (including **Production Central, Hollywood,** and **New York**), which contains many of the behind-the-scenes attractions, while the elongated Lagoon stretches off to the right, encircled by many of the thrill-based rides in **San Francisco, Springfield, World Expo,** and **Woody Woodpecker's Kidzone. The Wizarding World of Harry Potter—Diagon Alley** is on the far side of the lagoon.

After dark, if the park's open then, the water hosts the **Cinematic Spectacular,** narrated by Morgan Freeman. It's a quaint show featuring classic Universal clips projected onto waterfall screens, plus a modest taste of fireworks action. Shows like these aren't Universal's forte, but there's not a Disney-esque crush of spectators, either.

PRODUCTION CENTRAL

The area along the entry avenue (called both Plaza of the Stars and 57th St.) and to its left is collectively marked on maps as Production Central, but who are they kidding? Nowadays, those soundstages are used mostly for the odd local commercial and for haunted houses at Universal's fiendishly popular Halloween event.

The initial dream was much bigger. When the park was built, it was intended to be more like the original Hollywood location, where an amusement area grew up around a working studio. Newspapers at the time trumpeted Orlando as "Hollywood of the East" because year-round production could be accomplished here and at Disney–MGM Studios, and millions of tourists could be a part of the process. One of Universal's soundstages housed a working TV studio for Nickelodeon, the kids' cable channel, and

4

WHAT THE BASICS COST AT UNIVERSAL'S TWO PARKS

Parking: $17; $22 for closer "preferred" spaces; $30 for all-day valet

Single strollers: $15 per day

Double strollers: $25 per day

Kiddie Car (a stroller with a dummy steering wheel): $18; $28 double

Wheelchair: $12

ECV (electric convenience vehicle): $50

Lockers: $8 per day small (multi-entry)

Poncho: $8 adult, $7 kids

Regular soda: $3 / **Water:** $2.75 / **Beer:** $6.50

Universal Studios Florida

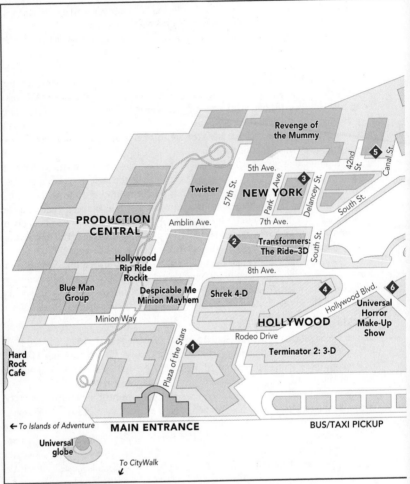

the game show "Double Dare" plucked families out of the park to compete on air. In front of the studio, a geyser of "green slime" (actually green water) gurgled in tribute to the Canadian show "You Can't Do That on Television" that helped make the channel's fortunes. (Today, that stage houses the equally messy Blue Man Group.) But the plan never took. It wasn't cost-effective to move productions here, celebrities didn't really relish working amidst a theme park, and state tax credits were often spotty.

The first block of Production Central is mostly shops, including the largest gift shop in the park, **Universal Studios Store,** on the left. Across from that are the tempting Art Deco buildings of Rodeo Drive, the spine of the Hollywood area and for my money the prettiest part of the park.

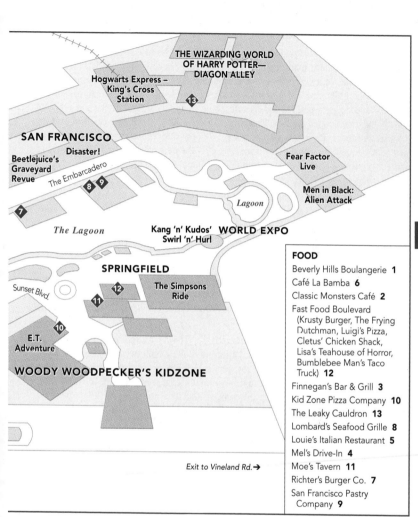

THE WIZARDING WORLD
OF HARRY POTTER—
DIAGON ALLEY

Hogwarts Express –
King's Cross
Station

SAN FRANCISCO

Disaster!

Beetlejuice's
Graveyard
Revue

The Embarcadero

Fear Factor
Live

Men in Black:
Alien Attack

Lagoon

The Lagoon

Kang 'n' Kudos'
Swirl 'n' Hurl

WORLD EXPO

SPRINGFIELD

Sunset Blvd.

The Simpsons
Ride

E.T.
Adventure

WOODY WOODPECKER'S KIDZONE

Exit to Vineland Rd. →

FOOD

Beverly Hills Boulangerie **1**

Café La Bamba **6**

Classic Monsters Café **2**

Fast Food Boulevard
(Krusty Burger, The Frying
Dutchman, Luigi's Pizza,
Cletus' Chicken Shack,
Lisa's Teahouse of Horror,
Bumblebee Man's Taco
Truck) **12**

Finnegan's Bar & Grill **3**

Kid Zone Pizza Company **10**

The Leaky Cauldron **13**

Lombard's Seafood Grille **8**

Louie's Italian Restaurant **5**

Mel's Drive-In **4**

Moe's Tavern **11**

Richter's Burger Co. **7**

San Francisco Pastry
Company **9**

Hollywood Rip Ride Rockit ★★★ RIDE   This is one advanced train: The 17-story height, vertical climb, hill-like loop, and near misses are just the start of it. Most advanced are its cars, outfitted with LEDs and in-seat speakers. Riders personalize their trip on screens embedded in the beltlike safety restraint, choosing the song that will play during the trip. Pick from a broad menu including country, rap, rock, and disco, but if you don't pick a song, it'll choose one for you. When the ride's over, you can buy a movie of the ride, along with your soundtrack. Lockers are required for loose items, but they're free for the wait time plus 20 minutes. Single riders get their own line, and it moves quickly. Note the novel boarding system that batches passengers together and sends them onto a moving sidewalk to catch up with the trains, which never stop moving forward. That first loop is also an original—the track twists to send the cars over the top of it before pulling them back on the inside again. Later on, you shoot through holes in the scenery in the New York session. Rockin'.

Despicable Me Minion Mayhem ★★ RIDE   The movies, if you don't know them, star a crotchety mad genius, Gru (voiced by Steve Carell), and his horde of nearly identical yellow henchmen (the Minions); their ride, which is considerably more charming than the films, give the little guys ample opportunity for some cartoon violence and giggly gags. The kid-friendly show/stationary ride takes place in a theater full of individual open-air ride platforms that have all the characteristics of motion simulators except claustrophobia. **Strategy:** An option for those prone to motion sickness is to request a car that doesn't move at all—the perfectly animated 3-D movie is immensely action-packed and is entertaining without it.

Shrek 4-D ★★ SHOW   The high-priced voices of the movie characters (Mike Myers, Cameron Diaz, Eddie Murphy) star in a snarky 12-minute, 3-D movie-cum-spectacle—filmed in "OgreVision." John Lithgow plays the ghost of the evil Lord Farquaad, who crashes Shrek and Fiona's honeymoon at Fairytale Falls with a few dastardly deeds. The chairs look like standard theater seats but they're tricked-up to goose sensations—don't worry; it won't make you ill. Well, unless fart jokes gross you out. It's a good one to do when the feet start aching, although the line can build in the afternoon. **Strategy:** Because the entertaining preshow is just as long as the movie, the Express Pass doesn't seem to buy you very much time. After the exit, visit **Donkey's Photo Finish,** featuring an interactive, robotic version of the movie's famous ass in his own stall; he interacts with kids and poses.

Transformers: The Ride—3D ★★ RIDE   This 2013 addition, an East Coast version of a ride that first appeared at Universal Studios Hollywood, repeats the technology and basic vehicle design of the gentler Adventures of Spider-Man next door at Islands of Adventure—that is, motion-simulator cars travel among sense-tricking rooms with 3-D projections. There difference is that here, the show method is pumped up with crisper animation, clearer sounds, and a whole lot of machine-on-machine violence and military-grade weaponry. But at heart, no matter how impressive the tech is, Transformers is still a Spider-Man update, down to key plot points. The mayhem is so frenetic you can't always tell which Transformer is which, but then again, you can't in the movies, either, so it hardly matters. You'll emerge feeling like you survived a 4-minute car crash. **Tip:** The clearest view is in the front row, and there's a fast-moving Single Rider line.

NEW YORK

When there's a park on your right, you've entered the New York area. In a display of geographic acrobatics, the park is an imitation of San Francisco's Union Square while straight ahead, at the end of 57th Street (the main entry avenue) is a little cul-de-sac that looks, through a camera lens, like Manhattan—except for the roller coaster that keeps roaring through.

The rest of the New York section is gussied up to look like the tenements of the Lower East Side or Greenwich Village and is worth a few photos. Actors playing **The Blues Brothers,** plus a female diva soul singer, show up on Delancey Street for regular jam sessions, and they're talented.

Twister . . . Ride It Out ★ SHOW   After several rooms of portentous preshow videos narrated by Helen Hunt and Bill Paxton, you finally enter a viewing area in a hangarlike chamber that's dressed to look like a Midwestern small town (gas station,

Don't miss if you're 6: Curious George Goes to Town
Don't miss if you're 16: Springfield
Requisite photo op: The rotating Universal globe out front
Food you can only get here: Butterbeer ice cream and Fishy Green Ale, Diagon Alley; Flaming Moe's and Duff Beer, Springfield

The most crowded, so go early: The Wizarding World of Harry Potter—Diagon Alley
Skippable: Fear Factor Live
Biggest thrill: Harry Potter and the Escape from Gringotts
Best show: Animal Actors on Location!
Where to find peace: On the lagoon

telephone pole, drive-in movie in the distance) on a weekend night. A storm approaches, rain begins to fall and, as you knew it would, a twister forms. Right before your eyes, a funnel cloud descends from the rafters and to the delight of many, wrecks the place. Sparks fly, roofs peel, and guess what happens to the gas station? Although people tend to shy away from the front row, don't, because you won't feel much more than mist and a light sucking sensation there (I'd tuck sensitive electronics away anyway). It's quite an original attraction, and it's another good one for a hot day, but little kids might lose their wits. **Strategy:** It runs continuously, but I wouldn't wait more than 20 minutes for it.

Revenge of the Mummy ★★★ RIDE   This brilliant ride is cutting edge with an easy start and a rollicking finish: Part dark ride, part roller coaster, it goes backward and forward, twists on a turntable, and even spends a harrowing moment stalled in a room as the ceiling crawls with fire. (It doesn't go upside-down.) To say much more would give away some clever shocks. I've told you what you need to know. **Strategy:** You must put loose articles in the lockers to the right of the entrance—they're free for the posted ride time plus 20 minutes, but after that they cost $3 every half hour, so although you'll probably want to ride again right away, don't. There are three lines: Express, standby, and single riders.

SAN FRANCISCO

Of all the Studios' areas, the San Francisco section has the least going on: one ride, one show. However, the restaurants are better than anywhere in the park. Once Harry Potter opens, though, expect it to be the park's main channel for sightseers.

Beetlejuice's Graveyard Revue ★ SHOW   Universal owns the rights to many classic movie monsters, and strangely, they appear in this rowdy '80s and '90s rock-'n'-roll show, presided over by the undead, naughty-minded Beetlejuice, who aims more for the funny bone than the jugular. Watching Dracula lead a dance chorus through "Smooth Criminal" will make you feel like someone slipped something into your Coke. **Strategy:** Unless you're a show person, you can skip this one, at least until you've knocked down some of the fresher attractions (or some liquor). The 20-minute performances happen a few times daily.

Disaster! ★★ SHOW/RIDE   In the preshow, a projected Christopher Walken, pretending to be a big disaster-movie director, interacts at length with a live actor. The technology is impressive, especially as his lifelike image rests his feet on boxes you can clearly see in front of you. Next, everyone files into an adjoining "soundstage" and

The **Delancey Street Preview Center** is marked on maps, but you can only get in by invitation (someone will approach you on the streets). That's where NBC-affiliated entities screen pilots and solicit audience opinions. On a quiet January day, I once earned $30 just for enduring a new show called "Psych." I broke it to them gently, telling them that it was clichéd and strained. Naturally, it became an eight-season smash on USA Network. You can't predict the demographic of the test audience they'll be looking for, so stop by and ask if you fit the profile du jour.

volunteers from the audience stand in for special-effect insert shots. Finally, everyone boards a tram mocked up to resemble San Francisco's BART subway—seats on the outside are the best. It travels down a tunnel and stops inside what appears to be a faithful re-creation of the Embarcadero station, albeit one that smells suspiciously of natural gas. Of course something goes horribly wrong. There's an earthquake. Hell is unleashed: rocking, flooding to within an inch of the train, the unexpected intrusion of a gas truck from the "street" above (with the required climactic explosion). The intent is to approximate a jolt measuring 8.3 on the Richter scale. Just as quickly as it began, everything halts and reassembles itself for the next "take" as your train whisks you out again. **Warning:** Claustrophobes abhor the BART bit, as do some nervous children.

THE WIZARDING WORLD OF HARRY POTTER— DIAGON ALLEY

From the outside, it appears to simply be a re-creation of some London landmarks, including a perfectly replicated Kings Cross station and some townhouses that would fool a lifetime resident of Bloomsbury (keep an eye on the curtains in the second balcony window of 12 Grimmauld Place, the shabby townhouse). You have the re-creation of the "Eros" fountain from Piccadilly Circus (unlike the original, this one is actually flowing), cab shelters selling Britannia souvenirs and jumbo hot dogs, and a three-level-tall **Knight Bus.** If its conductor is there, go have a chat with him, but don't be alarmed if the shrunken Jamaican head hanging above his steering wheel butts into the conversation.

Hidden behind the London facade, through some sidelong portals through brick, is the world's hottest theme park phenomenon of the moment, essentially a wholesale construction of 3 city blocks around Diagon Alley, where wizards go for their provisions. It's not so much a single attraction as it is a cluttered streetscape of shops, beverage and dessert stores, and painstaking design work that seals you off from the outside world. There are few right angles, but plenty of opportunities to spend lots and lots of cash. You could pass hours simply exploring details, from tricked-out window displays (the skeleton that imitates your movements from the window of Dystyl Phaelanges is a standout) to clever signage larded with inside jokes ("These Premises to Let: Reptiles/Arachnids Allowed").

The main thoroughfare is **Diagon Alley,** lined with the Leaky Cauldron restaurant, plus shops for wands, toys, and clothing. It leads dramatically to Gringotts Bank, which is crested by a petrified dragon that belches fire every few minutes. Gringotts is on **Horizont Alley,** a 2-block lane noted for its pet store, beer hall, and ice cream shop. On the left, it leads into **Knockturn Alley,** a fascinating indoor area that simulates a

4

Universal Orlando

UNIVERSAL ORLANDO, SEAWORLD & BEYOND

shady ghetto at night, right down to shifting clouds in a simulated sky and a tattoo parlor, Marcus Scarr's, where the animated sample designs writhe on the wall. Branching off from Diagon Alley on the right, you find **Carkitt Market,** a covered area recalling London's Leadenhall Market, where the principal show stage for the land is located. Performances include **The Singing Sorceress: Celestina Warbeck and the Banshees** (a talented but somewhat out-of-theme singer rendering such classics as "A Cauldron Full of Hot, Strong Love") and **The Tales of Beedle the Bard** (a street performance with puppets of two tales from the Potter spin-off book).

Reducio! Ways to Lighten Your Wallet at Diagon Alley

Nearly everything there is to do and taste comes with a price tag, and you can't get these experiences outside Universal's gates. It's extraordinarily easy to get swept along in the merchandising mesmerization. Some of the best bespoke purchasing potential includes these Potterized twists:

o **Gringotts Money Exchange, Carkitt Market.** Trade in "muggle money" (U.S. $10s and $20s only) for Gringotts Bank Rune Credit, a currency that you can use in both parks or, Universal hopes, take home as a souvenir for pure profit.

o **Ollivanders, Diagon Alley.** In addition to the same wand-selecting mini-show available at Hogsmeade (p. 120), you may purchase a $45 interactive wand used to activate more than a dozen tricks wherever you see a medallion embedded in the ground. Stand on it, emulate the wand motion depicted on it, and you'll make toilets flush, suits of armor animate, fountains squirt, and so on.

o **The Hopping Pot, Carkitt Market, and the Fountain of Fair Fortune, Horizont Alley.** Sip sweet concoctions for $5 each: Otter's Fizzy Orange Juice, Tongue Tying Lemon Squash, Peachtree Fizzing Tea, and Fishy Green Ale with "fish eggs" (actually blueberry boba) on the bottom. They also sell the classic Potter potable, Butterbeer (in a mug made for Diagon Alley, $12), and two beers unique to the park, Wizards Brew (a light lager) and Dragon Scale (a chocolatey stout), both $9

o **Florean Fortescue's Ice Cream Parlour, Diagon Alley.** Try a range of only-here flavors including Chocolate Chili, Clotted Cream, Earl Grey and Lavender, and a dangerously addictive soft-serve version of Butterbeer ($5 cup, $6 cone, $11 in a souvenir plastic cup).

o **Eternelle's Elixir of Refreshment, Carkitt Market.** Mix your choice of $4 "elixirs" (Draught of Peace, Fire Protection Potion, and so forth) with $4 "Gillywater" (water) and something magical happens (Universal just made $8 on sugar water).

o **Weasleys' Wizard Wheezes, Diagon Alley.** The new local toy shop (replacing the old Zonkos at Hogsmeade) sells $15 Pygmy Puff stuffed animals. When a purchase is made, the staff gongs a huge bell and announces a new adoption. Also buy the candies Ron would eat to get out of school: Puking Pastilles, Fainting Fancies, Fever Fudge, and Nosebleed Nougat ($7 each).

o **Magical Menagerie, Horizont Alley.** Where windows are filled with animated pets such as pythons and giant snails, procure the specialty souvenir: a plush version of Hermione's half-Kneazle cat Crookshanks ($25).

o **Shutterbutton's, Carkitt Market.** Via a green screen, put your family in the middle of a 3- to 4-minute DVD ($70), like a moving postcard exploring the Potter universe.

Harry Potter and the Escape From Gringotts ★★★ RIDE   Another genre-busting creation, this indoor ride plows new technological ground: part roller coaster, part motion simulator amid giant 3-D high-def screens. At times your respect for its razor's-edge complexity will overshadow the purity of the thrills, but it's still unmissable. The queue lingers in the sumptuous, echoing lobby of Gringotts Bank, where 10 robotic goblins pause long enough from their clerical duties to sneer at you, then your "identification" photo is taken (to sell to you later, of course) and you're taken by "lift" deep underground to begin the mine cart-like race through the vaults. Almost immediately, nasty lightning bolts from Bellatrix Lestrange (Helena Bonham Carter) put your course awry, sending you careening into the slithering presence of Voldemort (Ralph Fiennes). Can Harry, Ron, and Hermione save you in time? (What do *you* think?) There are some mild spins and drops, but you wear 3-D goggles the whole time, so it's not that rough, and it's less scary and height-restrictive than the Forbidden Journey ride at Hogsmeade. **Tip:** Locker use for small items is mandatory; they're free and to the right of the front door. There's a single-rider line that moves quickly, but you'll miss the entire pre-show, including the photo op and the lift.

Hogwarts Express ★★★ RIDE   Separate from Diagon Alley, through the vaulted brick interior of a shockingly accurate Kings Cross Station, you board the hissing, steaming, and, to all appearances, vintage steam train to Hogsmeade. You are assigned a six-person, upholstered compartment, the door shuts, and off you go. Out the window, England and Scotland scroll by while in the train corridor, you overhear conversations and see ominous shadows through frosted glass. In reality, you're traveling through Universal's backstage area, but you never see it. The technical prowess is nearly totally convincing, and even where it isn't, it's still dazzling. Within 4 minutes, you disembark at Islands of Adventure outside the gate to the other Wizarding World (if you require an upgrade to a park-to-park ticket, there are kiosks for the purpose). In the station, there's also a spot, done with mirrors and clever lighting, for you to re-create the moment when Harry and his fellow students walk through a brick wall to reach Platform 9¾. That photo op gets thronged, but there's a bypass if you don't want to wait for it.

WORLD EXPO

As Springfield expands, there's not much to this area except a ride and a dated show.

Men in Black: Alien Attack ★★ RIDE   Most riders enjoy this sassy riff on the Will Smith film franchise. After a superlative queue area that does a pitch-perfect, "Jetsons"-style imitation of New York's 1964 World's Fair (ironically, the one Walt Disney created so many wonders for), you discover the "real" tenant of the futuristic building: a training course for the Men in Black alien patrol corps. You board six-person cars equipped with individual laser guns. As you pass from room to room—expect lots of herky-jerky motions, but nothing sickening—your task is to fire upon any alien that pops out from around doorways, behind trash cans, and so on. If they peg you first, it sends your buggy spinning. Each car's point score is displayed on the dashboard, and the number accumulated by the end determines the climactic video you're shown—Will Smith will either praise you as "Galaxy Defender" or mock you as "Bug Bait." **Strategy:** The single riders' queue moves quickly, thanks to the odd number of seats in each row. Locker use for small items is mandatory, but free for the posted wait time plus 20 minutes.

Fear Factor Live ★ SHOW   Like the meat-headed NBC show, ordinary people do stunts (usually involving being dangled on wires, maybe eating food-grade mealworms) for the twisted pleasure of a whooping audience while an inane master of ceremonies eggs everyone on. If you're over 18 and want to volunteer as a contestant (first prize: polite applause), be there 70 minutes before your selected showtime and you'll go through a tryout including jumping jacks and a game of Simon Says. Contestants can't wear jewelry, and if your hands sweat when you're nervous, you will stink at the gripping challenges. This show goes dark in September and October.

SPRINGFIELD

After Diagon Alley, it's the most fun land in the Studios. The area is jammed with inside jokes from the longest-running comedy on TV. **Kwik-E-Mart** sells an array of bespoke souvenirs you can only get here, the **Duff Brewery** pours its signature quaff—the cause of, and solution to, all life's problems—plus Squishees, and the embiggened statue of frontiersman Jebediah Springfield lords over us all.

The Simpsons Ride ★★★ RIDE   It's easy to love this highly amusing, top-quality, motion-simulator "Thrilltacular Upsy-Downsy Spins-Aroundsy Teen-Operated Thrill Ride" that takes place in front of an 80-foot-tall screen. The premise, dense and ironic enough to please devotees of the FOX series, punctures Orlando itself: You join Homer's clan at Krustyland, a greedy theme park, on a roller coaster that's sabotaged by the evil Sideshow Bob (voiced by Kelsey Grammer). During the dizzyingly fast-paced 6 minutes, you zoom through predicaments that mock the theme park world, including skewers of Shamu, Pirates of the Caribbean, and "it's a small world." Add to that a giant killer panda bear and an extra layer of heightened sensory (like the whiff of baby powder—well, it makes sense when you ride). It's not too rough, but dehydrated people find it vaguely nauseating, and your brain may hurt from absorbing all the jokes. The queue area is so tongue in cheek and gag-packed that waiting is half the fun: Itchy and Scratchy furnish the gory safety warning and Krusty dispenses safety instructions such as "Wait here until someone comes and tells you to do something." Seats are four across, so families can ride together.

Kang & Kodos' Twirl 'n' Hurl ★ RIDE   Universal finally got its Dumbo ride. Here, silly slobbering aliens trick you into boarding a day-glow flying saucer (fitting two adults or one adult and two kids): "Please remain seated until the very end of the ride. You will know the ride has ended when your vehicle comes to a complete stop, or you have been eaten…I didn't just say that." As you rotate gently around, Dumbo-style, you use a joystick to pass in front of tentacle-shaped poles, triggering sounds of exclamation from the citizens of Springfield. Spoiler: You don't get eaten.

HOLLYWOOD

This Art Deco drag is a particularly good place to meet characters (Gru, Woody Woodpecker, the Men in Black) at odd times.

Universal Horror Make-Up Show ★★ SHOW   Learn how horror-movie makeup effects are accomplished in this terrific, 25-minute tongue-in-cheek exposé, conducted by a nerdy type in his workshop and his straight-man emcee. On paper, that seems like the kind of thing you might otherwise skip, but in truth park regulars love its wit and playful edge. For ribald ad-libbing and gross-out humor, the park suggests parental guidance for this one, but I find that most kids have heard it all before, and it's certainly true that seeing terrifying movie gore exposed as the make-believe it is can be a good reality check. Times are printed on your park map, and you can't get in once the show starts. Even if you skip it, there's something to see in the lobby: exhibits about great horror characters and make-up artists.

Terminator 2: 3-D ★ SHOW/FILM   Although the 12-minute film portion, a sort of minisequel to "Terminator 2," was made by extravagant director James Cameron with all his original stars (including Ah-nold and Linda Hamilton), it's hardly just another movie. It's got three screens, six 8-foot robots, gunfire, smoke bombs, and motorcyclists that seamlessly dive in and out of the filmed action. The film cost $60 million to make, which when it was produced in 1996 qualified it as the most expensive movie, per minute, in history, trumping Disney's equally bombastic "Captain EO." **Strategy:** This edgy, cynical show splits the eardrums with romping, stomping mayhem, so keep small children away unless they're hard cases. Those in the front rows will have to pivot their heads to see all the action.

Lucy: A Tribute ★★ ACTIVITY   Too overlooked is this one-room, walk-through exhibition of Lucille Ball memorabilia. Ever seen an Emmy? There are five, plus a Kennedy Center Honor and a model of the "I Love Lucy" set. Bet you didn't know it was painted black and white to look good on TV.

WOODY WOODPECKER'S KIDZONE

This is my pick for the best children's theme park playground area in Orlando. I've heard tales of 6-year-olds who threatened self-orphanization if they were dragged away within 4 hours. There's a ton to do, not least of which is **SpongeBob StorePants,** dedicated to merchandise and appearances by the absorbent doofus.

Animal Actors on Location! ★★★ SHOW   A troupe of trained dogs, cats, birds, and a horse anchor this charming 20-minute show (times are noted on the sign). Placing this show here was inspired, because small children get a thrill out of seeing common animals do tricks, and as a consequence, it's popular. Because it's in an amphitheater, you can also sneak out in the middle if you need to. But if you see only one emphatically punctuated household-pets-doing-cute-tricks-to-jaunty-music theme park show, make it SeaWorld's superior Pets Ahoy!

E.T. Adventure ★★ RIDE   Based on the 1982 Steven Spielberg movie, this endearingly weird indoor ride is rightfully in the kiddie area because it's not intense and the plot cannot tolerate scrutiny by a fully developed brain. Upon entering, guests supply their name to an attendant, who encodes the information on a pass you hand over when you board the ride. The indoor queue area is a fabulous reproduction of a thick, cool California forest at night. Vehicles are suspended from rails to approximate the sensation of cruising in a flock of bikes, and they sweep and scoop across the moonrise and even through gardens on E.T.'s home planet (remember, he was a botanist), where a menagerie of goofy-looking aliens, who miraculously speak English, have a party and greet us from the sidelines. At the climax, a grateful E.T. is supposed to call out your name as you fly home—hence those boarding passes—but in all my years of doing this ride, E.T. has spouted gibberish, so don't get your hopes up unless your name is Pfmkmpftur. **Strategy:** If the queue looks dense from the outside, return later—before park closing seems to be a charmed time for quick waits—since there are still more lineups indoors. In the **Toy Closet,** you'll find E.T. souvenirs. His "Talk to the Hand" T-shirt is perhaps a milestone in bad taste.

Fievel's Playland ★★★ ACTIVITY   Named for the hero of "An American Tail" (an obscure kiddie reference, and another '80s Spielberg movie), it's the most spectacular of several playgrounds in Kidzone. The concept is that your kids have been shrunk down to a mouse's size, and they're playing among giant everyday items like sardine cans and eyeglasses. They'll discover slides, nets, and tubes, but my favorite element is the easy water slide on a raft—so yes, make sure your kids have their swimsuits on. The ground is covered with that newfangled soft foam that all the modern playgrounds have. When I was a boy, we got concussions instead.

A Day in the Park with Barney ★ SHOW   The small indoor area that can be accessed through its own gift shop (plush Barney, $17), is technically the postshow area for a singalong show. The doors close at the start and stay closed until the ordeal is over. Frankly, being locked in a room with that sappy purple dinosaur and all those screaming babies constitutes a chamber of horrors for me, but little ones find it enthralling. Parents can find Duff Beer in Springfield nearby, if that helps. The play area mimics Barney's backyard with a waist-high counter for sifting through sand (so it won't get into shoes), a tree equipped with little slides, and a chance to have your picture taken with (and then buy it from) Barney the Capitalist Dinosaur.

Woody Woodpecker's Nuthouse Coaster ★★ RIDE   Kids can plainly see every drop before they commit to this straightforward thriller. It has no unpleasant surprises, unless you count hearing Woody's pecker as you go, and a run time of less than a minute.

Curious George Goes to Town ★★★ ACTIVITY   Welcome to the water playground that stole your child. This frenetic splash area is teeming with squealing children and positively soaked with streams of water from every direction—from squirt cannons, fountains, geysers, and, most importantly, from two 500-gallon buckets that, every 7 minutes, sound a warning bell and then drench anyone beneath them. The immoderate, virtually orgiastic scene is ringed by a perimeter of dry parents keeping an eye on their suddenly wild offspring. I enjoy joining them, because watching the children cheer and scamper when they hear the clang of the bucket's warning bell, and then watching them momentarily vanish in the deluge, is endlessly heartwarming. Through the wet area (there's a dry bypass corridor to it on the left) is the dry Ball Factory, where kids suck up plastic balls with light vacuums, pack them into bags, and then fire them at each other with weak cannons. It's not marked on the maps.

WHERE TO EAT AT UNIVERSAL STUDIOS

In addition to the random snack carts (including carts selling goliath turkey legs with chips for $11), there are counter-service and table-service restaurants in the park. None require reservations the way Disney's do. Kids' meals all come in under 300 calories. **Tip:** Meals do not *have* to come with side dishes. The potato chip bags served hold a mere 1⅛ ounces. Ask to subtract chips or fries from your meal deals and you'll save about $2. Cups good for unlimited refills at touchscreen Coke Freestyle machines, which mix soda to order using 126 flavors, cost $12 and are good for the day. Cups for standard beverages are $10 with $1 refills. **Remember:** Restaurants at CityWalk (p. 157) are a 5-minute walk from the park, so they're also options.

Classic Monsters Café ★★ AMERICAN   Indoor counter service on a nonscary B-movie set with some healthy options, such as rotisserie chicken with mashed potatoes and broccoli, wedge salad, double cheeseburgers, and ribs. Production Central. Combo meal $8 to $16.

Finnegan's Bar & Grill ★★★ IRISH/BRITISH   A sit-down, Irish-style pub good for a beer break, particularly after 3pm when a guitar singer performs. Scotch eggs ($6), split pea–and-ham soup ($5), Irish Cobb salad (it has corned beef), and bangers and mash are the kind of good things available, plus good strong ales. Park workers pick this place when they're off-duty. New York. Mains $11 to $22.

Louie's Italian Restaurant ★ ITALIAN   Straightforward counter service near The Mummy. New York. Slices $6, meatball subs $10.

San Francisco Pastry Company ★★ SANDWICHES   This lightly trafficked counter-service bakery across from Disaster!, does sandwiches and loaded croissants in addition to cakes and pastries, and healthier fruit plates and salads. San Francisco. Sandwiches $9.30, salads from $3.70.

Lombard's Seafood Grille ★★★ SEAFOOD/AMERICAN   An excellent, relaxing table-service choice that is surprisingly affordable: Fish tacos are $13, just three bucks more than a Quick Service meal, and other fish dishes, including the fish of the day, such as grouper, are in the mid-teens. Splashing fountains serenade, fish tanks adorn the dining room, and you can sit outside on the water if you like. Special diet options, such as quinoa with portobello mushroom, are well marked, and you can even get gluten-free table rolls. San Francisco. Main courses $13 to $20.

Richter's Burger Co. ★★ AMERICAN   A warehouselike dockside option that slings stacked burgers, marinated grilled chicken sandwiches, and for those weary of the greasy side of the plate, salads with grilled chicken. Periodically, the dining area rumbles (but doesn't move) to simulate quakes. Get the Aftershock double burger for $11 and an extra bun for $1 and you can feed two using the fixin's bar. San Francisco. Main courses $9 to $12 with fries.

The Leaky Cauldron ★★★ BRITISH   The fare at Diagon Alley's counter-service location is not mystical at all. It's plentiful and true to an English pub, serving British staples such as beef and Guinness stew, cottage or fisherman's pie, and banger (sausage) sandwiches. The ploughman's lunch for two ($20) has three types of cheese and Branston pickle, and although it's not on the menu, they'll do it for one for $10. Also get Butterbeer, Fishy Green Ale, and other Potter potables here. Mains $9–$15.

Fast Food Boulevard ★★★ AMERICAN   This mouthy indoor food court serves mostly standard food renamed with inside jokes and witticisms that puncture American culture. You could spend half your lunchtime just laughing at the dishes. **Krusty Burger** serves "meat sandwiches" such as the high-stacked double-bacon Clogger Burger with cheez sauce and curly fries and 6-inch Heat Lamp Dogs. **The Frying Dutchman** does Basket O' Bait fried fish and Clam Chowd-arr ($4). At the **Luigi's Pizza** area, get slices of Meat Liker's Pizza, and at **Cletus' Chicken Shack,** dig into the not-very-appetizing-but-accurate Chicken Arms (wings), Chicken Thumbs (tenders), and chicken-and-waffle sandwiches. Lastly, **Lisa's Teahouse of Horror** cuts out the clots with a cooler full of straight-up salads and wraps. You can also buy only-at-Universal treats such as **Lard Lad Donuts** (the platter-size Big Pink, coated with frosting, $5—a life-size Chief Wiggum figure enjoys one nearby) and Buzz Cola (no-calorie cherry cola). Springfield. Outside and across the way, there's the **Bumblebee Man's Taco Truck,** which closes by dinnertime. Main courses $8 to $14.

Moe's Tavern ★★★ BAR   A spot-on re-creation of Moe's, down to team pennants for the Isotopes and the purple TV on the wall, only without sleazy service by Moe. There is, however, a life-size Barney by the bar, ruefully contemplating his empty mug. Duff Beer is specially brewed for the park (in generous servings of regular, Lite, or Dry, $7–$8), but the kid-friendly specialty is a Flaming Moe's ($9), a nonalcoholic orange-flavored soda in a cup rigged with pellets that make it bubble and smoke (it's hard to breathe when you're sipping it). Springfield. Beverages $7 to $9.

In both its parks, Universal offers a simple meal plan. Dubbed the **Universal Meal Deal,** it entitles you to one main plate, one nonalcoholic beverage, and one snack, which can be used for ice cream, frozen beverages, and more. Adults pay $20 and kids $13; it only pays off if you were going to get that dessert anyway. Resort guests may avail themselves of a **Dining Plan,** good for one table-service meal, one quick-service meal, and a snack for $52 adults, $18 kids each day. The value is borderline, especially if you would ordinarily never have a table-service meal.

Kid Zone Pizza Company ★ PIZZA   Outdoor-only counter service for chicken fingers and fries, chef salad, and of course, pizza. It's the biggest food option near the children's play areas. Woody Woodpecker's Kidzone. Mains $8 to $10.

Mel's Drive-In ★★ AMERICAN   A '50s-style counter-service diner where fare leans toward chicken, burgers, and shakes. Air-conditioned seating has a view of the Lagoon. Hollywood. Main courses $8 to $11.

Café La Bamba ★★ BARBECUE   Its warren of dining rooms can make for a cool escape, but this chicken-and-ribs counter service location is only open in peak periods. Hollywood. Thurs–Sat, it's the location of the Superstar Character Breakfast ($26 adults, $13 kids 3–9). Mains $11 to $16.

Beverly Hills Boulangerie ★ SANDWICHES   An uncrowded choice for a reasonably healthy meal: sandwiches (turkey, roast beef, tuna) with potato salad and fruit. It does a soup-and-salad combo for $8. Hollywood. Sandwiches with sides $10.

Islands of Adventure

Islands of Adventure (IOA) ★★★ usually opens at 9am. In winter months, operating hours will end at around 6pm but in summer, they're often open to as late as 10pm. After you park ($15 and up), open your bags for inspection, take the moving sidewalks to CityWalk, and veer to the left, toward the 130-foot Pharos Lighthouse (it's just for show), you finally reach IOA. If you doubt whether your kids are tall enough to ride everything, there's a gauge listing requirements before the ticket booths.

ORIENTATION   IOA's 101 acres are laid out much like Epcot's World Showcase: individually themed areas (here, called "islands," even though they're not) arranged around a lagoon (called the Great Inland Sea). To see everything, you simply follow a great circle. The only corridor into the park, **Port of Entry,** borrows from the Magic Kingdom's Main Street, U.S.A., in that it's a narrow, introductory area where guests are submerged into the theme. In this case, you're gathering munitions for a "great odyssey," so, in theme park logic, it's where you do things like rent strollers and lockers and grab free maps. Most guests beeline through Port of Entry. Because attraction lines are shortest after opening, explore this area later, maybe before closing.

STRATEGY   Once you reach the end of Port of Entry, which way should you go? Right. That's the way to Harry Potter. Lines peak in late morning and early afternoon, then taper off again after that, but they're rarely short.

SHOPPING The park will send your souvenirs to the Islands of Adventure Trading Company, at the Port of Entry, for collection as you leave the park at the end of the day. The deadline for purchases changes, but it's usually about 2 hours before closing. To the right as you exit the park, there's a **small stand** selling marked-down items (the inventory changes, but I've seen $8 Marvel action figures, two-for-ones on plush Curious George dolls, and $40 sweatshirts for $22). It opens later in the day.

MARVEL SUPER HERO ISLAND

If Disney owns Marvel, how come Universal is allowed to have this island? The park licensed the brand in the 1990s, which gives it the right. Designs used the comic books of that period, which predates the film franchises of Spider-Man, the X-Men, Iron Man, and Fantastic Four, which is why characters don't look exactly the way you may be used to them. **Spider-Man** is sometimes one of them, but if you don't see him, head into the back of the Marvel Alterniverse Store, opposite the Captain America Diner. There, the hero has his own appearance zone where you can take your own photos (or buy one). The actor playing Spider-Man is one of the few who isn't clad in muscle-shaped padding—for the frank cling of his bodysuit, admiring members of the park's staff usually aren't far away. The **Comic Book Shop** is worth a stop. Surprisingly legit, the store carries the latest Marvel issues, compilation books, and collectible busts.

Incredible Hulk Coaster ★★★ RIDE Every minute or so, a new train blasts out of the 150-foot tunnel, over the avenue, and across the lakefront. Adding to the intensity, the track's hollow frame and nylon wheels generate an animal roar that can be heard throughout the park. The $15 million ride is quick—a little over 2 minutes—but it's invigorating. First, trains cruise into the inclined tunnel. Then, without warning, 220 aircraft tires accelerate trains from a standstill to 40mph in 2 seconds and shoot them into a zero G-force barrel-roll 110 feet in the air, which means passengers are already upside down even though they're still going up the first hill. What follows is unbridled mayhem, as you boomerang in a cobra roll and hit a top speed of 67mph through a tangle of corkscrews, loops, and misty tunnels. For many visitors, it's the first ride of the day, and its seven inversions are certain to work better than morning coffee. Loose items aren't allowed, so use the nearby lockers, good for the ride's posted wait time plus 20 minutes. **Strategy:** The single-rider line here is fruitful. A separate queue forms near the loading dock for the front row, but if you're low on time, wait instead for the front row on Dueling Dragons, where the exposed view gets you a lot more thrills. If you plan on buying a photo of your group on the ride, make sure you're all seated in the same line because shots are taken row by row.

Storm Force Accelatron ★ RIDE I can translate: Storm is the weather-controlling X-Man, so an Accelatron must be a 90-second spinning-tub ride, like Disney's teacups. Open, round cars spin on platters that themselves are on a giant rotating disk, and just to ensure maximum vomit velocity, each pod can be spun using a plate in the middle. **Strategy:** This ride is skippable unless you have insistent kids.

Dr. Doom's Fearfall ★★ RIDE Those twin 200-foot towers are fitted with rows of chairs that slide up and down them. The brave are rocketed 150 feet up at a force of 4Gs, where they feel an intense tickling in their stomachs, soak up a terrific view of the park, and bounce (safely) back down to Earth. The ride capacity is pretty low—you can see for yourself that each tower only shoots about 16 people up on each trip, with a reload period of several minutes in between—so either do this one early or very late so that waiting for it doesn't eat up too much time. You may hear the towers hiss like a snarling beast—it sounds like a Doctor Doom sound effect, but, in fact, it's part of

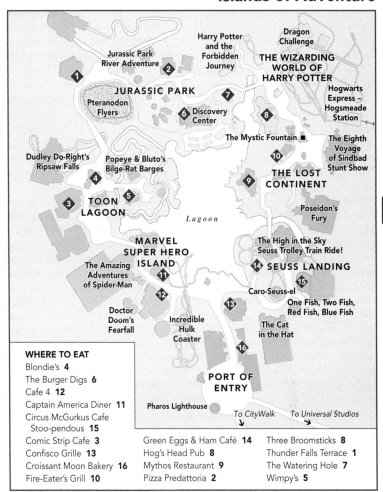

THE WIZARDING WORLD OF HARRY POTTER

Harry Potter and the Forbidden Journey

Dragon Challenge

Jurassic Park River Adventure ❷

❶

JURASSIC PARK

Pteranodon Flyers

❻ Discovery Center

Hogwarts Express – Hogsmeade Station

❼

❽

The Mystic Fountain ■

❿

The Eighth Voyage of Sindbad Stunt Show

Dudley Do-Right's Ripsaw Falls

Popeye & Bluto's Bilge-Rat Barges

❹

❺

TOON LAGOON

❸

THE LOST CONTINENT

❾

Lagoon

Poseidon's Fury

MARVEL SUPER HERO ISLAND

The Amazing Adventures of Spider-Man

⓫

⓬

The High in the Sky Seuss Trolley Train Ride!

⓮ **SEUSS LANDING**

⓯

Caro-Seuss-el

⓭

One Fish, Two Fish, Red Fish, Blue Fish

Doctor Doom's Fearfall

Incredible Hulk Coaster

The Cat in the Hat

⓰

PORT OF ENTRY

Pharos Lighthouse

To CityWalk ↓   To Universal Studios →

4

UNIVERSAL ORLANDO, SEAWORLD & BEYOND

Universal Orlando

WHERE TO EAT

Blondie's **4**
The Burger Digs **6**
Cafe 4 **12**
Captain America Diner **11**
Circus McGurkus Cafe Stoo-pendous **15**
Comic Strip Cafe **3**
Confisco Grille **13**
Croissant Moon Bakery **16**
Fire-Eater's Grill **10**

Green Eggs & Ham Café **14**
Hog's Head Pub **8**
Mythos Restaurant **9**
Pizza Predattoria **2**

Three Broomsticks **8**
Thunder Falls Terrace **1**
The Watering Hole **7**
Wimpy's **5**

the mechanism. A computer weighs each car before launch, and any excess compressed air is noisily expelled in the seconds before flight. **Strategy:** The seating configuration lends itself to lots of empty spaces, so the single-rider line moves much quicker than most.

The Amazing Adventures of Spider-Man ★★★ RIDE   The cliché "don't miss it" rightfully applies here. It fires on all cylinders, and the whole family can do it without fear. After passing through a simulation of the "Daily Bugle" newsroom (take special notice of the hilarious preride safety video, done as a pitch-perfect "Superfriends"-era cartoon), riders don polarized 3-D glasses, board moving cars, and whisk through a 1.5-acre experience. Mild open-air motion simulation, computer-generated 3-D animation, and a cunning sense trickery (bursts of flame, water droplets, blasts of hot air) collaborate to impart the mind-blowing illusion of being drafted into Spidey's battles against a "Sinister Syndicate" of supervillains including Doctor Octopus and the Green Goblin, who have disassembled the Statue of Liberty with an antigravity gun. Although the vehicles barely move as they make their way through the sets, you'll come off feeling as if you've survived a 400-foot plunge off a city skyscraper. Comics fans should keep a lookout for Spider-Man creator Stan Lee. He appears four times during the ride, and you'll hear him once. **Strategy:** Go early or late in the day to minimize waits. There's sometimes a single-rider line and it shoots past the slower standby queue. The middle of the front row is debatably the best place to sit.

TOON LAGOON

The next zone clockwise after Marvel Super Hero Island, Toon Lagoon, harbors two waters rides that are—both literally and figuratively—among the splashiest at any theme park. Both of them will drench you. If you're smart, you'll come just *before* it swelters, so that you'll be soaked and cool when the going gets rough.

Slow your pace when you reach the introductory section of Toon Lagoon, encountered after a brief zone of **midway games** (most: three tries for $5). Crawling with details, color, and fountains, it's the kind of place that reveals more the longer you look. Some 150 cartoon characters—some you'll recognize (Nancy, Annie, the Family Circus, Beetle Bailey) and some strictly for connoisseurs (Little Nemo in Slumberland, Zippy)—make two-dimensional appearances on the island, including inside the restaurants and on a soundtrack popping in and out of the action. Where you see a button or a possible trigger, press it or plunge it, because the environment has been rigged with sonic treats. Whimsical snapshot spots are worked in, too, such as the trick photo setup by the Comic Strip Cafe where you can pretend Marmaduke is dragging you by his leash. The deluge from the waterfall under Hagar's Viking ship provides cooling relief from the sunlight. Amidst all this, the **Boop Oop A Doop** Betty Boop store sells rare specimens. My sister-in-law found a 75th-anniversary cookie jar here that no other real-world store carried. Personally, I worry about the mental health of the clerks, who are subjected to a brain-melting loop of Boop's oops.

Dudley Do-Right's Ripsaw Falls ★★★ RIDE   Within this Technicolor snowcapped mountain, you'll find a wonderful perils-of-Pauline log-flume caper featuring Jay Ward's feckless Canadian Mountie bungling his rescue of Nell Fenwick from Snidely Whiplash. The winding 5-minute journey—ups, downs, indoor, outdoor, surprise backsplashes, chunky robotic characters—climaxes in a stomach-juggling double-dip drop that hurtles, unexpectedly, through a humped underground gully. Although the 75-foot drop starts out at 45 degrees, it steepens to 50 degrees, creating

---

The Best of Islands of Adventure

Don't miss if you're 6: The Cat in the Hat
Don't miss if you're 16: The Amazing Adventures of Spider-Man, Dragon Challenge
Requisite photo op: Hogwarts Castle
Food you can only get here: Butterbeer, Hogsmeade

The most crowded, so go early: Harry Potter and the Forbidden Journey
Skippable: Pteranodon Flyers
Biggest thrill: Incredible Hulk Coaster
Best show: Poseidon's Fury
Where to find peace: On the lagoon in Jurassic Park

a weightless sensation. Front- and back-seat riders get soaked, and anyone who didn't get soaked probably will when they double back to the disembarking zone, because that's when they'll face the gauntlet of sadistic bystanders who fire water cannons at passing boats. Ripsaw Falls is terrific fun. No one gets off it grumpy—the mark of amusement success. **Tips:** The ride often closes in January and early February for a scrub. There's an optional locker nearby—use it, because there's no boat storage. It's $4 for 90 minutes, which may allow you to also use it for Popeye & Bluto's barges. The **Gasoline Alley** shop, across the main path, sells $8 ponchos, but on Ripsaw Falls, you straddle the seat so your feet won't be easy to cover. Best to wear sandals.

Popeye & Bluto's Bilge-Rat Barges ★★★ RIDE   For my money, it's the best round-boat flume in the world because it's fun watching your loved ones get humiliated. You board 12-passenger, circular bumper boats that float freely and unpredictably down an outlandish white-water obstacle course—beneath waterfalls, through tunnels, over angry rapids, and past features designed to mercilessly inundate you. It's like playing Russian roulette with water, and everyone loses. This journey is considerably wilder, unquestionably wetter, and obviously more expensive to build than any others in the genre. The attention shows: Even the river's walls have been sculpted and painted in cartoon hues to resemble a wooden chute. It's diabolical and one of Universal's best. **Strategy:** There's a semiwaterproof cubby on board for personal belongings, but you'd be wise to slip your things into plastic bags, too, just in case. You may not go barefoot. For onlooker schadenfreude, there are 25¢ water blasters on overlooking walkways, but there are free ones on Me Ship, the Olive. Near the lockers ($4 for 90 min., which may be long enough use to use for Ripsaw Falls, too), you'll find step-in People Dryers that, for $5, bake and blow the water off you after your journey. (That works well, except on jeans.)

Me Ship, the Olive ★ ACTIVITY   An interactive ship-shaped playground for children just beyond the Barges' entrance, there's also a slide and some fun to be had with a piano in the cabin (play the notes on the sheet music for an orchestral surprise). One of my favorite things to do in Orlando is to spend awhile on the bridge beside the Olive, which overlooks Barge boats as they drift helplessly under a leaky boiler's funnel. Watching the gleeful alarm on people's faces, hearing the peals of laughter—the sublime delight of amusement park togetherness is repeated, again and again, from the vantage point of that bridge. I could stand there all day. I also love the shore of the sea nearby, which is private almost all the time.

JURASSIC PARK

Steven Spielberg was a creative consultant to Universal, the studio that nourished him, and this "island," the largest and greenest in the park, is presented practically verbatim from his 1993 movie. Once you pass through a proud wooden gate, John Williams' bombastic score becomes audible, and there it burrows until you move on to another area of IOA. When the park opened, the big boast was that all of the plants in this section were extant during the period of the dinosaurs, but it seems that's no longer the case. Still, the area has some 4,000 trees—half the number in the whole park—and if you stand quietly, you may hear rustling among some of them—a clever, Spielbergian touch.

Camp Jurassic ★ ACTIVITY   The only dedicated kids' zone of this part of the park is a self-guided tangle of rope bridges, slides, bubbling pools in caves, surprise geysers, water guns, spitting dinosaur heads, and thick greenery. It's easy to get lost here, and easier to get wet.

Pteranodon Flyers ★ RIDE   The hanging carts gently gliding on the nifty-looking track over Camp Jurassic constitute a very short (about 75 sec.) clacking route through the trees. Cool as it looks, it was poorly designed, fitting only two at a time, and huge lines are inevitable. In the business, that's called a poor "load factor." Facing irate crowds, Universal instituted a rule: No adult could ride without a child. That both prepared guests for the ride's tame deportment and cut down on the wait. Attendants may be willing to load child-free adults when the park is dead. **Strategy:** Skip this underwhelmer if the wait's more than 15 minutes.

Jurassic Park River Adventure ★★ RIDE   In that family-friendly Orlando tradition, the worst drop is clearly warned from the outside; gauge the 85-foot descent from behind the Thunder Falls Terrace restaurant, where river boats kick up quite a spray when they hit the water at 30mph. Before reaching that messy climax, boats embark on what's meant to be a benign tour of the mythical dinosaur park from the movie, only to be bumped off course and run afoul of spitting raptors and an eye-poppingly realistic T. rex who lunges for the kill. The dino attack is shrewdly stage-managed; note how, in true Spielberg fashion, you see disquieting evidence of the hungry lizards (rustling bushes, gashes in sheet metal) before actually catching sight of one. There's no logic as to which passengers will get drenched. In all honesty, you're much more likely to get soaked standing on the terrace of the restaurant than you are inside the boat, but the trip down is enough to blow your hat off. There's usually a delirious 12-year-old boy who stands in the splash zone for hours, giving himself a nigh-amphibious drenching.

Jurassic Park Discovery Center ★ ACTIVITY   Enter a convincing reproduction of the luxury lodge from the film, down to full-size skeletons in the atrium—downstairs, line up your camera just so, and you can snap a witty shot of a T. rex chomping a loved one's cranium. Hilarity with carnivores! Also seek out the scientist carrying a baby triceratops that hatched on the grounds; it flinches and reacts to your touch. You can also handle the ostrich-sized dinosaur eggs and slide them into nifty "scanners." Behind the center, there's a network of pleasant garden paths where you can take a break from the bustle of the park and chill out beside the lagoon.

THE WIZARDING WORLD OF HARRY POTTER—HOGSMEADE

When it opened in June of 2010, the 10-acre **Hogsmeade** ★★★ was rightfully hailed as the most significant achievement in American theme park design, detailed down to the souvenirs. It's as if the film set for Hogsmeade Village (the only British village for non-Muggles) and Hogwarts Castle have been transported to Florida, and indeed, it was designed by the same team. You don't have to know the books or the movies to enjoy the astounding level of attention: Stonework looks ancient, plaster was painted to appear moldy, rooftops and chimneys slouch in a jumble of snow-covered gables, and nearly every souvenir is a bespoke creation expressly for the Harry Potter universe. Even the restrooms aren't spared Moaning Myrtle's whine. Spend time going from shop window to shop window to take in the tricks. In Spintwitches Sporting Needs, a Quidditch set strains to free itself from its carrying case. At Gladrags, the gown levitates. At Tomes and Scrolls, Gilderoy Lockhart (Kenneth Branagh) vainly preens himself among his best-selling travel books.

Those stores are brilliant facades, but there are real shops that are just as unmissable (and invariably thronged). **Devish and Banges** is where you find Hogwarts school supplies in the colors of all four Houses, from capes to scarves to diaries to parchment, wax seals, and quills. (The seething "Monster Book of Monsters" is kept in a cage here.) In the window of **Honeydukes,** there's a macabre contraption in which a mechanical crow pecks out the gumball eye of a skeleton, which rolls through various chutes to be dispensed below, presumably for consumption. That signifies the wondrous candy store within, where colorful Edwardian-style packages contain Chocolate Frogs (they're solid, not hollow, but they'll still melt in the Florida heat), Fizzing Whizzbees, Bertie Bott's Every Flavour Beans (beware the vomit-flavored ones mixed in), Exploding Bon Bons, Peppermint Toads, and other confections that would faze even Willy Wonka.

The park's signature concoction, **Butterbeer,** is pulled from two keg-shaped carts in the walkways. The only place in the world you can buy it is right here or at the Harry Potter Studio Tour outside of London. Served frozen or unfrozen (I like it cold) with a creamy foam head on top, it tastes like a butterscotch Life Saver, and it's addictive. I once did laboratory analysis on it and found out that, surprisingly, it contains no more sugar than a Coke. It's $5 a cup, but for $12, you get a dishwasher-safe Butterbeer mug. **The Magic Neep** cart, between the Butterbeer stalls, sells **Pumpkin Juice** (really a Christmasy apple juice mix) in its unique pumpkin-top bottles for $7, along with actual fruit for $1.70 a piece.

Ollivanders ★★ SHOW   It's not on the maps because it can't handle big crowds, but the queue to the left of Dervish and Banges is for Ollivanders Wand Shop, stacked haphazardly to the dusty rafters with wands for every wizard. You enter in small groups, and the kindly shopkeeper selects one child from the group for a personalized wand selection—it selects *you*—accompanied by music cues and some fun tricks. Wickedly, an attendant then ushers your child, and that wand, directly toward the cash registers in the wand department at Devish and Banges, where you can also buy perfect replicas from nearly every major character of the Harry Potter universe (mostly $45), from Harry to Hermione to Snape to Voldemort to Bellatrix Lestrange to Luna Lovegood. They don't have price tags, but they do have stickers reading, preposterously, "This is not a toy." Treat them with care. Some are sturdy, but some, such as Professor McGonagall's, can break. **Tip:** If the line is too long, there are three more wand showrooms at Ollivanders on Diagon Alley at Universal Studios next door.

Harry Potter and the Forbidden Journey ★★★ RIDE   You will be drawn inexorably to the stunning re-creation of Hogwarts Castle, and within, you'll find a most technologically complex ride. I won't give away how it's done, but I will say it's an epic combination of motion-simulator movie segments and awe-inducing physical encounters as you travel on a jolting, four-person bench that has been enchanted by Hermione to transport you. This being Orlando, things quickly go wrong, and you encounter a dragon, Aragog the spider, the Whomping Willow, a Quidditch match, and Dementors, all in the space of 4 minutes. The mostly indoor queue is perhaps even more magical, taking you through Dumbledore's study and through the dim halls of Hogwarts, where real-looking oil paintings come to life and bicker with each other. At one point, fake snow falls on you, and a lifelike Sorting Hat supervises your arrival at the loading dock. It's a tour-de-force that takes the pain out of a long wait, and sometimes there's a tour-only route that lets you enjoy it without having to ride (ask). Once you're done, you go through Filch's Emporium of Confiscated Goods, a general-interest shop for Potteria. **Tip:** You'll save much frustration if you don't have bags. No loose articles are permitted. Lockers are free for the posted wait time plus 20 minutes, but using them is confusing. The single rider line lets you leapfrog much of the wait but you will miss most of the queue's excitement. A minority of people feel queasy after riding, but if you sense that happening, just close your eyes during the three movie portions and you should be fine.

Dragon Challenge ★★★ RIDE   This is a monster coaster of the first order, and one of Orlando's most thrilling, but it's not very Hogsmeade because it's actually a holdover from the pre-Potter years. Actually, it's two roller coasters, "inverted" so that passengers' feet dangle, entangled together for two different 145-second rides. Hungarian Horntail, in blue, has a cobra roll and its twistiness is perhaps (who can say?) more conducive to slight motion sickness for those who are prone to it. Chinese Fireball, in red-orange, has two more "elements" (maneuvers, in coaster-speak), and its first drop is slightly higher, but its course is slightly more jolty. The line for both snakes indoors through a castle before diverging before the twin loading zones, at which point you'll also have to decide if you want to wait longer to guarantee a front-row seat. The trains were designed to be dispatched together for near-misses on the course, but because naughty guests dropped loose items, seriously injuring others, that practice was ended. **Strategy:** The effect is best enjoyed from the front row or by keeping an eye on your feet. After you get off, ask an attendant if the "re-ride" line is up, because if it is, you won't have to go all the way out to line up again to try the other track. Note that guests of exceptional size may have to wait for the third row, where the larger seats are; if you're not confident that you'll fit, test out the standard seat located to the right of the main entrance to the queue. Locker use (free for the wait time plus 20 min.) is mandatory, and you'll find them at Hogsmeade Station.

Flight of the Hippogriff ★ RIDE   For kids too little for Dragon Challenge, you'll find a standard training roller coaster (also a rethemed holdover from pre-Potter years) that offers a glimpse of Hagrid's Hut from the queue. Don't expect more than a 1-minute figure eight with slight banking. The line is often exposed to the sun and the back seats feel the fastest. The long-legged should cross their ankles to fit more comfortably.

Hogwarts Express ★★★ RIDE   The journey from Hogsmeade to London in Universal Studios works just like the one coming here (p. 110), but you'll see different scenery and eavesdrop on different goings-on in the carriage. Hogsmeade Station is not as nice as Kings Cross at Diagon Alley—there's no AC and no fun tricks like the Platform 9¾ photo op—but trains carry 168 people at a time and new ones arrive just 3 minutes after the previous one departs. To board, you must have a park-to-park ticket, and there's a ticket upgrade booth out front for just that purpose.

THE LOST CONTINENT

The gist of the next island, the Lost Continent, is amorphous. Think of it as part Africa, part Asia, part Rome—anything exotic wrapped up in vagueness. It's being whittled away as Harry Potter grows.

The Eighth Voyage of Sindbad Stunt Show ★★ SHOW   Mounted a precious few times each day in an open-air stadium, usually in the afternoon (curtain times are marked on your map), it's fine for a stunt show, but it won't rock your world. You probably already suspect what you're getting here—a corny 20-minute, sound-effect enhanced banquet of macho men sword fighting and leaping in the pursuit of rescuing a princess who, it turns out, may or may not require male assistance after all. Buckles are swashed and cultural references are dropped like anvils. The climax, in which a man is lit on fire and plunges 30 feet into a pit, may alarm kids, but the production values are strong. **Strategy:** Attend this show if you'd like to sit for a while. Your IOA experience won't be lacking if you skip it.

Mystic Fountain ★★★ ACTIVITY Stop by briefly. If it's merely gurgling with recorded sound effects, all is quiet. But when least expected, it comes to life with wisecracks and sprays. Someone in an unseen booth interacts with anyone foolish enough to wander near—usually naïve children. As "Time" magazine put it when the park opened in 1999, the fountain exasperates with "the droll sarcasm of a bachelor uncle roped into caring for some itchy 10-year-olds." If you don't want to get doused, check the ground for slick spots to determine the fountain's spitting reach.

Poseidon's Fury ★★★ SHOW Despite its lowly status as a walk-through attraction, it has a stunning exterior, carved within a millimeter of reason to look like a crumbling temple. Young folk might be freaked out by the dark and the fireballs. Mature folk might disdain the vapid storyline involving a row between Poseidon and Lord Darkenon (who?). But it bemuses with an interesting (if fleeting) "water vortex" tunnel and some of its other special effects, such as walls that seem to vanish, are diverting. Like Sindbad, it's boisterous and pyrotechnic. **Strategy:** For the best views, head for the front of every room, especially the third one.

SEUSS LANDING

Nowhere other than Harry Potter is IOA's extravagance on finer display than this 10-acre section, which replicates the good Doctor's two-dimensional bluster with three-dimensional exactitude. Just try to find a straight line. From the lakefront, you can get a good look at what the designers accomplished. Notice how even the palm trees twist. They were knocked sideways near Miami in 1992's Hurricane Andrew, and because palm trees always grow upward, by the time they were scouted for IOA, they had acquired a perfectly loopy angle. Scout for hidden gags. Sprinkled around are Horton's Egg and, by the sea, the two Zaxes, which appropriate to their own book (a commentary on political rivalry in which they stubbornly face off while a city grows up around them), were the very first things placed in the park, and everything else was built around them. The area around the Mulberry Street Store hosts regular appearances by the Cat in the Hat and the Grinch, who looks as annoyed to be there as you might imagine.

High in the Sky Seuss Trolley Train Ride! ★★★ RIDE Everything on this island is appropriate for kids. The railway threading overhead is a cheerful family-friendly glide, narrated in verse. Like Dueling Dragons, there are two paths. The purple line surveys more of the area than the green line, which dawdles above the Circus McGurkus Cafe. The ride takes about 3 minutes and because there's so much to take in, time flies fast. You have to line up all over again if you want to do the other track.

Caro-Seuss-el ★★★ RIDE Its bobbing menagerie of otherworldly critters actually reacts to being ridden—ears wiggle, heads turn, snouts rise—making it delightfully over-the-top and appealing to kids who sniff at girly carousels. Beside the Caro-Seuss-el, seek out the quick but trenchant walk-through grove of Truffula Trees retelling Dr. Seuss' environmental warning tale, the **Street of the Lifted Lorax.**

One Fish, Two Fish, Red Fish, Blue Fish ★★★ RIDE Here we have another iteration (albeit a good one) of Disney's tot bait, Dumbo. Riders (two passengers per car normally, three if one of them loves the Wiggles) go around, up, and down by their own controls while a gauntlet of spitting fish pegs them from the sides—listen to the song for the secret of how to avoid getting wet, although the advice isn't foolproof.

There are benches good for watching little kids giggle malevolently when their parents get spritzed.

If I Ran the Zoo ★★★ ACTIVITY   Getting wet is part of the bargain, so there's a rack to keep shoes dry. The interactive playground for young children contains some 20 tricksy elements. Let your brood slide, splash in a stream, turn cranks, and play Tic Tac Toe on characters' bellies. Beware the cheeky fountain—it pays to follow all posted instructions in Seuss Landing. Thanks, Universal, for the hand sanitizer dispensers by the exit.

The Cat in the Hat ★★★ RIDE   Take a nonthreatening excursion through the plot of the famous storybook as viewed from slow-moving mobile "couches" (really a typical flat-ride car). The design racks up points for replicating the look of the beloved children's book with precision, even in three dimensions. The story is just as faithfully retold; it's clear from this sweet, 3½-minute ride that the family of Dr. Seuss (Theodor Geisel) had a strong influence in steering the execution of this section of the park. Parents will probably emerge feeling glad they tagged along. The gift shop after the offload platform is among the best in the park—Universal's red Thing 1 and Thing 2 shirts ($22) are as ubiquitous as Mouse ears. **Tip:** The vehicles spin a few too many times for some adults (kids don't seem to mind), but you can ask to have it turned off when you board.

WHERE TO EAT IN ISLANDS OF ADVENTURE

If the park closes at 6pm (like it does outside the summer and holidays), many restaurants will only be open from 11am to 4pm. But remember that **CityWalk** (p. 157) is a 5-minute walk from the park, so you can easily consider those places, too.

In addition to the random snack carts there's no use in listing here, there are counter-service and sit-down restaurants (including carts selling goliath turkey legs for $11) in the park. None require reservations the way Disney's do. Kids' meals all come in under 300 calories. **Tip:** Menu items do not *have* to be served with sides. The potato chip bags served with the posted meals hold a mere 1⅞ ounces. Subtract them, or fries, from your meal combos to save about $2.50. Cups good for unlimited refills at touchscreen Coke Freestyle machines, which mix soda to order using 126 flavors, cost $11 and are good for the day. Clockwise through the park from Port of Entry:

Croissant Moon Bakery ★ SANDWICHES   Lighter bites such as sandwiches and panini (with potato salad and fresh fruit), plus pastries such as cream horns and vanilla éclairs, can be snagged without much of a line. Nearby is the **Last Chance Fruit Stand** cart, which sells fruit cups ($3.80) and giant turkey legs ($10). Port of Entry. Sandwiches $9.50; soup and salad $12.

Confisco Grille ★ INTERNATIONAL   One of only two table-service locations in the park, the menu has an identity crisis—wood-oven pizzas, pad Thai, penne puttanesca, Tex-Mex wraps, fajitas—but that also means there is probably something for everyone in your group. The attached **Backwater Bar,** overlooked by nearly everyone and therefore ideal for sundowners, does happy hour from 4 to 7pm, when well drinks are just $4. Port of Entry. Main courses $9 to $17.

Captain America Diner ★ AMERICAN   This indoor counter-service location serves the usual burgers and chicken. Outside you'll find a **fruit stand** where pieces of whole fruit cost $1.30. Marvel Super Hero Island. Main courses $8 to $11 with fries.

Cafe 4 ★ PIZZA   Counter service with indoor seating for grabbing pasta as well as pizza by the individual pie. Marvel Super Hero Island. Pizza and pasta $7.50–$9.

Blondie's ★★ SANDWICHES   If you know that Dagwood is another name for a hero, you'll know who Blondie is, too. This indoor counter location does subs served with pickles and potato salad. It usually closes after lunch. Toon Lagoon. Mains $9.30.

Comic Strip Cafe ★★ INTERNATIONAL   Toon Lagoon's largest counter-service location offers four schools of food: burgers and dogs, pizza and pasta, Chinese, and fish and chicken. There's more indoor seating with AC here than anywhere else in this island. Toon Lagoon. Main courses $9 to $14.

Wimpy's ★ AMERICAN   It's the stand that furnishes its namesake's obsession (hamburgers), although the staff will not permit you to pay next Tuesday for a hamburger today, mostly because it opens only when the park is packed. Toon Lagoon. Main courses $8 to $11.

The Burger Digs ★ AMERICAN   The Discovery Center's indoor counter-service spot is upstairs, across from the dinosaur-theme toy store. Guess what it makes? There's a toppings bar, so you can load up, and to make it easier, it serves double cheeseburgers that you can convert into two meals with a second bun ($1). Jurassic Park Discovery Center. Combo meal $9 to $11.

Pizza Predattoria ★ AMERICAN   The menu is small but big on calories: pizzas, meatball subs, and chicken Caesar salad. It's counter service with outdoor seating. Jurassic Park. Nearby is the **Natural Selections** fruit cart. Mains $8 to $10.

Thunder Falls Terrace ★★★ BARBECUE   Watch the Jurassic Park boats splash down in the comfort of AC while noshing on food that's a cut above the rest: chargrilled ribs served with whole unhusked ears of corn, rotisserie chicken, and bacon cheeseburgers. Soups are just $3.50. Jurassic Park. Meals $10 to $16.

The Watering Hole ★★ BAR   Cocktails are served al fresco from this kiosk, which throws a happy hour from 3 to 5pm and 20 ounces of beer costs $4. Jurassic Park. Cocktails mostly $6 to $8.

Three Broomsticks ★★★ BARBECUE/BRITISH   The film tavern was gorgeously re-created, up to its wonky cathedral ceiling and down to the graffiti scratched in the timbers, as the only restaurant in this island, and the filmmakers reportedly liked the design so much they featured the set more prominently in later movies. The Great Feast feeds four for $50 with salad, rotisserie chicken, spareribs, corn on the cob, and roast potatoes. You can also go a la carte with shepherd's pie, fish and chips, or Cornish pasties with salad. **Hog's Head Pub** ★★★ is attached. Under the squinty gaze of a grunting mounted boar's head (it responds to tips), a selection of truly British quaffs (London Pride, Newcastle Brown, Strongbow cider) is pulled. There are two more beers of note: One is Hog's Head ale, a hoppy, only-here beer made by the Florida Brewing Company, and the other is Butterbeer, so if the line is long at the keg carts outside, you can grab a faster fix in here, where it's cool in more ways than one. (They won't spike it with rum. I've asked.) There's no happy hour here. Wizarding World of Harry Potter. Meals $9 to $16.

Mythos Restaurant ★★★ INTERNATIONAL   Mythos' cavelike interior, carved from that ubiquitous orange-hued fake rock that scientists should term Orlando Schist, commands a marvelous view of the lagoon (go around to the water, where few guests wander, to see the god holding the place up with his bare hands). You could sit and watch the Incredible Hulk Coaster fire all day from this subdued environment. Food many rungs higher man most theme park stuff, with pad Thai, wild mushroom meatloaf, pan seared mahimahi, and a risotto of the day, plus a healthy slate of sandwiches and salads. The Lost Continent. Reservations recommended. (✆ **407/224-4534.** Main courses $11 to $20.

"Doc" Sugrue's Desert Kebab House ★ MEDITERRANEAN Outdoor-only counter service spot serving its namesake in beef, chicken, and vegetables, plus hummus with veggies ($5). The Lost Continent. Main courses $7 to $9.

Fire-Eaters' Grill ★ INTERNATIONAL Outdoor-only counter service with the usual suspects: chicken fingers, chicken stingers (Buffalo chicken fingers), Italian sausage, and gyros. The Lost Continent. Meals with fries $8.30 to $9.

Circus McGurkus Cafe Stoo-pendous ★★★ AMERICAN Looking like a circus tent coated in cake frosting, it serves the usual burgers and pizzas, leavened with spaghetti and meatballs; chicken Caesar salad; and a fried chicken platter with mashed potatoes and corn on the cob so there's something for everyone. For dessert, the **Moose Juice Goose Juice** stand nearby sells Moose Juice (a tart orange mix) and Goose Juice (watermelon or grape) for $4.25. Meals $9 to $13.

Green Eggs & Ham Café ★ AMERICAN You can't miss it—it's the house-size slab of ham with a giant fork stuck into it. It sells burgers and, of course, sandwiches made of green eggs and ham ($7–$8), but it's rarely open unless it's super crowded, which is a shame. Seuss Landing. Main courses $8.

SEAWORLD ORLANDO

The second mighty theme park chain to set up shop in town, after Disney, was **Sea-World Orlando** ★★★ (Central Florida Pkwy., at International Dr., or exit 71 and 72 east of I-4; (✆ **800/327-2424** or 407/351-3600; www.seaworldorlando.com; adults $95, kids 3–9 $90, discounts of $15–$30 available online for entry Mon–Fri; parking $17; open 9am–7pm with extended hours in peak season), which began in San Diego in 1964 and opened in Orlando in 1973, scarcely 2 years after the Magic Kingdom. Although SeaWorld operates three American parks (the third is in San Antonio), its Orlando location has undoubtedly risen to become its most important. The Florida compound has an additional luxury theme park, **Discovery Cove** (p. 136), and a new water slide park, **Aquatica** (p. 136). SeaWorld is now the city's third genuine multiday theme park destination, after Disney and Universal.

At SeaWorld, the focus isn't on thrill rides or "magic"—it's animals, and thousands of them. Just about everything to see or do involves watching marine creatures in imitated habitats or performing in shows. Many tourists, particularly those over a certain age, claim SeaWorld as their favorite Orlando park, because there's a lot going for it: 200 acres of space for gardens, a compound that absorbs crowds well, an earnest educational component, and a refreshing lack of patronizing mythology.

The SeaWorld experience differs from other parks in that it's **show-based.** Your day here will revolve around the scheduling of a half-dozen regular performances in which animals (mostly mammals, but some birds, too) do tricks—except here, they're called "behaviors"—with their human trainers. Although there are rides, they're not in the true spirit of the place. SeaWorld's banner attraction is the Shamu show, and when you're not watching killer whales do back-flips, you're ambling through habitats stocked with other beautiful creatures. Whereas a day spent at Islands of Adventure or the Magic Kingdom might send you slumping home and reaching for the Calgon, it's unusual to come away from SeaWorld stressed. Thoughtfully, **schedules are posted**

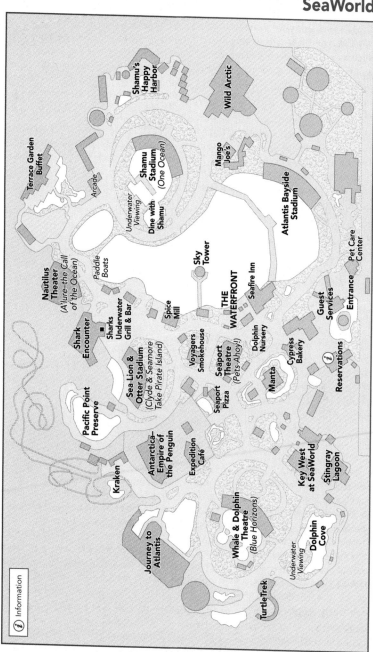

Ethical Entertainment? The "Blackfish" Controversy

Some conservationists say that SeaWorld's animals endure misery in captivity. Other conservationists laud SeaWorld for being an advocate for marine life. And therein lies the essential tug-of-war over this profit-generating amusement park. SeaWorld is hostile to accusations of mistreatment and exploitation—in 2013, the low-budget documentary "Blackfish" asserted that the 2010 death of its senior trainer Dawn Brancheau, which was witnessed by an audience at Shamu Stadium, was the result of inadequate care. (For its part, the Brancheau family distanced itself from the documentary, saying in a statement: "Dawn would not have remained a trainer at SeaWorld for 15 years if she felt that the whales were not well cared for.") As an anti-SeaWorld social media campaign grew and concert acts began cancelling appearances in the park, SeaWorld sharply rebutted some of the film's points, objecting to its lack of balanced reporting and complaining that the editing make it look as if the park stocks its park with animals collected from the wild, something it hasn't done for decades. Excepting a few aged animals that were born in the seas and rehabilitated from accidents in the wild, SeaWorld insists, most of its animals were born in captivity and raised by hand and so they would not know how to survive in the wild. The park says it has rescued some 22,000 animals to date, and points to its other conservation efforts, but "Blackfish" also alleges that the tanks at SeaWorld could never be large enough to contain marine mammals biologically programmed to roam wide territory—a charge that's harder to deny.

online a few weeks ahead of time so that if you're really anal, you can map out your day in advance; the various show schedules are under "Park Info."

If you're doing a full complement of the non-Disney parks, including both Universal parks, SeaWorld, Aquatica, Wet 'n Wild, and Busch Gardens, then you'll find value in the **FlexTicket,** also sold on SeaWorld's site ($320 adults, $300 kids 3–9 for all those parks), which gets you into all of them for 2 weeks. Details are on p. 236.

SeaWorld sells **Quick Queue Unlimited** ($20), which allows you to cut lines by entering through the exit, but lines are rarely long enough to warrant it. You can also buy the 6-hour **Expedition SeaWorld** VIP Tour (starting at $79 adult, $59 kids 3–9 in low season) that includes reserved seating to three shows, food, and Quick Queue.

TIMING YOUR VISIT You will spend quite a bit of time waiting for shows to begin. People show up early for seats, so it's smart to arrive at least 30 minutes ahead of show times. (It's also imperative that you wear a watch.) Crowds are lightest Tuesday and Wednesday. **Important:** If the forecast shows prolonged rain (as opposed to Florida's typical spot showers), reschedule your visit. Not only will you spend lots of time outside, but it's also harder to see marine animals when the surface of the water is pelted by raindrops—not to mention the fact that if there's so much as a twinkle of lightning anywhere in the county, these water-based attractions close faster than a shark's mouth on his dinner.

GETTING ORIENTED Once you park ($17, and more expensive "premium" spots aren't worth it) or get off the I-Ride (the stop is near the front gates), head for the lighthouse that marks the entrance. Inside, grab a placemat-size park map. On the back, printed fresh daily, is the **show schedule,** plus the opening times of all the restaurants and attractions. Shows usually begin an hour after park opening, and the blockbuster Shamu show, "One Ocean," has only a few presentations. I always prefer the last one because it's less crowded. On the off chance there's a space for a special interaction you'd like to do, the Guest Services and Reservations desk is the place to book. Otherwise, the Cape Cod–style entrance plaza is where you do the necessaries such as rent strollers and lockers. The area is really just a warm-up for the rest of the park

The pathways are lined with the odd "Animal Connections" enclosure—flamingoes here, turtles there—but those are really more like landscaping features than attractions, and some (but not all) aren't listed on the maps, so poke around. If you're interested in riding the park's thrill rides, the best time is when the Shamu show is scheduled, as it soaks up hundreds of people at once.

SeaWorld has a free **SeaWorld Discovery Guide app** (and free Wi-Fi in major park areas) that orients you, supplies show times, allows you to buy Quick Queue on the fly, and helps you remember where you parked. You can also enter your credit card number and make cashless purchases with a bar code.

The Best Shows

Feel free to be choosy about the shows you see, because if you load your plate with too many, you'll spend most of your in-between time hoofing it between amphitheaters— yet if I'm being honest, spreading SeaWorld over 2 days would be a bit much.

One Ocean ★★★ SHOW When the orcas start to fly, the crowd comes alive. Closed-circuit TV cameras capture and display the spectacle on four huge rotating screens as the animals thunder dauntingly through the water's surface, pointedly deluging entire seating sections in 52-degree water. It's quite a scene. The 25-minute show occurs on such a scale as to make it required viewing. Now that trainers are no longer permitted to swim with the orcas, there's lots of downtime during which loud, recorded rock music plays and the whales are nowhere in sight. Trainers fill the gaps with weak Temptations-style choreography and quasi-inspirational scripted gibberish ("Pass the word from generation to generation: A bright and beautiful future is in our hands . . ."). But you instantly forget about the flaws when the animals reappear to leap skyward and belly flop back into their tank. The stadium, which fits 5,000 and still fills early, is covered, but the sides may catch sun, so arrive at least 30 minutes early. **Strategy:** Soak zone seats offer excellent views of the animals hurtling through the 2.5 million-gallon, 36-feet-deep tank, and in case the splashes miss you, the dozens of fountain jets will finish the job. Seats near the shelflike front platform will also have a close-up view of a killer whale out of the water. Seats at the back of the stadium, higher than the central aisle, must rely on the TV cameras to make out what's going on underwater. Shamu Stadium.

The Best of SeaWorld

Don't miss if you're 6: Pets Ahoy!
Don't miss if you're 16: Manta
Requisite photo op: Orcas in flight, One Ocean, Shamu Stadium
Food you can only get here: Shamu ice-cream bar, carts parkwide

The most crowded, so go early: Believe, Shamu Stadium
Skippable: A'Lure, The Call of the Ocean
Biggest thrill: Kraken
Best show: One Ocean, Shamu Stadium
Where to find peace: Anywhere around the lagoon

Clyde & Seamore ★★ SHOW   SeaWorld's long-running Pirate Island show was retired in 2014, but Clyde and Seamore, a pair of sea lions, return in 2015 with a new spectacle. Their previous incarnation was a prototypical sea lion act: cheesy, anthropomorphic (animals doing double takes, saluting, and pretending to be choked by exasperated human companions), and slapstick. Their cute 25-minute presentation remains one of SeaWorld's most cherished franchises. **Strategy:** The worst seats are to the left as you face the stage (they have partial views), and the best are to the right, by the stone bridge. Sea Lion & Otter Theater.

Blue Horizons ★ SHOW   This bizarre spectacle about a little girl who "wants to explore the realms beyond imagination," whatever that means, somehow makes for a transfixing and very worthwhile 25-minute show. New Age poppycock makes it more like an acid trip at a carnival than anything else, which lends itself to loosely connected (but excellent nonetheless) stunts starring dolphins, parrots, a condor, and plenty of human acrobats hooked up to bungee cords and diving off high platforms. There's always something to see, and little to comprehend. Think of it as "Shark du Soleil." Dolphin Theater.

Pets Ahoy! ★★★ SHOW   Under-5s lose their minds at this indoor show, and you may, too—it's the show most worth seeing repeatedly. Although the furry cast is a deviation from SeaWorld's usual finny ones, the tricks are no less entrancing. A menagerie of common animals (cats, dogs, pigs, ducks, a skunk), most rescued from animal shelters, do simple tricks, and trigger tickling surprises on a rigged wharfside set. As the supercute gags multiply and compound in rapid succession (dachshunds pour out of a hot dog cart, a cat chases a white mouse in and out of hatches), and as more creatures are added into the mix precisely on cue, the amusement escalates. There's nearly no dialogue for its 20-minute run time. Afterward, trainers allow kids to pet some of the performers. **Strategy:** It's fun to sit under the catwalk (literally— cats walk on it) over the aisle between the first and second sections. This 850-seat theater fills well in advance of showtimes. Seaport Theater.

Smart Seating

Do try to be at shows at least a **half-hour early,** and for Shamu, add another 10 minutes to walk around the lagoon to the stadium. SeaWorld is not as controlling as—Disney about where you're permitted to sit, so the best seats go first. Furthermore, several shows ("Pets Ahoy!" especially) don't permit latecomers. At others, you can't get out easily until it's over.

   Three of the shows—"One Ocean," "Blue Horizons," and "Clyde and Seamore"—have a clearly marked **"soak zone"** in the front rows of the seating section. Bank on the first 10 rows as being the wettest. Don't take this warning lightly; you have no concept of how much water a 10,000-pound male orca can displace. Of course, sitting with your kids in the soak zone on a hot day is one of the great pleasures of SeaWorld, and most soak zone seating has the added advantage of affording side views into the tank where the animals prepare for their leaps and splashes. But for those with expensive hairdos, ponchos are sold throughout the parks, including at stalls beneath Shamu Stadium, for $8 ($7 kids). Keep your electronics somewhere dry, because salt water can fry their circuits.

A'Lure: The Call of the Ocean ★ SHOW   You mustn't feel bad if you miss this wordless, animal-free revue of arty human tumbling and caterwauling. The plot—something about an enchantress jealous of a stud-muffin fisherman—is as insubstantial as the bubbles that pour from the ceiling. It's mostly an opportunity to get into the air-conditioning. It's dark on Tuesdays and Wednesdays. Nautilus Theater.

The Rest of the Park

Dolphin Nursery ★★★ ACTIVITY   Between the entrance plaza and the Waterfront, the young mammals are kept with their mothers for the first few years of their lives before graduating to the larger Dolphin Cove elsewhere in the park. Much of the day, human trainers can be found here, feeding the adolescent animals and getting them acclimated to human interaction. A fence keeps you well away from the water.

Key West at SeaWorld ★ ACTIVITY   A sorta-reproduction of Front Street in the southernmost city in Florida features the **Stingray Lagoon,** a pool where you can lean over and feel the spongy fish. You can buy food to feed the rays for $5 per tray of about four fish, two trays for $9, or three for $13.

Dolphin Cove ★★★ ACTIVITY   Feeding times for the bottlenose dolphins (the schedule is posted) are regimented and crowded. Interested parties should collect in a zone near the feeding area about 30 minutes before the posted feeding time. You can take your own photos or SeaWorld will sell you a professional one for $20. Around feeding times, dolphins congregate at the trainers' dock, which can make seeing them from other parts of the tank difficult, so if you won't be feeding them, come between meals for a better look. Walk around the far side of the tank, and you'll find a little-used underwater viewing area with air conditioning.

TurtleTrek ★★ ACTIVITY/FILM   A circuitous entrance ramp brings you to a popular air-conditioned underwater viewing area for 1,500 Caribbean fish and sea turtles the size of coffee tables. If you look closely, you can tell which turtles are rescues—one lost her lower jaw from a fishing net, another gave a flipper to a shark near Bermuda. In the freshwater tank, much attention is paid to the manatee's status as one of America's most endangered animals, and, in fact, the sluggish creatures on display here were all rescued from the wild, where hot-dogging boaters are decimating their numbers. You'll be herded into a domed room where a (rather poorly) computer-animated 3-D film traces the life cycle of a sea turtle from its point of view. It's hard not to notice that 7-minute story hits the same beats as "Finding Nemo" (jellyfish fields, marauding birds, sharks prowling a shipwreck). You might be better off staying longer in front of the tank, where the view is more authentic. **Tip:** If you skip this, at least see the manatees in their habitat located out the attraction's exit.

Manta ★★★ RIDE   Rising above the park is SeaWorld's thrill-ride pride, a "flying coaster" ridden face-down and head-first, in a horizontal position. You board sitting upright, and after your shoulders and ankles are secured, you're tipped forward and the train is dispatched over curious pedestrians for the 2½-minute ride. The queue meaders through 10 aquaria containing cownose rays, spotted eaglerays, and octopi behind floor-to-ceiling windows, so you get a dose of sea life while you wait. Even nonriders can see rays through a separate entrance to the right of the ride's line. Speeds approach 60mph, with four inversions, in a fanciful approximation of what it feels like for a manta ray to swim. Manta is a pretty unique coaster experience, and it's solid fun. Lockers are $1 to $1.50 in quarters; there's a change machine. **Tip:** Because you're in "flying" position, no seat has an obstructed view.

To get the most out of a visit, try to be in the same place as the animal trainers, who frequently appear to nurture their charges. Ask questions. Get involved. They may even allow you to feed or stroke the animals (set aside another $25 or so for fish food). These zoologists love sharing information about the animals they have devoted their lives to. Feeding times are usually posted outside each pavilion's entrance; you may need to backtrack a few times to make the schedule, but the interaction will be worth the effort.

The Kraken End of the Park

Journey to Atlantis ★★ RIDE   On this 6-minute flume-cum-coaster ride (you can't see the brief coaster section from the front), getting drenched is unavoidable, as the 60-foot drop should warn. Riding isn't its only pleasure—it's fun to douse passing boats with coin-operated water cannons, too (Number 4 does the most damage to the unsuspecting). Atlantis is oddball. First you pass through a few rooms as if you're on a family-friendly dark ride (the robotics aren't great), and then one of the spirits turns against you sending you down the hill you saw outside, and finally the water gives way and your boat becomes, briefly, a roller-coaster car that escapes the evil sprite with no upside-down moments but yet another splashdown. Besides the drenching you can see from outside, there are a few other lap soakers and delightfully nasty splashbacks—ideal for hot days. **Strategy:** Front seats get wettest. Try to balance the weight; otherwise you'll list disconcertingly. Keep stuff dry in a nearby locker (four quarters; there's a change machine), and leave it there when you ride Kraken next door. Ponchos are sold nearby for $8; $7 for kids.

Kraken ★★★ RIDE   Take a 2-minute dose of testosterone. After you settle into your pedestal-like seat, the floor is retracted, dangling your legs while you undergo seven upside-down "inversions" of one sort or another. The coaster, which hits 65mph and drops 144 feet on its first breath-stealing hill, traces the shoreline of a pond behind the loading area and dives below ground level three times. **Strategy:** If you'd like to wait for a front seat, there's a special, longer line for it. Because it's floorless, you can't ride with flip-flops, but you may leave shoes on the loading dock and go barefoot (if you do that in the front row, which I recommend, you'll feel like you're about to lose a foot in the rails). Lockers cost 4 quarters; there's a change machine nearby at the lockers for Journey to Atlantis. Better yet, use one locker for both rides.

Antarctica ★★ ACTIVITY/RIDE   SeaWorld's 2013 addition was this 4-acre, iceberg-styled pavilion dedicated to penguins. View a colony of 245 Gentoo, Rockhopper, Adélie, and King penguins, first in a human-temperature room with a fascinating underwater viewing of the little birds zipping around underwater, and then, if you want, from a 30-degree area where they waddle helplessly on dry land. The ride, should you choose to try it out, takes you to the habitat in the reverse order. It's based on some cool trackless technology that allows cars, which will remind you of air hockey pucks, to roam the same room, even cross paths. Choose "Wild" or "Mild," although the wild version isn't much more intense than a few light spins and bucks. As rides go, it's fairly pointless, but it is unique. Don't confuse this exhibition with Wild Arctic, which contains the beluga whales and polar bears.

Pacific Point Preserve ★★★ ACTIVITY   Like Dolphin Cove, Pacific Point is an open-air, rocky habitat that encourages feedings, but here the residents are incessantly barking Californian sea lions and a few demure seals. There's a narrow moat between the tank and the walkway, but you're encouraged to lean over and toss the doglike animals fresh fish, which are sold for $5 per tray, $20 for five. More often than not, maurauding birds snatch what you toss. The area gets busy around Clyde and Seamore showtimes at the neighboring Sea Lion & Otter Theater.

Shark Encounter ★★★ ACTIVITY   The onetime Terrors of the Deep was given a more responsible name to further rehabilitate the public image of the much-maligned creatures within. It's one of the better exhibitions, with 60-foot acrylic tubes passing through 300,000 gallons of water stocked with sharks—the crowds are ushered along via moving sidewalks. Too many tourists scamper quickly through the smaller tanks before that dazzling main event, but they're missing some beautiful stuff, including barracuda, moray eels, lionfish, and the awesome leafy sea dragon, which looks for all the world like a floating clump of seaweed. Don't ignore the shallow tank in front of the building, as that's where the smaller species are kept. There, you can feed rays and tarpon shrimp for $5 a tray, two for $9, three for $13, and five for $20.

The Waterfront at SeaWorld

Sky Tower ★★★ OBSERVATION RIDE   Jutting above the lagoon—and topped to still-greater heights by a colossal American flag—is the 400-foot, old-fashioned "Wheel-o-vater" (that's what its interior label says) that rotates as it climbs 300 feet for a panorama. At the top, it slowly spins for two or three revolutions, giving you a good look around, before lowering you back to the Waterfront at the end of 6 minutes. You can point out the landmarks, including Spaceship Earth and the skyscrapers of downtown.

Shamu Stadium ★ ACTIVITY   The home to One Ocean has something to offer outside of show time. A few of the killer whales are visible in the **Shamu Up Close** viewing area that surveys one of their holding pods. Above the surface of that pen, the Dine with Shamu supper (p. 134) is held, separated by cargo netting from the water (reserve several weeks ahead).

Shamu's Happy Harbor ★★ ACTIVITY   Behind Shamu Stadium, kids have their own amusement area—and they get more rides than the grown-ups! The most obvious feature is the four-story cargo-net playground, but there are some and mild carnival-style rides: an underwater-themed **Sea Carousel** ★ topped by a 45-foot-wide pink octopus; a swinging-and-twirling tracked boat ride, **Ocean Commotion** ★; and the **Flying Fiddler** ★★, a bench that lifts kids 20 feet above the ground and then gently brings them back down in a series of short drops. Those rides join an 800-foot kiddie coaster with trains shaped like you-know-who (**Shamu Express** ★★), a ride

WHAT THE BASICS cost AT SEAWORLD

Parking: $17	**ECV:** $50 per day
Single strollers: $15 per day	**Lockers:** $8 (small) or $11 (large) per day
Double strollers: $25 per day	**Coke:** $2.70 / **Bottle of water:** $2.80 /
Wheelchair: $12 per day	**Cup of beer:** $7

with spinning cars attached to a stalk (**Jazzy Jellies ★**), a pirate ship (**Wahoo Two ★**) that doesn't do much, the teacup-style (**Swishy Fishies ★★★**), and the **Seven Seas Railway ★★** tiny train, where it's fun to make Daddy squish into the caboose.

The Shamu End of the Park

Wild Arctic ★★ ACTIVITY/RIDE   One of SeaWorld's most interesting exhibitions deserves more than it gets: marooned here, at the Nowheresville end of the park, when the only time it seems crowded is a half-hour after every Shamu showtime. As with Antarctica (which is different and has the penguins) there are two ways to get in. Either you opt for the motion-simulator ride that re-creates a turbulent 5-minute helicopter ride (well done for such an old ride, but its bumpiness makes me ill), or you much more quickly make straight for the swimmers after a short movie. After that, you can walk through at your own pace, enjoying first a surface view and then an underwater look at the Pacific walruses, polar bears (you won't see much—they sleep 16–18 hr. a day), and the parks' utterly beautiful white beluga whales, which look like swimming porcelain. There's probably more than a half-hour's worth of investigation here, including mock-ups of a polar research station and a fake "bear den" for young kids to explore. You'll also find it *very* cool, which makes it a blockbuster on hot days.

Where to Eat at SeaWorld

In case you were wondering, SeaWorld only serves sustainable seafood. There are also always vegetarian options. Prices are in line with everyone else's: $10 a meal, before a drink, is standard. Most places to eat are clustered in the center between the Waterfront and Kraken. All-you-can-eat food passes (one entree, one side or dessert, one nonalcoholic drink each time through line) cost $33 for adults and $18 for kids ($3 cheaper online); they're good at six of the counter-service locations.

Disney World has its Mouse-ear ice-cream bar, but at SeaWorld, you'll be served a variety shaped like Shamu ($3.60). Plastic drinking straws could choke the aquatic animals, so you don't get one. If you must have a straw, the $9 souvenir cups have them built in, and they grant $1 refills. More interesting are the Coca-Cola Freestyle fountains, which are touchscreen machines that allow you to blend your own brew from a range of 126 Coke flavors. Cups cost $10 and each time you refill it ($1). There's also a customizable Tourist Penguin version ($16) sold at Antarctica.

The headline meal event is **Dine with Shamu ★★**, served from noon to 2pm and from 4:30 to 6:30pm alongside the orca pools with the narration of trainers. Prices fluctuate by the day, but $34 for adults and $24 for kids is a peak rate. That's not bad to be near one of these massive creatures. It's important to book far ahead.

The newest counter-service location is **Expedition Café ★★★**, with non-A/C seating outside Antarctica, which, like the Antarctic Research Station, serves a range of food from many cultures: baked chicken, shrimp lo mein, gluten-free teriyaki chicken, spaghetti and meatballs, meatless lasagna, and "iceberg chef" salad.

The **Terrace Garden Buffet ★**, past the Nautilus Theater, is the only all-you-can-eat buffet. It piles on pizza, pasta, salads, and dessert—nothing daring, no caloric regard. Buy a ticket for $15 adults, $10 kids at the kiosk outside; it closes 90 minutes before the park does. Out front, don't miss the huge sculptures of sea life made out of plastic trash skimmed out of the ocean by the group WashedAshore.org. The other main restaurants serve high-quality food, too, but with less caloric regard. **The Seafire Inn ★★**, at the Waterfront, has some seating overlooking the lagoon and does fish and chips, pasta bowls, Caesar salads, and Mediterranean veggie wraps. Farther up the

Waterfront but with similar prices, the **Spice Mill Cafe ★★★** does stuff such as steak burgers, low-fat vegetarian chili, and grilled chicken salad, and it also has pretty water views. **Voyagers Smokehouse ★**, facing the Seaport Theatre's entrance, offers baby back ribs, spare ribs, and barbecue chicken, with a higher top price of $16.

Like Epcot's The Seas, the park devotes a section of an underwater viewing area to **Sharks Underwater Grill ★**, one of the park's premier tables. It doesn't particularly specialize in seafood. Despite some cute touches, such as a bar that's also an aquarium and chairs that look like sharks' teeth, prices like $27 for tempura shrimp and $28 for grilled chicken risotto strike me as too high (although salads are $9). But if you can square that with the incredible view, give it a shot. Some tables are right against the glass, but I think I prefer the ones farther back, which have a wider view.

For snacks, I suggest the **Cypress Bakery ★★★**, near the entrance. The carrot cake ($4) is huge, fluffy, and arguably among the best you'll have anywhere. The parks employees are hooked on it. It also sells snacks for special diets.

SeaWorld participates in the gruesome Orlando tradition of huge roasted turkey legs. Find them for $10 at Seaport Market, near Seaport Pizza (where you buy weak $8 individual pizzas) and at the Smugglers Feasts booth near Seafire Inn. Captain Pete's Island Hot Dogs in the Key West area has foot-longs such as one with key lime slaw ($9). At the Shamu end of the boardwalk, **Mango Joe's Cafe ★★** does a short menu of burgers and mango chicken salad.

Backstage Tours

As a place that prides itself on sharing conservation information—in fact, as a place that keeps animals on display, its reputation depends on it—**SeaWorld** (*©* **800/327-2424;** www.seaworldorlando.com) has Exclusive Park Experiences that are less about touting its vaunted design team, as Disney's are, and more for learning about animal care. In fact, they're dubbed "interactions." Because interactions sell out, always reserve—it can be done online—but if you forget, there's a Behind-the-Scenes desk at the entry plaza of the park for last-minute arrangements. Interactions involving swimming include a wetsuit and equipment, and end with a private, hot shower. There are about a dozen to choose from, from an on-dry-land dolphin meet to a sea lion spotlight, but these two are probably the most unforgettable experiences.

Beluga Interaction Program ★★★ ACTIVITY   Opportunities to squeeze into a wet suit and swim for 30 minutes in 55°F saltwater with the porcelain-white beluga whales simply don't come often. Participants don't have to be excellent swimmers, but they should be able to tread water, as they'll be maneuvering themselves in a deep tank to stroke and feed the gentle animals. Only about a half-hour is spent in the water; the rest of your visit, you'll become a pocket expert on belugas.

$119 per person, not including park admission. Minimum age 10. 90 min.

Marine Mammal Keeper Experience ★★★ ACTIVITY   The *ne plus ultra* for a SeaWorld or animal fan starts at 6:30am and leads you through a typical day for an animal keeper. The schedule may include food preparation (get ready for fishy fingers); helping the Animal Rescue and Rehabilitation Team look after manatees; standing over the vets' shoulders as they heal sick animals; and helping trainers interact with and train dolphins, pilot whales, or belugas. This is no put-on for shuffling bus tours; you participate in the work the day calls for, and there's a limit of just three people. Many people who have done this swear that it's money better spent than a ticket to Discovery Cove; you'll get in the water to care for dolphins and manatees, but you won't grab onto their fins for any gimmicky "swims."

$399, including lunch, T-shirt, and park admission for a week. Minimum age 13. 9 hr.

SeaWorld's Other Parks

Aquatica SeaWorld's water slide park is across International Drive from its parent park (a free, 3-min. van ride links it), and you can pay for admission as an add-on to your SeaWorld visit. While Typhoon Lagoon and Blizzard Beach are heavily themed, and Wet 'n Wild is tangled with bare-boned thrills, Aquatica is merely fresh and bright. It's a perfectly nice park, but the others have more tricks. The company entices tourists to swim with the fishes on the **Dolphin Plunge** slide, a tube that curls off a tower and then turns clear acrylic as it passes through a habitat for Commerson's dolphins. It looks exciting on paper, but in truth you're going too fast to see anything, even if the dolphins could be reliably near the tubes (they aren't) and there wasn't water splashing in your eyes (there is). There are 18 major slides, but because of duplications, only 7, including Dolphin Plunge, are really distinct experiences. The lazy river of **Loggerhead Lane** passes you by a big window into an aquarium. **Roa's Rapids** is novel in that it's a river with a very fast current meant to sweep your body along, without a tube. It's all fine, not scintillating, and bears the whiff of having been scaled down from something more notable. Aquatica does run with a smart, picnicky idea when it comes to meals: You can pay $15 adults, $10 kids for unlimited fare at the all-you-can-eat Banana Beach (chicken, pizza, hot dogs). Otherwise, Mango Market sells chicken tenders and sandwiches for the usual $10 per-meal price.

5800 Water Play Way, Orlando. ℂ **888/800-5447**. www.aquaticabyseaworld.com. Adults $55, kids 3–9 $50, online tickets $10 less, discounts for combination SeaWorld tickets, parking $12, $11 online.

Discovery Cove ★★★ THEME PARK   The most expensive park in town (prices shift by the season) is as an all-inclusive experience. Only around 1,000 people a day are admitted, guaranteeing this faux tropical idyll is not marred by a single queue. You can stop reading now if you don't want to get jealous—this is strictly a place for special occasions (or people spending strong foreign cash). Admission lanyards include breakfast, equipment rental, sunscreen, beer if you're of age, and unlimited lunch—a good one, too, such as fresh grilled tilapia (a fish that drew the short straw at SeaWorld, I guess). Discovery Cove, in fact, is more or less a free-range playground. When you arrive, first thing in the morning, you're greeted under a vaulted atrium more redolent of a five-star island resort than a theme park. Coffee is poured, and once you're checked in you're set loose to do as you wish. Wade from perfect white sand into **Serenity Bay,** feed fresh fruit to the houseguests at the **Explorer's Aviary** for tropical birds, snorkel with barbless rays over the trenches of **The Grand Reef,** swim to habitats for marmoset monkeys and otters in the **Freshwater Oasis,** or float with a pool noodle down the slow-floating **Wind-Away River,** which passes through waterfalls into the aviary, preventing the birds from escaping. Many guests elect to simply kick back on a lounger (there are plenty) on incredibly silky sand (imported, of course) at the natural-looking pool. Other than that, you read a book and relax. Since everyone wears free wetsuits or vests, there isn't much call for body shame or sunburned shoulders. When it's your turn—if you've paid extra—guests older than 5 can head to the **Dolphin Lagoon,** where in small groups of about eight you wade into the chilly water and meet one of the pod. Like children, dolphins have distinct personalities and must be carefully paired to people the trainers think they'll enjoy being with—many visitors don't realize that a dolphin can easily kill you, but many of these dolphins are docile, having dwelled at SeaWorld for decades. Here, the mostly hand-reared animals peer at you with a logician's eye while your trainer shows you basic hand signals. The climax of the 30-minute interaction is the moment when you grasp two of the creature's fins and it swims, you in tow, for about 30 feet. Naturally, a photographer is on hand for it all, so if you want images or video, you'll pay for that, too, pushing a day to $400. A second add-on experience, **SeaVenture** ($59, minimum age 10), places an air helmet on your head and brings you underwater to walk along the floor of The Grand Reef. Really, though, a day here is beyond divine.

6000 Discovery Cove Way, Orlando. ℂ **877/557-7404.** www.discoverycove.com. $169–$249, including free admission to SeaWorld and Aquatica for 2 weeks, plus $60–$150 for 30-min. dolphin interaction. Daily 8am–5:30pm.

LEGOLAND FLORIDA

Legoland Florida ★★, a 2011 newcomer, is not just the youngest Central Florida theme park. It's also the oldest. That's because it took over the historic property of Cypress Gardens, a park for botanical gardens and water ski shows on the cypress tree-lined shores of pretty Lake Eloise that helped put Orlando on modern tourist maps. For a glimpse of what things were like in the glory days, see Esther Williams' jaw-dropping heli-water-ski production number in MGM's "Easy to Love" (1953). Today, this extremely kid-friendly, soothingly mellow 150-acre park 45 minutes south of Disney World is a godsend for parents who crave a breather from the mechanical and authoritarian environment of Disney World. No other Florida park caters so completely to kids aged 2 to 12. Everything here is designed for little ones, from easy-to-tackle versions of adult rides to ample wide spaces for play.

Get your bearings, and take in the stirring views of the lake, on the **Island in the Sky** observation wheel, which reaches into the sky on a metal arm. Other park highlights include **Lost Kingdom Adventure,** an indoor target practice game in the style of a Lego-bright Indiana Jones tomb; **Coastersaurus,** a mild out-and-back wooden roller coaster suitable for grammar school lightweights; **Driving School,** the Ford-sponsored, trackless mini-auto course that teaches kids how to obey traffic rules; **Project X,** a wild mouse coaster perfectly situated for nonriders to take embarrassing shots of loved ones faces as they hurtle downhill; **Safari Trek,** a wholly adorable car ride past wild African animals made of Legos; and **Royal Joust,** a mini steeplechase-style plastic horse race for wee ones that just may be the cutest ride in the whole country. For a break from the excitement, the **Imagination Zone** as indoor Lego-building play zones and video game stations, and past that, a healthy portion of the carefully tended **Cypress Gardens Historic Botanical Garden** was preserved, complete with Spanish moss, cypress knees jutting from tannic water, old-growth banyans, and signs warning of alligators, which live in the lake. Suddenly, you remember Orlando is in Florida, which is sad, considering Florida made its tourist name by selling its natural wonders. For all that, and lots more like it, nothing competes with the fascination of **Miniland,** the sprawling tour de force display of Lego construction prowess that mounts exceedingly clever versions of American cities and landmarks. The longer you linger, the more touches you see: a moving escalator in a mock-up Grand Central Station, a Space Shuttle misting during takeoff, dueling pirate ships, a mini "Star Wars" cantina, the Bellagio's burping fountain, and marching bands in front of the Capitol. If you like those gags, stick around for the **Pirates' Cover Live Water Ski Show,** which replaces Cypress Gardens' pyramids of maidens with ski-jumping socket-headed Minifigure toy people. The park offers $10 round-trip shuttles from Orlando Premium Outlets, east of Downtown Disney (𝒞 **877/350-5346**). Because it closes by evening, arrive near opening time to get the most out of a day.

1 Legoland Way, Winter Haven. 𝒞 **877/350-5346.** http://florida.legoland.com. Admission $84 adults, $77 for kids aged 3 to 12, with discounts of up to $15 online; parking $14 ($12 online). Open daily from 10am to 5pm–8pm, depending on the day, closed Tues–Weds in low season.

PAST THAT turnstile IN THE SKY

Not all of Orlando's attractions have thrived. Tupperware Museum, we miss you. Kindly remove your Mouse ears to honor the forgotten fun—if not for an accident of time, you'd be vacationing here instead:

○ **Circus World (1974–86):** Started by Mattel as a walk-through museum dedicated to circus history (after all, most of the big top crews wintered in Florida), it collapsed under its own weight after competition with Disney tempted it into building too many rides. Also, clowns are scary.

○ **Boardwalk Baseball (1987–90):** Textbook publisher Harcourt, Brace and Jovanovich recycled Circus World in the image of Florida's other winter tradition, baseball, and the Kansas City Royals were enticed to train there. Few cared. On January 17, 1990, 1,000 guests were asked to leave.

○ **Xanadu (1983–96):** This walk-through "home of the future" was made by coating giant balloons with polyurethane—an early exercise in ergonomics. Sister homes in Gatlinburg and Wisconsin Dells were also built, but all outlived their curiosity value, and became,

in fact, quick homes of the past. You'll find the site near Mile Marker 12 of U.S. 192.

○ **JungleLand Zoo (1995–2002):** The demise of this low-rent Gatorland rip-off was hastened in 1997 by news coverage after a lioness escaped from her enclosure and went missing among Kissimmee's motels for 3 days. A few trainers got nipped by the gators, too. Bad news.

○ **Splendid China (1993–2003):** On 73 acres 3 miles west of Disney's main gate, China's wonders (the Forbidden City, a Great Wall segment containing 6.5 million bricks, and so on) were rebuilt in miniature. Who would blow $100 million on such a bad idea? The Chinese government, which pulled the strings.

○ **River Country (1976–2005):** Disney's first water park, incorporated into Bay Lake beside the Fort Wilderness Resort, simply wasn't fancy enough or big enough to satisfy guests anymore. Another issue: It turns out that the *Naegleria fowleri* amoebae growing in many Florida lakes can kill you. (Guests may no longer swim in *any* of Disney's lakes. Coincidence?)

BUSCH GARDENS TAMPA

Seventy miles southwest of Disney, and just 8 miles northwest of Tampa, **Busch Gardens Tampa** ★★★ (3000 E. Busch Blvd., at 40th St.; ✆ **888/800-5447;** www.buschgardens.com), dating to 1959, is a world-class theme park combining thrill rides with top-notch animal enclosures for gorillas, rhinos, and other rare creatures. New for 2014 was the terrifying **Falcon's Fury,** America's tallest drop tower that sends riders plummeting face-down. Its roller coasters, including the vertical drop of **SheiKra** and the sidewinding launch coaster **Cheetah Hunt,** are considered more thrilling than the multigenerational rides of Orlando. Although the park is worth a day's attention, relatively few Americans make the journey to another city, partly because their limited vacation days force them to restrict their movements. International visitors favor it more strongly. The park knows that coaxing visitors from Orlando is a problem, so if you have a paid admission ticket to Busch Gardens, it grants free round-trip coach transportation from Orlando with a paid ticket (✆ **800/221-1339**).

Admission to the park is $95 adults, $90 for kids 3 to 9, with $15–$30 discounts available online for pre-purchase or weekday entry. A 3 Park Unlimited Admission Ticket from SeaWorld also comes with a free round-trip bus ride from SeaWorld to Busch Gardens, and entry to both parks and Aquatica; it costs $149 adults and $141 kids when bought online. Busch Gardens also discounts its entry in the six-park version of the discounted Orlando FlexTicket (p. 236).

MORE ORLANDO ATTRACTIONS

When you're sick of parking trams and cattle-corral queues, it's time to divert yourself with something new. In many cases, actually, something old—some of these places are among the original attractions that sowed the seeds that grew the fertile vacationland Central Florida is today. Some attractions are beautiful, some are downright silly, but when you're on vacation, anything goes.

INTERNATIONAL DRIVE

The attractions around International Drive aren't plush—midways and sideshows, mostly—but they are the stuff of a quintessential family holiday and they won't break the bank. I-Drive is the only touristy area in Orlando where a car isn't necessary, not least because the I-Ride Trolley (p. 230) will tote you along, if you're tired of strolling.

CSI: The Experience ★ ACTIVITY   Scrutinizing a graphic murder scene: fun for the whole family! Turning tragedy into popcorn, this CBS-authorized whodunit turns you loose on one of three dioramas of slain corpses. You observe the details as closely as possible before taking your findings to a few touch-screen stations where you learn how investigators use forensics to find clues to crimes. Here's a sample line from one video, which features actors from the shows: "Ah, the smell of decaying flesh… It's an irresistible aroma to insects!" The satisfaction of solving the crime (it takes about 45 min.) may suit some visitors, although they may also have seen these facts addressed a hundred times in TV episodes. Still, the attraction's cheap convention-chair seating, Xeroxed handouts, and unadorned facilities make it seem like it could pull up stakes and skip town in an hour.

7220 International Dr., Orlando. Orlando.CSIexhibit.com. ℰ **407/226-7220.** $20 adults, $13 kids 6–11. Mon–Sat 10am–9pm, Sun 10am–8pm, last admission 45 min. before closing.

Fun Spot America ★ AMUSEMENT PARK   A recent recipient of immense investment and careful improvements, Fun Spot is Orlando's largest (15 acres), cleanest, best-lit midway-style diversion. Although it became famous for its four Go-Kart tracks (concrete, multilevel; the Quad Helix's stacked figure-eight turns make it a favorite, but the Conquest's peaked ramp is a pip), the spacious grounds are also stocked with a two-level arcade, a scrambler, plenty of snack bars, a Ferris wheel (Charlize

Orlando Area Attractions

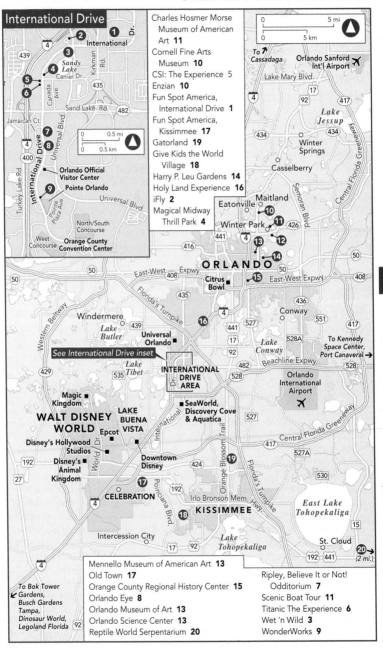

Charles Hosmer Morse Museum of American Art **11**
Cornell Fine Arts Museum **10**
CSI: The Experience **5**
Enzian **10**
Fun Spot America, International Drive **1**
Fun Spot America, Kissimmee **17**
Gatorland **19**
Give Kids the World Village **18**
Harry P. Leu Gardens **14**
Holy Land Experience **16**
iFly **2**
Magical Midway Thrill Park **4**

Mennello Museum of American Art **13**
Old Town **17**
Orange County Regional History Center **15**
Orlando Eye **8**
Orlando Museum of Art **13**
Orlando Science Center **13**
Reptile World Serpentarium **20**
Ripley, Believe It or Not! Odditorium **7**
Scenic Boat Tour **11**
Titanic The Experience **6**
Wet 'n Wild **3**
WonderWorks **9**

Theron rode it in "Monster"), and a section of kiddie rides. Additions in a hefty 2013 expansion include **White Lightning,** a smooth-as-silk wood-frame coaster that goes out and back, and **Freedom Flyer,** a wee version of a hanging, foot-dangling train. The 250-foot-tall SkyCoaster is the second tallest of its kind (the first is at Fun Spot's lesser location in Kissimmee, p. 148). Turn kids loose and take a breather.

5700 Fun Spot Way, Orlando. ℰ **407/363-3867.** www.funspotamerica.com. Pay-per-ride $6–$9, unlimited ride armband $30–$40 based on height. Generally daily 10am–midnight, winter weekdays noon or 2pm–midnight

iFly ★ ACTIVITY   Surprisingly, there seem to be as many hobby skydivers training in this vertical wind tunnel as there are curious out-of-towners. Visitors are strapped into jumpsuits and given a short training session on how to walk over the netting into the 125mph airflow—mastering the necessary arched-back, splay-legged posture can be tricky, but should you fail, there's a master diver with you to grab you by the sleeve and guide you into a series of adrenaline-fueled climbs and plunges. Or not—you can just hover there, if that's what floats your butt.

6805 Visitor Circle, Orlando. ℰ **800/759-3861** or 407/903-1150. http://orlando.iflyworld.com. $60 for 2 1-minute flights. Daily 10am–10pm.

Magical Midway Thrill Park ★ AMUSEMENT PARK   A small concrete area, which by night blares rock music and heaves with idle youth, this is a classic amusement

The Orlando Eye

There's no missing the new, 400-foot-tall observation wheel off of International Drive near Sand Lake Road. It's the **Orlando Eye** (www.officialorlandoeye.com), targeted at press time for a grand opening in spring 2015, and it comes attached to a passel of new attractions. One highlight is a 25,000-square-foot branch of the world-famous **Madame Tussauds** wax museum (www.madametussauds.com), a natural fit for I-Drive. Merlin Entertainments Group, which runs that, will also bring Florida its first **SEA LIFE Aquarium** (www.visitsealife.com), another common top-dollar worldwide brand, plus a slate of retail and restaurants. But undisputedly, the nucleus of the project is the Eye, the tallest structure in Central Florida, and 120 feet taller than the Statue of Liberty (but 20 ft. shorter than the attraction it mimics, the London Eye). The Swiss-made wheel has 30 air-conditioned capsule gondolas for 15 people each and a full revolution takes 20 minutes, but the experience is filled out with a 3-D sensory movie. Prepare for views of Universal just north, of a teeny Spaceship Earth to the distant west, and over Universal Boulevard to the east, of Lockheed Martin's off-limits military weaponry compound. Ironically, its installation in 1957 to serve NASA on the Space Coast set off the chain of events that established Orlando as a tourist hub—proving that with the Eye, Orlando comes full circle.

And just when you thought I-Drive couldn't squeeze in any more cars, in June 2014 a developer announced a new 570-foot-tall tower "Polercoaster" ride, the world's tallest, to be constructed by 2016 as the centerpiece of a new **Skyplex** development on the northeast corner at Sand Lake Road. There are a lot of hurdles before it becomes a reality, including approval from the FAA (yes, it would be that tall). Will all of these gargantuan additions be financially viable, or will they go under and become future Orlando Eyesores?

area built on adrenaline and rash decisions. The most obvious generator of regret is the world's tallest **Slingshot** ride ($25, not included on passes), a colossal fork strung with a pod. Two at a time sit inside, and are catapulted more than 200 feet into the sky, wailing to wake the dead. The 90-second adventure is so tense that it attracts concerned passersby. The circular swing ride, **Star Flyer** ($7), is scarier than it looks because the restraints feel inadequate for the 230-foot height it achieves—flimsy restraints being a necessary component of carnival thrills. The rest of the small plot is dominated by two thunderous, wooden Go-Kart tracks (the Avalanche track has slightly steeper ramps than the Alpine), a few minor rides including cheerless bumper boats, and a dirty arcade thronged with kids. Its unsophisticated virtues are something 11-year-old boys (and vacation-worn parents) appreciate.

7001 International Dr., Orlando. ℂ **407/370-5353.** www.magicalmidway.com. $7 Go-Kart rides, $3 midway rides, 3-hr. unlimited rides $25, all-day unlimited $32. Sun–Fri 2–10pm, Fri–Sat 2pm–midnight

Ripley's Believe It or Not! Odditorium ★ TOURIST MUSEUM   The ticketed equivalent of a forwarded e-mail joke, Ripley's is well-maintained and clean, but it's too expensive for the thin diversion it delivers. Mostly it consists of optical illusions, vaguely ominous specimens from foreign cultures, panels from the old Ripley's comic (does anyone under 60 even remember those?), and the odd coin-operated device. There are too many signs and fewer artifacts than you'll be expecting, unless you count a portrait of Beyoncé made out of hard candy. Don't set foot in it without at least harvesting coupons from any tourist brochure.

8201 International Dr., Orlando. ℂ **407/345-0501.** www.ripleys.com/orlando. $20 adults, $13 kids, $3 cheaper online. 4–12; daily 9am–midnight.

Titanic The Experience ★★ TOURIST MUSEUM   A 2012 infusion of more than 100 genuine artifacts from the *Titanic* itself—a teak deck chair to cookware to tile fragments to a boarding card—have done wonders for this permanent exhibition. For those interested in the topic, this theatrically presented museum, which walks guests chronologically from boarding to the abbreviated voyage to rediscovery, provides a balanced dossier of the sorry tale. There's a little conflation of Hollywood storytelling with history (at the replica of the First Class Grand Staircase, a piano rendition of "My Heart Will Go On" repeats *ad nauseam*), but there's still plenty of meat on this hambone. Join a regular tour, because guides are deeply knowledgeable and truly care; after the tour, you can backtrack for closer looks. The 2-ton slab from her hull, cast in an eerie light, makes for a moving epilogue.

7324 International Dr., Orlando. ℂ **407/248-1166.** www.titanictheexperience.com/orlando. $22 adults, $16 kids 5–11, $2 discounts online. Mar–mid-Apr, August 10am–8pm, mid-Apr–May, Sept–Feb 10am–6pm, June–July 10am–9pm, last admission 1 hr. before closing.

Wet 'n Wild ★★★ WATER SLIDE PARK   The best Orlando water park for pound-for-pound thrills, if not for style, is located smack in the middle of the I-Drive area. It's tough to top this, the world's first water theme park, which was opened in 1977 by George Millay, the same guy who started SeaWorld. This is the purist's paragon—a tightly packed coil of steel framework and get-to-the-point thrills. Most water is heated, RFID bracelets allow cashless purchases, and bigger rafts are hoisted up the ride scaffolds by conveyors. You needn't be an excellent swimmer—lifeguards monitor everything, even if most of them are still on Student Council. Parents tend to sit out the slides by hanging at the 17,000-square-foot **Surf Lagoon** or in the elaborate **Blastaway Beach** soak zone. Unusually, many of the coolest contraptions accommodate families who want to ride together. **The Black Hole** is a two-person raft (sorry,

SPRING training

Baseball is inextricable from Florida's calendar. Way back in 1923, the Cincinnati Reds began spring training in Orlando at Tinker Field and in the 1930s, the Washington Senators arrived in town and they stayed for the better part of half a century. A few teams in the so-called Grapefruit League (the Arizona trainers are the Cactus League) still call Orlando or its environs their temporary home, and in the preseason you can swing by to watch them practice or play exhibition games with visiting teams. Unlike at season games, players often mingle with fans—in fact, some teams' facilities were built to cozy proportions (you can leave the binoculars at home), with permanent interaction areas where you can collect autographs of the athletes before or after practice. Sometimes it feels like the spirit of old-time baseball, the one supplanted by high-priced players and colossal arenas.

Tickets (usually $15–$25) go on sale in January. Pitchers and catchers report first, in mid-February, and by the end of the month, the whole team is on hand. They play against other teams through March before heading to their home parks by April.

o **Atlanta Braves** (Disney's Wide World of Sports, 700 S. Victory Lane, Lake Buena Vista; ✆ **407/939-4263**). Since they took up residence in 1997 at Walt Disney World, the Braves can brag about having one of the nicest and largest (9,500 seats) training stadiums under the sun. Tickets for the 18-odd games, which are cheapest for the bleachers and the lawn, are sold through Ticketmaster (✆ **407/839-3900;** www.ticketmaster.com).

o **Houston Astros** (Osceola County Stadium, 1000 Bill Beck Rd., Kissimmee; ✆ **321/697-3200**). The smallest training park in the Grapefruit League (5,200 seats— still hardly tiny) has hosted the Astros since 1985. Team members make themselves available for fan greetings in their Autograph Alley. Tickets are sold through Ticketmaster (✆ **407/839-3900;** www.ticketmaster.com).

o **Detroit Tigers** (Joker Merchant Stadium, Al Kaline Dr., 2301 Lake Hills Rd., Lakeland; ✆ **866/668-4437**). Lakeland, between Orlando and Tampa on I-4, has hosted the Tigers since 1934, the longest relations for any major league team, and the team is such a local institution that their so-called "Tiger Town" training complex, built on the site of a World War II flight academy, has grown up with them (✆ **863/686-8075;** http://detroit.tigers.mlb.com).

soloists) that whisks blindly through a pitch-black tube, pierced momentarily by disorienting strips of lights. **Brain Wash,** a white-knuckle standout worth waiting for, drops rafts carrying two or four people 53 feet down the wall of a 65-foot-wide funnel that's turned on its side. On **Bomb Bay,** the park's scariest ride, riders step into an enclosed cylinder above a 78-degree chute that drops six stories as close to vertically as physics and lawyers will allow. A sadistic attendant peeks through a window to make sure your arms and legs are crossed, and without warning, hits the release button on a trap door, dropping traumatized riders down the flume below at wedgie speed. But the best ride is **Disco H$_2$O,** in which cloverleaf-shaped rafts (two to four people) are accelerated in a tube and sent spinning around an enclosed chamber where disco music plays and lights spin; eventually, the raft is washed out a chute. There are a dozen attractions beyond those, including the 2014 addition, 4 intertwined tubes called **Aqua Drag Racer.** The maintenance period is September to March, when flumes go out of rotation. **Tip:** It's part of the FlexTicket discount (p. 236).

6200 International Dr., Orlando. ✆ **800/992-9453** or 407/351-1800. www.wetnwildorlando.com. $56 adults, $51 kids 3–9, $10 less online, parking $13. Hours vary, but it generally opens at 9:30 or 10am and closes at 5pm in winter and as late as 9pm in the summer.

WonderWorks ★ TOURIST MUSEUM You know it's touristy because the facade looks like someone ripped a mansion out of the ground and turned it upside down. But the inverted motif doesn't continue very far into its doors. Instead, you get about 100 hands-on brainteaser exhibits not unlike what you'd find at a science museum or an arcade: an "earthquake simulator" box, a bubble-making area, all swarmed with children. Bring the Purell, because exhibits get smeary, and bring your patience, because some things will be broken. It's all about the children. And small kids love it—but then again, they have no sense of the value of a hard-earned dollar.

9067 International Dr., Orlando. ✆ **407/351-8800.** www.wonderworksonline.com. $25 adults, $20 seniors over 54 and kids 4–12, $7 per game of Lazer Tag, $10 ropes course, $10 motion simulator ride. Daily 9am–midnight.

North of Universal & Orlando

Holy Land Experience ★ THEME PARK The Trinity Broadcasting Network owns this bizarre Bible-themed, peculiarly American park. It has no rides, nor enough attractions to fill the hours—but there is a commissary serving Chick-fil-A. For oddity, there will never be its equal. Will there ever again be a theme park where major attractions are a wax museum of the Passion, a model of Jerusalem in the year 66, and a "Garden of Eden" strewn with animal mannequins? A cutout of Jesus was installed in the central lake as if he's walking on it. The day's climax comes when a handsome actor playing Christ drags himself to the top of a fake mountain to be "crucified" by villainous Romans. The act of entertaining people with a mock execution is actually more Roman than these guests perceive, but it brings some customers to tears anyway. If you have been to the real Holy Land, you will quickly grasp that this fantasy version of Israel comes from Charlton Heston movies—if Charlton Heston belted contemporary Christian power ballads. It's a one-of-a-kind place, for sure.

4655 Vineland Rd., Orlando. ✆ **800/447-7235** or 407/872-2272. www.holylandexperience.com. $50 adults, $35 for children 6–12, $20 for kids 3–5, free parking. Tues–Sat 10am–6pm.

Mennello Museum of American Art ★★ MUSEUM A rare museum with live-in pets (two cats, Red and Black are feline hosts) the Mennello is a repository for the luridly vivid paintings of Earl Cunningham, a chicken farmer and folk artist whose conceptions sometimes seem refreshingly naive, and then a moment later become brazenly modernist. Cunningham, who died in 1977 while running a curio shop in Saint Augustine, is now considered so important that the Smithsonian devoted an exhibition to him. The museum also hosts exhibitions of fine American folk art.

900 E. Princeton St., Orlando. ✆ **407/246-4278.** www.mennellomuseum.com. $5 adults, $4 seniors over 59, $1 students, kids 11 and under free. Tues–Sat 10:30am–4:30pm, Sun noon–4:30pm.

Orlando Museum of Art ★ MUSEUM Although this fixture of local pride is touted as *de rigueur* in much tourist literature, OMA takes less than an hour to see. Most of it is not particularly important, just high atmosphere, but of note are Robert Rauschenberg's "Florida Psalm," a collage paean to the state's fading tourism emblems;

Chuck Close's 1982 portrait of his wife done in fingerprints, and John James Audubon's Great Blue Heron. Temporary exhibitions up the par. Expect a pleasant outing, especially if you pair a visit with an amble around the surrounding Loch Haven Park.

2416 N. Mills Ave., Orlando. ℂ**407/896-4231.** www.omart.org. $8 adults, $7 college students and seniors over 64, $5 kids 6–18. Tues–Sat 10am–4pm, Sun noon–4pm.

Orlando Science Center ★MUSEUM   The center is an excellent (if expensive) example of its type, but it's still just a science museum aimed at children and school groups, and if you have one in your city, you should probably fill your scarce vacation time with other attractions. That's not to slam what it has: an inviting atrium; a dome

A Town of Psychics

George P. Colby was reared in the Midwest by Baptist parents, but incessant visions (and poor health) compelled him south, where in 1875, he came across land that, he said, appeared exactly as it had been shown to him by his spirit guide, Seneca. Soon after that, Colby enticed a group of refugees from chilly Lily Dale, New York—a town populated by spiritualists that still exists on the **Cassadaga** Lakes outside of Buffalo—to join him in the then-rural wilds of Florida. The winter "camp" of **Cassadaga ★★★** (exit 114 from I-4; www.cassadaga.org) was born. Nowadays, its residents offer a daily slate of services, laying-on of hands, and readings. The anachronistic town 40 miles northeast of Universal is untouched by development, and only accredited mediums may live among the ramshackle homes and Spanish moss. Tree-shaded, whitewashed, and more than slightly creepy, Cassadaga, on the National Register of Historic Places, is a bastion of metaphysicality in a region otherwise devoted to Christian fundamentalism.

Before setting out, check the town's website for the full list of events and psychics. When you arrive, consult the bulletin board in **Cassadaga Camp Bookstore** (1112 Stevens St., Cassadaga; ℂ **386/228-2880;** Mon–Sat 10am–6pm, Sun 11:30am–5pm) to see which mediums are available to take walk-in clients for readings or healings. Everything in town, including several gift shops for

gemstones and talismans, is within a few blocks, so park and explore. Because the rent's so cheap (the land is owned by the Southern Cassadaga Spiritualist Camp Meeting Association), services go for a fraction of what they cost in the outside world.

Historic walking tours leave from the bookstore twice a week (Tues at 2pm and Sat at 3pm; $15), but the coolest ticket is the **Nighttime Encounter Spirits** tour, on Saturday at 7:30pm ($25) where you bring your digital camera and go hunting for energy orbs. The next morning at 9:30, you can attend Lyceum—that's Sunday School for spiritualists—before Healing Service and church at the Colby Memorial Temple.

Residents shoo away outsiders at 10pm, so the only way to linger past the midnight hour is to stay at the town's old-fashioned inn: the 1928 **Cassadaga Hotel** (355 Cassadaga Rd., Cassadaga; ℂ 386/228-2323; www.cassadagahotel. net; $55–$65 Sun–Thurs, $70–$80 Fri–Sat, including continental breakfast; no guests under age 21), widely said to be haunted. Rooms (the cheapest ones don't have TVs or phone) are guaranteed to keep you anxiously listening for bump-in-the-night creaks. I asked the owner if I could take some photos of the time-warp lobby. "Sure, you're welcome to," she said, "but most people get a kind of orb or white light instead." I haven't found those, but my shots *did* come out blurry. I'm just saying.

that doubles as a movie theater; a NatureWorks area stocked with live baby alligators; a miniature KidsTown for kids under 48 inches tall to pretend to do grown-up things; a BeeHive Encounter (don't scientists use spaces between words?) area that feeds outside through a tube; a not-scary dinosaur zone full of reproduction skeletons and sandboxes where kids can dig for simulated fossils.

777 E. Princeton St., Orlando. ✆ **407/514-2000.** www.osc.org. $19 adults, $17 seniors age 55 and over and students with ID, $13 kids 3–11, parking $5. Daily 10am–5pm.

Orange County Regional History Center ★★★ MUSEUM   People who think Central Florida history began with Walt will have their eyes opened in this under-rated museum in a handsome 1927 Greek Revival former courthouse. Head first to the **fourth floor,** where the timeline starts 12,000 years in the past and work your way down. In 1981, a high school student rooting through lake muck found a Timacuan dugout canoe from around C.E. 1000, and now it is proudly displayed, as are mastodon teeth, pots from B.C.E. 500, and a 12-foot-tall oyster midden. As you advance through time, artifacts keep coming: saddles used by the forgotten Florida cowmen (the swampy ground made meat chewy, which Cuban customers liked), recipes for Florida Cracker delicacies (Squirrel Soup, Baked Possum), artifacts from the steamship tourist trade (in the 1870s, the St. John's River system was America's busiest one south of the Hudson), and a wall of gorgeous vintage labels from the many citrus companies that once dominated the area. The exhibitions are noticeably conflicted about the growth explosion wrought by the theme parks—the "Building a Kingdom" exhibition was created without Disney funding so it would have the freedom to be frank. An interesting sidelight is the retired Courtroom B, a handsome, wooden chamber out of "Inherit the Wind" silenced by cork floors and emblazoned with the slogan "Equal and Exact Justice to All Men." That was painted over the bench at a time when people were still being lynched here (there's a KKK robe in a nearby gallery), and until as late as 1951 in Orlando, black mothers had to give birth in the boiler room of the hospital. Some justice *was* served here: In 1987, Courtroom B tried the first case in America in which DNA evidence obtained a conviction.

65 E. Central Blvd., Orlando. ✆ **407/836-8500.** www.thehistorycenter.org. $12 adults, $9 kids 5–12, $10 seniors over 59. Mon–Sat 10am–5pm, Sun noon–5pm.

Winter Park & North Orlando

Winter Park has long been a bastion of wealth, particularly from New Money families who failed to find favor among the Old Money of the North. Its expensive tastes are represented by its lakefront mansions, its red-brick streets, and a few wrongly overlooked gems for true masterpieces.

Charles Hosmer Morse Museum of American Art ★★★ MUSEUM   The best museum in the Orlando area, and perhaps the finest in the state, presents an unparalleled cache of works by genius designer Louis Comfort Tiffany, from stained glass to vases to lamps, and even the lavishly decorated Daffodil Terrace and Reception Hall of his lost Long Island mansion, Laurelton Hall, and the bespoke fountains that ran through it. The Morse displays the best collection of Tiffany glass on the planet, including an entire room reconstructing the master's tour de force chapel, made for the World's Columbian Exposition in 1893. Once face-to-face with the uncanny luminescence of Tiffany's best work, even those previously knew nothing about him can't help but come away dazzled. The museum's founders also collected hundreds of other top-quality pieces from the Arts and Crafts movement, including sculpture, but the focus here is definitely Tiffany and his impeccable taste. Set aside an hour or more, though it's easy to combine a visit with a stroll through Winter Park's boutiques, as it sits among them.

445 N. Park Ave., Winter Park. ℂ**407/645-5311.** www.morsemuseum.org. $5 adults, $4 seniors, $1 students, free for kids 11 and under. Tues–Sat 9:30am–4pm, Sun 1–4pm, open until 8 on Fridays Nov–April. Free Fri 4–8pm Nov–Apr.

Cornell Fine Arts Museum ★ MUSEUM   Rollins College, whose graduates include Mister Fred Rogers, has long been a university of choice for parents with social aspirations for their children, and so it makes sense that its star exhibition hall would be bequeathed with such a fine collection in such a country-club setting. It's too small to showcase its impressive holdings, so even remarkable pieces (such as Vanessa Bell's portrait of Mary St. John Hutchinson) tend to rotate in and out of storage to make way for changing exhibitions, which spotlight a wide range of arresting works, from Matisse prints to 18th-century European portraits. A small but top-notch facility.

100 Holt Ave., Winter Park. ℂ**407/646-2526.** www.rollins.edu/cfam. $5 adults, free for students, sometimes free thanks to grants. Tues–Fri 10am–4pm, Sat–Sun noon–5pm.

South & East of Disney

Diversions get populist as you go south, and their character says more about eccentric Florida than imported wealth; two of Central Florida's most authentic reptile parks are roughly between Disney and the airport.

Bok Tower Gardens ★★★ GARDENS/HISTORIC SITE   About an hour south of Disney, the elegant, 250-acre gardens—designed by Frederick Law Olmsted, Jr., who worked on the National Mall and the Jefferson Memorial—are not often visited, which is too bad, because it's a big reason you're in Orlando at all: It was one of Central Florida's first world-famous attractions. They're genuinely tranquil and among the best surviving remnants of early-20th-century philanthropic privilege. The gardens (don't miss the water lilies, big enough to support a child) and their 205-foot, neo-Gothic Singing Tower were commissioned as a thank-you to the American people by a Dutch-born editor, Edward William Bok, publisher of "The Ladies' Home Journal" and a pioneer in public sex education. Bok was buried at the tower's base in 1930, the year after its completion and dedication by President Calvin Coolidge. The 57-bell carillon on the tower's sixth level sounds concerts at 1 and 3pm daily, and its 1930s Mediterranean-style Pinewood estate ($6 more) is open for tours. The sanctuary was enshrined in 1993 as a National Historic Landmark.

1151 Tower Blvd., Lake Wales. ℂ**863/676-1408.** www.boksanctuary.org. $12 adults, $3 kids 5–12. Daily 8am–6pm, last admission at 5pm.

Dinosaur World ★ TOURIST MUSEUM   An only-in-America roadside attraction, this is not someplace to pass hours—one will do, but it'll be a memorably weird one. Kids like to wander the jungly plot, happening upon more than 100 life-size versions of various dinosaurs, some 80 feet long. A labor of love by a Swedish-born man and his family, it's well kept, even if the foam-and-fiberglass models sometimes look more like aliens than reptiles. It's easy to catch on the drive to Busch Gardens.

5145 Harvey Tew Rd., at I-4's exit 17, Plant City. ℂ**813/717-9865.** www.dinosaurworld.com. $15 adults, $13 seniors over 59, $12 kids 3–12. Daily 9am–5pm.

Fun Spot USA ★ AMUSEMENT PARK   Fun Spot's flagship property is near Universal (p. 140) but this southern outpost delivers the same well-kept carnival-ride playground experience. There's a selection of basic rides that wouldn't be out of place

The standard tourist literature won't point them out, but pop history happened here:

o **Disney's Contemporary Resort, Walt Disney World.** On November 17, 1973, President Richard Nixon gave his "I'm not a crook" speech to a convention of Associated Press editors in the ballroom here, throwing gasoline on the fire of Watergate and bestowing him with his catchphrase of infamy.

o **Disney's Polynesian Resort, Walt Disney World.** While on vacation on December 29, 1974, John Lennon signed the document that officially dissolved The Beatles forever. No one is sure exactly which room he was staying in at the time.

o **1418½ Clouser Ave., in the College Park area.** In July 1957, 9 months before the publication of "On the Road," writer Jack Kerouac moved in with his mother, and he inhabited a 10×10-foot room with just a cot, a desk, and a bare bulb. Here, he wrote "The Dharma Bums," an exploration of personal spiritual renewal through a connection with nature. By the time he moved out in the spring of 1958, he was a literary superstar. The Kerouac Project (www.kerouacproject.org) now owns the home and invites writers to live rent-free in it for 3-month tenures.

o **1910 Hotel Plaza Blvd., Lake Buena Vista.** The very first building to be completed on Walt Disney World property was this low-slung glass-and-steel creation, considered painfully modern in January 1970. It was the Walt Disney World Preview Center, on what was then Preview Boulevard. Here, pretty young hostesses guided some one million visitors past artists' renderings, models, and films promoting Phase One of the resort that was being constructed. Naturally, the first souvenir shop at Disney World was also on the premises. The current tenant is a nonprofit organization promoting sports participation.

o **839 N. Orlando Ave., Winter Park.** In March 1986, the Canadian rock group The Band was in the midst of a disappointing reunion tour. After playing the Cheek to Cheek Lounge at the Villa Nova Restaurant, which stood here, pianist Richard Manuel, 42, returned to his hotel room at the Quality Inn next door and, when his wife briefly left the room, hanged himself in despair. The lounge site is now a CVS drugstore, and the motel is the Best Western Winter Park Inn.

5

MORE ORLANDO ATTRACTIONS

International Drive

beside a circus (the Hot Seat swings seated riders on the end of a big stick), a new wild mouse-style Rockstar Coaster with spinning cars, and a few multilevel Go-Kart tracks (the Vortex has 32-degree banking, the world's steepest) and racecar simulators. That 300-foot-tall skyline-scarring contraption is **SkyCoaster** ($40 a ride), which harnesses up to three would-be pants-wetters so that they're face-down, hoists them backward, and swings them forward at 80mph like wingless hang gliders.

2850 Florida Plaza Blvd., Kissimmee. Ⓒ **407/397-2509.** www.funspotattractions.com. Pay-per-ride $6–$9, unlimited ride armband $30–$40 (armband price based on height). Generally daily 10am–midnight.

Gatorland ★★★ ANIMAL PARK   Back in 1949, the reassuringly hokey Gatorland became Orlando's very first mass attraction, featuring Seminole Indians wrestling the animals for tourists, and the house-sized jaw at its entrance was a state landmark for Polaroids and Kodachrome. Back then, Florida was crawling with alligators—you would see them basking by the sides of the roads—but these days, the reptiles have been mostly evicted by development, so sanctuaries like these are the best places to see beasts (such as the newest resident diva, the 15-ft.-long, 1,400-lb. Bonecrusher II) in

Join the Club

Orlando is a world capital for miniature golf. Here, a flat, green fairway just won't do. Here, you play crazy golf under waterfalls, through caves, over motorized ramps, and even into volcanoes that "erupt" if you hit your shot. Putter around with one of these. The coupon booklets print discounts for all but Disney's courses; also check individual course websites for coupons.

○ **Congo River Adventure Golf** (www. congoriver.com): One of the best options, the challenging courses wind through man-made mountains speared with airplane wreckage—and there are live alligators in the pools! Play 18 holes for $12 adults, $10 kids. Two locations: 5901 International Dr., Orlando (© **407/248-9181**); and 4777 W. Hwy. 192, Kissimmee (© **407/ 396-6900**). Both open daily (Sun–Thurs 10am–11pm; Fri–Sat 10am–midnight).

○ **Disney's Winter Summerland** (outside Blizzard Beach, Walt Disney World; © **407/939-7529;** $12 adults, $10 kids; daily 10am–11pm; 50 percent discount on the second round): Two cute 18-hole courses themed around Christmas. The Winter side, piled with fake snow, has more bells and whistles (love that steaming campfire and that squirting snowman). Combine it with Blizzard Beach without moving your car. Summerland beats the other Disney course, **Disney's Fantasia Gardens** (same rates), themed to the movie "Fantasia," with its two courses: Fairways and Gardens. The Fairways course has challenging shots; Gardens is sillier. Find it by the Swan and Dolphin hotel duo.

○ **Hawaiian Rumble Adventure Golf** (www.hawaiianrumbleorlando.com): These tropical courses are threaded

with streams and waterfalls that could use a little upkeep. Play 18 holes for $10; 36 holes for $13. Two locations: 13529 S. Apopka Vineland Rd., Lake Buena Vista (© **407/239-8300;** daily 9am–11pm); and 8969 International Dr., Orlando (© **407/ 351-7733;** Sun–Thurs 9am–11:30pm and Fri–Sat 9am–midnight).

○ **Hollywood Drive-In Golf** (CityWalk Orlando, 6000 Universal Blvd., Orlando; © **407/802-4848;** www. hollywooddriveingolf.com; $14 adults, $12 kids 3–9; daily 9am–2am) The newest (2012) and coolest 36 holes in town, CityWalk's "haunted & sci-fi double feature" is kitted out, hilarious, and always surprising. Spinning vortices! Corkscrew ball elevators! At night, the lighting effects are impeccable. You can even download its own scorecard app and putt with an eyeball.

○ **Putting Edge** (Festival Bay, 5250 International Dr., Orlando; © **407/ 248-0700;** www.puttingedge.com; adults $11, kids 12 and under $8.50; Mon–Thurs 1pm–9pm, Fri noon–11pm, Sat 10am–11pm, Sun 11am–7pm). An 18-hole glow-in-the-dark course of fluorescent balls, holes, and decor.

○ **Pirate's Cove** (www.piratescove.net): Navigate wooden ships—a newly installed one is life-size—and falls of blue-ish water. Choose Captain's Adventure or Blackbeard's Challenge. Two locations: 8501 International Dr., Orlando (© **407/352-7378**), and 12545 S.R. 535, behind the Crossroads shopping center, Lake Buena Vista (© **407/827-1242**). Rates and hours the same: $12 adults, $11 kids 12 and under; open daily 9am to 11pm.

their ornery glory. Gatorland is rustic in a family-friendly way, as concrete pools have been replaced with natural-looking habitats, a sun-seared layout was molded into a pleasing nature walk, and stuff like a **wading bird rookery,** a **petting zoo,** and **zip line** (not worth the upcharge) were added. At regular showtimes, rangers, buzzed on their own testosterone, wrassle, tickle, and otherwise pester seething gators, and for a few extra bucks, they'll bring your children into the fray—safely, with a wad of rubber bands around the critters' snouts—for snapshots. These guys would be just as comfortable as Broadway actors as gator handlers; every show is staged to contain a near disaster to titillate and thrill tourists. Most of the fun is trawling the 110-acre plot on walkways as the critters teem ominously in murky waters underfoot. **Strategy:** It's easy to get the highlights in 2 or 3 hours, but don't miss the Jumparoo, when gators leap out of the water for suspended chunks of chicken meat. Bring a fistful of cash if you'd like to partake of extras such as being able to feed tamer animals such as tropical birds. And save a few bills for one of its 1960s-era vending machines, which press a miniature alligator out of injected hot wax right before your eyes—it's just one of many unmissable throwbacks here.

14501 S. Orange Blossom Trail, Orlando. ℂ **800/393-5297** or 407/855-5496. www.gatorland.com. $27 adults, $19 kids 3–12. Daily 10am–5pm

Give Kids the World Village ★★★ LANDMARK   Of the annual wishes granted by the Make-A-Wish Foundation and other wish-granting organizations for terminally ill kids, *half* of them are to visit Central Florida. Make-A-Wish turns to this nonprofit to fulfill those dreams, which it does for 196 families at a time and some 7,000 international families a year. No one is refused, and each family spends an all-expenses-paid week in their own villa, eating as much as they want and playing in a compound that looks like a second Magic Kingdom.

It's the most magical place you never knew existed. The 70-acre, gated operation is its own fantasy world with a 6-foot rabbit, Mayor Clayton, who provides nightly tuck-ins. Perkins Restaurants and Boston Market discreetly support the dining pavilion, which looks like a gingerbread house, and there's an Ice Cream Palace where no child is ever refused a scoop. Christmas falls every Thursday, when there's a parade, holiday lighting, and an appearance by Santa, who gives everyone a toy provided by Hasbro. The carousel is the only one in the world that a wheelchair can drive right onto, plus there's horseback riding, a small-gauge train route, miniature golf, and on and on.

As you can imagine, it depends on volunteers—to the tune of 1,200 slots a week. You don't have to commit to anything longer than a few hours and if you're there for dinner, you'll eat; just apply online about 2 weeks ahead and be at least 12 years old, although exceptions can be made for families who want to volunteer together. Mornings or evenings are best because the kids want spend their days at the theme parks, too. The workload is easy. That could mean turning person-size cards at the World's Largest Candy Land game, held Sunday nights on a board measuring 14,400 square feet. You could help at Mayor Clayton's surprise birthday party, thrown every Saturday, or at the "dive-in" movies screened weekly. You can spoon hash browns at breakfast (until about 11am), run the train, or serve dinner with a smile—the opportunities are virtually boundless and the staff matches talents with the right post.

Your mission is not to lavish pity or love, but to simply run the resort where families escape from hard times. You'll be a host, not a nurse. Not every child is sick—their brothers and sisters come, too, and many of them are starved for attention after their siblings' often long illnesses. You'll find that the village is quite a joyous place as families are, perhaps briefly, liberated from the burden of their lives. A favorite part of

Give Kids the World is the Castle of Miracles, where the rafters are covered with thousands of golden stars. Each star is affixed by a child on the last night of his or her stay. Years later, moms and dads sometimes return and ask to see, one last time, the star that their child left behind.

210 S. Bass Rd., Kissimmee. ℭ **407/396-0770.** www.gktw.org.

Old Town ★ AMUSEMENT PARK Walt Disney tried to extinguish honky-tonk, but it lives on, cotton candy and all, at his doorstep. Old Town is the kind of low-rent entertainment center you'd find rusting near a small town somewhere. Built to look like 4 blocks of a Main Street–style town, expect Americana to the extreme: beer-soaked ale halls, Old Glory T-shirts, and a gauntlet of no-name stores peddling impulse buys from baseball cards to puppets to pins to Western gear, plus a variety of special events (Fri and Sat for collector cars, Sun is country music). The area also has about 15 cheap rides, bumper cars, a just-renovated haunted house, a magic demonstration attraction, and **Windstorm,** a skeletal knot of metal tucked at the back of the park. It must be Orlando's least known roller coaster, which is not an injustice. Old Town may not be posh, and some people may even classify it as trashy, but kids like it, international tourists are fascinated by it, and the truth is that in the right frame of mind, it's a decent place to have a good time for less. You'll probably eat something fried.

5770 W. Irlo Bronson Hwy./U.S. 192, Kissimmee. ℭ **407/396-4888.** www.myoldtownusa.com. Free entry, pay per ride (various), unlimited rides $25. Daily 10am–11pm, rides open at 4pm.

Reptile World Serpentarium ★★ ANIMAL ATTRACTION Snake milking! What other enticement do you need? Truthfully, it's more of an unassuming biotoxin supply facility—and venom-collection wonderland—than a zoo. Begun in 1972 to collect poison for medical research and to save the lives of bite victims, its location 20 miles east of Disney tempted its operators into joining the ranks of tourist attractions 4 years later, and daily at noon and 3pm, you can thrill (safely behind glass) as George Van Horn grabs deadly serpents, plants their yawning fangs over the membrane of a venom-collection glass, and gets the creatures spitting mad. There are about 50 snakes on display (including an 18-ft. cobra and 11 types of rattlers) at any time, but obviously, this one's about venom spewing. Gotta admit—that's cool.

5705 E. Irlo Bronson Memorial Hwy./U.S. 192, St. Cloud. ℭ **407/892-6905.** www.reptileworld serpentarium.com. $8.75 adults, $6.75 kids 6–17, $5.75 kids 3–5. Tues–Sat 9am–5pm, Sun 10am–5pm.

KENNEDY SPACE CENTER

In the late 1960s, Central Florida was the most exciting place on Earth, all because of the moon. But the **Kennedy Space Center ★★★**, which was established in 1958 and ruled the tourist circuit with Disney in the 1970s, has been eclipsed by attractions based on fantasies. Now, KSC is usually hurting for visitors. Have some pride, America!

Start a full day near opening time. A few miles before reaching the actual visitor center, you'll pass the **United States Astronaut Hall of Fame.** Because they see it first, people make it their first stop, but you're going to be getting plenty of similar information on your tour, so only stop here on the way out if you're still yearning for spacemen. Instead, proceed to the Visitor Center proper. There, many are waylaid by the retired rockets, IMAX films, and simulators, but again, that's not the best stuff. Proceed instantly to the newly opened, $100 million permanent home of the **space shuttle** *Atlantis.* Hanging 26 feet off the ground at an angle of 43.21° (like the numbers in a launch countdown), she's still covered with space dust, and she now tips a wing at

The end of the space shuttle program has enabled previously off-limits areas to be opened for visits. Availability shifts, but on a variety of additional tours (generally $25–$30 adults, $19 kids 3–11), there's always something that's not on the standard KSC Bus Tour.

You can visit the shuttle's launch pad, the Launch Control Center used in the shuttle's last 21 liftoffs, and Launch Complex 34, the site of the 1967 Apollo tragedy. You'll also get up to speed on NASA's current projects.

everyone who comes to learn about her on the many interactive displays that surround her. This state-of-the-art, hyper-engaging interactive exhibition explaining how she worked can easily consume 2 hours, but don't dally too long. Board the can't-miss **bus tour,** which leaves every 15 minutes until about 2:15pm and takes most people around 4 hours—be warned that the last buses don't leave you enough time to browse. Coaches, which are narrated by both video segments and a live person, zip you around NASA's tightly secured compound. Combined with the nature reserve around it, the area (which guides tell visitors is one-fifth the size of Rhode Island) is huge but you'll be making three stops not too far away—still, hope for good weather, since you'll be in and out of doors. Each stop allows you to disembark, explore, and then catch the next bus. The system can be slow, but it at least lets you linger where you want. From the first stop, the **LC-39 Observation Gantry,** you'll have a view, across a few miles, of the two launch sites used by the shuttle and by the Apollo moon shots, and you'll receive an intelligent explanation of the preparation that goes into each shuttle launch. Ever wonder why you saw a lot of sparks by the shuttle engines during launch, or why water appeared to be pouring out the bottom? You'll find out why. (If you'd like to get much closer to the launch pads, you have to pay another $25 adult/$19 kids for the Up Close tour, but that's only for die-hards.)

Back on the bus, you'll buzz by eagles' nests, alligator-rich canals, and the absolutely titanic **Vehicle Assembly Building,** or VAB, where the shuttle—which NASA folk call "the orbiter"—was readied; the Statue of Liberty could fit through those doors. The second bus stop, the **Apollo/Saturn V Center,** begins with a full-scale mock-up of the "firing room" in the throes of commanding Apollo 8's launch, in all its window-rattling, fire-lit drama. The adjoining museum contains a Saturn V rocket, which is larger than you can imagine (363 ft. long, or the equivalent of 30 stories), and the chance to touch a small moon rock, which looks like polished metal. The presentation in the **Lunar Theatre,** which recounts the big touchdown, is well produced and even includes a video appearance by the late, reclusive Neil Armstrong.

Once you've completed the standard bus tour, it's up to you whether you want to plumb the sillier, kid-geared business at the Visitor's Complex—it's hard to absorb physics lessons from mewling computerized fowl at **Angry Birds Space Encounter** seriously when you've just heard from Mr. "One Small Step for Man" himself (although that's the point at which some kids engage). By this point, much of it will be redundant, and some of it is pure malarkey, but take the time to check the 42-foot-high black granite slab of the **Astronaut Memorial,** commemorating those lost; **Early Space Exploration,** where you'll see the impossibly low-tech Mission Control for the Mercury missions (they used rotary telephones!), plus some authentic spacesuits from the Gemini, Mercury, and Apollo series. You can also try the $60-million **Shuttle**

5

MORE ORLANDO ATTRACTIONS

Kennedy Space Center

Launch Experience, in which 44-person motion-simulator pods mimic a 5-minute launch. For an extra fee, you can try truly professional equipment on the **Astronaut Training Experience (ATX),** described below.

Because the government commandeers the surrounding land as a buffer, there is nowhere else to eat within a 15-minute drive, and food is expensive. The center points out that it uses no public funding for its tourist amenities, but I still think charging $16 for two hot dogs and two drinks is gouging. Good hospitality isn't rocket science.

Route 405, east of Titusville. ℭ **866/737-5235.** www.kennedyspacecenter.com. Admission is $50 adults, $40 kids. Daily 9am to between 5 and 7pm, depending on the season. Astronaut Hall of Fame: open at noon and shares closing times with the Center. Bus tours every 15 minutes, last one at 2:15pm.

Kennedy Space Center Special Tours

Lunch with an Astronaut   One of the coolest benefits of visiting the Space Coast in person is the chance to meet a real astronaut, many of whom have retired to the same area where they once worked. At times, you'll have seen headliners such as Jim Lovell and Story Musgrave making the rounds. Typically, these guys (and a very few women) love basking in fandom and in reliving old tales of glory—and unlike out-to-pasture sportsmen, these old-timers really did risk their lives the way heroes are supposed to—so these small-group sessions are geared toward questions.

ℭ **866/737-5235.** www.kennedyspacecenter.com. $30 adult, $16 kids 3–11, not including required admission. Daily at noon.

Astronaut Training Experience ★★★ ACTIVITY   KSC dubs the program ATX, but you could call it Space Daycamp. You'll test a few of the pieces of astronaut equipment, such as the multi-axis trainer (which spins your body within a series of interlinked concentric circles to test your equilibrium), a gravity chair, and a spell in a full-scale mock-up of the shuttle. Nothing is as intense as what astronauts experience, but it's still plenty rigorous for most terrestrials, and the facilitators can answer nearly any question you can launch at them. There's also a milder version, ATX Family, appropriate for younger children. The standard version is called Core.

Astronaut Hall of Fame, 6225 Vectorspace Blvd., Titusville. ℭ **866/737-5235**. www.kennedyspace center.com. $145; minimum age 7; 7 hr.

Be There for Liftoff

Although the Space Shuttle has flown into history, NASA still launches unmanned rockets. Because launches are often postponed, it would be dangerous to plan a trip to Orlando just to catch one, but then again, if there's a launch when you're in town, it would a shame to miss it. Kennedy Space Center maintains an updated schedule online at **www.kennedyspacecenter.com/events**. The general public is not permitted to flood NASA turf during the actual events, but Titusville, a town at the eastern end of S.R. 50, is a good place to get a clear, free view, as you'll be across the wide Indian River from the pad. Even if you can't leave Orlando for a launch, you can still see the fire of the rockets ascend the eastern sky from anywhere in town. Night launches are even more spectacular.

NIGHTLIFE IN ORLANDO

After nightfall, the exertion of visiting theme parks has turned most visitors into exhausted puddles, and then the resorts mop up the remaining guests at their on-premises nightspots. But these novel nighttime destinations are worth the rally:

Enzian ★★★ CINEMA This thoughtfully programmed cinema would be the envy of any city in America. Before the movie, you kick back at its Brazilian walnut patio bar, watching the sunset paint the Spanish moss red. Some of the drinks come from the private cellars of the Enzian's founder, the granddaughter of an Austrian princess. The relaxation continues inside at a large single-screen cinema, where a selection of art films and documentaries is shown, plus Hollywood biggies. Unlike multiplexes, there aren't rows of seats, but lollipop-colored levels of tables with cushy seating. Servers take your order (if you have one—eating's not required) before the movie and after the lights dim, your meal arrives surreptitiously and the air fills with the aroma of popcorn and truffled fries. After the show, a 20-minute drive has you back at Disney World.

1300 S. Orlando Ave., Maitland. ✆ **407/629-0054.** www.enzian.org. Tickets $10 adults, $8 seniors/students.

Howl at the Moon Saloon ★★ BAR The 15-strong chain is good fun: a saloon delivered as a theme park experience, where dueling pianists outdo each other for laughs and virtuosity (expect to hear "American Pie"), and the patrons, mostly over 35 and white, clap earnestly to the beat. The theme resorts have their own dueling pianist joints: Jellyrolls at Disney's BoardWalk (p. 156) and Pat O'Brien's at Universal's CityWalk (p. 158).

8815 International Dr., Orlando. ✆ **407/354-5999.** www.howlatthemoon.com. Sun–Thurs 7pm–2am, Fri–Sat 6pm–2am, piano show starts 1 hr. after opening; cover $10.

Icebar ★ BAR The gimmick: a bar made of 50 tons of ice, from the chairs to the frozen goblets. You're loaned gloves and a cape for warmth. The Arctic cocktailerie is only the size of a hotel room, dotted with ice sculptures, and aglow with cobalt lighting, and when you've had enough, there's a larger, room-temperature lounge where you can continue the party.

8967 International Dr., Orlando. ✆ **407/426-7555.** www.icebarorlando.com. $30 including 2 drinks, $20 without drinks. Sun–Wed 7pm–midnight, Thurs 7pm–1am, Fri–Sat 7pm–2am.

Minus5° Icebar ★ BAR Put on your parkas, because it's another frigid icebar. This newcomer, part of a chain with locations in Vegas and Manhattan, gradually changes color thanks to a flashy lighting system and ultimately, it depends not on local revelers but on on convention crowds. Before 9pm, you can bring kids.

Pointe Orlando, 9101 International Dr., Orlando. ✆ **407/704-6956.** www.minus5experience.com. Sun–Thurs 5pm–1am, Fri 5pm–2am, Sat 1pm–2am.

Parliament House Orlando ★★★ BAR/THEATER/DISCO There's nothing else in America quite like it. In 1975, a dying Johnson-era, 130-room motel was revitalized as an amusement megacenter for gay folks. Its rambling size—10 acres, including a beach on a small lake out back—justifies it as a hangout not only for gay guys, but also for the friends who love them, women who want to dance without being accosted, and open-minded straight guys. Think of it as a fabulous entertainment minimall: There's the Footlight Theater for cabaret and drag hosted by longtime resident mistress Darcel Stevens; a diner; a pool; a disco, which gears up around 9pm; a video bar; and a scuzzy cubby called Western Bar, for leather-and-jeans-wearing guys who play pool and, um, know how to handle a stick. The scene is unexpected when you consider that its operators are a straight couple with six kids and that Orlando politics are still controlled by conservative Christians. It's considered a nucleus of Florida gay life, and when it entered rough financial waters in recent years, some locals advocated for it to be landmarked.

410 N. Orange Blossom Trail, Orlando. ✆ **407/425-7571.** www.parliamenthouse.com. Cover and hours vary.

Player 1 Orlando ★ BAR   Right outside the east Downtown Disney-area door of WDW, is this spot where you can play video games all night long. Reasonable drink prices, a large beer selection, and a huge inventory of totally free games for superfans and nostalgics alike (consoles to cabinet), make it a fun addition to the Orlando leisure scene.

8562 Palm Parkway, Lake Buena Vista. ✆ **407/504-7521.** www.facebook.com/player1orlando. Cover $5. Mon–Fri 5pm-2am, Sat–Sun 4pm–2am.

NIGHTLIFE AT THE RESORTS

After a long day trooping through the parks, your wish list for nightlife may begin and end with a hot bath. But if, once the fireworks fizzle, you're still ready to party, the amusement giants are happy to serve into the wee hours (1 or 2am daily). These play-grounds rock on every night, even if the dance floors happen to be desolate. Their offerings have been concocted by committee to appeal to as wide a spectrum of visitors as possible, and their playlists and decor alike are designed for the masses, but those who surrender to it are bound to have fun.

Walt Disney World

Between the Swan and Dolphin hotels and Epcot, **Disney's BoardWalk** (no admission required) is a lesser entertainment district (p. 94) though it's no match for the **Downtown Disney** area (p. 94). It can be reached from Epcot's International Gateway side entrance, but if you park at Epcot, be careful because once the park closes, you can't cut through to the parking lot. At the very least, BoardWalk is a scrubbed-down ideal-ization of 1930s Atlantic City that makes for a pleasant backdrop for an evening stroll on the water. Most visitors grab an ice cream and stick around for a half-hour or so. Its two clubs thump along, sometimes in lonely desolation, although patronage depends greatly on what conventions are staying at the adjoining hotels and if participants are in a party frame of mind.

Atlantic Dance Hall ★   Appearances to the contrary, it is not a place where they might shoot horses (that concept failed), but an under-patronized DJ dance club for Top 40, '80s, and videos. Its clientele seems to consist of tipsy trade-show attendees from the Swan and Dolphin hotels next door. Hip it's not, and nostalgic it ain't, which is too bad, because its Art Deco interior holds such promise and its spacious wood floor feels good to dance on.

✆ **407/939-2444.** disneyworld.disney.go.com. No cover, minimum age 21. Tues–Sat 9pm–2am.

Jellyrolls ★   The brightest entertainment option at BoardWalk is Disney's chal-lenge to the Howl at the Moon Saloon (p. 155): Dueling pianists jam, audiences sing along and try to stump them with requests, and the mood is light. Pianists start at 8pm and the space usually starts to fill up after 9pm, so arrive earlier for a table. There's no food beyond popcorn and the like.

✆ **407/560-8770.** disneyworld.disney.go.com. $12 cover, minimum age 21. Daily 7pm–2am.

Don't Stop the Party

For more nighttime fun with the whole family, see "Orlando After Dark with Kids," on p. 95, but if you're craving a night out without the tikes check out the box on babysitting (p. 175) for childcare options.

Rix Lounge ★ Far from this planet, in a hotel catering to conventions, you stumble into this misplaced cocktail lounge. An illuminated, amberlike bar and lots of seating nooks make you think you're getting Miami swank, but the action depends entirely on whether a convention is on, when it rollicks with up-for-it partiers. Otherwise it's dead. It's also appalling that any cocktail bar in Florida should serve premixed mojitos by pipe through a tap, as this place does, but at Disney, you greedily lap up whatever nightlife you can get.

Disney's Coronado Springs Resort, 1000 W. Buena Vista Dr., Orlando. © **407/939-3806.** www.rixlounge.com. Daily 6pm–midnight.

Universal Orlando & CityWalk

CityWalk ★★ Universal Orlando's 30-acre nightclub mall takes fewer pains than Disney to present a wholesome face to the public. In fact, there's an upscale tattoo parlor. Nights here, in the front yard shared by both Universal theme parks, were designed with jellybean colors and rock-concert panache but they attract locals as well as tourists and therefore have a sharper edge. The drinks seem stronger, too. The liveliness is bolstered partly by regular concerts at its Hard Rock Live venue. There is no charge to enter the common area, which is a boon because that allows anyone to tour around before deciding whether they want to pay to enter any clubs. Buying a $12 **CityWalk Party Pass** from any of the kiosks at the complex grants you unlimited admission to any and all of them on a given night; the clubs usually open after 9pm and are otherwise $7 a pop. Some of them serve food during the day and turn into nightspots late, and others open only in the evening. All Universal park tickets with multiday admission automatically come with one Party Pass. The Party Pass also is available with the addition of a movie ticket at the AMC Universal Cineplex (see below), which is part of the complex. That combo costs $16. Finally, there's a package that buys a prix-fixe dinner at eight of CityWalk's restaurants with a ticket to the cineplex for $22. Grab a "Times & Info" guide, which maps the stores and restaurants and lists the current happy hour times and specials. Many clubs only admit patrons 21 or older because drinking is permitted outdoors anywhere in CityWalk.

6000 Universal Blvd., Orlando, exit 75A coming on I-4 from the west, or exit 74B coming from the east. © **407/363-8000.** www.citywalkorlando.com. $12 admission to all clubs; daily 11am–2am. parking $17 before 6pm, $5 6pm–10pm, free after 10pm, excluding event nights.

Blue Man Group ★★★ Three taciturn, bald, blue guys get into hilarious mischief, play with bizarre homemade toys, and trash their custom-made theater—get a seat in the first four rows in the so-called "poncho section" (you'll get a plastic cloak) if you think it'd be a blast to be splattered with goo. (It is.) If you've gone to the parks for the day, the Blue Men won't require driving; guests can start drinking cocktails whenever they want and even bring them into the theater, accessible to both CityWalk and Universal Studios (it's practically beneath the Rockit coaster).

© **888/340-5476.** www.universalorlando.com. Adults $69–$84, kids from $29, $10 discount online. Dinner packages for $15 more. 1 hr. 45 min.

5

MORE ORLANDO ATTRACTIONS

Nightlife at the Resorts

157

Bob Marley—A Tribute to Freedom ★★   You often get live music for the $7 cover, but mostly it's an easygoing place to kick back, eat, and listen to recorded reggae—an antidote to the high-energy clubs around it.

📞 **407/224-3663.** www.universalorlando.com.

CityWalk's Rising Star ★   This karaoke joint has a spin: You get a band and backup singers. Like all karaoke, the more you drink the more ridiculously fun it gets. Cover is $7, usually charged after 9pm.

📞 **407/224-2189.** www.universalorlando.com.

the groove ★   Sleek and state-of-the-art; this DJ dance club is also middle-of-the-road; music skips from the '70s (Tues) to the '80s (Sat) to recent hits. The cover is $7, and it opens at 9pm.

📞 **407/224-2165.** www.universalorlando.com.

Jimmy Buffett's Margaritaville ★★   Live music nightly in a touristy environment that's first about the cheeseburgers in paradise, secondly about margaritas (there are three bars), and thirdly about island music. Get there before the live music starts at 10pm to avoid the $7 cover charge.

📞 **407/224-2155.** www.universalorlando.com.

Pat O'Brien's ★★   It's "an authentic reproduction of New Orleans' favorite watering hole," which is cool to see, and although its Hurricane rum drinks could make you see double, there are truly two dueling pianists playing nightly. O'Brien's serves good food, but if you can't get a seat (or don't want one), you can also grab a drink through a window facing the street. This spot is among the most popular here—the party starts at 4pm—and kids can join in. Cover is $7, usually after 9pm.

📞 **407/224-3663.** www.patobriens.com.

Red Coconut Club ★★   A vanilla version of an ultralounge, it mixes stylish cocktails and cultivates the most intimate atmosphere at Universal Orlando. It's the district's most upscale venture. Tapas are $8.

📞 **407/224-2425.** www.universalorlando.com.

Hard Rock Live ★★   A 3,000-seat, top-of-the-line live-music arena attached to the famous burger joint is one of Orlando's primary concert and comedy venues. The second-floor seating is spacious and has good sightlines; for some concerts, the first floor is converted to a dance floor or to standing room. You can't miss it—it looks like the Roman Coliseum. Check with website to see what'll be on during your visit.

📞 **407/351-5483.** Ticket prices vary. www.hardrock.com/live.

OUTDOOR ORLANDO

Picture an old-fashioned steamship, not unlike the "African Queen," puttering along a narrow river of clear spring-fed water beneath a cool canopy of oak trees. Alongside the vessel, a few docile manatees nibble contentedly on river grass. As the steamship breaks through a curtain of Spanish moss, it enters a wide, warm lake teeming with long-necked birds. The passengers sigh.

It's hard to believe, but that's what Central Florida really is. Well, was. Although it was a harsh land with arid soil and mosquitoes in flocks, cypress and oak grew along the lakes and provided welcome shade. Modern-day developers have cleared away everything but the lakes, ripping out the absorbent natural vegetation. (And people wonder why they feel so hot and sinkholes are common.)

When you tire of artificial rocks that conceal loudspeakers, remember that Orlando is adored for natural beauty, starting with its year-round warmth, and for wide, blue skies chased by billowy clouds. Central Florida's development explosion only kicked in a generation ago, and some people were smart enough to rope off land from destruction. We're only beginning to understand how important the wetlands are to the ecosystems farther south and how runoff in Orlando affects drinking water downstate.

The tropical conditions mean botanical gardens support a wider array of plants than many others in the country. Look around, and you'll find examples of the land's primacy—natural springs that Ponce de Leon once toured, swamps where alligators lurk beneath bladderwort and spatterdock, and marshy preserves thronged with migrating birds. And should all of that scenery bore, you can speed by it on bracing boat tours or observe from the above in a balloon or hang glider.

Blue Spring State Park ★★ NATURE RESERVE   You stand a fair chance of seeing manatees here, especially in the morning on a cold day. The creatures venture up the St. Johns River from the Atlantic Ocean to seek out the warmth of the springs of this 2,600-acre park, which maintain a constant 72°F temperature even in winter. From mid-November through March 15, all boating, swimming, and snorkeling are suspended while the big guys (more than 75 in some years) are in residence. An exception is made daily at 10am and 1pm, when a **2-hour guided boat tour** (*(C)* **407/330-1612;** www.sjrivercruises.com; $22 adults, $20 seniors, $16 kids 3–12) is given, and the park also coughs up a few nature trails and canoe rental. Find it 60 miles north of Disney from exit 114 off I-4; go south on U.S. Rte. 17-92 to Orange City, and then make a right onto West French Avenue (there are signs).

2100 W. French Ave., Orange City. *(C)* **386/775-3663.** www.floridastateparks.org/bluespring. $6 per car. Daily 8am–sundown

De Leon Springs State Park ★★★ NATURE RESERVE   Florida has some 300 springs, and 27 of them discharge more than 60 million gallons of pure water a day. In fact, Florida has more springs than any other American state, so it's easy to conclude that natural springs are more authentically Floridian than pretty much anything else you might see in Orlando, and there's no more enjoyable place to experience them than here. The Spanish, Seminoles, and prepresidential Zachary Taylor all fought over this spot of land, and Audubon saw his first limpkin here. (Remember *your* first time?) It's impossible to overstate the importance of the St. Johns River on the development of Florida— before rail, everybody used it—and, like the Nile, it's one of the few world rivers to flow north, not south. On this segment of the river, there are 18,000 acres of lakes and marshes to canoe (boats can be rented by the hour), a concrete-lined area to swim in, and 6 miles of trails to forge as you try to spot black bears, white tail deer, swamp rabbits, and, of course, 'gators. It gets cooler: At its general store–style **Old Spanish Sugar Mill** (*(C)* **386/985-5644;** www.planetdeland.com/sugarmill; Mon–Fri 9am–4pm, Fri–Sat and holidays 8am–4pm), you make your own all-you-can-eat pancakes on griddles built into every table ($4.95 per person, but they'll cook you other things, too). Niftier still, the designated swimming area beside the Griddle House, is in a spring-fed boil—30 feet deep in spots—that remains at a constant 72°F, year-round. To reach it, take I-4 north, exit for Deland, and 6 miles north of Deland on U.S. 17 turn left onto Ponce DeLeon Boulevard for 1 mile. Get there early, because when the weather sizzles, it gets busy.

601 Ponce de Leon Blvd., Deland. *(C)* **386/985-4212.** www.floridastateparks.org/deleonsprings. $6 per carload. Daily 8am–sundown.

Disney Wilderness Preserve ★ NATURE RESERVE   To gain permission to develop swampland, Disney was required to set aside more. Now protected by the Nature Conservancy, the 12,000 marshy acres, once a ranch, constitute part of the headwaters for the Florida Everglades, and they're scarred by barely more than a 2-hour, 3-mile walking trail through scrub and cypress habitats. It's a shame the businesslike hours keep people from enjoying it.

2700 Scrub Jay Trail, Kissimmee. ✆ **407/935-0002.** www.nature.org. $3 adults, $2 kids 6–17; Sun–Fri 9am–5pm.

Harry P. Leu Gardens ★ GARDENS   Botanical gardens seem dull on paper, yet once you find yourself within one, inhaling perfume and being warmed by the sun, you're in no hurry to leave. So it is with this 50-acre lakeside escape just north of downtown that gives visitors an inkling of why so many Gilded Age Americans wanted to flee to Florida, where the fresh air and gently rustling trees were a tonic to the maladies inflicted by the industrial North. Here you'll find Florida's largest formal rose garden (peaking in Apr); a patch planted with nectar-rich blooms favored by migrating butterflies; a large collection of camellias that bloom in late fall; and the lush Tropical Stream garden, crawling with native lizards and opening onto a dock where freshwater turtles swim and ducks bob.

1920 N. Forest Ave. ✆ **407/246-2620.** www.leugardens.org. $10 adults, $3 kids, free the first Mon of the month. Daily 9am–5pm.

Tibet–Butler Preserve ★ NATURE RESERVE   Located more or less between Disney and SeaWorld (it's incredible it hasn't been turned into a golf course yet), it's the closest to the parks: about 5 miles north of the Lake Buena Vista hotel area. The 438-acre spread is combed by 4 miles of well-maintained boardwalks and trails (which close when flooded) that will give you a soothing respite among the cypress swamps and palmetto groves that once dominated this area.

8777 C.R. 535, Windermere. ✆ **407/876-6696.** Free. Wed–Sun 8am–6pm.

Wekiwa Springs State Park ★★★ NATURE RESERVE   The closest major spring to Orlando (just 20 min. north, off I-4's exit 94) is, despite encroachment by suburbs and malls, one of the prettiest preserves in the area. When you think of Florida, you don't normally picture rambling rivers, but the 42-mile Wekiva (yes, spelled differently than the park's name and pronounced "Wek-*eye*-va") is federally designated as "Wild and Scenic," meaning it hasn't been dammed or otherwise despoiled by development, despite the fact it's just northwest of Orlando's sprawl near Apopka. The springhead, fed by two sources, flows briskly and thrillingly over rock and sand, and some people come to fish, but most agree that its canoeing is among the most spectacular in the state. **Wekiwa Springs State Park Nature Adventures** (✆ **407/884-4311;** www.canoewekiva.com) rents canoes ($17 for 2 hr.). Developers would love to sink their bulldozers' claws into this paradise; in fact, so much water is being siphoned from it that its flow is expected to diminish by 10 percent by 2025.

1800 Wekiwa Circle, Apopka. ✆ **407/884-2008.** www.floridastateparks.org/wekiwasprings. $6 per car. Daily 8am–sundown.

Boat Tours

The real Florida Everglades don't begin until south of Lake Okeechobee, which is why you'll hear Central Florida referred to as the *headwaters* of the Florida Everglades. Orlando-area swamps are still home to a wide diversity of life forms, though.

Christmas, Florida, a blip on S.R. 50 between Orlando and Titusville, usually isn't much to write home about: farm supplies, roadkill. Unless, of course, it's the holiday season, when people come from far and wide to give their cards a Christmas postmark from the local post office. You'll find the P.O. at 23580 E. Colonial Dr./S.R. 50 (*𝄐* **407/568-2941;** Mon–Fri 9am–5pm, Sat 9:30am–noon).

Boggy Creek Airboat Rides ★ TOUR Airboats use powerful, backward-facing propellers to skip through shallow bogs, and they're a common form of eco-entertainment in Florida, particularly farther south in the Everglades. Though much wildlife is spooked by the din made by boat and plane alike (you'll get ear mufflers), many water snakes and alligators appear too thick-headed to care, so you should see a few on one of the continuously running 30-minute tours—boat skippers will cut the engine and float near the critters. The boats don't operate in the rain. The wildlife spotting is better in South Florida, but this'll is a long-running crowd-pleaser. Coupons are commonly distributed. One-hour night tours ($52 adults, $48 kids 3–12) are also available, but require reservations; check the website for times.

2001 E. Southport Rd., Kissimmee. *𝄐* **407/344-9550.** www.bcairboats.com. 30-min. tours $27 adults, $21 kids 3–12. Daily 9am–5:30pm.

Scenic Boat Tour ★★★ TOUR This Winter Park institution has been showing visitors glorious lakeside mansions since 1938, when they were in their heyday of attracting wealthy snowbirds from the North. Three of Winter Park's seven cypress-lined lakes, which are connected by thrillingly narrow, hand-dug canals, are explored in a 1-hour, 12-mile tour narrated by salty old fellas. The lakes are flat and relaxing, with plenty of bird life, and your guide will pay particular attention to the works of James Gamble Rogers II, a virtuosic architect responsible for many of the area's finest homes. Among the high points is a glimpse of the modest condominium where Mamie Eisenhower spent her waning years and 250-year-old live oaks. You'll find this charmer 3 blocks east of the shops on Park Avenue. Bring sunscreen because the pontoons are exposed.

312 E. Morse Blvd., Winter Park. *𝄐* **407/644-4056.** www.scenicboattours.com. $12 adults, $6 kids 2–11, cash only. Hourly departures 10am–4pm daily.

Golf

Golf courses do great damage to an ecosystem as precarious as Central Florida's, but the sport is nonetheless a major draw. Some of the brightest names in golfing, including Tiger Woods, Annika Sorenstam, Ernie Els, and Nick Faldo, have called Orlando home, as does cable's Golf Channel (which isn't open to visitors). In January, Orlando is home to the annual PGA Merchandise Show (www.pgashow.com), held in January at the Convention Center.

Every self-respecting resort has a course or three (the new Four Seasons opened its course in September 2014), as do luxe condo developments. There are some 170 courses around town, and the competition has caused rates to plummet in recent years, although some still command around $150. The booking websites **TeeOff.com** and **GolfNow.com** both sell discounted tee times, driving rates down further. Some courses give priority to players who stay in their hotels, either through advantageous tee times, early reservations privileges, or cheaper fees. Prices can be steeper in high season (Jan–Apr), and they may be lowest in the fall and early winter. They usually sink to

5

MORE ORLANDO ATTRACTIONS

Outdoor Orlando

about half the day's rate for "twilight" tee times, which start around midafternoon. Club rentals cost $40 to $60. Reservations are all but required and most courses have a dress code and even an age minimum, so always ask.

DESTINATION COURSES

From pedigrees by well-known designers to clubhouses that operate more like spas, these fashionable courses are the theme parks of the fairway set. Tee time at these pricey greens fill quickly because the courses have national reputations. Count on paying about $10 per hole.

Arnold Palmer's Bay Hill Club & Lodge   Designer: Arnold Palmer, who owns it and also oversees the golf school. This guests-only course regularly receives the most accolades from experts. There's a full map of every hole on its website.

9000 Bay Hill Blvd., Orlando. ℂ **888/422-9445.** www.bayhill.com. 18 holes.

ChampionsGate Golf Resort   Designer: Greg Norman. Headquarters of the **David Leadbetter Golf Academy** (ℂ **888/633-5323;** www.davidleadbetter.com), this resort and handsome high-rise hotel is 10 minutes south of Disney.

1400 Masters Blvd., ChampionsGate. ℂ **407/787-4653.** www.championsgategolf.com. 36 holes.

Mystic Dunes Golf Club   Designer: Gary Koch. Located 2 miles south of Disney, it has steadily won "Golf Digest" praise. Elevation changes up to 80 feet over the course of play.

7600 Mystic Dunes Lane, Celebration. ℂ **407/787-5678.** www.mysticdunesgolf.com. 18 holes.

Reunion Resort & Club   Designers: Jack Nicklaus, Arnold Palmer, Tom Watson. Top designers and a golf school overseen by Annika Sorenstam—all a 10-minute drive south of Disney.

7593 Gathering Dr., Kissimmee. ℂ **407/396-3199.** www.reunionresort.com/golf. 54 holes.

The Ritz-Carlton Golf Club Orlando, Grande Lakes   Designer: Greg Norman. This **Golf Digest School** (ℂ **800/875-4347**) is taught by PGA and LPGA professionals. Family golf packages are often available.

4040 Central Florida Pkwy., Orlando. ℂ **407/393-4900.** www.grandelakes.com. 18 holes.

Shingle Creek Golf Club   Designer: David Harman. Local near the convention center, Shingle Creek is also home to a school overseen by Brad Brewer.

9939 Universal Blvd., Orlando. ℂ **866/996-9933** or 407/996-9933. www.shinglecreekgolf.com. 18 holes.

Villas of Grand Cypress   Designer: Jack Nicklaus. In 2012, this club, right next to Disney in Lake Buena Vista, was noted one Orlando's best golf resorts by the readers of "Condé Nast Traveler," who know about such things.

One North Jacaranda, Orlando. ℂ **407/239-1909.** www.grandcypress.com/golf. 45 holes.

Walt Disney World Golf Courses   Disney has been closing courses or parceling them to other resorts, but there are currently four left, including the Lake Buena Vista (once a PGA tour host), the recently refurbished Palm, and the Magnolia (the one with the sand bunker shaped like Mickey). Oak Trail (9 holes; $38) is the better choice for family outings. Greens fees include golf cart, when available, and kids under 18 get half off full tee time rates at the 18-hole courses. All courses opened with the resort in 1971, and if truth be told, their maintenance is spotty.

Walt Disney World. ℂ **407/938-4653.** www.disneyworldgolf.com. 63 holes.

MORE AFFORDABLE COURSES

Unlike the aforementioned courses, these don't have big marketing budgets and they don't always come attached to celebrity names, but they nevertheless are high-quality courses you can enjoy at sensible prices.

Celebration Golf Course   In the Disney-built town next door to the Disney-built world, English master designer Robert Trent Jones, Sr. and his son pocked their course with water hazards on 17 of its 18 holes.

701 Golf Park Dr., Celebration. ✆ **407/566-4653.** www.celebrationgolf.com. 18 holes.

Errol Estate Golf & Country Club   Golf for $22! The course, mostly through quiet Florida forest with several dogleg-shaped runs and a variety of elevations, is worth more. Its Lake Course is long but easy, while its Grove Course is known for being its trickiest because of dense trees and hills. The club is 20 miles north of Disney in Apopka.

1355 Errol Pkwy, Apopka. ✆ **407/886-5000.** www.errolestategcc.com/golf. 27 holes.

Hawk's Landing Golf Club   Because it's part of the Orlando World Center Marriott resort on World Center Drive by Disney, it crawls with convention-goers who keep prices high. Water is in play on 15 of the 18 holes, and the par-71 course carries a slope rating of 131.

8701 World Center Dr., Orlando. ✆ **800/567-2623.** www.golfhawkslanding.com. 18 holes.

Highlands Reserve Golf Club   This highly praised public course, with a fair mix of challenges and cakewalks, is a strong value, charging a top rate of $45, and its twilight rates kick in as early as noon. It's about 10 minutes southwest of Disney.

500 Highlands Reserve Blvd., Davenport. ✆ **863/420-1724.** www.highlandsreserve-golf.com. 18 holes.

Hunter's Creek Orlando   Former cattle-grazing land was transformed into a wavy course with a good gimmick: 13 lakes were created as water hazards for 13 of the holes. The fairways are long, so prepare to drive hard. It's near the airport.

14401 Sports Club Way, Orlando. ✆ **407/240-4653.** www.golfhunterscreek.com. 18 holes.

MetroWest Golf Club ★   This Marriott Golf–managed course is the work of Robert Trent Jones, Sr., famous for tight greens protected on both sides by sand traps, trees, or water. In late 2013, it was "redesigned to make the game faster and more enjoyable for everyday golfers," as its owners put it. Considering it's one of the city's most popular courses, let's hope that $1.5 million was well spent. It's less than 3 miles north of Universal Orlando.

2100 S. Hiawassee Rd., Orlando. ✆ **407/299-1099.** www.metrowestgolf.com. 18 holes.

Orange County National Golf Center and Lodge   At this wide-open complex (922 acres, unspoiled by houses—atypical around here), fees peak at $89 for 18 holes, depending on time of year and day of the week (Mon–Thurs are cheapest). Holes have five sets of tees, allowing you to choose a game that ranges between 7,300 yards and a little over 5,000. It's among the developments north of Walt Disney World.

16301 Phil Ritson Way, Winter Garden. ✆ **407/656-2626.** www.ocngolf.com. 45 holes.

Royal St. Cloud Golf Links   Aiming to recall Scotland's great links—there's even a stone bridge that looks like it was built during the days of William Wallace, not in 2001—this modest club, 25 miles east of Disney, charges $19–$22 for morning fees.

Its fairways are noted for being wide, well groomed, and firm, and planners promise you'll use "every club in the bag."

5310 Michigan Ave., St. Cloud. ⓒ **877/891-7010** or 407/891-7010. www.stcloudgolfclub.com. 27 holes.

Timacuan Golf and Country Club   There are five sets of tees, adapting this exceptionally well-groomed course from 7,000 to 5,000 yards, and unusually, designers were careful to leave its handsome Old Florida features (undulating fairways, Spanish moss, wetlands) mostly intact. Only 3 holes are riddled with water, which might make it easier for kids. The greens were renovated in 2013. Lake Mary is 10 miles north of downtown.

550 Timacuan Blvd., Lake Mary. ⓒ **407/321-0010.** www.golftimacuan.com. 18 holes.

Hot-Air Ballooning & Hang Gliding

Florida is well suited to hot-air ballooning for many of the same reasons that it's ideal for golf: flat, even topography and often placid morning weather. A trip involves a very early start—6am is common. You'll be finished with your hour-long ride by the time the theme parks get cranking.

Magic Sunrise Ballooning   More intimate than its supersized competition, with just 2 to 4 people in the basket with the pilot, this company, flying since 1987, greets landings with a champagne toast.

603.N. Garfield Ave., Deland. ⓒ **866/606-7433.** www.magicsunriseballooning.com. $215 per person for 2–4 people, $125 kids under 90 lbs., no kids 5 or under.

Orlando Balloon Rides   In business since 1983, its flagship balloon, launched as the world's largest in 2011, is 11 stories tall and its basket fits an incredible 24 people. It meets at a hotel near the main Disney entrance.

2900 Parkway Blvd., Kissimmee. ⓒ **800/634-4774.** www.orlandoballoonrides.com. $185 adults, $95 kids 10–15, $10 less online.

Wallaby Ranch   In flat Central Florida, where there are no mountains that don't contain roller coasters, hang gliders can't soar from cliffs. Instead, they're launched by ultralight "aerotugs," to an altitude of 2,000 feet.

1805 Deen Still Rd., Davenport. ⓒ **863/424-0070.** www.wallaby.com. Tandem flights $175.

SHOPPING

Orlando is a hotbed for outlet activity, partly because international visitors, with their often-superior currencies, are prone to buying frenzies. Like most modern outlet malls, not all of the items you find for sale here will have come from higher-priced "regular" stores; much of the stock has been specially manufactured for the outlet market (although "Consumer Reports" doesn't think the quality is substantially different from retail). You'll usually find prices between 30 and 50 percent off sales at retail stores, and after the holiday rush, when stores need to ready for the new lines, discounts go deeper. All the best ones are village-style outdoor malls and most stay open for longer-than-usual hours: Monday to Saturday from 10am to 11pm, Sunday 10am to 9pm.

Outlet Malls

Orlando Premium Outlets International Dr. ★★★ OUTLET MALL   The most dangerously tempting outlet in town is a stupendous 180-store (give or take) open-air village where it is very unlikely you will come away empty-handed. Many times of year, the place vibrates with 40-percent discounts, luring tourists by the hordes. Nearly every conceivable brand has a presence here, but the chief threats include Neiman Marcus Last Call—a clearance center that sells genuine department store castoffs from its namesake stores, Bergdorf Goodman, and the Horchow catalog—Saks Fifth Avenue Off 5th, Calphalon, Coach, Ann Taylor Factory Store, Puma, Nike Factory Store, Guess? Factory Store, Eddie Bauer Outlet, Kenneth Cole, Fossil, Reebok Outlet Store, Hugo Boss Factory Store, Calvin Klein, Brooks Brothers Factory Store, Kate Spade New York, Tumi, Victoria's Secret, and Juicy Couture. There's a Disney's Character Warehouse to undercut your souvenir bill. Weekdays are quietest, and parking is most ample around back. The website lists sales by store.

4951 International Dr., Orlando. ℭ **407/352-9600**. www.premiumoutlets.com.

Orlando Premium Outlets Vineland Ave ★★ OUTLET MALL   Being just a mile east of Disney property has its perks—its owners tout it as the most productive outlet center in America, with sales exceeding $1,000 per square foot. That's why at press time, it was about to cut the ribbon on a 110,000-square-foot expansion of a property that already had 550,000 square feet and 150 stores. Among the goods: Armani Outlet, Banana Republic Factory Store, Barney's New York Outlet, Gymboree, and Burberry. One popular shop, because it's so close to the Mouse House, is Disney's Character Premiere, for cast-off official theme park souvenirs. Steel yourself during the weekend; the competition for parking approaches Olympian difficulty. It's 10 minutes from Downtown Disney; the turnoff is just south of I-4's exit 68 on S.R. 535/Apopka Vineland, by Bahama Breeze. The I-Ride Trolley (p. 230) touches down here ostensibly every 20 minutes.

8200 Vineland Ave., Orlando. ℭ **407/238-7787**. www.premiumoutlets.com.

Lake Buena Vista Factory Stores ★ OUTLET MALL   The third-best outlet shopping in town is a strip mall–style collection of about 50 stores, not all of which are owned by famous brands. The offerings here, about 2 miles south of the Downtown Disney gate, are not as shimmering as those at its two rival outlet malls, but they're decent, especially for kids. There are enough names you know (including Tommy Hilfiger Kids, Carter's for Kids, Old Navy Outlet, OshKosh B'Gosh, and Aéropostale) to warrant a quick trip. The Disney Character Outlet has some bargains (half-price mugs, shirts, toys, and some souvenirs dated from a few years ago), and there's a Travelex office for currency exchange. The mall provides a free daily shuttle to and from major hotels around Disney and I-Drive; they leave between 9am and 2:50pm and return in four batches from 12:55 to 7pm (6pm on Sun).

15657 S. Apopka Vineland Rd. (S.R. 535), Orlando. ℭ **407/238-9301**. www.lbvfs.com. Mon–Sat 10am–9 and Sun 10am–7pm.

Downtown Disney

Downtown Disney ★★, Walt Disney World's main free area for restaurants and shopping, ambles along the shore of Village Lake a few miles east of Epcot, in a traffic-clogged zone on the eastern edge of park property. At the easternmost section, the Marketplace section is dominated by stores selling every variety of Disney-themed merchandise you can imagine.

As of this writing, Downtown Disney is receiving a drastic overhaul. By 2016, it will be known as Disney Springs, with more corporate restaurants and shops added and the old, Disney-created Pleasure Island concept extracted like a wart. Downtown Disney/Disney Springs will remain a place to grab dinner (alas, no cheaper than elsewhere in the World), buy souvenirs, and maybe bowl or catch a Cirque du Soleil show. Parking is free but maddening, although a new structure to open in 2015 will hopefully assuage that. In the meantime, hunting for a space here will be a less-than-magical experience that sometimes requires parking across the street, so consider taking the free Disney bus or ferry from elsewhere in the resort.

The district has three zones; because of the size, it's helpful to know which one you're heading for because the walk between them can be up to 15 minutes. The busiest and easternmost area is called the Marketplace (it's nearest to the DTS bus stop), and it's for shops and restaurants. The westernmost zone is the West Side, and it leans toward nightlife and entertainment, with a Cirque du Soleil show, **Splitsville Luxury Lanes** bowling, and a 24-screen cinema (p. 94). Between them is the focus of the Disney Springs redevelopment, and it will eventually be divided into The Town Center and The Landing.

Shops at the **Marketplace** (℡ **407/939-3463**) are almost pure Mouse, and nearly all of them sell candy, too. Stores are themed for maximum souvenir sales, including one for toys and games **(Once Upon a Toy),** one for Christmas and holiday decorations **(Disney's Days of Christmas),** one for high-end collectibles **(the Art of Disney),** one for kitchen tools **(Mickey's Pantry),** one for urban wear **(Tren-D),** one for stationery and albums **(Disney's Wonderful World of Memories),** and **Disney's Pin Traders,** a hub for collectors of the park's badges where you can also buy MagicBands. Don't bother looking for a bookstore to browse the range of titles pertaining to Walt and what he accomplished. Disney closed its bookstores.

The Marketplace's tent-pole is the big kahuna of Disney merch: **World of Disney,** the largest souvenir department store in the resort, crowned by a giant Stitch burping water onto passersby. It's a rambling cathedral-roofed barn stocked from rug to rafter with every conceivable Disney-branded item—a Villains room, a room for men, one for candy, one for the latest branding craze, and so on. You'll find stuff here you won't find at other Disney stores here or at home. Yet sometimes, the same toys and DVDs cost $7 at box stores while Walt Disney World wants $20 or more. Before purchasing, always ask if any item you want is a "park exclusive"—that means it's only available here. Otherwise, you could do a lot better if you got it back home. Despite its status as the chief Mouse mart, World of Disney still may not have what you want. That's because it's the only store that offers annual passholders a discount, which means the most obsessed fans clean the shelves here first. It also may not carry items that might be sold at another store at the Marketplace (tree ornaments, for example, or toys). Disney's merchandise distribution is bureaucratic; shopkeepers virtually beg superiors for restocking, and even then it can take weeks.

Very few stores sell non-Disney plunder. **Ghirardelli Soda Fountain & Chocolate Shop** is one of the few non–San Francisco locations run by the chocolate-making stalwart. It has a pricey sundae shop and a boutique where $1/12$-oz. samples are freely dispensed. Kids can't be separated from the **Lego Imagination Center** store (still here despite the fact the toymaker now brands a competing park, p. 137), where children can play with kits for free, or **Build-A-Dino** which does for reptiles what Build-a-Bear does for teddies. **Basin** sells bath products for those teeny hotel room tubs. The resort's shopping list has seismically dumbed down since the 1970s, when fascinating international goods were imported for the area then called the Lake Buena Vista Shopping Village.

Bibbidi Bobbidi Boutique ★★★ SALON   Little girls bask in the star treatment as they are lavished with glittery, pink makeovers as princesses for $55 (Coach package with hair and a sash; add nails for $5) to more than $240 (gown, wand, photos), overseen by a kindly "Fairy Godmother-in-Training." *Warning:* The dresses are hot and scratchy, so bring a change of clothes if the sun is strong. Boys are steered to the Pirates League in Adventureland, where similar gender roles are ascribed. There's also a salon in the Magic Kingdom in the Castle, but you'll need a park ticket for that and slots are scarcer.

World of Disney, Marketplace. ℡ **407/939-7895.** www.disneyworld.com/style. Daily 9am–7pm. Minimum age 3. Reservations required.

The Pin Culture

One of the most special souvenir traditions on Disney turf is the collection of little enamel and cloisonné pins featuring every known character, ride, movie, and promotional event. When the Haunted Mansion was refurbished, pins were made that contained tiny snippets of Madame Leota's original crystal ball. Sometimes it seems it's easier to get your hands on a pin than it is to find a bottle of water—there's even a pavilion that sells nothing but pins at Downtown Disney. They are usually worn on lanyards, and when cast members clock in for their shifts, they replenish their pin supply at a special window in the backstage area—a dozen to a lanyard at all times. The rule is that if a cast member is wearing almost any pin you want (barring ones commemorating employment milestones), you're allowed to ask them to trade it for one of your own and they're not allowed to refuse if the pin is legit. Universal sells a fair supply, too, but the craze is fiercest at Disney, where the backings are shaped, of course, like a mouse head.

Other Interesting Stores

If you feel moved to learn more about Florida history, the book selection isn't massive. The bookstore at the **Regional History Center** (☏ **407/836-8594;** p. 147), however, is a good start. You'll find a **Barnes & Noble** (Venezia Plaza, 7900 W. Sand Lake Rd., Orlando; ☏ **407/345-0900;** daily 9am–11pm) among the terrific restaurants of Sand Lake Road west of I-4 and at the Florida Mall (8358 S. Orange Blossom Trail, Orlando; ☏ **407/856-7200;** Sun–Thurs 9am–8pm, Fri–Sat 9am–11pm).

Artegon Orlando ★ MALL   This ongoing real estate tragedy at the top end of I-Drive is struggling to wake from a nightmare that began when it opened in 2001. In 2014, $70 million was sunk into reinventing a bleakly undertenanted mall as a space for a farmer's market, beer hall, and bazaar for artisans making one-of-a-kind stuff. No matter what happens with that scheme, the anchor stores remain interesting: The beloved **Ron Jon Surf Shop** out of Cocoa Beach; a **Sheplers Western Wear** for honing that proto-American look; a **Toby Keith** bar and grill for faking an attitude; and the camping-and-fishing megastore **Bass Pro Shops Outdoor World** so gargantuan it must be seen to be believed. For minor entertainment, there's the **Putting Edge** glow-in-the-dark minigolf course (p. 150).

5250 International Dr., Orlando. ☏ **407/351-7718.** www.artegoneorlando.com. Mon–Sat 10am–9pm, Sun 11am–7pm.

Eli's Orange World ★★ SHOP   Agra has the Taj Mahal and Sydney has its opera house—Orlando has a 60-foot-tall orange. Back when most of this land was orange groves, Florida roadsides were full of this kind of souvenir catch-all, stacked high with oranges and grapefruits in their red mesh bags, but the citrus industry cashed out for McMansions. Fruit changes by the season: Fall is for navel and ambersweet oranges, January sees honeybell tangelos, and February through May sees a procession of oranges, honey tangerines, and Valencia oranges; Indian River grapefruit is available year-round. A timeshare hawker tries to pitch to marks, and shelves also teeter with the sort of corny Florida souvenirs that time forgot, including shellacked alligator heads and local jellies. Sure, there are *lots* of schlocky, fluorescent-lit barns selling junky souvenirs on U.S. 192 and I-Drive—but this is *landmark* schlock.

5395 W. U.S. Hwy. 192, Kissimmee. ☏ **800/531-3182** or 407/239-6031. www.orangeworld192.com. Daily 8am–9:40pm.

Theme Park Connection ★★ SHOP   There's no other shop like it in the world. Here, Disney liquidates stuff it can't use anymore, including costumes, props, retired souvenirs, signs, and even entire ride vehicles. Disney nuts are a rabid bunch, so the businesslike staff can hold out for top dollar, but this merchandise is unquestionably fascinating and one-of-a-kind. It's a few miles east of I-4 off Sand Lake Road.

2160 Premier Row, Orlando. ✆ **407/284-1934.** www.themeparkconnection.com. Mon–Fri 10am–5pm, Sat 10am–3pm.

CRUISES FROM PORT CANAVERAL

Cruise lines depart from Port Canaveral (www.portcanaveral.com), an hour east of Orlando, so it's easy to combine a cruise of a few days with the theme parks. Parking costs about $20 a day or $120 a week, and there's nothing to do at the port.

As usual, you won't find many discounts from Disney, although MouseSavers.com tells which departures are going cheap. Quotes from specialty agents are often hundreds lower than those the lines themselves offer, and prices of $100 a night or less can be had if you book through a specialist. Check **Cruise Brothers** (✆ **800/827-7779;** www.cruisebrothers.com), **Cruises Only** (✆ **800/278-4737;** www.cruisesonly.com), and **Online Vacation Center** (✆ **800/780-9002;** www.onlinevacationcenter.com). Don't quit before you consult a terrific site called **Cruise Compete** (www.cruisecompete.com), on which multiple cruise sellers jockey for your business by offering low bids.

Carnival Cruise Lines ★ CRUISE   Considered a low-rent line, it's noisy and atwitter with neon, like the inside of a pinball machine. Think "Real Housewives of the Atlantic Ocean." Carnival is popular with families, teens especially like it, and there are few pretensions. Each ship has a twisting water slide that has also become a line signature. Carnival sails the *Sensation* and the *Liberty* on 3- and 4-night Bahamas runs, and the *Liberty* does weeks to San Juan. In 2015, the *Sunshine* joins the ranks.

✆ **800/764-7419.** www.carnival.com.

Disney Cruise Line ★★★ CRUISE   These high-quality, casino-free ships, the newest of the port's fleet, include character appearances, fireworks at sea, and top-drawer entertainment. The hallmark is the kids' program, and in a brilliant touch, waiters follow you no matter the restaurant you're in (one restaurant, by the way, changes from black and white to full color as you dine). The *Magic,* DCL's original ship, and the *Dream* and *Fantasy,* the line's newer and larger additions, sail for weeklong Eastern and Western Caribbean trips and 3- and 4-night Bahamas jaunts. Disney packages trips with theme park stays and provides seamless transitions between the two, although because it's a Disney package it won't give you the best deal on the Walt Disney World portion.

✆ **800/393-2784.** www.disneycruise.com.

Royal Caribbean International ★ CRUISE   It's the line for young couples and teens, with active diversions such as rock-climbing walls. It hits the sweet spot between the gaudy tackiness of Carnival and the twee branding of Disney. The principal ship is *Enchantment of the Seas,* a Vision-class ship from 1996 (no ice rink, no sheet wave machine) that's among the line's most manageable, at 2,664 passengers. It offers 3- and 4-night Bahamas runs. *Freedom of the Seas* (2006) does weeklong trips to the Western Caribbean, and *Explorer of the Seas* joins in the deep winter months.

✆ **866/562-7625.** www.royalcaribbean.com.

DINING AROUND TOWN

You don't need a guidebook to decide if you want to eat at a chain restaurant—and Orlando is crawling with those, in plain view, everywhere. But you might use help locating family-run small businesses or fledgling brands that aren't backed by multi-million-dollar ad campaigns. These are the worthy discoveries you might not otherwise have noticed among the clamor of plastic and neon signage.

That's not to say corporate food can't have local provenance. In Orlando, even supersized brands have a pedigree: Darden, which owns Olive Garden and LongHorn Steakhouse, is based here, and so is Hard Rock Cafe. But for those, you already know what you're going to get. Frommer's wants to show you more original flavors.

Pretty much every restaurant is open for lunch and dinner. Don't expect places to accept checks—credit cards are Orlando's cash. Also, this is a town where it bears asking for discounts. Turnover is high, so everybody's angling for business.

In addition to our recommendations, check out Scott Joseph's Orlando Restaurant Guide (**www.scottjosephorlando.com**) by longtime food critic Scott Joseph, which describes high-quality places to eat in the "real" Orlando north of the tourist zone. In September, dozens of high-quality area restaurants band together for **Orlando Magical Dining Month** (www.orlandomagicaldining.com), when three-course (appetizer, entree, dessert) prix-fixe dinners cost $33.

Prices are classified based on the price range for a main course at dinner:

- Inexpensive: $10 or less
- Moderate: $11 to $16
- Expensive: $17 or over

OUTSIDE THE DISNEY PARKS

These are the restaurants on resort property but not inside a ticketed park. For places inside the theme parks, plus info on the Disney Dining Plan, see chapter 3. Some of Disney's best restaurants are in its hotels, accessible to anyone. Well, not anyone: folks with deep pockets, soon to be empty. Disney's most affordable hotels don't offer much beyond food courts, but its most expensive hotels support a fine restaurant or two.

Reservations are a necessity for Disney's table-service restaurants. Walk-ins are accepted, but you may be turned away. Slots open 180 days in advance, and families throw themselves into it early as if they're Panzer units invading Poland. Obnoxiously, Disney slaps you with a $10 cancellation fee if you fail to show up for your reservation, and taking your credit

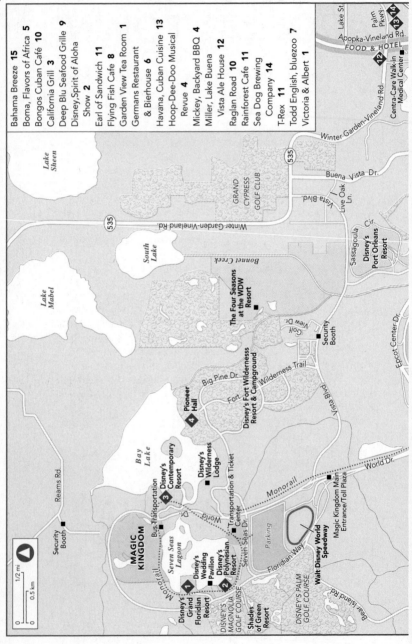

Bahama Breeze **15**
Boma, Flavors of Africa **5**
Bongos Cuban Café **10**
California Grill **3**
Deep Blu Seafood Grille **9**
Disney,Spirit of Aloha Show **2**
Earl of Sandwich **11**
Flying Fish Cafe **8**
Garden View Tea Room **1**
Germans Restaurant & Bierhouse **6**
Havana, Cuban Cuisine **13**
Hoop-Dee-Doo Musical Revue **4**
Mickey, Backyard BBQ **4**
Miller, Lake Buena Vista Ale House **12**
Raglan Road **10**
Rainforest Cafe **11**
Sea Dog Brewing Company **14**
T-Rex **11**
Todd English, bluezoo **7**
Victoria & Albert **1**

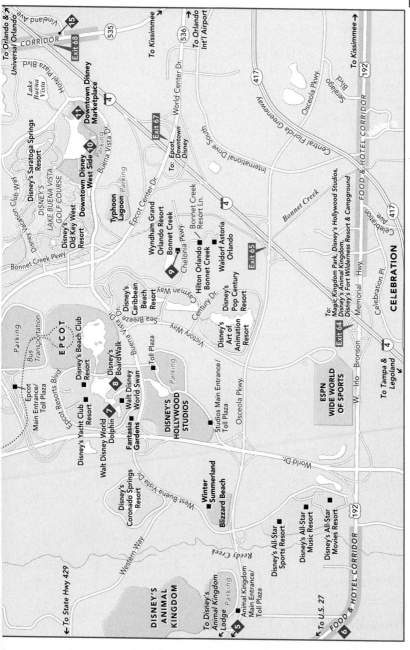

card details for that purpose can turn a simple booking into an 8-minute dialogue. All Disney's restaurants have the same contact details ((C) **407/939-3463** [DINE]; http://disneyworld.disney.go.com/dining). You can sometimes get around that by making a reservation using its app. Parking is free with a reservation. Reservationists have schedules of other resort events (such as fireworks times) and will help you plan around them.

The nicest restaurants within Disney's hotels generally serve from 5 to 10pm, as it's assumed patrons will eat lunch in the parks. Some are more special than others, and many more have no point of view or care mostly about the convention crowd, so focus your booking attentions on these (all unfortunately in the Expensive category).

EXPENSIVE

Boma—Flavors of Africa ★★★ AFRICAN   Make a reservation here and you get a big bonus: a fine excuse to visit Disney's Animal Kingdom Lodge and pay a visit to the animals in its backyard paddocks, floodlit after dark—think of the high price as an admission fee for that. Dinner is a good time, too: A 60-item buffet menu, served in a dramatically vaulted dining room of thatching and bamboo, is not all African. It runs the gamut from roast chicken and beef to African-themed delights such as watermelon rind salad, curried coconut seafood stew, and *bobotie* (a moussaka-like pie of ground beef from South Africa). There's an atmospheric wood fire, with plenty of chefs on hand to answer questions and plenty of options for less adventurous tongues.

Disney's Animal Kingdom Lodge, 2901 Osceola Pkwy., Bay Lake. (C) **407/939-3463.** www.disneyworld.com. Adults $39–$43, kids $18–$20. Daily 7–11am and 4:30–9:30pm.

California Grill ★★★ AMERICAN   For 1 blowout night with a view, the best choice is this just-renovated and much-beloved space on the 15th floor of the mod Contemporary Resort. The wine list is extensive (250 by the bottle, 80 by the glass, 10 types of sake), and the fusion-style menu, helmed by Chef Brian Piasecki, is bright and seasonal—the 24-hour braised short rib with truffle-whipped potatoes goes for richness, and sushi is a popular sideline here. Book as soon as you can—the maximum is 180 days before—and get a window seat for the fireworks. The music for the show is even piped in to the outdoor viewing platforms, which are practically on top of Tomorrowland. After dark, Cinderella Castle is lit by a shifting palette of indigos and emeralds. Plus, a dinner here is a fantastic excuse to have a stroll through the atrium of Disney World's most iconic hotel.

Disney's Contemporary Resort, 4600 N. World Dr., Lake Buena Vista. (C) **407/939-3463.** www.disneyworld.com. Main courses $34–47.

Deep Blu Seafood Grille ★★ SEAFOOD   A 2014 chef change hasn't done much to diminish this spacious resort restaurant's mandate for gourmet seafood-based creations. It repeatedly makes the list of the city's best choices for dishes such as crab mac and cheese, calamari "fries," and some divinely soft crab cakes that are plated as savory fall-apart patties, bucking most kitchens' tendency to over-fry. You can pair wines with every course, or try one of the house cocktails, most of which advance a tropical theme by being based on one fruit or another. You'll find Deep Blu in the massive Wyndham development close to Downtown Disney/Disney Springs on the south side of Disney property; turn left at the second Wyndham-marked entrance.

Wyndham Grand Orlando Bonnet Creek, 14651 Chelonia Parkway, Orlando. (C) **407/390-2420.** www.deepbluorlando.com. Mains $29–$45. Daily 5:30pm–10pm.

Garden View Tea Room ★★ HIGH TEA   The pseudo-Victorian space with a garden gazebo feel delights little girls with its range of high teas—tea cozies, china, and all. The most extravagant option, the My Disney Girl's Perfectly Princess Tea Party, costs $250 for an adult and child together and includes a visit from Aurora.

Disney's Grand Floridian Resort & Spa, 4401 Floridian Way, Lake Buena Vista. ℂ **407/939-3463.** www.disneyworld.com. High tea without characters $14–$38. Daily 2–4:30pm.

Jiko—The Cooking Place ★★ AFRICAN   The a la carte fine dining room across the hall from Boma is considered by many to be one of the resort's most romantic spot. It serves entrees that are very good, too (plus flatbreads—Disney's top restaurants have a love affair with flatbreads), but they often cost what the entire banquet does at Boma. The food coming from the open kitchen is pan-African, but waiters are sometimes too eager to adulterate to pander to American palates. That said, there are some delicious twists such as sweet tamarind butter for the bread, frisky amuse-bouches (prosciutto-wrapped pineapple, cucumber sorbet), and crispy beef *bobotie* spring rolls. Animal Kingdom Lodge also has one of the largest lists of South African wines in all of North America. When you're here, you also get to see the animals in the view area at the Lodge.

Disney's Animal Kingdom Lodge, 2901 Osceola Pkwy., Bay Lake. ℂ **407/939-3463.** www.disney world.com. Main courses $29–$46. Daily 7–11am and 4:30–9:30pm.

Todd English's bluezoo ★ SEAFOOD   A rare Disney restaurant overseen by a culinary celebrity; in this case, Todd English, known for rich flavors. Eaten among witty colored-glass baubles that suggest being underwater, the menu changes but the focus is fresh fish. The nightly herb-rubbed "dancing fish" is grilled on a spinning skewer (watch them spin alongside the raw bar); the light clam chowder comes infused with bacon; and the 2-pound "Cantonese" lobster is painted in a sticky soy glaze that must be shared. The Lounge serves a bar menu.

Walt Disney World Dolphin Hotel, 1500 Epcot Resorts Blvd., Lake Buena Vista. ℂ **407/934-1111.** www.swananddolphin.com/bluezoo. Mains $30–$43. Daily 5–11pm.

Victoria & Albert's ★★★ FRENCH   Disney's flagship restaurant is the destination for honeymoons, anniversaries, proposals, and gourmands. The company puts much stock in Chef Scott Hunnel, a multiple James Beard nominee who sources ingredients personally and also oversees the top-tier restaurants on Disney Cruise Line. Praised as the only AAA five-diamond restaurant in Central Florida, a citation it has earned since 2000, the 65-seater lays on its indulgent seven-course menu (amuse-bouches, osetra caviar, Iwate Japanese beef with oxtail jus, pheasant consommé) presented to you under cloches like a parade of debutantes. It's so theatrical you just have to swoon. It's like the Very Fancy Restaurant where a character might take a date on a sitcom, which adds to the theater. The resort's most exclusive reservation is here: the four-table Queen Victoria's room, where a private 10-course meal is served behind closed doors for $210 per person before wine. It sells out. Reserve 180 days ahead.

Disney's Grand Floridian Resort & Spa, 4401 Floridian Way. Lake Buena Vista. ℂ **407/939-3463.** www.victoria-alberts.com.com. Prix-fixe from $135, wine pairings from $65. 10-course Chef's Table prix-fixe from $210, wine pairings from $105. 2 nightly seatings, 1 for Chef's Table and Queen Victoria's room. Jacket required for men (loaners available), no children under 10 permitted.

Downtown Disney/Disney Springs

In these restaurants, none of the food is as spectacular as the interior decor, and unless you come at lunch when prices drop by a third, you will pay something to the tune of $15 for a burger. Welcome to Disney!

Downtown Disney charges extreme prices ($30 a plate) but doesn't give your money back to you in skilled cuisine. Although none serve foul food, most of the restaurants coast along by sponging from steady foot traffic. That means you can count these places out, although you will be pressured not to: **Fulton's Crab House,** in a mock riverboat berthed solidly in concrete; the fair-to-average **Portobello Country Italian Trattoria,** with an Italian theme; and the Asian-fusion **Wolfgang Puck Grand Café** (it also has a walk-up window for quick bites, and there's also an "LA Bistro" version at Universal's CityWalk), a tired **Planet Hollywood** in need of euthanasia, and **House of Blues. Ghirardelli Ice Cream and Chocolate Shop** is a rare offshoot of the San Francisco treasure, but it only does desserts (although its candy shop always gives away tablet-size free samples).

EXPENSIVE

Bongos Cuban Café ★ CUBAN   This place proudly reminds you it was co-founded by Gloria and Emilio Estefan, the Cuban-born power couple of Latin music, and that boast is a portent that the focus will be on music and not on food. The dishes (ceviche, plantains, yucca, and lots of grilled or lightly fried fish and meats) are generally unsuccessful, and such inattention to signature Cuban dishes is abrasive when you've paid this much, but there's some festivity in the hypersugary decor, which makes the building look like it's been overtaken by giant, washed-out pineapples, palms, and drums. At night, there's often a (loud) live band, and the upstairs patio is an appealing place to hang out with a rum drink, earning a gentle recommendation.

Downtown Disney West Side. ℂ **407/828-0999.** www.bongoscubancafe.com. No cover. Mains $15–$30. Free self-parking.

Raglan Road ★★★ IRISH   This is the only restaurant at Downtown Disney that wins acclaim from food critics in the wider area. Of all the chefs working Downtown Disney, contemporary Irish chef Kevin Dundon has the most imagination and the most consistent standards. Here, Irish staples are turned into sprightly new visions, including whiskey marmalade-glazed steak with basil oil, beef stew infused with Guinness, and good old fish and chips. Although the massive dining area is styled after an Irish pub, it's 20 times noisier. There's free live music most nights, and often step dancers. If you only want fish and chips, get it on the south side of the building for about $8 less at the counter-service **Cookes of Dublin** ★, run by the same people.

Downtown Disney. ℂ**407/938-0300.** www.raglanroad.com. Mains $17–$29. Daily 11am–1:30am.

Rainforest Cafe ★ AMERICAN   Another over-the-top themed doozy where families dine in a faux jungle with lions, pythons, elephants, and other robotic animals that periodically spring to life, interrupting dinner and stoking wild behavior in small children. Think of it as the Jungle Cruise with napkins. Like so much in Orlando, it has no culinary specialization, instead opting to be all things to all eaters: burgers, salads, pizzas, capped by a gift shop with stuffed animals. Because Rainforest exists across America, pick T-Rex. There's a second location at the front gate of Animal Kingdom.

Downtown Disney Marketplace. ℂ **407/827-8500.** www.rainforestcafe.com. Mains $19–$31. 11am–10:35pm.

T-Rex ★ AMERICAN   Nothing is a more surefire theme park-style diversion than life-size robotic dinosaurs planted amongst the tables. Every so often, the ceiling (at least, the one outside the simulated ice cave) is lit with a projected meteor shower and, for your amusement, the destruction of all prehistoric life forms is briefly simulated. Pass the ketchup. It's so silly it seems like a joke in a movie. You can probably predict the fare: Bronto Burgers, Artifact Stack fried onion rings, and to end it all, the $17 Chocolate Extinction, a fudge cake sundae for two or more people.

Downtown Disney West Side. (✆ **407/828-8739.** www.trexcafe.com. Mains $18–$33. Daily 11am–11pm.

INEXPENSIVE

Earl of Sandwich ★★ SANDWICHES   The most affordable option at the Downtown Disney Marketplace area, minus McDonald's, is located to its extreme east: a branch of a 27-location franchise based in Orlando. Here, you can easily grab a made-to-order 6-inch sandwich, made with fresh ingredients and toasted on the spot. There are more than a dozen hot and cold selections, from roast beef to turkey with stuffing, plus nine salads, and everything's six bucks. It's hard to believe such good prices exist in Disney World. Then again, Disney doesn't run it.

Downtown Disney Marketplace. (✆ **407/938-1762.** www.earlofsandwichusa.com. Sandwiches $6. Daily 8:30am–11pm.

Disney's BoardWalk

BoardWalk is a lakefront promenade that's merely notionally themed to an old-time pier. You'll find a few midway games, occasional buskers, and ice cream and margarita stores—not much, and most of its menus pander with the standard burgers-and-such variety. The **ESPN Club** serves food as an excuse to bask in the blare of countless TV airing live sports while **Big River Grille & Brewing Works** serves food because you need something to wash down with its microbrews (and happily, doesn't accept reservations, so if other places are jammed, try there). The newest restaurant here is **Trattoria al Forno,** a place for pastas, hand-made mozzarella, and Neopolitan-style pizzas. Postmeal strolls, as ferries serenely cross water and Epcot twitters in the near distance, are pretty, and they're reason enough to come. You can park at the BoardWalk Inn and get your parking validated or you can walk there via Epcot's World Showcase, 10 minutes away, where, it must be said, the dining is much more fun.

Rent-a-Poppins

Parents: I know you came to Orlando to spend some time with your family, but I also understand that you might need to get away from some of them for a few hours. If you're staying in a luxury resort hotel, the management may offer some kind of paid babysitting or supervised kids' club service. If not, there is always **Kid's Nite Out** (✆ **800/696-8105;** www. kidsniteout.com; $16/hr. for the first child, $2.50 for each additional child). It is insured, bonded, and licensed, and it would appreciate a few days' warning for reservations for in-room sitting. Expect $10 to $12 in transportation fees. Five Disney resorts including the Polynesian and Animal Kingdom Lodge operate supervised clubs (✆ **407/939-3463;** call at least 2 days ahead) for potty-trained kids ages 3 to 12 starting at 4:30pm and ending at midnight. These cost $12 per hour per child, which includes a simple meal during dinnertime and a 10pm snack, and are sometimes open to people who aren't staying in a Disney hotel. The new Four Seasons resort offers free babysitting as part of its hefty nightly tariff. Although your kids would love it, I do *not* recommend depositing your offspring at the gates of the Magic Kingdom and speeding off rather than paying a babysitter, as actress Tracy Pollan's father once did to her.

EXPENSIVE

Flying Fish Cafe ★★★ SEAFOOD   To say this is one of the most underrated restaurants on Disney property is not to say it's a knockout. But its kitchen is careful to source truly fresh food and deliver a good time in a theme-parky environment. Impeccably prepared seafood (grouper, mahimahi) is its principal domain, but it also does plenty of land-based meats. You can choose between a table or a stool facing the invigorating fire in its open kitchen. The entree of note is the memorable potato-wrapped red snapper, which should tell you about the carbohydrated concessions a fresh-ingredient kitchen must make to keep the booths packed in Orlando.

Disney's BoardWalk. ℂ **407/939-5100.** www.disneyworld.com. Mains $28–$39. Daily 5:30–10pm.

Universal Orlando

Although **Mythos** (p. 125) and **Lombard's** (p. 114) are the only table-service restaurants inside the Universal theme parks worth a detour, there are worthwhile dining options in Universal Orlando that are outside the parks—ones for which you don't need a park ticket. Universal's hotels have upscale restaurants, while the CityWalk outdoor party mall, located between the resort's main parking garage and the entrances to the parks, attracts locals with no intention of proceeding to the thrill rides.

After dark, CityWalk has windows serving stuff like Fat Tuesday booze slurpees, plus the slowest Burger King on the crust of the earth. Its table-service restaurants are loud, cavernous, family-friendly, often with faux antiques bolted to the walls. You'll want to arrive before 9pm, because some of these places charge covers after then. Everything closes by 2am. (For CityWalk's nightlife, see p. 157.)

If you intend to linger at CityWalk for the nightlife (parking is $5 from 6–10pm and free after 10pm unless there's a big event on), there are a few package deals that combine a meal, including a beverage, with a movie and entry to the clubs. The **Meal and Movie Deal** (ℂ **407/224-2691**; $22) pairs dinner at one of seven restaurants with a movie at CityWalk's ABC multiplex, and can be purchased at the CityWalk Guest Services window. Conveniently, you don't have to enjoy both meal and movie on the same day.

Entrees cost more than they would outside Universal; they're mostly priced in the teens, with burgers sliding in around $13. So although none of these places are at the top of my list for a value meal, and only one of them is a true gourmet experience, you may find yourself patronizing one after a long day at the parks. Call ℂ **407/224-3663** for more information, unless there's a different number listed. You know what you're gonna get at **Bubba Gump Shrimp Company, Hot Dog Hall of Fame,** the Neopolitan-style **Red Over Pizza Bakery,** or **NASCAR Sports Grille,** but these are the more interesting choices. You may (but don't have to) make reservations online:

EXPENSIVE

Emeril's Orlando ★★ CREOLE   The highest standard of fare at CityWalk is a modern New Orleans menu with its heart in meats, with flavors typified by preparations such as gin and molasses brine (for its pork). The wine list could send you reeling even before you have a single sip—the back wall of this loftlike space displays a 10,000-bottle aboveground cellar built to dazzle. Happily, it offers a kids' menu (including a petite filet mignon), which makes adult pleasures more possible.

CityWalk. ℂ **407/224-2424.** www.emerils.com. Reservations suggested. Mains $11–$26, 3-course lunch menu $22. Daily 11:30am–3pm; Sun–Thurs 5–10pm; Fri–Sat 5–10:30pm. Free valet parking for lunch.

Emeril's Tchoup Chop ★★★ PACIFIC RIM   Should Emeril's be full, Lagasse oversees a second restaurant at the Royal Pacific Resort, a few hundred yards away, that's actually more compelling. Pronounced "chop chop," it serves ostensibly Hawaiian creations, meaning there's a touch of Asian in the meaty offerings including garlic grilled tiger shrimp and banana leaf-wrapped pork loin shoulder. The daffy colors of the high-ceilinged dining room, exuberantly embellished by David Rockwell in rich orange and cobalt glass, are more a nod to Orlando's boundless showmanship than a portent of a saccharine meal.

Royal Pacific Resort, 6300 Hollywood Way, Orlando. ℭ **407/503-2467.** www.emerils.com. Mains $18–$39. Daily 11:30am–2:30pm; Sun–Thurs 5–10pm; Fri–Sat 5–11pm.

MODERATE

Antojitos Authentic Mexican Food ★★★ MEXICAN   Banish beany burritos and trashy Tex-Mex at this peppy new addition to CityWalk that conjures up the flair of Mexican street food. Downstairs is casual (food like tempura shrimp BBQ tacos with mango salsa, adobo chicken chimichangas), upstairs a little more refined (dry-aged coffee-crusted ribeye, slow-roasted pork loin).

CityWalk. ℭ **407/224-2106.** www.universalorlando.com. Downstairs mains $12–$20, upstairs mains $14–$29. Food daily 11am–midnight.

Bob Marley—A Tribute to Freedom ★ CARIBBEAN   Jamaican food (spicy jerk chicken, fried plantains, even oxtail) done passably, but stick around for when it turns into a reggae nightclub with a dance floor.

CityWalk. ℭ **407/224-3613.** www.universalorlando.com. Mains $10–$17. $7 cover after 9pm. Food served Sun–Thurs 4pm–10pm, Fri–Sat 4pm–11pm, bar open to 2am.

The Cowfish ★★ BURGERS/SUSHI   Sushi made with burger components, burgers made like sushi. This offbeat concept, rendered with a cocktail bar and some interactive screens to pass the time, opened in 2014. It actually works, and it's fun.

CityWalk. ℭ **407/224-3613.** www.thecowfish.com. Mains in the mid-teens. Daily 11am–midnight.

Hard Rock Cafe ★★ AMERICAN   Hey, look! It's . . . well . . . a Hard Rock Cafe. Granted, the world's largest (600 seats) and possibly the loudest. You've probably already sampled the Hard Rock shtick on offer at 163 of them: a casual tavern done up with music memorabilia (like Madonna's infamous "Like a Virgin" wedding dress and BOY TOY belt buckle, in the gift shop) and out back, a slab from the Berlin Wall. Fun fact: The company's headquarters is just 3½ miles north of here.

CityWalk. ℭ **407/351-7625.** www.hardrock.com. Mains $13–$32. Daily 11am–midnight.

Jimmy Buffett's Margaritaville ★★ AMERICAN   Because it's nearest to Islands of Adventure at the park's closing time, it gets jammed with park-goers clamoring for margaritas and grub like Cheeseburgers in Paradise. In late afternoon, there may be a strummer on the "Porch of Indecision," and after 10pm, the indoor area morphs into a three-bar club with a band and that $7 CityWalk cover. Across the way, under a 60-foot Albatross plane, the *Hemisphere Dancer,* is the **Lone Palm Airport** for margaritas and appetizers on the go.

CityWalk. ℭ **407/224-2155.** www.margaritavilleorlando.com. Mains $13–$25. $7 cover after 9pm. Daily 11:30am–2am.

NBA City ★ AMERICAN   The Hard Rock for basketball nuts, with a similarly wide-ranging burgers-and-pasta menu, except there are jerseys instead of Stratocasters on the walls. Turn kids loose in an interactive area to test their jumping and free-throw skills.

CityWalk. ℭ **407/363-5919.** www.nba.com/nbacity. Mains $11–$34. Sun–Thurs 11am–10:30pm; Fri–Sat 11am–11:30pm.

Pat O'Brien's ★★ SOUTHERN Like its bawdy Nawlins namesake, it does Cajun-style dishes such as shrimp gumbo, étouffée, and jambalaya, optionally served with a fat rum Hurricane cocktail in the hand. The potent drinks account for a clientele with fewer kids, but there is a kids' menu.

CityWalk. ✆ **407/224-3663.** www.patobriens.com. Mains $12–$18. $7 cover after 9pm. Food daily 4pm–2am.

Vivo Italian Kitchen ★★ ITALIAN In a contemporary open-kitchen setting, dine on house-made pasta (from the classics to modern inventions such as Fiochette stuffed with gorgonzola and pear), fresh mozzarella, braised short ribs, and cured meats.

CityWalk. ✆ **407/224-7223.** www.universalorlando.com. Dinner mains $11–$32. Sun–Thurs 4pm–11pm, Fri–Sat 4pm–midnight.

U.S. 192 & Lake Buena Vista

If you want truly inexpensive eats and lighter crowds, you *must* depart the theme park turf. Just for a short while—it doesn't hurt. Around Disney, two major zones present every chain restaurant known to familydom. The Disney South zone, U.S. 192, goes both east and west from Disney's southern gate. The eastern zone, Lake Buena Vista, is a mile east of the traffic-snarled Downtown Disney area. The two zones are linked by a few miles of Interstate 4, making it easy to shift from one to the other. But you don't need our help to find chain restaurants. Here are the best places you wouldn't otherwise know about.

EXPENSIVE

Columbia Restaurant ★★★ CUBAN Not everything in Celebration, the Disney-built town just east of Walt Disney World, is fake. The original location of this palatial restaurant opened in Tampa in 1905, and this outpost bustles as boldly as its daddy. The hot, fresh Cuban bread is so delicious you'll want to fill up on it, but don't, because portions are giant. Tampa was a major arrival city for Cubans, and their tradition holds sway with flavorful grilled steaks and chicken, paella, mojitos and sangrias, and big fish fillets. My favorite, the 1905 Salad is mixed tableside with ham, cheese, lettuce, olives, greens, and a garlicky wine vinegar dressing that won't help you consummate any courtships but is deservedly on sale by the bottle in the gift shop.

649 Front St., Celebration. ✆ **407/566-1505.** www.columbiarestaurant.com. Tapas plates $10; main courses $20–$27. Daily 11:30am–10:30pm. Reservations recommended.

MODERATE

Bahama Breeze ★★ CARIBBEAN Although this is a smallish corporate chain, it has local provenance: Darden, which owns it (along with the Olive Garden, and LongHorn Steakhouse), is based in Orlando, a 10-minute drive from this location. This concept is its most Floridian, which you will notice when you hear the live steel drums as you approach. Rum cocktails are served on the outdoor patio, and food includes burgers, Cuban sandwiches, rice bowls, Jamaican jerk chicken, coconut shrimp, and other filling quasi-island favorites. I'm all about the fish tacos and the spicy West Indies Chicken Curry made with coconut milk and served with naan and pineapple chutney, but for something mellower, a cup of black bean soup is just $4.

8735 Vineland Ave., Orlando. ✆ **407/938-9010.** www.bahamabreeze.com. Main courses $10–$22. Sun–Thurs 11am–midnight; Fri–Sat 11am–1am. Second location: 8849 International Dr., Orlando. ✆ **407/248-2499.** Sun–Thurs 11am–1am; Fri–Sat 11am–1:30am.

Bruno's Italian Restaurant ★★★ ITALIAN A true find. Your temptation would normally be to drive past this place since it shares a building with dog-ugly gift

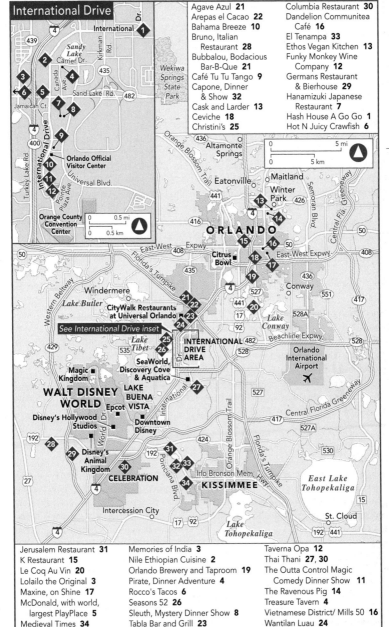

International Drive

- Agave Azul **21**
- Arepas el Cacao **22**
- Bahama Breeze **10**
- Bruno, Italian Restaurant **28**
- Bubbalou, Bodacious Bar-B-Que **21**
- Café Tu Tu Tango **9**
- Capone, Dinner & Show **32**
- Cask and Larder **13**
- Ceviche **18**
- Christini's **25**
- Columbia Restaurant **30**
- Dandelion Communitea Café **16**
- El Tenampa **33**
- Ethos Vegan Kitchen **13**
- Funky Monkey Wine Company **12**
- Germans Restaurant & Bierhouse **29**
- Hanamizuki Japanese Restaurant **7**
- Hash House A Go Go **1**
- Hot N Juicy Crawfish **6**

- Jerusalem Restaurant **31**
- K Restaurant **15**
- Le Coq Au Vin **20**
- Lolailo the Original **3**
- Maxine, on Shine **17**
- McDonald, with world, largest PlayPlace **5**
- Medieval Times **34**
- Memories of India **3**
- Nile Ethiopian Cuisine **2**
- Orlando Brewery and Taproom **19**
- Pirate, Dinner Adventure **4**
- Rocco's Tacos **6**
- Seasons 52 **26**
- Sleuth, Mystery Dinner Show **8**
- Tabla Bar and Grill **23**
- Taverna Opa **12**
- Thai Thani **27, 30**
- The Outta Control Magic Comedy Dinner Show **11**
- The Ravenous Pig **14**
- Treasure Tavern **4**
- Vietnamese District/ Mills 50 **16**
- Wantilan Luau **24**

shop that's garishly painted with killer whales, but inside, it's the food that's killer. There's a lot of junky pasta in the tourist zone, but it's the rare Italian table where the owner is not only cooking with pride, but he's also actually Italian. In this one modest room, Bruno loads his generous plates with garlicky goodness, from his puttanesca to his buttery rolls, and he also does pizzas, calzones, and fresh cannoli. Ask about the daily specials, which include bracciole or a concoction called "eggplant Pavarotti," a rich piling of eggplant, ricotta, spinach, crabmeat, shrimp, and vodka sauce. Delivery is available to the vacation homes of Disney South.

8556 W. Irlo Bronson Hwy., Kissimmee. ✆ **407/397-7577.** www.brunos192.com. Main courses $9–18. Daily 11:30am–10pm.

Germans Restaurant & Bierhouse ★★ GERMAN   A giddy and welcome respite from the chain-dominated stretch of U.S. 192 west of Disney, this family-run 2014 newcomer celebrates everything authentically Teutonic, from bratwurst to strong German draught beers to cheese-and-meat plates, all with a fun-loving, family-friendly twist. The curry wurst, for example, is available in spicy or "what the hell," and a lunchtime option is the "schnitzel burger." Waitresses wear pigtails and leiderhosen— in Orlando, there's Epcotty showmanship in everyone.

7868 W. Irlo Bronson Hwy., Kissimmee. ✆ **407/507-2649.** www.germans-orlando.com. Main courses $14–18. Mon–Sat 11:30am–1:30pm and 5–10:30pm.

Havana's Cuban Cuisine ★★ CUBAN   It would be a shame to come to Florida without tasting authentic Cuban food. Downtown Disney only does touristy Cuban, but this modest family-run place nearby is hosting the real thing—tender *bistec palomilla* (thin-pounded steak with sautéed onion), aromatic *congri* (red beans and rice), and specials such as red snapper in garlic sauce. For dessert, the milk-soaked *tres leches* cake makes you wish you could start again for another round. It also does pressed sandwiches, a Cuban standard, for $9. Beware the green hot sauce—it'll knock you back. The decor is plain (rust-orange walls, reproduction travel posters), but there's heartiness is in the food.

8544 Palm Pkwy., Orlando. ✆ **407/238-5333.** www.havanascubancuisine.com. Main courses $9–$25. Mon 5–10pm; Tues–Sat 11:30am–10pm; Sun noon–9pm.

Sea Dog Brewing Co. ★★ SEAFOOD   Hidden in back of a strip mall facing I-4, this new arrival hails from Maine, where seafood matters but decorum doesn't. So expect a kid-friendly, relaxed joint serving good chowders (Bahamian conch, New England clam), conch fritters, salads, burgers, and dinners ranging from pot roast to broiled haddock. It's all designed to be served with more than a dozen Sea Dog beers by Shipyard Brewing Company in Maine, which you can also buy here by the case to fill your hotel room's fridge.

8496 Palm Pkwy., Orlando. ✆ **321/329-5306.** www.seadogbrewing.com. Main courses $10–$17. Mon–Thurs 4pm–1am; Fri–Sat 11:30am–2am, Sun 11:30am–1am.

INEXPENSIVE

El Tenampa ★★★ MEXICAN   From the outside, you'd swear it was just a grungy mini-mart best avoided, but inside, you discover a family-friendly hideaway of slotted-pot lanterns, hand-carved thrones, and big plastic cups in orange, magenta, and lime. Menus are bilingual but Spanish-first, which tells you about its main clientele, and because Mexican families show up in droves, you also know the food is authentic and good. The fresh *aguas frescas* (rejuvenating sweet water drinks, eight flavors ranging from tamarindo to limon) flow freely, and portions are big and reliable. You'll start with the free salsa and delicate corn chips that are still shiny and hot from the fryer, but don't fill up, because guacamole is a mere $4, whole fish $10, chicken mole with rice and beans only $8, and hefty burritos but $6.50. At its market next door, sample the Mexican popsicles at its *paleteria* and take away homemade pastries for under $1.75. Even Orlando residents, few of whom would dare head to this part of town, are delighted by what they find here.

4565 W. Irlo Bronson Memorial Hwy./U.S. 192, Kissimmee. ⓒ **407/397-1981.** www.eltenampa mexican.com. Main courses $6.50–$13. Sun–Thurs 10am–9pm; Fri–Sat 9am–10pm.

Jerusalem Restaurant ★★ MIDDLE EASTERN   Unknown to tourists, a growing Muslim immigrant community calls Kissimmee home (you'll see a few halal grocery stores around this area), and this family restaurant is one of the benefits: a friendly choice hidden in an elbow of a quiet strip mall, embellished with bougainvillea, stone walls, and a gurgling fountain. Lunch specials (11am–3pm) get you kebabs for $9, which go for $14 by dinnertime, but wraps (including falafel, shawarma, and—in a nod to the tourists—Philly steak) start at just $6. I love the garlicky hummus ($5.50) and *kibbeh* fritters made of beef, cracked wheat, pine nuts, and seasonings ($6). Couscous dishes start at $13.

2920 Vineland Rd., Kissimmee. ⓒ **407/397-2230.** www.facebook.com/jerusalemrestaurant orlando. Main courses $6–$17. Daily 11am–11pm.

Miller's Lake Buena Vista Ale House ★ AMERICAN   The Ale House has 65 locations and counting. There are a few locations in town, including on International Drive, but this location attracts Disney cast members who raise 1 of 75 beers after their shifts are finished. This is the kind of publike sports bar Florida does well—big room, lots of TVs, beers on special by the bucket—with a menu of finger foods like burgers, wings, nachos, and sandwiches. The Ale House's Zingers are boneless chicken wings, a trick of science to be rivaled only by the ones conjured by your future cardiologist.

12371 Winter Garden Vineland Rd., Lake Buena Vista. ⓒ **407/239-1800.** www.millersalehouse. com. Main courses $8–$10. Mon–Sat 11am–2am; Sun 11am–midnight.

International Drive & Convention Center

This is a major hotel and entertainment center, so many visitors find themselves here. The stretch of Sand Lake Road west of Interstate 4 is known, somewhat self-deprecatingly, as "Restaurant Row." It's true that some of the city's most popular date-night restaurants are scattered among the shopping centers on this street.

EXPENSIVE

Christini's ★ ITALIAN   Christini's, a fixture since 1984, is much more expensive than most Italian places and it doesn't permit young children. Those facts qualify it as a special occasion restaurant and not one to grab a bowl of spaghetti. Picture a prototypical high-end Italian splurge and you've got it: wandering accordion player, sommelier, lifetime waiters alert to your every twitch. It does pasta well, but guests tend to praise its meats, particularly the tender *osso buco,* above all. Reservations are recommended, and the dress code is business casual at the least.

7600 Dr. Phillips Blvd., Orlando. ⓒ **407/345-8770.** www.christinis.com. Main courses $23–$57. Daily 6–11pm.

Funky Monkey Wine Company ★★★ AMERICAN   The menu is everchanging at this beloved locally owned eatery that stocks nearly eight dozen types of wine, but count on spry twists such as asiago fries, "Monkey Balls" of seasoned rice served with cream cheese and spicy mayo dipping sauce, coconut curry poached shrimp, and a full slate of fresh sushi. It's upscale without taking itself too seriously, a mode that proves itself Sundays at 12:30pm when a highly amusing Drag Gospel Brunch show entertains diners.

9101 International Dr. at Pointe Orlando, Orlando. ℂ 407/418-9463. www.funkymonkeywine. com. Sushi rolls $8–$16, main courses $21–$40. Reservations recommended. Mon–Thurs 11:30am–11pm, Fri–Sat 11:30am–midnight, Sunday 11am–2pm and 5–11pm. Second location: 912 N. Mills Ave., north of downtown Orlando.

Lolailo The Original ★★ SPANISH   Lolailo's Galician cuisine rises above its mundane-appearing strip mall location, and its interior, with its burnished copper bar and Victoria Arduino espresso machine, elevate the mood, too. Both excellent tapas (grilled octopus, piquillo peppers) and mains (lamb, traditional cured ham) are available, but paella is not (unless you're there for Sun brunch) because this is Spanish cuisine that celebrates delicate ingredients, not piles of rice. Finish with the *elogia al vino,* a surprising dessert of ice cream, custard, and red wine reduction.

7637 Turkey Lake Rd., Orlando. ℂ 407/730-8948. www.lolailo.com. Tapas $7 to $18, main courses $22–$40. Tues–Sat 11am–10pm; Sun 11am–3:30pm.

MODERATE

Agave Azul ★★ MEXICAN   Hidden in a strip mall, as so many of Orlando's most surprisingly delicious places to eat are, Agave Azul cultivates a following with classic Latin dishes, from gourmet to Tex-Mex (ceviches, taqueria, a few types of guacamole including one with shrimp and goat cheese) in a soothing, modernist environment with lots of space, huge booths, and a gentle indoor fountain. The margaritas pack a wallop—the drinks here come stronger than the attentively measured pours elsewhere. It's right around the corner from Universal.

4750 S. Kirkman Rd., Orlando. ℂ 407/704-6930. www.agaveazulorlando.com. Main courses $9–$20. Mon–Thurs 11am–10pm, Fri–Sat 11am–11pm.

Bubbalou's Bodacious Bar-B-Que ★★ BARBECUE   Real barbecue done the way devotees like it, from cornbread stuffed with gooey butter pads to fall-off-the-bone ribs proven to stain shirts. There's no pretense at this tidied-up dive: Order at the counter and eat at picnic-style tables stocked with paper towel rolls and squirt bottles of sauce going from "sweet" to "killer." Get the standards: Texas brisket, pulled pork, ½ chicken, fried catfish, even gizzards. Sandwiches go for $7, but add any 4 sides (like baked beans, black-eye peas, Brunswick stew, or crunchy cole slaw) for $4 more. Or opt for meat by the pound ($11–$14), and take it back to the gang.

5818 Conroy Rd., Orlando. ℂ 407/295-1212. www.bubbalouscatering.com. Main courses $8–$14. Mon–Thurs 10am–9:30pm; Fri 10am–10:30pm; Sat 10am–9:30pm; Sun 11am–9pm.

Café Tu Tu Tango ★★ INTERNATIONAL   Fun, festive, and noisy in a good way, this casual tapas-style hangout flies high with an artist theme. Actual artists somehow concentrate on painting at easels amid the frolic of tables, cocktails, and nightly entertainment of belly dancing, salsa, or flamenco dancing. Their works fill the walls up to the rafters while boisterous diners spill out into the front patio. Despite the gimmick, chef Tiffany L. Sawyer's food is locally sourced from sustainable ingredients and packs flavor. I love the chili-lime marinated chicken skewers with corn pudding and almond pesto and the pork belly Reuben, although the Cajun chicken egg rolls are popular. This may also be one of the only mainstream Orlando restaurants to serve the animal that once owned these parts, the alligator: Try it as spiced gator bites with key lime mustard, or in gator jambalaya; clichés aside, it's kinda like chicken.

8625 International Dr., Orlando. ✆ **407/248-2222.** www.cafetututango.com. Tapas $8–$10. Sun–Thurs 11:30am–11pm; Fri–Sat 11:30am–1am.

Hanamizuki Japanese Restaurant ★ JAPANESE
The theme parks never saw a fish they didn't want to batter-fry. So here, the fresh sushi, chicken and salmon teriyaki, and udon or soba noodle soups make for a refreshing palate-cleanser. The blonde wood and fabric decor conforms neatly to your expectations of a soothing Japanese restaurant—it draws a steady trade of Japanese visitors hungry for a taste of home—and so does the rest, from the greeting when you walk in the door to the deep bowls of flavorsome soup. The fun Ishiyaki Mix Steak allows you to grill meat and vegetables on a hot stone placed on your table. Best of all, because of a tucked-away location in a strip mall near the Kings Bowl Orlando, it's rarely crowded. At lunchtime, it adds ramen to the menu.

8255 International Dr., Ste. 136, Orlando. ✆ **407/363-7200.** www.hanamizuki.us. Main courses $8–$14. Tues–Sat 11:30am–2pm; Tues–Sun 5pm–10:30pm.

Hash House A Go Go ★ AMERICAN
Hash House's claim to fame is shocking immoderation. Dishes are laughably immense, piled as high as Jenga games, and the outcome could be just as messy if you attempt to eat all you are served. Everything on the down-home menu, which the restaurant calls "Twisted Farm Food," sounds like a good idea mostly in retrospect: 1-pound burgers (stuffed with the likes of bacon and cheese, if you dare), towers of fried green tomatoes, a platter of fried chicken and waffles deserving of its own area code. This is destination food. The HH is an import from the casino culture of Vegas, where it began, which makes sense: This is a meal with a high risk-reward ratio, and you can bet there'll be leftovers.

5350 International Dr., Orlando. ✆ **407/370-4646.** www.hashhouseagogo.com. Main courses $10–$15. Sun–Thurs 8am–10pm, Fri–Sat 8am–11pm.

Hot N Juicy Crawfish ★ SEAFOOD
Sometimes when you're in Orlando, you just want to rip your meal apart with your bare hands, and for those times, there's this place, where as soon as you sit down they slap a bib on you and let you loose on the shellfish. Some are market price, but crab usually sells for a pound in the mid-teens, shrimp for $12 a pound, and mussels for $9 a pound. A few accents such as fried calamari, po' boys, and corn fritters are available for further kicks, but don't expect a fork. Vegetarians, give this place wide berth; this is for the vivisectors among us.

7572 W. Sand Lake Rd., Orlando. ✆ **407/370-4655.** www.hotnjuicycrawfish.com. Main courses $9–$15 a pound. Sun–Thurs noon–10pm; Fri–Sat noon–11pm.

Memories of India ★★ INDIAN
Overcoming a bland name with flavorful pan-Indian food and a cheerful staff, it has seen its following build. At lunch it prepares *thali,* a platter combining basmati rice, bread, *raita* (yogurt with cucumbers and tomatoes), pickle (relish), a meat dish, a *papadum* (thin wafer), and, at this place, dessert (I like the pulpy mango ice cream)—all for $6.95 to $9.95. The tandoori and naan (a dozen kinds) are made in a clay oven. The Lamb Kada Masala, cooked in ginger, garlic, spring onion, and gravy, is consistently strong. It's a few blocks west of International Drive, in the ignoble Bay Hill shopping plaza, and Universal Orlando staffers often come here for lunch.

7625 Turkey Lake Rd., Orlando. ✆ **407/370-3277.** www.memoriesofindiacuisine.com. Main courses $11–$16. Mon–Fri 11:30am–2:30pm and 5:30–10pm; Sat 11:30am–2pm and 5:30–10pm; Sun 11:30am–2:30pm and 5:30–9pm.

Nile Ethiopian Cuisine ★★★ ETHIOPIAN   Nile's owners are so friendly and eager to share their cuisine they have made themselves a devoted fixture on I-Drive. They even offer a few hutlike booths in which you can sit on the ground to eat, East Africa–style. It's a positive experience for families. Everyone tears off a piece of spongy injera bread to scoop up various stews and meats (beef, lamb, chicken, vegetarian) collected on a platter. You can even request a traditional coffee ceremony, in which beans are brewed in a *jabena* pot at your table and the eldest in your party is served first. Ethiopian cuisine is made with infused oil, not butter, so the vegetarian options are truly vegan, and with advance notice, the injera can be made gluten-free. It's memorable and not daunting.

7048 International Dr., Orlando. ✆ **407/354-0026.** www.nile07.com. Main courses $12–$15. Mon–Fri 5–10pm; Sat–Sun noon–10pm.

Rocco's Tacos ★★ MEXICAN   Every night's a party at Rocco's, a loud, popular, tequila-drenched upscale hangout where friends meet to kick back with margaritas and dig into guacamole mixed tableside. After sunset, flaming torches illuminate its lakeside terrace, and deeper into the night, a DJ spins, and occasionally Rocco himself appears to dance on the bar and pour tequila. It serves all kinds of Mexican entrées, but its specialty is the fajita-like *molcajetes,* marinated and slow-cooked for hours and served in a lava rock bowl to keep them hot longer.

7468 W. Sand Lake Rd., Orlando. ✆ **407/226-0550.** www.roccostacos.com. Main courses $12–$24. Sun–Mon 11am–11pm, Tues–Weds 11:30am–11:30pm, Thurs–Fri 11:30am–1am, Sat 11:30am–midnight.

Seasons 52 ★★★ AMERICAN   This culinary experiment has spread nationwide, but this was its first location. The point of the menu, which changes to make use of seasonal crops, is that no dish clocks in at more than 475 calories (although none will leave you hungry). Servings aren't particularly teeny—the food is just really good, thoughtfully made, and never sees a deep fryer. That's something you'll thank your waiter for after a long week in the theme parks. The desserts come in single-serving shot glasses, but mind they don't catch you licking the glass.

7700 Sand Lake Rd., Orlando. ✆ **407/354-5212.** www.seasons52.com. Main courses $13–$20. Sun–Thurs 11:30am–10pm; Fri 10am–11pm; Sat 11:30am–11pm.

Tabla Bar and Grill ★★ INDIAN   Be encouraged when an Indian restaurant is full of young Indian-Americans having a good time. Knowing that fact might help entice you inside, because its unappealing location in a tatty Days Inn might otherwise deter you. Tabla rises above that. Chef Sajan does the standards (pulling from various traditions like Parsi and Hyderabadi and the dosa of South India), but he also plays around (chocolate samosas and *janat e paan,* a kulfi dessert with glazed *paan*). Start with fresh-made tomato cream soup just like they serve on Indian Railways ($4 for a huge bowl). At lunch (11am–2:45pm), there's an ample all-you-can-eat buffet ($8 weekdays, $13 weekends with champagne), and there's always a full bar where mango-themed drinks are a specialty. There's a good feeling here, like being at a club that only you were smart enough to know about.

5827 Caravan Court, Orlando. ✆ **407/248-9400.** www.tablabar.com. Main courses $7–$15. Daily 11:30am–3pm and 5–11pm.

Taverna Opa ★★ GREEK   It would be hard not to find something to eat, from tapaslike *meze* (hummus with garlic chunks and hot pita bread, *taramosalata, keftedes* meatballs), salads, hearty wood-fired and long-marinated meats and grilled fish, and *moussaka* (an eggplant lasagna with béchamel). There's no resisting the party that starts after 7pm or so—waiters and customers alike toss napkins and dance on the tables as belly dancers and "Zorba" dancers (their term) swirl. Kids really get into it. Lunches are more subdued, and mains are $10 cheaper.

9101 International Dr. at Pointe Orlando, Orlando. © **407/351-8660.** www.opaorlando.com. Meze $5–$12, main courses $15–$27. Sun–Thurs noon–11pm; Fri–Sat noon–2am.

Thai Thani ★★ THAI A strip-mall anchor store by SeaWorld channels Chiang Mai with wood carvings, brass, and powerfully romantic private booths. Popular with locals (it recently added a Celebration location near Disney), it serves Thai food suited to newbies—the lemongrass soup is tame, with few chilies, which proves the chef is holding back—but more advanced eaters should choose from the "spicy dishes" section to get the full flair of the cuisine—I like the Thai chili jam stir-fried with veggies and your choice of protein. Finish with Thai Grandma Ice Cream: coconut ice cream with sticky rice and peanuts ($7). Lunch is about $5 less.

11025 S. International Dr. © **407/239-9733.** www.thaithani.net. Main courses $11–$16. Daily 11:30am–11pm. Second location near Disney: 600 Market St., Ste. 100, Celebration. © **407/566-9444.** Daily 11:30am–11pm.

INEXPENSIVE

Arepas el Cacao ★★ VENEZUELAN This local success story started in 2010 as a family-run food truck that rapidly cultivated a following that funded the launch of several brick-and-mortar locations. The specialty is simple: handmade corn flatbread (*arepas*) that's overstuffed with meats, veggies, and your choice of sauce, from creamy to spicy. It's simple, filling, and honest, and it's made even more satisfying when you pair it with tropical juices such as blackberry or mango. You'll find it just east of the Universal complex. *Note:* It's lunch-only.

5389 S. Kirkman Rd., Orlando. © **321/252-2226.** www.arepaselcacao.com. $6–$8. Daily 9am–4pm.

McDonald's ★ FAST FOOD You've seen one McDonald's, you've seen them all, right? Not this one—otherwise why mention it? It serves the usual junk food, of course, but there's also a huge array of options such as burritos, pastrami, chimichangas, pastas, panini, and pizzas. That's odd enough, but it also claims to operate the largest PlayPlace in the world. Looks accurate: You'll find tube slides, a 500-gallon aquarium, and some 100 arcade games with a prize center. Keep kids wowed for the price of fries.

6875 Sand Lake Rd., Orlando. © **407/351-2185.** www.mcfun.com. Main courses $5–$8. Daily 24 hr.

Miller's I-Drive Vista Ale House ★ AMERICAN There are a few locations of this family-friendly, popular sports bars in town, including at Lake Buena Vista (p. 181), and another at 5573 S. Kirkman Rd. near Universal, but this location is among the largest, with several cavernous rooms that open up to the nightlife on I-Drive. Hang out at a high-top table with a bucket of beers—something is always on special—cheer when your team scores, and dig into family-friendly finger foods like burgers, wings, oysters, pastas, sandwiches. There's even steak and potatoes ($15–$19) and lobster tails ($18 for two) if you're feeling hearty.

8963 International Dr., Orlando. © **407/370-6688.** www.millersalehouse.com. Main courses $8–$10. Daily 11am–2am.

Orlando Brewing and Taproom ★★★ BREWERY Because it's buried in an industrial area, you have to know about it to find it. There's no food served, either—if you want some, they'll hand you a binder of delivery menus—but that doesn't mean there isn't some delicious cooking happening. At least 24 beers (ales, IPAs, stouts—it changes according to how the brewers experiment) are on tap at 42°F and served at a copper-top bar. The quick rise of the brewery, which has been certified organic, has been remarkable. Orlando's best hotels (including Disney's) and restaurants now serve it. Most days at 6pm, the owners grant a free 30-minute tour of the beerworks, where quaffs are made without pasteurization (like the Old World) for sale within 2 weeks. The bar area is simple but convivial, like a rec room your dad might have slapped up in the basement, and uncluttered by televisions or pool tables.

1301 Atlanta Ave., Orlando (just east of the Kaley St. exit off I-4, exit 81). ☎ **407/872-1117.** www.orlandobrewing.com. No food; beer only. Mon–Thurs 3–10pm; Fri–Sat 1pm–midnight; Sun 1–9pm.

Downtown Orlando

The neighborhood east of downtown, Thornton Park, hosts a few well-publicized bistros and sidewalk cafes, but with prices around $12 a plate for lunch and $20 for dinner, there are no money-saving revelations among them. Instead, try these.

EXPENSIVE

Cask & Larder ★★ SOUTHERN Like its sister gastropub restaurant down the street, the Ravenous Pig (p. 187), it's dedicated to ever-changing dishes based on seasonal ingredients. The difference here is that Cask & Larder is less about picking meat off an animal's bones as it is about home-brewed beer by a resident brewmaster and a casual vibe. But you can eat, and comfort food is the thing—it could be fried chicken (a staple), country fried rabbit (yes), or an addictive potted pimento cheese topped with "ham jam" (ham that's been cooked down with honey). Rich touches prevail, such as the vanilla butter slowly melting atop the cornbread, which arrives in its own iron skillet, and the mac and cheese jolted with pickled mustard seeds.

565 W. Fairbanks Ave., Winter Park. ☎ **321/280-4200.** www.caskandlarder.com. Mains $14–$27. Daily 5–10pm, Sun 10:30am–3pm. Reservations recommended.

K Restaurant ★★★ AMERICAN Kevin Fonzo's mastery of rich flavors using Southern bistro classics and local ingredients made him a star of Orlando cuisine, and his upscale but casual showplace is one of the city's best for gourmet flavors without pretentiousness. The menu changes but almost always includes a steak tartare (sometimes served with brussels sprout kimchee), fried green tomatoes, and the K Filet dusted with wild mushrooms and accompanied by a wildly scrumptious cabernet sauvignon sauce. Ask to be served by the long-running and much-loved Rocky, who's famous in these parts. This uproariously flamboyant merry-maker carries with him a leather wallet full of photos from his colorful past, and he's got a hundred funny stories for each one. There's a big wine list, too.

1710 Edgewater Dr., Orlando. Krestaurant.net. ☎ **407/872-2332.** Main courses $18–38. Tues–Fri 1:30–2pm, Mon–Tues 6–9pm, Weds–Sat 6–10pm.

Le Coq Au Vin ★★★ FRENCH Longtime Chef Louis Perrotte hand-picked his protégé Reimund Pitz to take the reins at this classic French romantic restaurant, an Orlando institution since 1976. Diners, many of whom are here celebrating a special occasion, feel more like they're guests in a home than paying patrons, an illusion that's extended by its mostly residential neighborhood. Pitz is classically trained as a French chef, so you get the complicated flavors (a well-marinated coq au vin, a daily selection of game meat, Grand Marnier soufflé) that the prices demand, plus Gallic staples such as frog legs and vichyssoise. Some dishes come in ample half portions that can cost two-thirds what larger servings do. A three-course prix-fixe menu goes for $35.

4800 S. Orange Ave., Orlando. ☎ **407/851-6980.** www.lecoqauvinrestaurant.com. Main courses $19–39. Tues–Sat 5:30–10pm; Sun 5–9pm.

The Ravenous Pig ★★★ SOUTHERN James and Julie Petrakis have won renown for knowing just when to deploy bacon and in what amount, a talent dear to me, and they have been rewarded by operating one of the city's most influential dining choices. Expect a beer-friendly yet sophisticated evening where the food is gourmet without pretentiousness. The menu changes seasonally but always features traditional farmhouse meats—in the form of frites, say—and some perennial Southern comfort dishes with an upscale spin, like shrimp and grits with Gruyere biscuits. The Petrakis' cookbook, on sale here, is all about exploiting the best of Florida's ingredients.

1234 N. Orange Ave., Winter Park. ⓒ **407/628-2333**. www.theravenouspig.com. Mains $14–$30. Tues–Sat 11:30am–2pm, 5:30–10pm. Reservations recommended.

MODERATE

Cevíche ★ TAPAS For a lively night out, head to Church Street Station, a revitalized pedestrian district of red-brick warehouses, gas-lit lamps, and late-night lounges. This rococo dining hall feels like it was plucked off Las Ramblas in Barcelona. The menu, also true to Spain, is piled with more than 100 tapas dishes, most $6 to $10, including daring-for-Orlando meats (quail, crispy chicken livers, oxtail), standard ones (chorizo, veal, lamb chops), and plenty of vegetable and fish choices. And, of course, there's ceviche (I like the tuna, with garlic, lime, onion, and a touch of jalapeño). Because everything's meant to be shared, the energy is social and vibrant. Things get loud when the flamenco band clacks and strums, so enjoy the evening on the front patio. Then club-crawl on Church Street late into the night.

125 W. Church St., Orlando. ⓒ **321/281-8140**. www.ceviche.com. Tapas $8–$12. Sun–Mon 5–10pm; Tues–Thurs 5pm–midnight; Fri–Sat 5pm–2am.

Maxine's on Shine ★★ INTERNATIONAL Hidden in a residential neighborhood (blink and you've passed it), it's a labor of love by its owners, who frequently emerge from the kitchen to party with guests. There's a good wine list plus a tiny stage hosting a roster of entertainment ('70s karaoke one night, classical piano the next). Chicken Maxine blends pan-seared diced chicken with shallots, mushrooms, a Marsala wine cream sauce with penne pasta, but on Sundays at 7pm, I go for the Magical Mystery Meal Tour, when $25 buys three courses, plus a glass of wine, as long as you agree to let the chef serve you whatever inspires him that day. As you depart, a sign thanks you for helping "this little restaurant's dreams come true."

337 N. Shine Ave., Orlando. ⓒ **407/674-6841**. www.maxinesonshine.com. Mains $14–$24. Tues–Thurs 5–10pm; Fri–Sat 11:30am–11pm; Sun 10am–10pm.

INEXPENSIVE

Dandelion Communitea Cafe ★★★ VEGETARIAN/VEGAN When you hang out at Dandelion, you feel like you're a part of something. That's because it's as much a neighborhood hangout as it is a cafe. Once a private home, hardwood floors and cabinets were left intact, and now diners of all ages (including kids) roam. A huge selection of tea is served with menu items made with local ingredients. There's no meat, and nearly everything is gluten-free. The signature dish is the Giddyup ($9, but only $5 on Mon), a filling nacho bowl of tempeh chili piled with blue corn chips, diced tomatoes, scallions, and cheese. My favorite is Henry's Hearty Chili, the most flavorful veggie chili I've ever had ($4 a cup). Twice a month, on the new and full moon, people gather here to "express your true self with music, rhythm, dance and trance." If you don't travel with your own bongo, they'll lend you one.

618 N. Thornton Ave., Orlando. ⓒ **407/362-1864**. www.dandelioncommunitea.com. Main courses $8–$9. Mon–Sat 11am–10pm; Sun 11am–5pm.

A GASTRONOMIC TOUR OF little vietnam

Just north of Orlando's downtown, along a stretch of 1950s storefronts around Colonial Avenue and Mills Avenue, a thriving Vietnamese area (variously called Little Vietnam, ViMi, and Mills Fifty) is flourishing. Many people fled here upon the fall of Saigon, and Vietnamese dissident Thuong Nguyen Cuc Foshee has been an Orlando resident since the time of the Vietnam conflict. Diners can find cheap meals here, true to Vietnam's reputation for nuanced flavors. Park anywhere (most buildings hide secret lots behind them) and explore on an empty stomach.

The quickest meal is banh mi, addictive baguette-style sandwiches stuffed with thinly sliced veggies (cucumbers, daikon, carrots), cilantro, hot peppers, a buttery secret sauce, and meats such as roast pork, pâté, or meatball (or tofu). They're shockingly cheap: $3 to $4, hot, and made-to-order. The best are at **Bánh Mì Nha Trang,** hidden in an ancient strip mall (1237 E. Colonial Dr.; *©* **407/346-4549;** Mon–Wed and Fri 10am–7pm, Sat–Sun 10am–6pm), where they barely speak English but are improbably friendly—every transaction ends with a chipper "See you tomorrow!" Also get them at the counter beside checkout at

Tiên-Hung Market (1108 E. Colonial Dr.; *©* **407/422-0067;** daily 9am–6pm), a catch-all for Asian groceries.

At most of the area's Vietnamese restaurants, where entrees range $8 to $12, menus drone on like a Russian novel, but if you're wise to it, each place has its specialty. **Phó 88** (730 N. Mills Ave.; *©* **407/897-3488;** www.pho88orlando. com; daily 10am–10pm) excels with pho beef noodle soup; bowls seem as large as hot tubs, with many flavors vying for dominance. Its two enormous spring rolls could fill an average stomach for $3.25. The specialty at Ánh Hông (1124 E. Colonial Dr.; *©* **407/999-2656;** daily 9am–9:30pm), on the corner of Mills, is tofu (especially fried), while **Viet Garden** (1237 E. Colonial Dr.; *©* **407/896-4154;** Sun–Thurs 10am–9pm, Fri–Sat until 10pm) wows with its crispy noodle dishes. Neophytes prefer the mass appeal of **Little Saigon** (1106 E. Colonial Dr.; *©* **407/423-8539;** www.littlesaigon restaurant.com; daily 10am–9pm), which has several dining areas with yellow walls and red tablecloths that place it as slightly more upscale than its somewhat utilitarian one-room neighbors—but its food is just as good.

Ethos Vegan Kitchen ★★ VEGAN   As one of the only fully vegan restaurants in Central Florida, Ethos garnered such a loyal following it recently moved and expanded. That's because when vegan cuisine is all that you do (even the cheese qualifies), you have to be skilled at making it taste good, too—and Ethos succeeds. Among the favorites are pecan-encrusted eggplant, pumpkin seed pesto penne pasta, and 10-inch pizzas. Kelly and Laina Shockley, who run it, are assiduous about ingredient sourcing and proudly pay their servers a living wage (not minimum wage). Specials change according to seasonal crops, and there's always a soup of the day. About a third of the menu is gluten-free.

601-B New York Ave., Winter Park. *©* **407/228-3898** or 407/228-3899. www.ethosvegankitchen. com. Mains $8–$15. Mon–Fri 11am–11pm; Sat–Sun 9am–11pm.

Dinnertainment

Besides "America's Got Talent" and "Dancing with the Stars," there may be no purer form of vaudeville left in America than the Orlando dinner show. Part banquet and part spectacle, most of these guilty pleasures involve stunts, audience participation, and plenty of noise. Most of them are mounted in arenas lined with bench seating and long tables, and while the show grinds on, waiters scurry around, distributing plates of banquet food the way Las Vegas dealers deal blackjack cards. These shows are immoderate and tacky to the extreme, but they're an intrinsic part of the Orlando scene. Nowhere else on Earth—at least not since Caligula's Rome—will you find so many stadiums in which to stuff your face while fleets of horses, swordsmen, and crooners labor to amuse you. Dinnertainments aren't top values, but they certainly represent the delight of Orlando's shtick.

Most times of the year, most of these shows kick off daily around 6 or 7pm, but during peak season, there may be two shows scheduled around 6 and 8:30pm. Upon arrival, crowds are corralled into a preshow area where they can buy cocktails and souvenirs, and endure hokey comedy routines—feel free to be slightly tardy, and feel free not to buy anything, as drinks come with dinner. Most shows will be mopping up by around 9:30pm, so schedule a visit on a night when you don't intend to catch theme park fireworks. Most of them also serve kids' standards (chicken fingers, hot dogs, and so on) for picky children. Soft drinks, draft beer, and wine (the cheap stuff, watered down) are unlimited. Bring a sweater if you're sensitive to air-conditioning, and bring enough cash to tip your server because gratuities aren't included. **Money-saving tip:** The free coupon books and discount ticket suppliers should be your go-to for cheap prices on dinner shows. There are so many deals floating around for the banquets held off theme-park property that only a stooge pays full price. The ones thrown by the theme parks, though, generally don't discount. In fact, they tend to sell out, so book those as far ahead as you sensibly can.

IN ORLANDO & KISSIMMEE

Capone's Dinner & Show ★ ITALIAN

Kardashian-generation girls pretend to be 1920s flappers and warble to recorded music in this affordable dinnertainment effort. Dinner's a bog-standard steam table buffet of lasagna, spaghetti with meatballs, pizza, nuggets, and a few token nonpasta choices, such as a hot meat carving station. This troupe's own brochures and website promise half-off discounts, which grant the price I list, but I've never seen the so-called full price quoted, let alone charged.

4740 W. Irlo Bronson Hwy., Kissimmee. ℂ **800/220-8428.** www.alcapones.com. $29 adults, $32 kids 4–12. Nightly, some 1pm shows.

Medieval Times ★ AMERICAN

The long-running coach-tour favorite, at which your waitress is called a "wench," is also an attraction in eight other North American cities, qualifying it as the McDonald's of dinnertainment. You eat spare ribs and chicken with your hands while the jousters compete in an arena. For $10 more ($8 online), the Royalty Package gets you front-row seating, a free program, and a souvenir DVD. Its "castle" is located a few miles east of Disney on U.S. 192, in a downtrodden area of Kissimmee. It's also always discounted by brochures to the tune of $15 less.

4510 W. Irlo Bronson Hwy., Kissimmee. ℂ **866/543-9637** or 407/396-2900. www.medievaltimes. com. $63 adult, $37 kids 12 and under. Nightly.

The Outta Control Magic Comedy Dinner Show ★★ PIZZA More affordable and easygoing than its dinnertainment competition, the show mounted by the WonderWorks science/video playground targets kids—and parents weary of over-produced, overpriced glitz. Unlimited pizza, salad, beer, wine, and soda are distributed while buddy-buddy magicians engage in family-friendly jokes, tricks, mindreading, and improv. Discount coupons get $2 off.

WonderWorks, 9067 International Dr., Orlando. ✆ **407/351-8800.** www.wonderworksonline.com. $25 adults, $20 kids 4–12 and seniors. 6 and 8pm.

Pirate's Dinner Adventure ★★ AMERICAN For kids who just can't get enough Jack Sparrow–like misbehavior, there's this high-energy eye-popper, set on an 18th-century galleon amid a 300,000-gallon lagoon—the arena is the most spectacular of all the Orlando dinnertainments. Expect a circus of rapier duels, rope swinging (lots of it), trampolining, singing, and arrrghing. Although the show provides lots of oppor-tunity for participation (each of six sections roots for its assigned buccaneer, kids get onstage), it treats female characters like sexy livestock. That may account for why its most devoted demographic appears to be 12-year-old boys. Production values are fairly high. Buying online yields discounts of $5 a ticket, but many of the free bro-chures dispensed around town are good for as much as $15 off.

6400 Carrier Dr., Orlando. ✆ **800/866-2469** or 407/248-0590. www.piratesdinneradventure.com. $66 adult, $40 kids 3–11. Nightly.

Sleuth's Mystery Dinner Show ★★★ AMERICAN After mingling with a few zany characters and watching the show, which takes about an hour and contains at least one murder, you confer over dinner with your tablemates, grill the suspects, and, if you feel confident, accuse a killer. The cases change nightly, so you can attend several times without duplicating your experience. Actors seem to be having fun, and they'll even tone down the grown-up jokes if they see young children in the crowd, although these low-budget shows are clearly more suited to adults. As for audiences, they appear to be grateful for a rare chance to employ their brains in this town. Beer and wine are included, too. Lots of brochures offer discount rates.

8267 International Dr., Orlando. ✆ **800/393-1985** or 407/363-1985. www.sleuths.com. $58 adult, $24 kids 3–11, $3–$7 less if booked online. Nightly.

Treasure Tavern ★★ AMERICAN The people behind Pirate's Dinner Adventure also put on a 2-hour mix of burlesque, circus and magic tricks, contortionists in garters, clenching male abs, and dancing. It's for those 18 years old and over (although if you're older than 14, you can come with a grown-up). The concept is that Gretta, the bawdy proprietor of the Treasure Tavern, has assembled a band of misfits who she puts to work entertaining you. Think "Cabaret" meets "Benny Hill." Because kids are cut out, food is a cut above—the standard meal is beef tenderloin. Servers are referred to as "rum girls." (I said it was adult, not sophisticated.)

6400 Carrier Dr., Orlando. ✆ **877/318-2469.** www.treasuretavern.com. Tickets $66. Tues–Sat nights, doors open at 7pm.

AT THE THEME PARK RESORTS

Disney's Grand Floridian resort does afternoon tea time bookings for little princesses (✆ **407/939-1947**), but these are the parks' dinner shows for the whole family.

Disney's Spirit of Aloha Show ★ POLYNESIAN The chicken-and-ribs luau presided over by fire twirlers, hula dancers, and the like has been going strong for years in an open-air theater on Seven Seas Lagoon. Bookings begin 6 months ahead, and usually the last people to reserve are shunted to the rear tables, which can feel like they're actually as distant as the Cook Islands; the tables that are farthest away are the least expensive. It bores some kids, but it has its adult adherents (although most of them cite not its educational qualities but its food—pineapple-coconut bread being at the top of their lists). It's on the monorail line from the Magic Kingdom, which means it's easy to catch the fireworks after early shows.

Disney's Polynesian Resort. ⓒ **407/939-1947.** www.disneyworld.com. $59–$74 adults, $30–$40 kids 3–9. Tues–Sat 5:15 and 8pm.

Gospel Brunch ★ AMERICAN

There is no plot, and it's not sanctified, but the live music is jumping and the cuisine combines Southern and breakfast foods. The morning show fills first. Still, because so many House of Blues throw these, you can't say it's very Orlando.

House of Blues, Downtown Disney West Side, 1490 E. Buena Vista Dr., Lake Buena Vista. ⓒ **407/934-2583.** www.hob.com. $53 adults. Sun at 10:30am and 1pm.

Hoop-Dee-Doo Musical Revue ★★ AMERICAN

Book 6 months out, not necessarily because it's the best, but because it's Disney's most kid-friendly dinner-tainment, which makes it crazy popular. Six-performer shows put on a hectic and helter-skelter music-hall carnival of olios and gags, which elementary-school age children usually find riveting, and much quarter is given to recognizing birthdays and special events. The headlining menu item is ribs served in pails—enough said? I prefer seats in the balcony, overlooking the stage (the cheapest, anyway).

Pioneer Hall at Fort Wilderness Resort. ⓒ **407/939-1947.** www.disneyworld.com. $59–$70 adults, $28–$36 kids 3–9. Shows scheduled from late afternoon to evening.

Mickey's Backyard BBQ ★ AMERICAN

The dinner show choice for very young children is patronized by rope tricksters and taxi-dancing costumed characters wearing Western-style gear. More informal than the Hoop-Dee-Doo in that it takes place under an open-air pavilion (come dressed for humidity), the event serves pass-able buffet-style picnic food, but the toddler factor makes it chaotic, and for some cruel reason, seating is first come, first served. You might be less disappointed if you see this as a photo op with Mickey and not as a proper show.

The Outdoor Pavilion at Fort Wilderness Resort. ⓒ **407/939-1947.** www.disneyworld.com. $60 adults, $30 kids 3–9. Thurs and Sat Mar–Dec.

Wantilan Luau ★★★ POLYNESIAN

Universal's weekly 2-hour luau is held in a covered pavilion. It, like Disney's Spirit of Aloha Show, has fire dancers and hula girls aplenty, but it trumps the rest for authenticity: Food includes pit-roasted suckling pig, with spiced rum–infused pineapple puree, and a Pacific catch of the day; mai tais are included in the price. Should kids be grossed out by carving meat off the pig, there's a tamer children's menu. The show is more culturally documentary than Disney's, too, as it's attentive to the differences between the various Pacific islanders it represents. You can walk from both Universal parks.

Royal Pacific Resort. ⓒ **407/503-3463.** www.universalorlando.com. $63 adults, $35 kids 3–9. Sat at 6pm, some Tuesday nights.

CHARACTER MEALS

A character meal is a rite of passage. Usually all-you-can-eat and often buffet, it guaran-tees face-to-fur time with beloved costumed characters. Always, *always book ahead*—as soon as you can.

At Disney, meals are themed by location; at the Cape May Café, characters wear beach outfits, and at Chef Mickey's, they emerge in chef's aprons and do a towel-twirling dance. (Reading that, it sounds a little like a Chippendales show, not a Chip 'n' Dale show, but rest assured it's all preschool-friendly.) The characters (six to eight headliners make appearances) won't actually be eating with you, but they'll circulate, working the room the way a good host does, and signing autographs. This, as kids and grown-ups binge on a smorgasbord that would give Jillian Michaels apoplexy—Mickey-shaped waffles topped with M&Ms and all—comes the day's first sugar crash.

Prices vary, but they're a little cheaper at hotels than inside theme parks. When a breakfast is held inside a park, you'll still have to proffer an admission ticket. However, for breakfast, your name will be on a VIP list and you'll be admitted through the gates early (it's fun to walk through an empty park). Try to book the earliest seating available so that by the time you're done, you'll be among the first in line for the rides; you'll also have first crack at the stroller rentals. Tips are not usually included.

Cinderella's Royal Table, inside Magic Kingdom's Cinderella Castle, is the big "get"—there are some intense parents out there with freakishly fast speed-dial fingers, because that place always sells out 180 days early. Also try Chef Mickey's, which is a one-stop monorail ride away from the Magic Kingdom, and the Tusker House, a good start for the early day at Animal Kingdom. Less prestigious addresses, such as the buffet breakfast at the Beach Club near Epcot, can be smart choices, particularly because they tend not to be as crowded and you're likely to have lots more one-on-one time with the stars.

Inside Disney Parks

Cinderella's Royal Table   The most difficult reservation (reserve 6 months ahead at 7am Orlando time) features Cinderella, with possible appearances by her Fairy Godmother and other Princesses. The price includes five souvenir photos.

Cinderella Castle, Fantasyland, The Magic Kingdom. ✆ **407/939-1947.** www.disneyworld.com. Meals $54–$72 adults, $35–$43 kids 3–9, plus park admission. All three meals.

Crystal Palace   Winnie the Pooh and his friends, and a visible kitchen.

Crystal Palace, Main Street, U.S.A., The Magic Kingdom. ✆ **407/939-1947.** www.disneyworld.com. Meals $25–$38 adults, $14–$18 children kids 3–9, plus park admission. All three meals.

Dining with an Imagineer   When your kids have outgrown furry friends, there's still this exceptional mealtime meet-and-greet. Over a four-course meal, groups no larger than 10 hang out with a longtime Disney Imagineer—an art director, designer, or engineer—and have the chance to ask them anything about the mechanics of the resort. At lunch, you need a ticket to Disney's Hollywood Studios, but at dinner, it takes place at the Flying Fish Cafe (p. 176) at the nonticketed Disney's BoardWalk.

Hollywood Brown Derby, Disney's Hollywood Studios or Flying Fish Cafe, Disney's BoardWalk. ✆ **407/939-1947.** www.disneyworld.com. Lunch adults $61, kids 3–9 $35, plus park admission; dinner $85, kids under 14 not recommended.

Garden Grill   Appearances by Mickey, Chip 'n' Dale, and Pluto.

Garden Grill, The Land, Epcot. ✆ **407/939-1947.** www.disneyworld.com. Meals $37–$42 adults, $18–$20 kids 3–9, plus park admission. Dinner.

Princess Storybook Dining   Appearances by the Princesses in the Norway section of Epcot. The price includes photos of your party.

Akershus Royal Banquet Hall, Norway, Epcot. ✆ **407/939-1947.** www.disneyworld.com. Meals $41–$55 adults, $25–$30 kids 3–9, plus park admission. All 3 meals.

Playhouse Disney's Play 'N Dine Appearances by Handy Manny, Jake, Doc McStuffins, and Sofia the First.

Hollywood & Vine, Echo Lake, Disney's Hollywood Studios. ✆ **407/939-1947.** www.disneyworld. com. Breakfast or lunch $25–$32 adults and $14–$17 kids 3–9, plus park admission.

Donald's Dining Safari Appearances by Mickey, Goofy, and Chip 'n' Dale.

Tusker House Restaurant, Africa, Disney's Animal Kingdom. ✆ **407/939-1947.** www.disneyworld. com. Breakfast and lunch $29–$35 adults and $16–$19 kids 3–9, plus park admission.

At Disney-Area Hotels

Chef Mickey's Served by Mickey, Goofy, Donald Duck, and Pluto.

Chef Mickey's, Disney's Contemporary Resort. ✆ **407/939-1947.** www.disneyworld.com. Breakfast or dinner $33–$42 adults, $18–$22 kids 3–9.

Cape May Café Appearances by Goofy, Minnie, and Donald Duck.

Cape May Café, Disney's Beach Club Resort. ✆ **407/939-1947.** www.disneyworld.com. Breakfast $27–$31 adults, $14–$17 kids 3–9.

Good Morning Breakfast with Goofy & Pals Appearances by Goofy and friends; began serving in mid-2014.

Ravello, Four Seasons Resort Orlando at Walt Disney World. 10100 Dream Tree Blvd. ✆ **800/267-3046.** www.fourseasons.com/orlando. Breakfast Thurs, Sat, and some Tues. $38 adults, $18 kids 3–12, including photo.

Supercalifragilistic Breakfast Appearances by a variety of characters, including Mary Poppins.

1900 Park Fare, Disney's Grand Floridian Resort and Spa. ✆ **407/939-1947.** www.disneyworld. com. Breakfast $23–$27 adults, $13–$15 kids.

Cinderella's Happily Ever After Dinner Appearances by Cinderella, Prince Charming, Fairy Godmother, and others.

1900 Park Fare, Disney's Grand Floridian Resort and Spa. ✆ **407/939-1947.** www.disneyworld. com. Dinner $38–$43 adults, $19–$21 kids.

'Ohana Character Breakfast Appearances by Mickey, Pluto, Lilo, and Stitch.

Disney's Polynesian Resort. ✆ **407/939-1947.** www.disneyworld.com. Breakfast $22–27 adults, $13–15 kids.

Garden Grove Appearances by Goofy, Pluto, and others.

Garden Grove, Walt Disney World Swan. ✆ **407/939-1947.** www.disneyworld.com. Breakfast on weekends, dinner nightly. Breakfast or dinner $21–$36 adults, $13–$17 kids.

Universal Orlando

Superstar Character Breakfast Universal's sole character meal has characters from "Hop" and "Despicable Me." It's a good way to get the jump on Harry Potter crowds, too.

Cafe La Bamba, Universal Studios. ✆ **407/224-7554.** www.universalorlando.com. Breakfast $26 adults, $13 kids, plus park admission. Thurs–Sat 8am.

ORLANDO'S HOTELS

7

Orlando has more than 116,000 hotel rooms, a staggering figure. Some 57 million visitors come every year for theme parks, conventions, and outdoor recreation, making the city the world's most popular family vacation destination.

As you can imagine, with numbers that large, competition can be fierce, and at some properties, quality can be lax. A little too often, you find yourself shrugging and saying, "Eh, it does the job." Most of Central Florida's monolithic hotel architecture steals and inflates Europe's palatial traditions; often on such a scale that even a Texan would blush. You'll find arcades, frescoes, columns, Spanish tiles, arched windows, and marble . . . but knock on the columns. They're hollow. Get close to the marble. It's often painted on. And the rooms are just rooms. That's why Orlando's resorts, as much as they charge, rarely achieve true opulence. Here, when you pay for a fine hotel, you're mostly paying for mood. I'll help you look beyond the set dressing to find the best value for you—which may not end up being a hotel at all.

Following are a few key questions to ask yourself to help you choose accommodations in Orlando:

How much space would I like to have? If you have kids with you, will a single hotel room supply the elbowroom everyone needs? Disney's most affordable hotel rooms, for example, have a maximum occupancy of four people in two double beds, so if your group exceeds that number, you'll have to rent two rooms or upgrade to something more expensive. For most families, renting a home or condo solves the space issue, and usually for less money.

Will I have a car? Unless you're a Disney-only type of person, you should have one. The rival resorts plot to keep you on property. Cars can speed you away from their clutches, saving your sanity and your pocketbook. They enable you to see both Disney *and* Harry Potter as well as Orlando's many appealing diversions.

How much time do I plan to spend at my accommodations? If your schedule will be jammed and you're planning to use your room only to hit the sack, then why pay more than you have to? Do you *really* need a fitness center after slogging around the 1.3-mile path of Epcot's World Showcase all day? No, you don't.

Then, grill your hotel about their true value: **Is there a resort fee?** It's increasingly common, and they effectively increase the rate. **Is there a parking fee?** It's another way to hide the true cost of a stay. **What's in the breakfast?** If it's "continental", it could be just instant coffee and a mound of stale croissants. **What's the view?** Properties boast of fireworks views, but neglect to mention they're from 8 miles away.

GETTING THE BEST RATES

Ask any hotel what it charges, and you're unlikely to get a straight answer. Almost all hotels in Orlando delight in changing their rates according to how full they are, but the emptier the hotel is, the more likely it'll be that rates are at their lowest. As a rule of thumb, prices are lowest when kids are unlikely to be in school (summers, spring break), and followed by the light periods in late January, September, October, and early December. Weekends see slightly higher prices, too, because Florida residents drop by. The prices in this guide represent an average rate.

The good news is that Orlando's average nightly rate is $110, which is cheaper than the national average, so you're already working at an advantage. Primary websites that collect quotes from a variety of sources (whether they be hotel chains or other websites) include **Expedia.com, Hotels.com, Kayak.com, Mobissimo.com, Momondo.com, Orbitz.com,** and **Travelocity.com.** Always canvas multiple sites. The bidding areas on Hotwire.com and Priceline.com are more likely to get you the best rates in the month before you travel; hotels hold out for higher prices until then. Then call the local number of the hotel, not the toll-free one (which may connect to an office far away), to see if they'll do even better. Also check **Hotelcoupons.com** for current discounted rates for some of the cheapest motels in town (no promises about their quality, and that hotels frequently refuse to honor the lowest rates if they hit 75–80 percent occupancy).

Another reliable way to get a cheaper room is to buy your reservation along with an **air/hotel package.** No domestic company operates charter flights to Orlando anymore, but several packagers buy cheap hotel rooms in bulk and sell them with scheduled airfare. Check **Lastminute.com** (☎ 866/999-8942), **Funjet** (☎ 888/558-6654; www. funjet.com), as well as some of the vacation wings of major airlines such as **Southwest Vacations** (☎ 800/243-8372; www.southwestvacations.com), **JetBlue Getaways** (☎ 800/538-2583; www.jetblue.com/vacations), **Delta Vacations** (☎ 800/800-1504; www.deltavacations.com), and **American Airlines Vacations** (☎ 800/321-2121;

Theme Park Shuttles: Going Your Way?

Almost all of the hotels located off theme park property tout some kind of "free" shuttle service to the major parks (often covered by your resort fee). When they work, they're a dream, but you need to know that most are restrictive. Many run once or twice a day, on their schedule, and you must book ahead. A typical hotel shuttle may leave for the Magic Kingdom twice a morning and return at, say, 5 and 10pm. Shuttles may provide only one run per direction which drops after the park has opened for the day and returns before it closes, wasting valuable time. Sometimes, hotels will provide shuttles to one area (Disney or Universal/SeaWorld) but not the other. Ask.

Many hotels share shuttles. They can be dirty, worn, and crowded, and you might have to stop at up to a half-dozen other places on your way. If you're hungry, thirsty, tired, or your kids are restless, bring your best Zen face.

Before settling on a hotel based on its advertised rides, ask questions:

1. What time do they leave and return?
2. Which theme parks are not covered?
3. How many other hotels share the same shuttle?
4. Is there a fee? (That $30 for two could have been used to rent a car.)

www.aavacations.com). Internationally, **Virgin Holidays** (www.virginholidays.co.uk) is a huge player, with lots of customer service reps available on the ground should things go wrong. Increasingly, these websites may even sell hotel-only deals using their negotiated rates. Use the properties on its specials page, though, because prices often come out higher in searches.

Few of these players will truly discount a Disney hotel, although they may package Disney products without discounts. If they do, be careful to parse the pricing and compare it to a la carte options—Disney packages are notorious for fees, wasting money, and including more than you could possibly need. Even if you do want a Disney hotel, price be damned, book your Disney hotel separately from tickets or airfare— "room-only," on a separate phone call—because it gives you more scheduling flexibility with Magic Your Way tickets and room-only cancellation rules are far kinder. Don't accept *any* package from a Disney receptionist, even if it's for harmless trinkets, unless you're okay with paying a $200 fee for cancellations made 44 to 2 days ahead; room-only bookings have no penalties for cancellations made 5 to 6 days ahead. When it comes to non-Disney hotels, though, package away, because that's where some great deals live.

Conventions make last-minute bookings risky, but Orlando's **Official Visitor Center** (8723 International Dr.; *⌀* **407/363-5872;** www.visitorlando.com; daily 8:30am–6:30pm) will help you find something. You're also likely to find a room (grotty though it may be) on U.S. 192 east of I-4.

ORLANDO'S HOTELS

Every hotel in this book has a swimming pool (because of liability issues, few are much deeper than 5 ft.), Wi-Fi, and air-conditioning, and almost every hotel offers shuttles to at least some theme parks, although fares around $5 to $10 per person may apply. Pretty much every hotel is kid-friendly. In fact, you should expect even the top-end places to be crawling with scampering, shouting children hopped up on a perpetual vacation-permitted sugar buzz. If you crave peace, steer toward a rental home or one of the splurgy resort hotels that lean more toward the convention trade, in which case the rugrats will be replaced by mobile phone-wielding conference-goers in chinos.

Following are the categories and price ranges for the hotel rooms in this chapter:

- Inexpensive: Up to $95 a night
- Moderate: $96 to $175
- Expensive: $176 and up

Note: Prices in this book don't include taxes, which for hotels add as much as 14.5 percent to your bill depending on the municipality in which you're staying.

Inside Walt Disney World

Some people don't mind spending twice Orlando's going rate so they can be on Disney property near the resort's storied "magic," but they are hard-pressed to explain what that actually means, though it probably has to do with the sensation of security that well-planned theming elicits. But strictly from a non-pixie-dusted consumer-advice standpoint, there are advantages and disadvantages to saying on property. How many of these considerations are important to you—or justify the expense?

DISNEY PRICING SEASONS

Unlike most hotels, which price dynamically, Walt Disney World's hotel rates are fixed by a calendar. The seasons you need to remember are, in descending order of expense: **Holiday, Peak, Summer, Regular, Fall,** and **Value.** The major price spikes, when

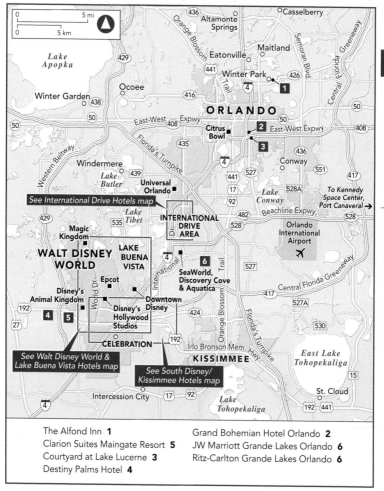

The Alfond Inn **1**
Clarion Suites Maingate Resort **5**
Courtyard at Lake Lucerne **3**
Destiny Palms Hotel **4**

Grand Bohemian Hotel Orlando **2**
JW Marriott Grande Lakes Orlando **6**
Ritz-Carlton Grande Lakes Orlando **6**

charges as much as double, are around spring break, Easter, and the late December holidays—put simple, when school is out.

Likewise, there are three categories of hotel: **Deluxe, Moderate,** and **Value,** plus Disney Vacation Club apartments. Ergo, the get the cheapest room, book a Value resort during a Value period.

SEASONS The dates for each season shift annually and are tweaked per property, but they follow the same pattern on the calendar. For 2014, the schedule shook out like this, including the weekday price of a Value hotel room so you'll know the bottom line of the lowest-priced room (on weekends, prices pop up as much as 25 percent):

o **Value season:** Jan 2–Feb 13, Aug 17–Sept 26. Value price: $96
o **Fall season:** Sept 13–Dec 12. Value price: $110.

Walt Disney World & Lake Buena Vista Hotels

7

B Resort **10**
Barefoot'n Resort **4**
Best Western Lake Buena
  Vista Resort Hotel **11**
Blue Heron Beach Resort **8**
Comfort Suites Maingate East
  at Old Town **5**
Gaylord Palms **3**
Hawthorn Suites Lake Buena Vista **16**
Holiday Inn Express
  Lake Buena Vista **15**
Hyatt Regency Grand Cypress
  Resort **12**
Meliá Orlando Suite Hotel
  at Celebration **2**
Nickelodeon Suites Resort **7**
Quality Suites Lake Buena Vista **16**
Radisson Hotel Lake Buena Vista **13**
Radisson Resort Orlando
  Celebration **1**
Staybridge Suites Lake Buena Vista **14**
WorldQuest Resort **6**
Wyndham Lake Buena Vista **9**

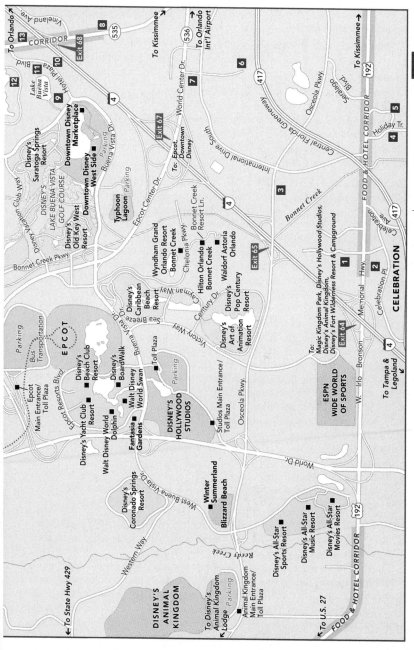

To Orlando
Vineland Ave.
CORRIDOR
Exit 68
535
8

To Kissimmee

536
To Orlando Int'l Airport
6

To Orlando
Hotel Plaza Blvd
Lake Buena Vista
10 11 12
9

Downtown Disney Marketplace
Downtown Disney West Side
4
Exit 67
World Center Dr.
7

Disney's Saratoga Springs Resort
LAKE BUENA VISTA GOLF COURSE
DISNEY'S
Buena Vista Dr.
Parking

Disney Vacation Club Way

Disney's Old Key West Resort

Typhoon Lagoon

Epcot Center Dr.

To: Epcot, Downtown Disney

International Drive South

Central Florida Greenway

Osceola Pkwy.

417

Bonnet Creek

3

Exit 65

4

Wyndham Grand Orlando Resort Bonnet Creek

Chelonia Pkwy.

Bonnet Creek Resort Ln.

Hilton Orlando Bonnet Creek

Waldorf Astoria Orlando

Disney's Caribbean Beach Resort

Century Dr.
Century Way
Cayman Way
Sea Breeze Dr.

Disney's Pop Century Resort

Disney's Art of Animation Resort

Victory Way

To: Magic Kingdom Park, Disney's Hollywood Studios, Disney's Animal Kingdom, Disney's Fort Wilderness Resort & Campground

Memorial Hwy.
W. Irlo Bronson
Exit 64
4
To Tampa & Legoland

1
2

Celebration Pl.
Celebration Ave.
417
CELEBRATION

FOOD & HOTEL CORRIDOR
192
To Kissimmee
Holiday Tr.
5
4

Bonnet Creek Pkwy.

Parking

EPCOT

Bus Transportation
Epcot Resorts Blvd.
Epcot Main Entrance/ Toll Plaza

Disney's Beach Club Resort
Disney's BoardWalk

Buena Vista Dr.

Toll Plaza
Parking

Walt Disney World Swan
Walt Disney World Dolphin
Disney's Yacht Club Resort

Fantasia Gardens

DISNEY'S HOLLYWOOD STUDIOS

Studios Main Entrance/ Toll Plaza

Osceola Pkwy.

World Dr.

ESPN WIDE WORLD OF SPORTS

Disney's Coronado Springs Resort

West Buena Vista Dr.

Winter Summerland
Blizzard Beach

Reedy Creek
Western Way

To State Hwy 429

DISNEY'S ANIMAL KINGDOM

To Disney's Animal Kingdom Lodge

Animal Kingdom Main Entrance/ Toll Plaza
Parking

To U.S. 27

Disney's All-Star Sports Resort
Disney's All-Star Music Resort
Disney's All-Star Movies Resort

192
FOOD & HOTEL CORRIDOR

199

- **Regular season:** Feb 23–Mar 6, Apr 27–May 29. Value price: $105.
- **Summer season:** May 30–Aug 2. Value price: $150.
- **Peak season:** Feb 13–23, Mar 7–Apr 12, Apr 21–26, Dec 12–18. Value price: $152.
- **Holiday season:** Dec 19–Jan 1. Value price: $190–$198.

MouseSavers.com and **TheMouseForLess.com,** both post codes of all current known discounts. In general, AAA and military service may help cut costs.

AMENITIES   All Disney hotels, regardless of class, have touches that provide relief for families, including shallow kiddie pools at each resort, coin laundries, and playgrounds. Wi-Fi is free. There will always be somewhere to eat, although at Value resorts it will be a food court. Disney Transportation System (DTS) shuttle buses (p. 230) serve all resorts for free, and every property is protected by gated security that checks every visitor against the guest list. And, of course, every resort has at least one souvenir store—usually more.

YAY! THE BENEFITS OF STAYING ON DISNEY PROPERTY

- For those without cars, there's **free bus, monorail, and ferry transportation** throughout the resort. This is the biggest consideration for most people. (Then again, it's free to *everyone* at Disney, guest or not.)
- **Free parking** at the theme parks (normally $17 per day for a car).
- The right to make **Fastpass reservations** 60 days ahead (instead of 30).
- Each day, during **Extra Magic Hours,** one or two parks open an hour early or up to 3 hours past closing for the express use of Disney hotel guests. The major attractions, but not all of them, will be open during this period, and lines tend to be shorter than when general admission takes effect.
- Free coach transfers to Orlando International Airport through **Disney's Magical Express** program. See p. 229 for its drawbacks.
- **Every room has a small balcony or patio** (except at Value resorts).
- The right to **charge purchases** on your room key card or MagicBand.
- The right to have in-park **shopping delivered to your room.** (The delivery lag time is such that you should be staying for at least 2 more nights.)
- Three or four timed **kids' activities** a day, albeit some at a charge.
- **Wake-up calls** feature Disney characters.
- Sometimes staff (called "Mousekeeping") leaves **towels shaped like animals** (a Disney tradition).
- **Free wheelchair rental.**
- **Guaranteed admission** if parks are full.
- Option to purchase soft drink **mugs** ($16) that you may refill endlessly while at the hotel.

BOO! THESE THINGS ABOUT STAYING WITH DISNEY STINK

- **"Free" resort transportation doesn't mean "fast."** Routes can be circuitous and waits can be aggravating, and you may have to stand.
- **Rates are 40–70 percent higher** than off-property rooms of comparable quality.
- **Stingy occupancy limits.** Most rooms add $10 a night for each person past the limit of two up to the room's stated maximum capacity, so an $105 room will in fact be $125 if four people over 18 stay there. Value and Moderate resorts cap occupancy at four (not including a babe in a crib) and Deluxe cap at five. Families larger than four must rent two units, doubling the expense, but if you have seven or more people to accommodate, it gets ugly.

How to Save on Lodging

- o **Come during low season.** Hotel prices are trimmed then.
- o **Avoid holidays.** If the kids are out of school, you might pay double.
- o **Make sure the room can fit everyone in your party.** Otherwise you'll have to rent two, doubling costs.
- o **Always get a quote directly from the hotel.** It might be lower.
- o **See what's on offer from a packager.** They have purchasing power.
- o **Plug Kissimmee into Web searches.** It's cheaper than Orlando.
- o **Good locations also save on food.** Are there affordable restaurants nearby?

- o **Haphazard room assignment.** In busy times, families with multiple rooms may get split apart. Requests for specific locations may not be honored.
- o Disney resorts are so large (often, 2,000 rooms) that **lines,** even for a cup of coffee, are an endless nuisance and **sprawling layouts are confusing** to small children, to say nothing of their parents. Disney has turned the failing into profit: It charges $15 more for "Preferred" rooms nearer the lobby.
- o Counterintuitively, the more affordable a room is, they more you could use a rental car. Value rooms are about as **far from the action** as many off-property hotels. The Value resorts, in particular, are a good 15-minute drive from the Magic Kingdom (no farther than a decent vacation home).
- o **Safes** are tiny (laptops won't fit). In-room cooking is made difficult in that the most affordable rooms lack **microwaves** or **coffeemakers.**
- o The most affordable Disney hotels also **don't have restaurants.** They have food courts (burgers, sandwiches, pasta—all at theme park prices of around $10) and the only room service item is pizza. This is less of a problem if you intend to save money by eating off property anyway.

DELUXE RESORTS

No one who has experienced a true luxury hotel can seriously attest that Disney's quality standards compare. They're 3-star hotels in fancy dress. Sure, they have sit-down restaurants, spas, lounges, and elaborate pools (their main calling card). But rooms and service are nothing special. What Disney's Deluxe hotels mostly have is uplifting theming—a prevailing mood—that makes a stay memorable, and it's a genuine thrill to be so near a theme park, to get such fantastic views of the Magic Kingdom or African animals—there's just something special about it. Yes, you can certainly pay less than the $239 to $1,018 you pay to sleep in just a standard room. But for many people, they're more than just a place to sleep.

Most Deluxes enable you to dart out of the parks easily. Three are by the Magic Kingdom on the monorail line encircling the Seven Seas Lagoon: the Contemporary (the most iconic), the Grand Floridian (the fanciest), and the Polynesian (the most private and also nearest the stop for Epcot). A fourth, Wilderness Lodge, is linked to the Magic Kingdom by ferry, while the Beach Club, Yacht Club, and BoardWalk are walking distance from Epcot's side door. Only Animal Kingdom Lodge is marooned by roads, but it has other one-of-a-kind perks that counterbalance that.

For an extra $100 to $150, Disney sells "club-level" concierge-style rooms in a restricted area of certain hotel with a private lounge stocked with free food and beverages. In some hotels, club level entitles you to better views or to buy additional experiences, such as a custom tour of the savannah area at Animal Kingdom Lodge.

Disney's Animal Kingdom Lodge ★★★
No grander lodge ever existed on the African veldt, and the higher tariff returns to you in the form of a 24-hour safari. The hotel is built within a system of paddocks, so if you've got a Savannah view (they start at $409—careful that you don't accidentally book a Standard one overlooking the parking lot), when you look out of your window, you'll see whatever genial African animal is loping by at that moment, be it a giraffe, an ostrich, a zebra, or a warthog. You'll find a game-viewing guide beside your room service menu. Because animals tend to be active in the early morning, when families are gearing up for their days, the idea works well. Like the Contemporary, anyone can visit, even if they're not staying here; there's even a public viewing area straight out the back door of the awe-inspiring vaulted lobby. Its principal drawback is its distance from everything except for Animal Kingdom; all connections are by road.

2901 Osceola Pkwy., Bay Lake. ℰ **407/934-7639** or 407/938-3000. www.disneyworld.com. 1,293 units. $319–$652 nonclub double. Extra person $25. Children 17 and younger stay free in parent's room. Free parking. **Amenities:** 2 restaurants, cafe, lounge, babysitting, supervised children's program, club-level rooms, health club and limited spa, heated outdoor pool, kids' pool, room service, free Wi-Fi.

Disney's Beach Club/Disney's Yacht Club ★★★
Both excellent choices, these sisters are on a pond across from the BoardWalk entertainment area and a short stroll out the International Gateway exit of Epcot's World Showcase, which brings the fun close to your room, although you can't watch IllumiNations from it. Their shared 3-acre pool area, Stormalong Bay, has a crazy water slide coming off the mast of a pirate ship, plus sandy shores. (It's easily the best pool on Disney property, and it's restricted to guests.) The difference between them is nearly negligible—so much so that many guests think they're one giant hotel, but the Yacht Club has slightly nicer furnishings, bigger balconies, attracts slightly fewer families with kids, is a tad quieter, and is at 10-minute stroll from Epcot instead of 5. Other than that, it's a toss-up.

1800 Epcot Resorts Blvd., Lake Buena Vista. ℰ **407/934-7639** or 407/934-8000. www.disneyworld. com. Beach: 583 units. Yacht: 630 units. $400–$743 nonclub doubles. Extra person $25. Children 17 and younger stay free in parent's room. Free parking. **Amenities:** 2 restaurants, grill, 4 lounges, babysitting, supervised children's program, health club and small spa, 3-acre pool and play area, 2 outdoor heated pools, kids' pool, room service, 2 lighted tennis courts, free Wi-Fi.

Disney's Contemporary Resort ★★★
Nothing says, "I'm at Disney World" more than the awesome sight of that monorail sweeping dramatically through its glassy Grand Canyon Concourse, which it does every few minutes on its way to and from the Magic Kingdom. The building itself, one of the first two to open in 1971, has transitioned from "dated" to a midcentury architectural treasure, and indicative of the revolutionary methods that Walt Disney World hoped to pioneer: The United States Steel Corporation helped design it; its modular, prefabricated rooms were slotted into place by crane. The brilliant idea was that when rooms required renovation, the capsules could simply be removed like drawers, but in practice, they fused to the steel frame, so renovations are done the old-fashioned way. The current look: soothing putty and slate business-class colors. The best rooms are high up in the coveted A-framed Contemporary Tower, but there are stylish low-level Garden Rooms along Bay Lake, too, by a surprisingly blah pool, that are about $150 cheaper. Rooms on the west of the tower face the Magic Kingdom itself—from the 9th floor, the *ne plus ultra* of Disney views—and every water-view room takes in the nightly electrical parade that floats

after dark. Even if you can't stay here, this is the best hotel to tour. Drop by to see the 90-foot-tall, stylized mosaics of children by the visionary Imagineer Mary Blair, which encapsulate the late-'60s futurist optimism out of which the resort was born. If money were no object, this would always be a top choice.

4600 N. World Dr., Lake Buena Vista. ℭ **407/939-6244** or 407/824-1000. www.disneyworld.com. 1,008 units. $378–$801 nonclub double. Extra person $25. Children 17 and younger stay free in parent's room. Free parking. **Amenities:** 3 restaurants, grill, 4 lounges, babysitting, concierge-level rooms, small health club and spa, 2 outdoor heated pools, kids' pool, free Wi-Fi.

Disney's Grand Floridian Resort & Spa ★★

It's strange to spend $600 a night on a hotel room and then have to walk outside in the rain to reach the building it's in, but from a value standpoint, that tells you a lot. This is the Disney hotel with snob appeal, since the whole point is to put on a costume of exclusivity and luxury (two things Walt despised, which is why *his* hotels had populist themes) and brag about it when you get home. So it's encrusted with upper-class affectation, from high tea to a pianist tinkling away in a very pretty lobby (chandeliers, glass dome, wedding-cake balconies). It can't help but strum your imagination of what a white-glove Victorian grande dame hotel might have felt like, but anyone can enjoy that on a day visit without paying insane rates for what amounts to a 3-star room. There *are* vacation-making pluses I'd unreservedly celebrate here if money were no object, such as next-door access to the Magic Kingdom, gourmet restaurants, and an atmosphere more romantic than at any other Disney hotel.

4401 Floridian Way. Lake Buena Vista. ℭ **407/934-7639** or 407/824-3000. www.disneyworld.com. 900 units. $549–$1,018 nonclub double. Extra person $25. Children 17 and younger stay free in parent's room. Free parking. **Amenities:** 5 restaurants, grill, 3 lounges, character meals, babysitting, supervised children's program, club-level rooms, health club and spa, heated outdoor pool, kids' pool, room service, 2 lighted tennis courts, free Wi-Fi.

Disney's Polynesian Resort ★★★

The 25-acre hotel, thickly planted and torch-lit by night, was one of the first two hotels planted here, back when the South Pacific tiki craze was still swinging, and the longhouse-style thatched-roof complex remains one of the most transporting of the Disney resorts. The most expensive rooms glimpse the Magic Kingdom across the Seven Seas Lagoon (there's an on-site monorail station for it), but most have greenery views. Everyone can enjoy the volcano-themed swimming pool with water slide tube and a beach with some of the softest white sand you ever sank your toes into (no swimming in the Lagoon, though). It's a notch better for families, as there's an on-site child-care facility, the Epcot monorail is steps away, and rooms are on the big side, sleeping five. An easy favorite. *Note:* Until March 2015, the pool area will be under renovation and guests will receive a free ticket and transportation to Blizzard Beach in compensation.

1600 Seven Seas Dr., Lake Buena Vista. ℭ **407/939-6244** or 407/824-2000. www.disneyworld.com. 853 units. $482–$981 nonclub double. Extra person $25. Children 17 and younger stay free in parent's room. Free parking. **Amenities:** 3 restaurants, cafe, 2 lounges, on-site babysitting, supervised children's program, club-level rooms, nearby health club and spa (at Grand Floridian), 2 heated outdoor pools, kids' pool, room service, free 7:30pm marshmallow roast, free 9pm outdoor movie, free Wi-Fi.

Disney's Wilderness Lodge ★★

This effective riff on Yellowstone's woody Old Faithful Lodge, swaddled by oaks and pines, is picturesque but disconnected from the rest of the park—the Magic Kingdom, 10 minutes away by ferry, is the only thing easy to reach if you don't have your own car. Most of its tricks are in its dramatic atrium lobby: giant stone hearth, springs that flow to a thronged, geyser-themed pool area out back. Because of the surrounding woods, rooms are a little dark, but they have adorable rustic touches headboards carved with woodland creature finials.

901 W. Timberline Dr., Lake Buena Vista. ☏ **407/934-7639** or 407/938-4300. www.disneyworld.com. 909 units. $325–$609 nonclub room. Children 17 and younger stay free in parent's room. Valet parking $12, free self-parking. **Amenities:** 3 restaurants, 2 lounges, babysitting, club-level rooms, health club and limited spa, 2 spa tubs, 2 heated outdoor pools, kids' pool, room service, free Wi-Fi.

Walt Disney World Swan and Dolphin ★   Many people choose them so they can use rewards points from the outside world—that's the main appeal to the Starwood-run Swan and Dolphin, which are linked by a footbridge over the lake they share. Former Disney CEO Michael Eisner controversially allowed outside corporations to intrude on resort property and the result was these dated designs distinguished mostly by splashy exterior set pieces—like the 56-foot tall dolphin fish statues. The ceilings are a little bit low, the staff a little bit distracted, but the location never quits: You can walk to Epcot in 15 minutes and Hollywood Studios in 20, avoiding the bus, which is a good thing for Swan guests since sometimes DTS arrives there after having filled up at the Dolphin. The Dolphin is essentially a business hotel for conferences, although it strives to welcome families, too (rooms fit five and its grotto pool is inviting). Some rooms in the Dolphin's Center Tower have terrific views into Epcot. Everything lacks the tonal fantasy at Disney-run hotels, but guests get the same perks as at a Disney-run hotel, except for DisneyExpress from the airport and the ability to make park purchases by room key or MagicBand: Separate is not equal.

1500 Epcot Resorts Blvd., Lake Buena Vista. ☏ **407/934-4000.** www.swandolphin.com. 1,509 units. Swan: $239–$505 nonclub double, plus $20/night resort fee. Dolphin: $219–$579 nonclub double, plus $20/night resort fee. Extra person $25. Both: Resort fee $20 per night. Children 17 and younger stay free in parent's room. Self-parking $15, valet parking $23. **Amenities:** 4 restaurants, cafe, grill, 5 lounges, character meals, babysitting, free domestic phone calls, supervised children's program, club-level rooms, health club and spa, 5 heated outdoor pools, room service, 4 lighted tennis courts, Wi-Fi included with resort fee.

MODERATE RESORTS

The next category up from Value is Moderate, easily $182 to $284 for a double, if not more. Compared to Value, what do you get for the extra dough? Put simply, the main pools have more elaborate themes with slides and there are usually a few additional, simple pools; rooms measure 314 square feet instead of 260 square feet (so 2 ft. wider); most have two sinks instead of one (both outside the shower/toilet room); all rooms have a small balcony or patio with seating (though most have no view to speak of), and you can rent a bike or a boat on the premises. The upgrade doesn't win you the right to fit more people: Rooms mostly fit four, plus one child under 3, same as the Value class.

Moderate properties feel more resortlike when compared to the glorified motels of the Values, but at heart, they're still glorified motels, with exterior corridors (close your drapes) and windowless bathrooms. You'll still be eating mostly in high-priced food courts located at a main building that might be quite distant from your room. Although the bedrooms aren't really much plusher than the Value properties, you will sense more breathing room and personality to the grounds since Disney has been pouring money into glorifying its Moderate pool areas.

Disney's Caribbean Beach Resort ★   Like Coronado Springs, this resort is sprawling with a central pond—1.4 miles around!—except there's an island theme. Rooms (mostly full beds) are the Moderate category's largest (by a little) and fresh; Disney spent a ton theming some rooms to "Pirates of the Caribbean" (beds like ships, carpet like decking) that cost $44 to $72 more than a regular room. The main Old Port

Royale pool area emulates a waterfront Spanish fort and has a giant tippy bucket, so you can see why families favor this property. The resort's principal drawbacks are a lack of elevators and the fact no other major areas connect to it. At least Port Orleans, for nearly the same money, has boats that go to Downtown Disney; from Caribbean Beach, all connections are by road, so it's strongly recommended to have a car here.

900 Cayman Way, Lake Buena Vista. ℂ **407/934-7639** or 407/934-3400. www.disneyworld.com. 2,112 units. $162–$298 standard double. Extra person $15. Children 17 and younger stay free in parent's room. Free parking. **Amenities:** Restaurant, food court, lounge, arcade, heated pool, 6 smaller pools in the villages, kids' pool, free Wi-Fi.

Disney's Coronado Springs Resort ★★
Built to attract convention crowds with a vibe to match, it nonetheless has fans for its subdued tone. The well-planted grounds, done in a hacienda style around a pond, are far-flung (some rooms are a 15-min. walk from the lobby), and rooms, with kings or queens, have a single sink, as at the Values. The food court is above average, though, as is the pool area (the Dig Site) themed after a Mayan pyramid, and there's a cocktail lounge, Rix, with a semblance of sophistication. The hotel is about 10 minutes' drive from any parks. If you need a room accessible for those with disabilities and the cheaper hotels are out of such units, you can try here, where there is an inventory of 99 rooms.

1000 Buena Vista Dr., Lake Buena Vista. ℂ **407/934-7639** or 407/939-1000. www.disneyworld.com. 1,921 units. $167–$298 double. Extra person $15. Children 17 and younger stay free in parent's room. Free parking. **Amenities:** Restaurant, grill/food court, 2 lounges, arcade, health club and limited spa, 4 outdoor heated pools, kids' pool, free Wi-Fi.

Disney's Fort Wilderness Resort & Campground ★★
Not to be confused with the Wilderness Lodge, an imitation of Yellowstone Lodge, this 780-acre wooded enclave near Magic Kingdom consists of campsites, mobile home–style cabins with decks and grills that sleep six, and RV spots. Camping under the thick pines is far and away the cheapest and most distinctive way to sleep on property, but it's twice the market rate, and without equipment (tents are $30, cots $4, if a group hasn't booked them first). The nightly marshmallow roast and outdoor Disney film screenings are perennial hits.

3520 N. Fort Wilderness Trail, Lake Buena Vista. ℂ **407/934-7639** or 407/824-2900. www.disneyworld.com. 784 campsites, 408 wilderness cabins. $55–$139 campsite/RV double, $330–$562 wilderness cabin double. Extra person $2 campsites, $5 cabins. Children 17 and younger stay free in parent's room. Pets $5 (full hookup sites only). Free parking. **Amenities:** Restaurant, grill, lounge, babysitting, extensive outdoor activities (archery; fishing; horseback, pony, carriage, and hay rides; campfire programs; and more), 2 outdoor heated pools, kids' pool, 2 lighted tennis courts, free Wi-Fi.

Disney's Port Orleans Riverside and French Quarter ★★
An unwieldy name for an unwieldy property. It's actually two resorts, both built on a canal and awkwardly fused together. The French Quarter (1,000 rooms), built along right angles on simulated streets, purports to sorta imitate the real one in New Orleans. Riverside (2,048 rooms), where buildings are more successful pastiches on magnolia-lined Mississippi-style homes (Magnolia Bend, where princess-themed "Royal Rooms" have touches such as headboards with push-button light shows; $30–$40 surcharge) and rustic cabins (Alligator Bayou, where trundle beds sleep five), is the nicer of the two, as it has more water for rooms to face (though the privilege will cost you another $30 a night) and is the locale for most activities for the two resorts. The main pool at Riverside is less elaborate than French Quarter's, although it has five pools to French Quarter's one. The properties are far enough apart (about 15 min. walking) that many people choose to use the free boat service linking them. The boats will also take you

to Downtown Disney—the trip is one of the most pleasant, least known free rides at Disney World—but the parks are served only by buses.

2201 Orleans Dr., Lake Buena Vista. ✆ **407/934-7639** or 407/934-5000. www.disneyworld.com. 3,048 units. $162–$288 double. Extra person $15. Children 17 and younger stay free in parent's room. Free parking. **Amenities:** 2 restaurants, grill/food court, 2 lounges, 6 heated outdoor pools, 2 kids' pools, free Wi-Fi.

Shades of Green ★★★ Operated as a golf resort for 21 years before being handed to the military as the only Armed Forces Recreation Center (AFRC) in the continental U.S., it's the best deal on WDW soil if you or your spouse is an active or retired member of the U.S. military (a full list of eligibility requirements is posted online). Standard rooms are among the largest at Disney (just over 400 sq. ft.) and suites accommodate up to eight. All rooms have balconies or patios, and pool or golf-course views. Bonus: You can walk to the monorail and the Magic Kingdom.

1950 Magnolia Palm Dr. (across from the Polynesian Resort), Lake Buena Vista. ✆ **888/593-2242** or 407/824-3400. www.shadesofgreen.org. 587 units. $93–$131 double (based on military rank); $250–$275 6- to 8-person suite (regardless of rank). Extra person $15. Children 17 and younger stay free in parent's room. Free parking. **Amenities:** 2 restaurants, cafe, 2 lounges, health club, arcade, 2 heated outdoor pools, kids' pool, 2 lighted tennis courts, free Wi-Fi.

VALUE RESORTS

Although the Mouse pushes you toward its most expensive hotels by making them so cool, Disney, in fact, has more Value rooms, 9,504 of them, more than many midsize cities have in total—available for $106 to $236. The T-shaped building blocks with outdoor corridors can feel at times like thin-walled battery hen hutches, with noisy plumbing and seething with kids who don't realize how sound carries (especially when school groups and cheerleader meets are in town). The walk to each hotel's lobby/food building can be a marathon. There are elevators.

FACILITIES Value rooms are motel-style, often of standard cinder-block construction. They come with two full beds, but a few have kings (request one when you reserve). Rooms fit four (there's a $10 daily charge for each third and fourth adult over 17), plus one child under 3—a full room would be a mighty tight squeeze. If your party is bigger than that, spring for a 6-person Family Suite, which is usually just two rooms

---

The "Good Neighbor" Policy

Scattered throughout town as far as the International Drive area are properties Disney has certified as "Good Neighbor" (www.wdwgoodneighborhotels.com). The appellation is mostly meaningless. It means that hotel will have shuttles, can sell Magic Your Way tickets, and screens a mesmerizing 24-hour "Must Do Disney" channel featuring the insanity-inducing Stacey Aswad, the world's most nose-wrinklingly perky Disney fan (she's a Juilliard-trained performer, and to her, everything is "amazing"), and her Top Seven favorites at each park. To be brutally honest, most Good Neighbor hotels are mediocre. Something about the added business that comes with the distinction makes a hotel care a little less about hustling for business. Only the Good Neighbor properties on the west side of Apopka Vineland Road (mostly on Hotel Plaza Blvd.) enjoy half-hourly shuttles; the rest don't. Legoland's version, with its own shuttles, are **"Bed & Brick"** hotels (✆ **800/979-9983**). But don't select a hotel just because it's a Good Neighbor hotel. Choose it because it's the hotel for you.

with a door banged through and a minikitchen (little fridge, microwave, coffeemaker) added. Those are at the All-Star Music resort and Art of Animation, where the design is more spacious, but at $202 (lowest price at Music) to $252 (lowest price at Animation), you can do *much* better outside the World.

The food court, front desk, and sundries shop are all in the same building by the bus stops to the parks, and some rooms are a 15-minute walk away.

TRANSPORTATION No Value or Moderate resort is connected to anything by monorail. Roads are your only option for those categories, be it a bus or your car.

Disney's All-Star Movies/Disney's All-Star Music/Disney's All-Star Sports ★ Depending on your point of view, at the Value resorts, Disney treats you either like a second-class guest or an average American family on vacation. The fun is in the outdoor areas, not in the rooms, which are only faintly themed. Their setup is identical—an expanse of concrete-block buildings at the edge of the property studded with enormous emblems, as if a giant had spilled the Legos in his toy box. But because they're older (they opened in the late 1990s) and there's no enlivening pond, they are the last-choice Values. At the very least, sinks are outside of the toilet-and-shower room, which eases life for multitasking families. Of the three, I prefer Movies, not just because it's the youngest (opened 1999) and because its decor is laden with Disney-specific iconography while its sisters stick to musical and sports-equipment icons. Disney shuttle buses also tend to stop there last on their circuit of the three, which cuts transportation time. Then again, some choose Sports for the same reason, as it's the first stop and so it's easier to get a seat there. (That concern says a lot about the Value resorts.) The Music is the only one with suites fitting six people.

Buena Vista Dr., Lake Buena Vista. ✆ **407/934-1936.** www.disneyworld.com. 1,920 units each. Standard rooms $96–$198, family suites $249–$445, 3rd and 4th adult $10. Children 17 and younger stay free in parent's room. Free parking. **Amenities:** Food court, lounge, arcade, babysitting, 2 outdoor heated pools, kids' pool, free Wi-Fi.

Disney's Art of Animation Resort ★★★ This attractive 2012 addition benefits from theming more lavish than at other Values, including a spot-on Radiator Springs pool area. Family Suites have two bathrooms, convertible couches, and demi-kitchens (no stove). Standard "Little Mermaid" rooms are gorgeously and whimsically themed, too—better than at other Values. Other suites draw on "Finding Nemo" (where there's the Big Blue pool, WDW's largest) and "The Lion King." Unfortunately, 6-person suites cost 2½ times more than basic 4-person Value rooms, which is hard to justify.

1850 Century Dr., Lake Buena Vista. ✆ **407/938-7000.** www.disneyworld.com. 1,120 suites, 864 standard units. Standard rooms $100–$191, 6-person family suites $254–$433. Free parking. **Amenities:** 3 pools, food court, kids' pools, arcade, free Wi-Fi.

Disney's Pop Century Resort ★★ The largest Value resort (opened 2002) is a fair choice, with smallish (260 sq. ft.) rooms with one sink and one mirror, and for dining, a heaving central food court with quality akin to the average mall's. As if to counteract such dormlike austerity, the boxy sprawl of T-shaped buildings, some of which face a pleasant lake, is festooned with outsized icons of the late 20th century: gigantic bowling pins, yo-yos, and Rubik's Cubes—which kids think is pretty cool.

1050 Century Dr., Lake Buena Vista. ✆ **407/938-4000.** www.disneyworld.com. 2,880 units. Rooms $96–$198. Free parking. **Amenities:** Food court, 3 pools, kids' pools, arcade, free Wi-Fi.

DISNEY VACATION CLUB

Disney sells timeshares, too. Since this isn't a real estate guide, there's no need to go into the fact after you crunch the numbers, **Disney Vacation Club (DVC)** is economical only for people who never want to vacation anywhere that isn't Disney. The company rents its empty villa units to walk-up customers who have no intention of signing any dotted lines. So far there are 11 DVC properties in Orlando (grafted onto the major hotels), plus stand-alone properties including **BoardWalk Villas, Saratoga Springs Resort & Spa,** and **Old Key West,** serving hundreds of thousands of DVC investors. That number is a result of heavy promotion around the resort and even inside the theme parks themselves, which Walt surely would have detested as a fantasy-killer. During value season, the simplest studio with a kitchen costs an insane $327 (at Old Key West, the cheapest) a night, and in high season, it costs $431 a night. Bay Lake Tower ranges $492 to $1,006. Knowing that for that money, you could get week's stay at a condo no farther away than Animal Kingdom, or even 10 rooms on Disney property, I cannot in good conscience suggest you spend your money renting a DVC room. I have, though, now informed you they're available.

Non-Disney On-Property Hotels

The best way to think of these choices is "location without immersion." While some visitors find the Disney-run hotels cloying, these properties are permitted to run their own shows on Disney turf, supplying convenience and often, higher standards. Technically, the Bonnet Creek resorts are not on Disney property, but you use Disney roads to get into them so you'd never know the difference.

EXPENSIVE

Four Seasons Resort Orlando at Walt Disney World Resort ★★★ In mid-2014, Orlando's most genuinely luxurious resort opened deep inside the custom-built gated community of Golden Oak, within sight of the Magic Kingdom. Four Seasons' largest property in the world offers luxury as no other Disney hotel does it: Chandeliers were inspired by fireworks blooms and rooms come with walk-in closets and marble bathrooms. The par-71 golf course, once Disney's Osprey Ridge but now renovated by Tom Fazio, is also a bird sanctuary. To see the fireworks from your balcony, you must spring for a "Park View Room," which are $200 more than a "Lake View Room" on the lower floors, or opt for a meal at the rooftop Capa restaurant. As part of that sky-high rate, daytime babysitting is free. If you can afford this pampering, go for it.

10100 Dream Tree Blvd., Godlen Oak. ☏ **800/267-3046.** www.fourseasons.com/orlando. 434 units. From $545 for a standard double, no resort fee, valet parking $26 (no self-parking). **Amenities:** 3 restaurants, pool, children's pool, 5-acre "Explorer Island" splash zone and water slide, lazy river, spa, tennis courts, fitness center, fitness center, sundries shop, character breakfast, frequent Disney shuttle, free standard Wi-Fi, high-speed Wi-Fi (fee).

Hilton Orlando Bonnet Creek ★ Linked to the Waldorf Astoria by a convention hall and set in 482 mostly unbuilt acres, this is a favorite of large groups and one of Hilton's biggest properties. Rooms lack balconies, but they retain that reliable and unsurprising Hilton standard, and it's on Disney property, which counts for a lot. The 3-acre pool area is done in contemporary stonework—a bit like riding a lazy river in a hotel bathroom—and is abuzz with cocktails and activities. Overall, it's a fine place to disappear unnoticed in an upscale resort experience but not necessarily romantic or special. Shuttles to the Disney parks are plentiful and free.

14100 Bonnet Creek Resort Lane, Orlando. ☏ **407/597-3600.** www.hiltonbonnetcreek.com. 1,001 units. $139–$309 for a standard king, plus $22/night resort fee. Parking $16/night. **Amenities:** 6 restaurants, coffee bar, pool bar, pool with activities, Disney shop, golf course, business center, fitness club, spa (at neighboring Waldorf Astoria), game room, free Disney shuttles, Wi-Fi ($17 a night for full speed)

Waldorf Astoria Orlando ★★★ The first time the Waldorf expanded its brand outside of Manhattan it was in Orlando, and if the original's Upper East Side ethic has now been gilded with Florida's tropical colors, the service standard is noticeably higher than at most other Orlando luxury hotels. Between the Rees Jones-designed par 72 golf course, the formally arranged adults-only swimming pool, the high-end Bull & Bear steakhouse, and the sink-deeper-into-slumber beds, this is the best choice of all the Bonnet Creek properties. If the price is similar to the Hilton, book here; for the same money you'll get perks such as bathrobes, better views of distant fireworks, and much more attentive service. You may use the lazy river of the Hilton next door.

14200 Bonnet Creek Resort Lane, Orlando. ✆ **407/597-5500.** www.waldorfastoriaorlando.com. 498 units. $209–$449 double queen. $25/night resort fee. Parking $16/night. **Amenities:** 5 restaurants, pool, kids' activities, spa, fitness center, golf course, golf club, free Disney shuttles, free Wi-Fi.

Wyndham Grand Orlando Resort Bonnet Creek ★ This resort caps off a development of more than 1,000 timeshare villas around a pretty 10-acre lake at the south end of Disney property. When you stay here, you can roam the campus, dipping into pools themed after Caribbean fortresses and pirate ships, barbecuing dinner on public grills. It's a sweet setup, and the fact it's so well-located among Disney's parks makes it better. Be warned that if you book it via a discounter (it's often discounted), it may try to place you in the living room of a half-rented suite; refuse. The **Deep Blu Seafood Grille** (p. 172) is a restaurant highlight.

14651 Chelonia Parkway., Orlando. ✆ **407/390-2300.** www.wyndhamgrandorlando.com. 400 units. $149–$249 standard room, plus $18/night resort fee. Parking $16/night. **Amenities:** 4 restaurants, coffee bar, pool with access to 5 others, 2 lazy rivers, spa, fitness center, kids' activities, gift shop, jogging trail, game room, free Wi-Fi.

MODERATE

B Resort ★★★ The onetime Royal Plaza Hotel, convenient to both I-4 and Downtown Disney, completed a gut renovation in the summer of 2014. Every thread and surface is new, and in place of a tired hotel you have an airy Miami-flavored resort suffused in whites and clean lines. King rooms are much larger than double-queen ones, but all are sizable, and higher-floor ones in the "Stunning" (that's the name) 17-story tower claim views. Ringing the zero-entry pool, "Chic" rooms come with bunk beds to make family stays more fun. The Florida-based company that runs it wants to plow new Disney territory by providing a stylish stay that's still family-friendly and affordable, and it succeeds with fun gimmicks such as loaner iPads and Aveda toiletries. The ground-floor restaurant, American Q, does a riff on barbecue; chandeliers are made out of Mason jars and diners pick buffet items from the flatbed of a Ford F1 pickup truck.

1905 Hotel Plaza Blvd., Lake Buena Vista. ✆ **407/828-2828.** www.BResortLBV.com. 394 units. Doubles from $159–$189. Resort fee $20/night. Parking $16/night, valet parking $21/night. **Amenities:** Restaurant, pool bar, pool, tennis courts, spa, fitness center, sundries shop, free Disney shuttle, free Wi-Fi.

Best Western Lake Buena Vista Resort Hotel ★ Another motel-grade tourist machine on Hotel Plaza Boulevard, the congested road leading to Downtown Disney, this 18-story hotel is older and could use a brush-up (you have to request a fridge or microwave, for example, and there are few electrical sockets). But it distinguishes itself by having a balcony for every room and charging a resort fee of only $10 a day, which is better than the other joints on this strip. It's a fair mid-budget option if you can score a deal online (to pay three digits would be a stretch), and if you're lucky, your room will be high enough to offer fireworks views.

2000 Hotel Plaza Blvd., Lake Buena Vista. ℂ **407/828-2424.** www.lakebuenavistaresorthotel.com. 325 units. $89–$125 2-queen rooms, plus $10 for sleeper sofa. $10 parking with $13 resort fee. **Amenities:** 2 restaurants and a snack bar, pool with children's pool, arcade, fitness center, sundries shop, frequent Disney shuttle, free Wi-Fi.

Wyndham Lake Buena Vista ★ The Wyndham gets passing, but not flying, marks. Rates bottom out at $84 but are usually in the low $100s for the full hotel enchilada, including an aging fitness center, two big pools, shuttles that depart every 30 minutes, minifridges in the rooms, and the only sanctioned Disney character breakfast on Hotel Plaza Boulevard (3 mornings a week). The polished lobby makes everything seem more luxurious than it is, but the kid-friendly staff boosts the value even considering its $18 daily resort fee. Ask for a Tower Room on the west side (floors 9–19) for a limited view of Lake Buena Vista.

1850 Hotel Plaza Blvd., Lake Buena Vista. ℂ **407/828-4444.** www.wyndhamlakebuenavista.com. 626 units. $84 doubles with courtyard view, $115 doubles in tower. $18/night resort fee, $15/night parking. **Amenities:** Restaurant, 3 lounges, character breakfast (Tues, Thurs, Sat), babysitting, children's activity program, health club, spa tub, 2 outdoor heated pools, 2 lighted tennis courts, complimentary bus service to WDW parks, transportation to non-Disney parks for a fee, Wi-Fi.

Inside Universal Orlando

There are four hotels on Universal property, all operated by the Loews hotel group (a fifth, the 1,000-room, Caribbean-themed Sapphire Falls Resort, opens in summer 2016), and they all feel more like true resorts whereas Disney's have a busier feel. There are strong advantages that come with the higher prices. First, all hotels are within 15 minutes' walk of the parks, and three are connected by a free boat that runs continuously into the wee hours. Rooms have wet bars with coffeemakers, two phones, and turn-down service (rare at Disney). Also, every guest can use their room key to make charges throughout the resort, they get into Harry Potter an hour early, and at three hotels, they can join the Express line at the two parks' best attractions—that perk has the effect of freeing up a vacation schedule. Guests can also drink and dine all night at CityWalk next door without having to drive or wait for a bus. Use the hotels' website to find Hot Deals, which grants discounts of 20 to 30 percent on specified nights; the website also posts floor plans of all room types.

The Universal property is hemmed in by lots of real-world restaurants where prices are realistic, and free shuttles to SeaWorld and Wet 'n' Wild are provided once a day. So unlike cloistered Disney, when you're at Universal, you're linked to the real Orlando, and there's more food flexibility. At Easter and during the December holidays, rates are $150 higher than the lowest price.

EXPENSIVE

Hard Rock Hotel ★★★ Besides being the city's most convenient hotel for any theme park—the two parks are both a 10-minute walk away—the Hard Rock has more perks for the money than most of the city's similarly priced hotels. Rooms have genuinely funky furniture, tons of mirrors, two sinks (one in and one out of the bathroom), two big beds, and music systems. The ginormous pool, which imitates a beach gently descending to depth, has not only a substantial water slide but also underwater speakers through which you can hear the party music. (They really bring out the finger cymbals in "Livin' on a Prayer.") The halls are lined with rock memorabilia (whoa: the gold-lion-head necklace Elvis was wearing when he met Nixon!). The Hard Rock really walks the rock walk: On the last Thursday of the month, the lobby is taken over by the rollicking Velvet Sessions (www.velvetsessions.com) concert series for well-known acts, which have recently included Bret Michaels, Taylor Dayne, and Survivor.

5000 Universal Blvd., Orlando. ✆ **888/832-7155** or 407/503-7625. www.hardrockhotel.com. 650 units. Rooms $254–$259. Parking $20/night, valet parking $27/night. **Amenities:** 3 restaurants, cocktail lounge, Emack & Bolio ice cream shop, babysitting, supervised children's program, club-level rooms, fitness center, pool with activities and bar, free Wi-Fi.

Portofino Bay Hotel ★★ Universal's priciest and most romantic option faith-fully re-creates the famous Italian fishing village, down to the angle of the boat docks and bolted-down Vespas. Beyond that spectacular gimmick (said to have been Steven Spielberg's idea, like much at Universal), rooms are of a particularly high standard—standard ones are a generous 450 square feet, have top-end beds, and were fully reno-vated in 2013. But because the resort is the farthest of the four from the parks (about 20 min. by boat or foot), it tends to appeal to couples, but a few kids' rooms are decked out in a "Despicable Me" theme.

5601 Universal Blvd., Orlando. ✆ **888/430-4999** or 407/503-1000. www.universalorlando.com. 750 units. Double queen or king rooms $279–$359. Parking $20/night, valet parking $27/night. **Amenities:** 3 restaurants, Mandara spa, 3 pools with activities and bar, nightly opera show, free Wi-Fi.

Royal Pacific Resort ★★★ The least expensive luxury option at Universal does an apt impression of the South Seas in the 1930s. It's more luxurious yet cheaper than the Disney Polynesian, with a lush pool area (sandy beach, winding garden paths, interactive water play area) and a sophisticated, wood-and-wicker look. The standard is high: very soft robes, cushy beds with fat pillows, and marble-top chests. It's right over the road from Islands of Adventure; many rooms have a panorama of it. In any other city, the Royal Pacific might be everyone's favorite resort. Here, though, its subtler charms get lost in the crowd.

6300 Hollywood Way, Orlando. ✆ **888/430-4999** or 407/503-3000. www.universalorlando.com. 1,000 units. Guest rooms $224–$294. Parking $20/night, valet parking $27/night. **Amenities:** 3 restaurants, sushi bar, cocktail lounge, pool with activities and bars, free Wi-Fi.

MODERATE

Cabana Bay Beach Resort ★★★ Universal's fourth hotel, a 2014 newcomer, is much larger and $100 cheaper than its sisters and it brilliantly plays the role of affordable family vacation hotel by embracing it: It kitsches it up as a retro 1950s fam-ily hotel. Geometric fabrics, teals and lemons, swooping Space Ace architecture, a doo-wop soundtrack, a Jack LaLanne-branded gym, and a 10-lane bowling alley all wink at the midcentury vacation genre. Things may *look* old but they're decidedly modern, down to the ample outlets in the bedrooms, gated parking, and AC that's whisper quiet. In fact, this is the nicest "value" hotel the theme parks have to offer. Uniquely, bathrooms are lined up along the side of the rooms, galley-style, and the toilets are separate from the sink and tub, making mornings easier on families. On the north end of the complex, where a motor court theme prevails, you'll find 600 family suites with kitchen areas (microwave, no stove) that sleep six somewhat tightly, two on a sofa bed. The south courtyard, where the Miami Beach theme and lazy river are, you find standard rooms in 7-story towers. The music never stops in the two ginormous pool areas, fueling the family-friendly party. Its Bayliner Diner is better than it should be for a food court. All in all, the lower price opens Universal to a new group of visi-tors, but there's a trade-off: no Express pass privileges (you do get into the parks early), and to reach the action, you'll have to either walk 15 minutes or take a shuttle.

6550 Adventure Way, Orlando. ✆ **888/273-1311** or 407/503-4000. www.universalorlando.com. 1,800 units. Standard rooms from $119–$134, family suites $174–$284. Discounts for extended stays. Parking $10/day. **Amenities:** Food court, Starbucks, 10-lane bowling alley with food, 2 pools, 2 pool bars, water slide, lazy river, fitness center, free standard-speed Wi-Fi (full-speed $15/day).

U.S. 192 Area Accommodations

The lowest rung in the Orlando tourist ladder both in class and price, U.S. 192 is where you'll find the most affordable (if often the most tired) motels close to the Disney zoo. Most were built in the 1970s boom and settled into the budget category. These places are technically located in the town of Kissimmee, which posts tourist info at **www. experiencekissimmee.com**—check it for regular deals. In this region, shuttles are often available to Disney, but not always to SeaWorld or Universal.

EXPENSIVE

Bohemian Hotel Celebration ★★ The Kessler Collection, which operates chic, art-laden boutique hotels in Savannah, Asheville, and other Old South enclaves, also runs this romantic fantasy come true. The civilized, full-service 115-room property evokes funky Florida and gets the pace and look just right. The lakeside setting is soothing and private—there's nothing on the opposite shore but trees and quiet. Furnishings are tropical, almost postcolonial (four-posted beds, wicker-paddle ceiling fans); the halls are filled with slightly skewed artwork that is a hallmark of the Kessler brand; there's a cool martini-style bar; and the restaurant's Kessler Chophouse is gourmet and worthy of a date. Right out the front door is Celebration's easygoing waterfront downtown, ripe with nonchain boutiques and restaurants, and Disney is a 5-minute drive away, which is a good thing since there is no provided shuttle (another reason this place isn't suited to kids).

700 Bloom St., Celebration. *(Ⓒ* **888/249-4007** or 407/566-6000. www.celebrationhotel.com. 115 units. $139–$209 lake-view king or queen. Daily $15 valet parking or $10 self-parking. **Amenities:** Pool, restaurant, fitness center, cocktail lounge, free Wi-Fi.

Gaylord Palms ★ The Gaylord, run by Marriott, is geared to meetings, so although its scenery is spectacular, so are its incidental charges. Beneath its mighty glass atrium is a 4.5-acre Florida-themed ecosystem of gator habitats, caves, indoor ponds, sand sculptures, restaurants, and a full-size sailboat—all that makes for an attraction unto itself, and to face it, you'll pay about $20 extra. Rooms, renovated in 2012, sleep five and sport unusually nice granite-lined bathrooms. Even if it weren't nestled against Disney property, you could happily never leave, what with the on-site Cypress Springs mini water park, sports bar with two-story screen, adults-only pool, weekend brunches with Shrek, and the Relâche Spa & Salon. It also schedules family activities and an annual holiday ICE! extravaganza (p. 235). Look on its Web page for last-minute rates that can save $25 or so.

6000 W. Osceola Pkwy., Kissimmee. *(Ⓒ* **407/586-2000.** www.gaylordhotels.com/gaylord-palms. 1,406 units. $169 king or double-queen rooms. $20 daily resort fee. $26 valet parking; $18 self-parking. **Amenities:** 2 pools, fitness center, spa, 5 restaurants, sports bar, fitness center, arcade, room service, free local phone calls, character breakfast, park shuttles (Disney free), free bottled water, free Wi-Fi.

Hyatt Regency Grand Cypress Resort ★★ Probably the most complete self-contained resort near Disney, the stepped tower packs every conceivable amenity into a lush 1,500-acre campus located practically within Walt Disney World: 45 holes of golf, an unforgettable waterfall-and-cavern studded lagoon pool, trails wrapping around a private lake, horses, and top-floor views of the fireworks at Epcot and the Magic Kingdom, even from the corridor. Better yet, many of its extras (kayaks, paddleboats, parking close to the building) are free, if you consider free as "included in a high daily resort fee." I've seen $85 Priceline bids accepted. Contrary to its decidedly '80s atrium construction (and a parrot who was allowed to remain in the lobby long after the hotel's previous tropical decor was eliminated), rooms—maximum

South Disney/Kissimmee Hotels

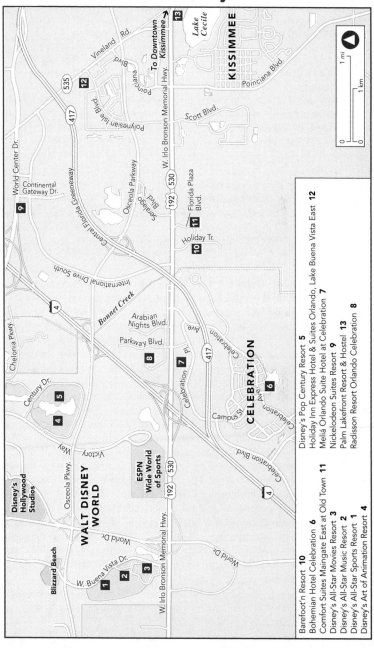

Disney's Pop Century Resort **5**
Holiday Inn Express Hotel & Suites Orlando, Lake Buena Vista East **12**
Meliá Orlando Suite Hotel at Celebration **7**
Nickelodeon Suites Resort **9**
Palm Lakefront Resort & Hostel **13**
Radisson Resort Orlando Celebration **8**

Barefoot'n Resort **10**
Bohemian Hotel Celebration **6**
Comfort Suites Maingate East at Old Town **11**
Disney's All-Star Movies Resort **3**
Disney's All-Star Music Resort **2**
Disney's All-Star Sports Resort **1**
Disney's Art of Animation Resort **4**

Winning at Priceline Roulette

Instead of pecking around Priceline and making blind bids that may waste you money, use one of my three secret-weapon sites, **BiddingTraveler.com, BetterBidding.com,** and **Bidding ForTravel.com,** to find out what recent bids have been accepted. Then you'll get a sense of how low you can go. Using it one low season, I read about a $40 success story for an off-Disney two-star property. I dared to offer Priceline $29—and got my deal. Next, I shopped for rental cars. Although the major renters were offering around $25 a day on their own sites, Priceline accepted a bid of $16, through Alamo. That made for a total of $35 a day for both hotel *and* car—not bad. Three-star hotels go for $40 to $50, and four-stars for $60 to $70, even in summer.

guests: 4—have an almost Asian sleekness with rain showers, chaise lounges, and adapter panels to play multimedia on the 37-inch HDTV.

1 Grand Cypress Blvd., Lake Buena Vista. ⓒ **800/233-1234** or 407/239-1234. www.hyattgrand cypress.com. 815 units. $139–$239 king or double queen, plus $25 daily resort fee. Valet parking $25, self-parking $17. **Amenities:** Pool, babysitting, kids' club, business center, gift shop, babysitting, 3 year-round restaurants, 3 cocktail bars, coffee bar, game room, golf course, rock climbing wall, fitness center, salon, beach, free park shuttles, included Wi-Fi.

Nickelodeon Suites Resort ★★★ The anima-psychedelic image of the basic-cable staple Nickelodeon is kid heaven, with over-stimulation at every turn. The 777-unit, multimillion-dollar hotel, with one- to three-bedroom suites arranged around two courtyards, is so much fun that kids have been known to forget about going to the theme parks. Not only does it have facilities to make a kid's head explode, but it's also got more activities than Disney's moderate hotels. In the two astounding splashdown areas (the less elaborate one, the Oasis, operates only in high season), water cannons blast, a 400-gallon bucket regularly spills water over squealing kids, and 13 slides and flumes twist. Half the hotel comprises of "premium deluxe" rooms kitted out with eye-popping SpongeBob and Dora decor and cost $25 more than "superior" rooms, which are not. It's acts like a theme park: food court, 3,000-square-foot arcade, character breakfasts with Nick icons, a studio for "Double Dare" live game shows in which parents might get "slimed," a cinema for sensory movies, and a kiddie spa. The three-bedroom suites, which sleep up to eight, come with equipped kitchens (so do one-bedroom kitchen suites), two-bedrooms just have a microwave and mini-fridge, while all KidSuites have a kids' bunk room (doorless) with video games. Everything has a pullout double, too. It's a good choice if you plan to spend recharge time back at base (it's wickedly close to Disney turf) or want to let kids off the leash, as security is superb—it's gated and everyone wears wristbands. As you can imagine, it gets pretty noisy. Its website posts last-minute rates that sometimes halve costs. Don't forget that sky-high $30-a-day resort fee, which bumps this otherwise flawless option into the expensive category.

14500 Continental Gateway, Orlando. ⓒ **800/972-2590** or 407/387-5437. www.nickhotel.com. 777 units. Low-season rooms $109 (1-bedroom) to $350 (3-bedroom), high season rooms $209 (1-bedroom) to $599 (3-bedroom). $30-a-day resort fee. Free parking with resort fee and $17/night for additional vehicles. **Amenities:** 2 pools with splash playgrounds and slides, cinema, arcade, souvenir shops, kid's spa, adult cocktail lounge, restaurant and food court, basketball court, character breakfasts, character appearances, park shuttle, babysitting, teen lounge, live entertainment, free Wi-Fi.

MODERATE

Holiday Inn Express Hotel & Suites Orlando–Lake Buena Vista East ★★★ Nicer than its price point should permit, this hotel is clean, impeccably run, attractively appointed in a Spanish style, and located 10 minutes from Disney, out of the fray yet close to food options, and offering a very high quality for the price. Family suites are not divided by proper walls, but by waist-high partitions. This hotel, which opened in 2004 as a La Quinta, has a small arcade with air hockey for kids, and rooms have minifridges and free Internet access. It's enough to make you forget (or resent) all those other worn-down Holiday Inn Expresses. Right outside its driveway, there's a Walmart and, unusual for Florida, a smattering of Halal grocery stores.

3484 Polynesian Isle Blvd., Kissimmee. ℂ **800/423-0908** or 407/997-1700. www.hielbv.com. 148 units. From $98 king, $103 double queen, $111 2-bedrooms with king and 2 twin beds. **Amenities:** Pool, free breakfast, business center, game room, park shuttles, fitness room, free parking, free Wi-Fi.

Meliá Orlando Suite Hotel at Celebration ★★★ Curvy-walled and cloistered, this 240-room hotel arrived on the scene in 2008 (as the Mona Lisa—her grinning image still greets guests in the lobby) and remains a peaceful, well-kept secret. Fittings are top-notch and modern, with fully equipped kitchens including full-size fridges plus dishwashers. Units also have a little patio, with a queen-size pullout to sleep more people. Protected by the hotel's four curving buildings, a perfectly round vanishing-edge pool ringed with funky red pyramid umbrellas recalls South Beach style, lending the sensation of an upscale resort, so it's not the best choice for rambunctious kids. Getting a pool view adds about $20. The location beside the jungle of U.S. 192 very near Disney is prime, but not a lot of people seem to know about it. The best prices are through its own website.

225 Celebration Place, Celebration. ℂ **888/956-3542.** www.meliaorlando.com. 240 units. $120–$219 1-bedroom suite sleeping 4, 2-bedroom suites sleeping 8 $30 more, $219–$269 family suite sleeping 8. $15-a-day resort fee. Free parking. **Amenities:** Pool, restaurant, park shuttles, shuttles to Celebration village, bottled water, free continental breakfast, free Wi-Fi.

Radisson Resort Orlando Celebration ★★ Cheaper than its sister hotel in Lake Buena Vista, this property aims squarely at the family crowd with a sports lounge, an active grotto pool area with a 42-foot rock slide, and rooms that have two double beds or one king each. It's also one of the fresher choices in town, having just enjoyed a 2014 renovation that poured $10 million into improvements, fitting it with pillow-top mattresses and granite-counter bathrooms. Adding to the convenience, it's a few hundred yards off U.S. 192, giving you all of its convenience but none of its nuisances, and there's an Action Car Rental office right across the lot.

2900 Parkway Blvd, Kissimmee. ℂ **800/634-4774** or 407/396-7000. www.radisson.com/lakebuenavistafl. 718 units. Rooms from $79 plus $20/night resort fee. Free parking. **Amenities:** Restaurant, pool, business center, small fitness center, sand volleyball, lighted tennis and basketball courts, free Epcot shuttle, free Wi-Fi.

INEXPENSIVE

Barefoot'n Resort ★ These lemon-colored one-bedroom villas a block off chain restaurant–lined U.S. 192 are everything you need in simple, condo-style accommodation. Rooms come with queen beds, washer and dryer, DVD players, and a sofa sleeper, but you choose between having a fully equipped kitchen with a dishwasher and bar seating or larger bedroom with a spa tub and a partial kitchen. You take care of your own cleaning during your stay. The very sunny pool area has a grill and also faces a pond that's home to brown ducks and a little alligator, Crocky. The tiny resort, which is in good shape and recently renovated, faces the Old Town amusement area, but the drifting music isn't bothersome. If you book by phone, there's no minimum stay requirement.

2754 Florida Plaza, Kissimmee. ☏ **877/978-3314.** www.barefootn.com. 42 units. 1-bedrooms $89–$95. Free parking. **Amenities:** Pool, hot tub, security gate, outdoor barbecue, free Wi-Fi.

Clarion Suites Maingate ★★   A superior-level motel organized around its pool, the Clarion has a quiet, pseudo-resort feel (it's set away from the bustle of U.S. 192 but near enough to its restaurants) that makes it popular with scrimpers. All rooms come with a small fridge, microwave, and pullout sofa (hence the "suites" distinction of the hotel's name), queen beds, and sleep up to six people. During the week, rooms facing the parking lot usually cost the least, and ones facing the landscaped, free-form courtyard pool cost $10 more. Prices on weekends are about $10 higher, and continental breakfast, with a few plusses such as waffles, is always included. Kids get excited when they look down its driveway and see the summit of Expedition Everest at Disney's Animal Kingdom peeking over the trees nearby.

7888 W. Irlo Bronson Hwy., Kissimmee. ☏ **888/390-9888** or 407/390-9888. www.clarionsuites kissimmee.com. 150 units. $83–$109 doubles. Free parking. **Amenities:** Pool, restaurant, Disney shuttle, free breakfast buffet, game room, barbecue grills, sundries shop, free Wi-Fi.

Comfort Suites Maingate East at Old Town ★★   A good choice for families with kids, it's tucked just off the main drag of U.S. 192, a few miles east of Disney, and both the restaurants and the carnival-style amusements of Old Town are mere steps from the door—but not so near that the noise is truly annoying. The best rates are for "standard rooms" with either a king or queen bed, but you can get a "deluxe" two-bedroom one for about $40 more, and all rooms are on the large side with mini-fridges and microwaves for basic meal preparation. The elevators can be overwhelmed when it's at capacity. Up your occupancy by two by using the pull-out couch that's standard in every unit. AAA membership chops rates slightly.

2775 Florida Plaza Blvd., Kissimmee. ☏ **888/784-8379.** www.comfortsuitesfl.com. 198 units. $79–$169 1-room suites. Free parking. **Amenities:** Pool with poolside bar, 24-hr. fitness center, sundries shop, game room, business center, free park shuttles, free hot breakfast buffet, free Wi-Fi.

Destiny Palms Hotel ★★   Standards are high considering it's at the affordable end of the motel spectrum, and although the decor is less than pristine (it could be classified as "Early '80s Beige"), the staff keeps things spotless, and that's what you want. Rooms, all of which are nonsmoking, come stocked with a toaster oven, mini-fridge, free Wi-Fi, and a continental breakfast upgraded with eggs, oatmeal, pancakes, and waffles. King rooms face the north parking lot and are on the small side while double queen rooms look south on some pleasing old-growth Florida woods. The east-facing pool (it, too, is motel-simple) also faces the trees, which keeps this place from feeling hemmed in. Coupons from the tourist circulars often halve prices to $30 to $40.

8536 W. Irlo Bronson Hwy./U.S. 192, Kissimmee. ☏ **407/396-1600.** www.destinypalmshotel.com. 104 units. $60–$70 doubles plus $3.50-per-night resort fee. Free parking. **Amenities:** Pool, free continental breakfast, free local calls, free Wi-Fi.

Palm Lakefront Resort & Hostel ★   Meet the absolute cheapest respectable option in town. The facilities, cinder-block construction, and past-its-prime stretch of U.S. 192 will put pampered types off, but there are major plusses for a budget property, starting with attentive upkeep and a convivial international clientele. It backs up to Lake Cecile with its own dock, and there's also a pool in the giant backyard, where there's also a barbecue pit. You'll find simple private rooms with cable TV, private bathrooms, and twin beds, plus a family room sleeping five ($15 per person). Across the street, there's a Publix supermarket for munitions (the hostel has an equipped kitchen), and the $2 city bus to Disney goes right past the front door. You can't hope for more for rock bottom.

4840 W. Irlo Bronson Hwy./U.S. 192, Kissimmee. © **407/396-1759.** www.orlandohostels.com. $36 doubles $36, $19 dorm beds. Free parking. **Amenities:** Pool, barbecue, shared kitchen.

Lake Buena Vista

Roughly speaking, Lake Buena Vista is the area where the eastern end of Walt Disney World around Downtown Disney/Disney Springs meets exit 68 off I-4. LBV, as it's nicknamed, is more compact and higher-class than the comparable cluster of Kissimmee hotels along U.S. 192, a few miles south near Disney's southern gate. One of its magnets is the Crossroads shopping center, walkable from most points, where you'll find plenty of restaurant chains and a high-priced grocery store. For breathing room, the best part of Lake Buena Vista is Palm Parkway, a lightly trafficked, winding, tree-lined avenue of fairly new corporate hotels. It's a secret shortcut that avoids I-4. Drive north on it and you'll pass a turnoff for SeaWorld, a Walmart, a Whole Foods, the restaurants of Sand Lake Road, and eventually you'll hit Universal.

LBV is so compact that you could theoretically walk to Downtown Disney and from there use the free Disney bus system, obviating the need for a rental car. Or you could take a taxi to each Disney park (although doing so would not save you much more than getting an inexpensive rental car). Such convenience comes with a trade-off: You'll often pay higher prices than you have to in Kissimmee or on I-Drive, and traffic stinks. Free shuttles around here tend to go to Disney but not to Universal or SeaWorld.

See the map on p. 198 for locations of the properties below. Also investigate the **Crowne Plaza Orlando—Lake Buena Vista** (12390 S. Apopka Vineland Rd., Orlando; © **800/439-4745;** www.ihg.com), which was slated to open after a gut renovation in October 2014, too late for review. It's one of the newest choices.

MODERATE

Blue Heron Beach Resort ★   Ignore the deceptive "beach resort" part; you stay at this mid-priced condo-style property to get above it all. These two high-rise towers overlook Lake Bryan, furnishing the illusion that you're only person in the city and not a mile off Disney property. Units are huge but not artistically furnished, have a private balcony, a washer/dryer, a sleeper sofa, two bathrooms (even in one-bedrooms), and a kitchen so well equipped it even has a blender (margarita time!). There are bunk beds in the hall to increase sleeping capacity for families. The best value is the two-bedroom units, which have perspectives of both the lake to the west and of Disney to the east; from high floors, you can see fireworks.

13428 Blue Heron Beach Dr., Lake Buena Vista. © **407/387-2200.** www.blueheronbeachresort. com. 283 units. $99–$129 1-bedrooms, $129–$199 2-bedrooms, plus $12 resort fee. Housekeeping $15–$25 per service. **Amenities:** Pool with hot tub and kids' area, Disney shuttle, fitness center, game room, free parking. free Wi-Fi.

Holiday Inn Express Lake Buena Vista ★★   At first, the six-story hotel doesn't look like much more than a concrete box the color of orange sherbet, but it's got a number of advantages over other hotels. First, its location is near both Disney and plenty of restaurants on the westernmost stretch of quiet Palm Parkway. Rooms are spotless and come with microwaves and fridges, plus balconies made truly private by concrete walls. The pool, found out back where sounds of frolic at its one-story rock

Credit or Debit?

If you use your debit card (instead of a credit card) as collateral against any purchases you may make during your stay, your card may be charged $50 to $250 (or more) *per day*, whether you actually charge anything to your room or not. This policy can seriously deplete your checking account, leaving you with far fewer funds than you might realize—and you won't see a credit back to your account until *up to 10 days after* you have checked out of your resort. Ask about your hotel's policy.

waterfall and short slide won't disturb other guests, is open until midnight—ideal for postpark wind-downs. This old-school, reliable hotel comes with no surprises.

8686 Palm Pkwy., Orlando. ✆ **800/465-4329** or 407/239-8400. www.hiexpress.com. 200 units. $109–$149 double. Free parking. **Amenities:** Pool, free buffet breakfast, business center, free local calls, free Epcot shuttle, fitness room, kids eat free, free Wi-Fi.

Radisson Hotel Lake Buena Vista ★★★ Gleaming, professionally run, and consistently top-notch for a nonresort hotel. Rooms feel current and are packed with the latest modern conveniences such as HDTVs, iPod docks, free Internet, minifridges, and microwaves. Size is beyond the average, too: Bathrooms are spacious, and in a 2007 gut renovation, old balconies were incorporated as sitting areas with pullout couches, so a superior room can sleep up to five. There are a few downers, such as tricky entry that requires some U-turning, a dull but sunny pool area, and infrequent free shuttles, but those bummers are entirely offset by the quality of the rest and by the fact it's a short, safe walk to the many restaurants of the Crossroads shopping center. Its website often offers the best prices.

12799 Apopka Vineland Rd. ✆ **800/967-9033** or 407/597-3400. www.radisson.com/lakebuenavistafl. 196 units. Rooms $99–$165. Free parking. **Amenities:** Pool, small fitness center, restaurant, free Wi-Fi.

Staybridge Suites Lake Buena Vista ★★ A little bit north of the Hotel Plaza Boulevard gate to Disney World, and close to lots of restaurants, you'll find these apartment-like quarters (there are two TVs and the kitchens even have dishwashers), which were renovated in recent years. The three-level buildings don't have elevators, but overlook that fact and avoid the ground-floor rooms, which are darker and less private. The full breakfast is free and plentiful, and you can eat it indoors or out. There's also a well-used pool in one of the courtyards. Expect rates along the lines of $140 for a one-bedroom with a king-size bed (sleeps four), or $30 more for a two-bedroom (sleeps six), with prices rising $20 to $40 when it's busy. The Disney shuttle is free. Home or condo rentals are cheaper, but you won't find many of those so close to Disney grounds, and those also come with cleaning fees and minimum stays.

8751 Suiteside Dr., Orlando. ✆ **407/238-0777.** www.sborlando.com. 150 units. $110–$145 1-bedrooms sleeping 4 and $110–$176 2-bedrooms sleeping 8. Free rollaways and cribs. Free parking. **Amenities:** Full breakfast, heated pool, spa tub, business center, sundries shop, free Wi-Fi.

WorldQuest Resort ★★★ A richly appealing facility that looks and feels like a luxury condo complex. Surrounded by nothing but trees and peace, yet only a mile from Disney property, its five-floor buildings gather around a lush, fountained pool area. Each unit is a fresh, contemporary apartment complete with full fridge and freezer, fully equipped kitchens you could bake a cake in, screened-in furnished balconies, DVD player, and a master bathroom that's the size of some hotels rooms elsewhere in town. Here's a major downside: It has no full restaurant and it's too isolated to walk anywhere, so you must use a car. Bookings made on Travelzoo waive the resort fee, and Expedia often packages it for less than you could get directly.

8849 WorldQuest Blvd., Orlando. © **877/987-8378** or 406/387-3800. www.worldquestorlando.com. 238 units. $129–$189 2-bedroom/1-bathroom suites, add $20 for a 3rd bedroom; 3-night minimum stay or a $39 fee; $15-per-night resort fee. Free parking. **Amenities:** Pool with cabana bar, security gate, fitness center, sundries shop, free continental breakfast, free Disney shuttle, free Wi-Fi.

INEXPENSIVE

Hawthorn Suites Lake Buena Vista ★   The decor is a touch dated (no flatscreen TVs, for example), but the management is attentive and hard-working, so this L-shaped property, arranged around a quiet and uncomplicated kidney-shaped pool, is all you could need for a home base. The special appeal of this place is its full kitchens, standard in all rooms, with dishwashers, stoves, cookware—what you need to cook for yourself and save. All suites are one-bedroom suites, and the cheapest ones have two queen beds. Monday through Thursday afternoons, free cocktails are served, and on Wednesday from 5:30pm to 7:30pm, there's a "Manager's Reception" serving a free hot dog or hamburger.

8303 Palm Pkwy., Orlando. © **866/756-3778** or 407/597-5000. www.hawthornlakebuenavista.com. $79–$159 double. 120 suites. **Amenities:** Pool, hot tub, small fitness center, breakfast buffet, park shuttle, game room, business center, sundries shop, free local calls, free Wi-Fi.

Quality Suites Lake Buena Vista ★★   Fronted by three-story-tall palm trees, these mini-apartments could be called simple but inviting. Probably because it's a pipsqueak among lions, its attentive managers charge a competitively low price and even throw in a cooked breakfast. All rooms, which are larger than the average, have two TVs and fully equipped kitchens with a big fridge, toaster, microwave, dishwasher, and stove—a rarity among hotels that usually make do with microwaves alone, and a lifesaver when it comes to saving money on dining. The hotel is close enough to the Disney parks to make for a realistic lunch break, and the basic pool is open until 11pm, so you can use it for end-of-the-day soaks.

8200 Palm Pkwy., Orlando. © **800/370-9894** or 407/465-8200. www.qualitysuiteslbv.com. 123 units. $79–$139 doubles. $159–$249 2-bedroom units sleeping up to 8. Free parking. **Amenities:** Pool and hot tub, fitness room, Disney shuttle, free buffet breakfast, free local calls, business center, game room, grills, sundries shop, free Wi-Fi.

International Drive, Universal

I-Drive is probably the best place to stay if you don't have a car because it's central, well connected, and full of competing places to eat. It's also the only hotel zone with a semblance of street life. If you stay here, you'll be in the thick of the family-friendly come-ons, amusement halls, minigolf, and theme bars. You'll need wheels to reach Disney (most hotels offer shuttles, but not always to Disney, and not always for free), although Universal is just across I-4 to the north and the dirt-cheap I-Ride Trolley (p. 230) links you with SeaWorld. On many nights around dinnertime, car traffic can clog I-Drive, but there's a workaround: Universal Boulevard, a block east, bypasses the mess. Get ready for change: The new Orlando Eye, open by 2015, has hotels preparing with new coats of paint—and some of them now charge guests for parking.

EXPENSIVE

Hyatt Regency Orlando ★   Until 2013, it was a spinoff of the famed Memphis Peabody Hotel but now it's a Hyatt to its conventioneering core. Expect gleaming glass, echoing marble, sculptural waterfalls, luxuriously appointed bathrooms, ankle-level lights that switch on when they sense your movement, and other high-end touches that appeal to business travelers. Walking to I-Drive's restaurants is easy (driving out of the remote parking structure, not so much), and the free-form tropical pool is gorgeous, but in sum it feels more like a place where expense accounts are spent than where cherished memories are made.

9801 International Dr., Orlando. © **407/284-1234.** http://orlando.regency.hyatt.com. 1,641 rooms. $185–$425 doubles for up to 4 plus resort fee of $20/night. $16 self-parking, $26 valet, **Amenities:** 3 restaurants, cocktail bar, pool with children's area, spa, babysitting, free Wi-Fi for one device.

JW Marriott Grande Lakes Orlando/Ritz-Carlton Grande Lakes Orlando ★★★
A true resort and a smart choice for a well-rounded vacation, the two luxury towers form a city unto themselves, and indeed, the JW's profile rises like a citadel in a 500-acre plot east of SeaWorld. The JW's 24,000-square-foot pool area, landscaped with fake rocks, jungle greens, and a ¼-mile lazy river, is the poshest outside of the Disney water slide parks, while the Ritz's is formal and refined. The JW's rooms has tile floors and slots for plugging your MP3 player into the plasma TVs. Yes, like many fancy convention hotels, it's a nickel-and-dime experience—everything costs you. As long as you know that in advance, the hotel's upscale amenities (gurgling lobby fountain, echoing bathrooms with separate bathtub and shower, palatial beds, narrow balconies on many rooms) are pleasing, even if the remote location 15 minutes from the parks means you'll have to drive somewhere every time your stomach rumbles if you want to escape resort pricing. At the Ritz-Carlton attached by a corridor, the three-level, 40,000-square foot spa is well reviewed and in the rooms, the pamper factor is yet a notch higher. Both have unobstructed views of a Greg Norman–designed golf course and a nature reserve; west-facing rooms take in sunsets and SeaWorld in the distance. **Primo,** Chef Melissa Kelly's restaurant at the JW, and **Norman's,** Chef Norman Van Aken's ode to Florida flavors at the Ritz, are two top-of-the-line restaurants that would be a credit to any resort.

4040 Central Florida Pkwy., Orlando. © **800/576-5760** or 407/206-2400 for the Ritz; © **800/576-5750** or 407/206-2300 for the JW Marriott. www.grandelakes.com. JW: 1,000 rooms, Ritz: 584 units. $183–$599 double. No resort fee. Valet parking $25; self-parking $18. **Amenities:** 7 restaurants, 3 lounges, babysitting, kids' activities, spa, sundries shops, club-level rooms, health club, golf course, 2 outdoor heated pools, kids' pool, 3 tennis courts, transportation to non-Disney parks for a fee, Wi-Fi ($15).

MODERATE

Drury Inn Suites ★★★
A top pick. The popular privately owned Missouri-based hotel group expanded to Orlando in July 2012 on an ideal plot—drive around the corner to Universal, down Palm Parkway to Disney, or go on foot to the restaurants of I-Drive or Sand Lake Road. Design is fresh in rust browns and greens, rooms are wider than the industry average, and there are tons of free extras. So friendly is this brand that every day at 5:30pm, it hosts a "Kickback" with free food, beer, and wine. You could make a dinner out of it, and retire to a room that is newer and cleaner than just about any other budget property in Orlando right now. The king-bed category has only a shower; the others have tubs.

7301 W. Sand Lake Rd., Orlando. © **407/354-1101.** www.druryhotels.com. 238 units. $109–$146 1-king or 2-queen rooms. Free parking. **Amenities:** Indoor/outdoor pool, free hot breakfast, free soda and popcorn, 24-hr. fitness room, business center, free local calls, pets permitted for free, free Wi-Fi.

Four Points by Sheraton Studio City ★
Because it occupies one of those dated cylindrical towers that were briefly in vogue in the early 1970s, the ideally located property has slight novelty that doesn't translate to luxury. It's just an interesting mid-priced

International Drive Hotels

Avanti Resort **12**

Cabana Bay Beach
Resort **5**

Drury Inn Suites **8**

Fairfield Inn Orlando
InternationalDrive/
Convention Center **9**

Four Points by Sheraton
Studio City **6**

Hampton Inn Orlando
Convention Center **14**

Hard Rock Hotel **2**

Hyatt Place Orlando
Universal **3**

Hyatt Place Orlando/
Convention Center **13**

Hyatt Regency Orlando **16**

La Quinta Inn International
Drive **10**

Portofino Bay Hotel **1**

Rosen Inn **7**

Rosen Inn at Pointe
Orlando **15**

Royal Pacific Resort **4**

Sonesta ES Suites **11**

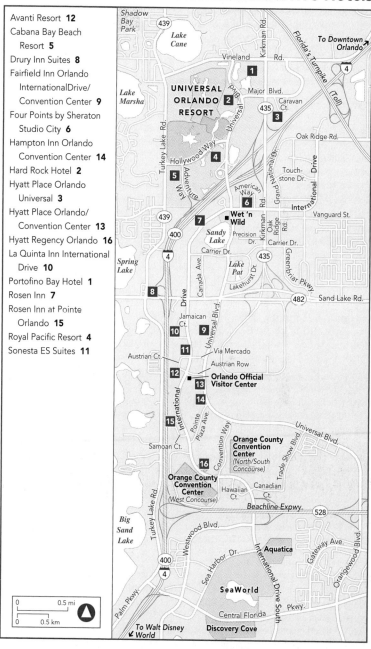

choice. Because rooms are carved out of the floors like pie pieces, they're more spacious than the norm, and many have two queen beds. Request a room that doesn't face east, as the floodlights from the minigolf joint next door are blinding. The top floors have spectacular views of I-Drive, Wet 'n Wild (to the west), and Universal (just over I-4 to the north). It's not luxury, but it approximates it, and views in Orlando are rare at any price (particularly the $48 I've seen turn up in blind Hotwire bookings). Breakfast's $10, but there's an IHOP next door.

5905 International Dr., Orlando.℃ **888/625-4988** or 407/351-2100. www.fourpointsorlandostudio city.com. 301 units. $99–$119 doubles. Free parking. **Amenities:** Pool, pool bar, restaurant, cocktail lounge, business center, park shuttles, free Wi-Fi.

Hyatt Place Orlando Universal ★★★

You check in at a kiosk that spits out your key, and without delay, head to a huge semipartitioned room with giant beds and a sitting area, plus an extra pullout sofa. If you're not familiar with the standardized brand, it has up-to-date design, a 42-inch HDTV you can plug a laptop or a iPod into, granite bathrooms, wet bar, free continental breakfast, Wi-Fi, and plenty of space for five (six if two sleep on the pullout), all from $89. Seriously, why can't they all be like this? A second location at I-Drive isn't within spitting distance of Universal's gates as this one is, but it is nearer to more places to eat (8741 International Dr., Orlando; ℃ **407/370-4720**; http://orlandoconventioncenter.place.hyatt.com; 150 rooms, $127–$209 rooms two double beds). Both underwent 2013 renovations.

5895 Caravan Ct., Orlando.℃ **407/351-0627.** http://orlandouniversal.place.hyatt.com. 151 units. $87–$179 rooms with 2 double beds, $20 more for king bed. Free parking. **Amenities:** 24-hr. prepared meals, fitness center, free park shuttle, free breakfast, free Wi-Fi.

Rosen Inn at Pointe Orlando ★★

One of the largest budget-priced properties outside of Disney's Value developments (so expect family noise) this former Quality Inn sprawls over 2 well-located city blocks and six Nixon-era buildings (renovated 2010). I-4 runs along the western side, resulting in a constant hum. You'll see rates for as little as $50 a night on sites such as Otel.com, so don't pay three figures. Respectably affordable units, which come with a fridge, microwave, and two double beds, have smoked-glass windows, which helps create privacy given the external corridor construction, but doesn't help illuminate the bathrooms in the back. Rooms in the A building are near the lobby but suffer daytime noise from the sightseeing helicopter pad next door; opt for something in the F building, which is a 10-minute walk/2-minute drive from the lobby and has the most rooms hidden from I-4. Parking is gated but free. You'll feel like you're back on an '80s vacation with Dad just by walking past the three big pools, where kids work off their postpark highs. Many eateries are within walking distance on I-Drive. Universal is 10 minutes north, SeaWorld 5 minutes south.

9000 International Dr., Orlando.℃ **800/999-8585** or 407/996-8585. www.roseninn9000.com. 1,020 units. $99–$129 rooms with 2 doubles. Free parking. **Amenities:** 2 pools, playground, restaurant, bar, free local calls, free shuttle to Universal and SeaWorld, charged shuttle to Disney, free Wi-Fi.

Sonesta ES Suites ★★

In anticipation of the I-Drive Live project, this well-located all-apartment hotel, near plenty of places to eat and arranged around a courtyard pool, was just lavished with a gut renovation, so there are fewer moderate properties that are as current. All units will have new kitchens with new appliances, just-installed furniture, fresh carpeting, and bedding, a booth for family meals, and lots of added electrical outlets for recharging. Suddenly a dowdy '80s holdover has become a barely slept-in mid-priced darling. The staff is unusually dedicated, and some have been running this property for years.

8480 International Dr., Orlando. ✆ **407/352-2400.** www.sonesta.com/orlando. 146 units. 1-bedrooms $124–$189, 2-bedroom/2-bath $30–$40 more. Free parking. **Amenities:** Free breakfast, pool, spa tub, bar, sundries shop, small fitness center, free park shuttles (for Disney, connect via Epcot), free Wi-Fi.

INEXPENSIVE

Avanti Resort ★ Let's be frank: This is just an EconoLodge that got an extreme makeover. It still has the creaky bones of a motel, with small bathrooms, exterior corridors, and an echoing central pool. Yet because of its renovation, and those up-to-date mellow colors and cool laminate floors, it's one of the fresher faces on I-Drive and consequently a good value. Double queen rooms sleep up to 4 and have fridges and microwaves, and the location makes it easy to walk to a slate of cheap places to eat. But it's not a "resort" by any stretch. It's an upgraded motel, but a nice one at that.

8738 International Dr., Orlando. ✆ **855/828-2684.** www.avantiresort.com. 652 units. Doubles $65–$119, plus $8/night resort fee. Free parking. **Amenities:** Restaurant, coffee bar, pool, fitness room, sundries shop, business center, game room, free local calls, park shuttles, free Wi-Fi.

Fairfield Inn Orlando International Drive/Convention Center ★★★ A 2013 newcomer, it's as sparkling clean and pristine, with a terrific location by the Orlando Eye, which you can walk to. Expect large rooms in yellows and oranges, outlets galore, and large counters and desks to spread out on. On the east, rooms face nothing but greenery. True, the elevators and breakfast buffet can get a tad overwhelmed in the mornings and you have to ask for a room with a mini-fridge or you may not get one, but overall, it's a real find, as bright and as fresh as you could wish for an affordable hotel. Management cares, too; without knowing me, it phoned me 10 minutes after my check-in to ask how I was settling in. Hotwire can bring its rate into the $70s.

8214 Universal Blvd., Orlando. ✆ **407/581-9001.** www.marriott.com. 160 units. $94–$159 doubles. Free parking. **Amenities:** Pool, free breakfast buffet, sundries shop, free Wi-Fi.

Hampton Inn Orlando Convention Center ★★ It may be just like every other Hampton Inn you've ever seen (they must make these buildings from kits), but that doesn't detract from the fact the place is in good shape, there are plenty of restaurants and a multiplex within walking distance, and the cheerful staff runs a tight ship. Stays include a bountiful all-you-can-eat breakfast, including a few hot dishes; there's also a 24-hour lobby booth selling snacks and sundries. I have personally witnessed front-desk clerks offering to beat competitors' prices. Ask for a room on the south side, as these don't face other nearby buildings.

8900 Universal Blvd., Orlando. ✆ **800/426-7866** or 407/354-4447. www.orlandoconventioncenter. hamptoninn.com. 170 units. $79–$160 doubles or rooms with 2 double beds. Free parking. **Amenities:** Pool, free hot breakfast, fitness room, sundries shop, free Wi-Fi.

La Quinta Inn International Drive ★ A veteran four-floor motel with external corridors and the usual minor noise inconveniences of the category, it's not a bad choice if you want a clean, basic place off I-Drive. Windows are on the large side, and most face an interior heated pool cloister instead of the whoosh of Interstate 4. The rooms facing I-4 tend to drive some guests nuts, so request accordingly. Don't believe the rack rate; you can get this place for $49 using the coupon books around town.

8300 Jamaican Ct., Orlando. ✆ **800/753-3757** or 407/351-1660. www.orlandolaquinta.com. 200 units. Doubles from $89. Free parking. **Amenities:** Pool, bar, free breakfast, free local calls, free Wi-Fi.

Rosen Inn ★ When you drive up to this concrete tower, you may be concerned. It is, after all, upgraded from what was once the largest Rodeway Inn in America. But fear not: This is value. It's clean and on a lively bend of International Drive near

Wet 'n Wild and 2 minutes' drive from Universal, which makes eating cheaply a breeze. The pool is heated when it's cold, security is always around, there's a pub, you can get free Wi-Fi in the lobby ($9 with wires upstairs), and all rooms have a microwave and refrigerator. It's dated, but all you need. The rate sometimes attracts noisy kids on school break, but on balance, you can't do better at this price.

6327 International Dr., Orlando. ☏ **800/999-6327** or 407/996-4444. www.roseninn6327.com. 315 units. Rooms with 2 doubles from $70. Free parking. **Amenities:** Pool, park shuttle, 2 restaurants, pub, park shuttles, business center, game room, free Wi-Fi.

Around Downtown Orlando

For years, travel writers have been begging tourists to spend more time in downtown Orlando and Winter Park, just north. There's charm, museums, great food, antiques, ritzy shopping, a student culture, and a relaxed vibe that could make you wish you lived in Florida. Sadly, they've been wasting ink. The theme parks won the war. Because it's a 30-minute ride north of Disney on I-4 (yes, you should have a car for these), a hotel would have to be pretty special to convince a tourist to choose it over one that's nearer. Orlando has a few, where you can find welcome respite from the hurdy-gurdy and plastinated smiles of the tourist zone—and a breather from children.

EXPENSIVE

The Alfond Inn ★★ In 2013, Rollins College opened the boutique hotel using a $12.5 million donation; its income will endow a scholarship program. That makes it both the newest fine property in town and the one with the biggest incentive to keep quality high. Its Southern restaurant and hopping cocktail bar, planted courtyard, and modern rooms striped in teal, wood, and lime are designed to appeal to sophisticated palates, something that its fantastic public art collection underscores. These gleaming new facilities are 3 blocks from the shopping of Park Avenue and the Morse Museum (p. 147), making it an instant keystone of the Winter Park scene. It's probably too far if you've got a heavy theme park schedule, but it's ideal for explorations around town.

300 E. New England Ave., Winter Park. ☏ **407/998-8090.** www.thealfondinn.com. 112 units. Doubles $159–$249. Valet parking $18, no self-parking. **Amenities:** Pool, restaurant, lounge, fitness center, pets permitted, free Wi-Fi.

Grand Bohemian Hotel Orlando ★★★ Yes, Orlando *is* sophisticated. Because the hotel's owner, Richard Kessler, is something of a dilettante, its common areas are decorated with eccentric artwork—it's part hunting lodge and part *commedia dell'arte,* including six original drawings by Gustav Klimt, and in the lobby, there's a storefront gallery. An L.A.–style pool terrace keeps sunbathers far above city traffic, and lighting is so muted in its rooms, the dark woods so dark and fabrics so indigo, that a dusky, drowsy atmosphere is created even on days when the Florida sun could blister pavement. By night the Bösendorfer Lounge is a stylish martini nightspot with a following and some epic neo-romantic paintings by William Russell Walker. For a city about fake Spanish country clubs and golf resorts, the Grand Bohemian's urban panache is welcome, and its lounge areas tend to attract local artists (and frequent wedding parties of young professionals) who live more like they're in Manhattan, Chicago, or San Francisco.

325 S. Orange Ave., Orlando. ☏ **866/663-0024** or 407/313-9000. www.grandbohemianhotel.com. 250 units. Standard room $179–$269 for up to 4, weekends $20 more. Extra person $25. Valet parking $24, no self-parking. The garage is 2 blocks west on Jackson St. **Amenities:** Restaurant, 2 lounges, club-level rooms, health club, heated outdoor pool, room service, shuttle to the theme parks for a fee, Wi-Fi ($10).

MODERATE

Courtyard at Lake Lucerne ★★
Despite a name that might have you expecting something corporate, Orlando just doesn't have rooms this individual anymore. South of downtown, near highways that go everywhere, you'll find a rare B&B, and rarer still, it preserves the feeling of Old Florida. There's a reason local couples favor it for weddings: Under Spanish moss, this hideaway of calm preserves four homey buildings of varied historic styles. Top of the line is the city's oldest documented house, 1883's Norment Parry Inn, which believe it or not has the cheapest rates here because not everyone likes sleigh beds and claw-footed tubs; you'll sleep in an elegant four-poster bed among Victorian-era European antiques. I. W. Phillips House recalls Key West because its wooden wrap-around verandah overlooks tropical plantings. Wellborn Suites is Art Deco, less elegant, but with kitchenettes. All rooms have TVs, phones, and private bathrooms.

211 N. Lucerne Circle E., Orlando. ℭ **407/648-5188.** www.orlandohistoricinn.com. 30 units. Doubles $99–$225. Some rooms do not permit kids. Free parking. **Amenities:** Free breakfast, free Wi-Fi.

Home Rentals

RENTAL AGENCIES

In most destinations, the main way to obtain a vacation rental is to contact the owner directly. This is an option in Orlando, and the prominent online databases operate here, including **Airbnb.com, FabVillas.com, FlipKey.com, HomeAway.com, Housetrip. com,** and **Vacation Rentals by Owner** (www.vrbo.com).

But there are also accredited companies that take the risk out of a rental—ones that actually inspect your potential home and give you support on the ground. In addition to being selected for their reputations, longevity, and inventory, these companies have satisfactory listings with the Better Business Bureau of Central Florida. Check on any company's background for the past 3 years at www.orlando.bbb.org.

A good rental agency will matchmake your needs and budget to the most suitable property. Your credit card will usually be charged a deposit ($200–$300 or 1 night's rent is standard) a month or two ahead of time, and if you cancel, you're unlikely to see that again. You'll also have to pay a one-time fee that goes toward insurance or cleaning; $50 to $80 is normal, which makes stays of a single night less economical. Perks like pool heat or grills may incur a surcharge, which is normal. Also ask your rental agency what it supplies and what you'll need to buy. Clean bath towels and sheets are supplied, but maid service won't be unless you pay extra. Many rental agencies no longer require you to pick up keys. Instead, front locks are equipped with keypads.

Alexander Holiday Homes The family-run outfit has been renting since 1981, when the industry was in its infancy. It reps some 250 properties, most of them within 10 miles of Disney. Using its website's Hot Deals, prices go as low as $65 for a two-bedroom condo, and you stay for less than a week. Annoyingly, its website doesn't reveal availability windows; you have to call.

1400 W. Oak St., Ste. H, Kissimmee. ℭ **800/621-7888** or 407/932-3683. www.floridasunshine.com. Wi-Fi $25. Pet-friendly.

All Star Vacation Homes Frommer's favorite Orlando vacation home renter has an in-house design team that cuts no corners in furnishing each of its hundreds of homes, with lots of woods, quality fabrics, and dried flowers—the completeness elevates the offerings above the competition. All units, which go up to purpose-built 14-bedroom mansions, are keyless and have a pool, and most are within 6 miles of

Disney. Three-bedroom condo units sleeping up to eight, with a themed kids' room, start at $125 a night, or $75 less than what it costs to squeeze eight into two Disney Value rooms. Or you could have a whole 3-bedroom house for $209. Prices go up as you add treats such as home cinema rooms, arcade rooms, multiple master bedrooms, and so forth. Full six-bedroom houses start at $289—you can split that among 14 people if you've got a full house. *Reminder:* A standard room at the Disney's Polynesian, sleeping five tightly, can't be had for less than $482.

1132 Celebration Blvd., Celebration. ℂ **888/619-2302** or 321/281-4966. www.allstarvacation homes.com. No pets.

Award Vacation Homes   Award's inventory is thickest around Hwy. 27, a newly developed corridor 15 minutes west of Walt Disney World via U.S. 192 (via Disney's Western Way back entrance). That distance is a price advantage, as its neighborhoods are serviced by grocery stores that are not as overpriced for tourists as other ones are. For three-bedroom, two-bath places, rates start at $118.

1536 Sunrise Plaza Dr., Clermont. ℂ **800/338-0835** or 352/243-8669. www.awardvacationhomes. com. No pets.

Florida Sun Vacation Homes   Another upfront business, it rents homes ranging from two to seven bedrooms in the Disney area (the Windsor Hills development in particular), with three-bedroom starting prices of $69 in low season and popping to $149 in high season. All of its properties have a pool or a spa (or both). Minimum stays of 3 nights are common, and like many companies, it asks that you reserve and pay at least 6 weeks in advance.

7802 W. Irlo Bronson Hwy./U.S. 192, Kissimmee. ℂ **800/219-1282** or 407/938-0228. www.florida sunvacationhomes.com. No pets.

IPG Florida Vacation Homes   IPG began by serving British vacationers before branching out into Florida, and now its inventor is among the largest, dealing in dozens of home developments south and west of Disney, particularly Bella Piazza, Highlands Reserve, Windsor Hills, and the Villas at Island Club. Two-bedroom condos run from $120 to $160, often less; even something as big as six bedrooms can cost a mere $288.

9550 W. U.S. 192, Clermont. ℂ **800/311-7105** or 863/547-1050. www.ipgflorida.com. Pets w/$400 fee.

Lowery's Vacation Homes   Around since 1985, Lowery's reps plenty of inexpensive, tasteful properties in the usual developments, and its website includes 360-degree tours of each property. It's a good fallback in busy seasons. Rates here can be sensational—how about $95 a night for a three-bedroom condo? The largest home available has seven bedrooms.

7864 W. Irlo Bronson Hwy., Kissimmee. ℂ **800/569-3797** or 407/397-0088. www.moremouse.com. Pet-friendly.

VillaDirect   Founded in 1998, it manages some 350 Orlando-area properties in a hodgepodge of styles and quality levels. Condos sleeping six start around $62, although prices in the $80s are more common. Its office is open 7 days, and a majority of its inventory is near Animal Kingdom, but it also has a few near SeaWorld. Helpfully, its website posts videos for each of its vacation home communities.

6129 W. Irlo Bronson Hwy., Kissimmee. ℂ **877/259-9908** or 407/397-9818. www.villadirect.com. No pets.

PLANNING YOUR TRIP TO ORLANDO

Orlando hosts some 57 million people a year, and the people who run the airports, hotels, and theme parks are specialists in moving them from one location to another—the whole system is set up to make it foolproof—so you probably won't get lost in a mire of confusion. You will, however, need to take care of some nitty-gritty details, from flights to transportation.

GETTING THERE

BY PLANE   Orlando is served by 44 airlines, so thankfully, competition keeps airfares among the lowest on the East Coast. Nearly 35 million people fly in or out of Orlando International Airport (MCO) each year, or nearly 96,000 a day. Strategies for finding a good airfare include:

Primary websites that collect quotes from a variety of sources (whether they be airlines or other websites) include **CheapOAir.com, Expedia.com, Kayak.com, Lessno.com, Mobissimo.com, Momondo.com, Orbitz.com,** and **Travelocity.com** (which runs Expedia searches). Always canvas multiple sites, because each has odd gaps in its coverage because of the way they obtain their quotes. Then compare your best price with what the airline is offering, because that price might be lowest of all. Some sites have small booking fees of $5 to $10, and many force you to accept nonrefundable tickets for the cheapest prices. Sounds odd, but you can often save money by booking between roughly 6 weeks in advance if you're flying domestically and 2 to 3 months ahead if you're coming from abroad.

The main airport, **Orlando International Airport** (www.orlandoairports.net), is a pleasure. If, on the way home, you realize you neglected to buy any park-related souvenirs, fear not, because Disney, SeaWorld, Kennedy Space Center, and Universal all maintain lavish stores (located *before* the security checkpoint, so budget enough time). The airport, 25 miles east of Walt Disney World, was built during World War II as McCoy Air Force Base, which closed in the early 1970s but bequeathed the airport with its deceptive code, MCO. I don't know how they do it, but the late-departure rate of 17 percent is among the lowest in the country, even though the airport is America's 13th busiest. Midmornings and midafternoons can be crowded for outgoing passengers, weekends can be clogged with cruise passengers, and mid-afternoon summer thunderstorms sometimes create delays.

The main terminal is divided into two sides, A and B, so if you can't find the desk for your airline or transportation service open on one side, it may be on the other side. Several rental car companies are right outside, no shuttles required.

Rental car companies at MCO:

Alamo: ✆ 800/327-9633; www.alamo.com

Avis: ✆ 800/831-2847; www.avis.com

Budget: ✆ 800/527-0700; www.budget.com

Dollar: ✆ 800/800-4000; www.dollar.com

Enterprise: ✆ 800/325-8007; www.enterprise.com

E-Z Rent-A-Car: ✆ 800/266-5171; www.e-zrentacar.com

Hertz: ✆ 800/654-3131; www.hertz.com

L & M Car Rental: ✆ 407/888-0515; www.lmcarrental.net

National: ✆ 800/227-7368; www.nationalcar.com

Thrifty: ✆ 800/367-2277; www.thrifty.com

Also keep in mind Hertz-owned **Firefly** (✆ 888/296-9135; www.fireflycarrental. com), which can offer lower prices than most of its competitors because its vehicles are older and well-used.

Very few airlines (Allegiant, Icelandair) use **Orlando Sanford International Airport** (www.orlandosanfordairport.com), or SFB, 42 miles northeast of Disney. It's connected to the Disney area by the Central Florida GreeneWay, or S.R. 417—the trip takes about 40 minutes and there are tolls, so new arrivals should have U.S. dollars. European visitors might fly into **Tampa International Airport** (www.tampaairport. com), or TPA, 90 minutes southwest.

BY TRAIN Amtrak's (✆ **800/872-7245;** www.amtrak.com) Silver Service/Palmetto route serves Orlando and Kissimmee. Trains go direct between New York City, Washington, D.C., Charleston, and Savannah.

Transportation to & from MCO

BY RENTAL CAR Get a car. Otherwise, theme park resorts conspire to hold you prisoner. If you intend to experience the "real" Orlando or its rich natural wonders, get a car. If you want to save huge amounts of money on meals, if you ever want to take a breather from the theme parks' relentless plastic personalities—get a car.

Economy rental cars start around $15 to $25 a day. Test the waters at a site such as Kayak, Orbit, or Travelocity, which compare multiple renters with one click. Priceline and Hotwire have been known to rent for as little as $15 a day.

If you rent a car from the airport be alert as you **exit the airport**—you must decide whether to use the south exit (marked for Walt Disney World) or the north exit (for SeaWorld, Universal, the Convention Center, and downtown Orlando). Whichever route you take, you will pay a few dollars in tolls, so have loose change. Also, at toll booths, stay to the right, where the cash windows are; the others are for e-passes.

If you're staying on Disney turf, a budget-saving solution is to rent a car for only the days you'd like to venture off property. To that end, **Alamo** (✆ **800/462-5266;** www. alamo.com) and **National** (✆ **800/227-7368;** www.nationalcar.com) operate satellite agencies within the Walt Disney World Resort: one at the Car Care Center near the parking lot of the Magic Kingdom. Alamo is also at the Buena Vista Palace Hotel east of Downtown Disney. Renting away from the airport incurs taxes of around half of those charged by renting (or even merely returning) a car at the airport, where they're over 20 percent. Always fill up *before* driving back to the airport. Gas stations near the airport's entrance have been nabbed for gouging. Stations inside Walt Disney World charge a competitive price, but one not as low as outside the tourist zone.

Agencies may not rent to those under 25. **Action Car Rental** (3719 McCoy Rd., Orlando; ℂ 877/535-7117 or 407/240-2700; www.actionrac.com) will, but it charges them $10–15 more a day. Most companies won't rent to anyone older than 85.

BY SHUTTLE   Mears Transportation (ℂ 407/423-5566 or 855/463-2776; www. mearstransportation.com) is the 800-pound gorilla of shuttles and taxis; it sends air-conditioned vans bouncing to hotels every 15 to 20 minutes. Round-trip fares for adults are $32 ($24 for kids 4–11, kids 3 and under free) to the International Drive area, or $36 per adult ($27 for kids) to Walt Disney World/U.S. 192/Lake Buena Vista. You'll probably make several stops because the vans are shared by other passengers.

If you have more than four or five people, it's more economical to reserve a car service (do it at least 24 hr. ahead) and split the lump fee; an SUV for up to 7 would be $110 to $150. Try Mears, **Tiffany Towncar** (ℂ 888/838-2161 or 407/370-2196; www.tiffanytowncar.com), or **Quicksilver Tours** (ℂ 888/468-6939 or 407/299-1434; www.quicksilver-tours.com), which often volunteers to toss in a free 30-minute stop at a grocery store so you can stock up on supplies.

If you have a reservation at a Disney-owned hotel, you have the right to take the company's airport motorcoaches (also known as **Disney's Magical Express,** run by Mears). By offering the perk, the Mouse makes it seem simple by sending you tags for your luggage, which you affix before leaving home, and telling you everything will be taken care of from there. By the time you board the bus to the resort, you'll already have waited in two long lines—the first of many, many lines you'll endure, so get used to it—and then you'll stop at up to five other hotels first. Your bags may not meet up with you again for 6 to 8 hours, so hitting a park right away may be difficult. When you depart for home, you must be ready 3 to 4 hours before your flight. Magical Express is free, but it costs you. It lulls you into not renting a car, which means you'll probably never leave Disney property again and you'll have to rely on the park's slow buses for your entire vacation.

BY TAXI   Taxis are not the best bargain. The going rate is $2.40 for the first ¼ of a mile or the first 80 seconds of waiting time, followed by 60¢ for each ¼ of a mile. Taxis carry five passengers. It'll be about $70 to the Disney hotels, $60 to Universal, not including a tip, which is cheaper than a town car but not a rental.

GETTING AROUND

BY CAR   Probably 90 percent of what a tourist wants to do lies within a 10-minute drive of Interstate 4, or I-4, as it's called. That free highway runs diagonally from southwest to northeast, connecting Walt Disney World, SeaWorld, the Convention Center, Universal Orlando, and downtown Orlando. I-4 is technically an east-west road linking Florida's coasts, so directions are listed as either west (toward Tampa and the Gulf of Mexico) or east (toward Daytona Beach and the Atlantic Ocean). Once you've got that down, you'll be set. Exits are numbered according to the mile marker at which they're found. Therefore, the Disney World exits (62, 64, 65, and 67) are roughly 10 miles from Universal Orlando's (74 and 75), which are about 9 miles from downtown (83). If you know the exit number, you can figure out distance.

If you stray much onto minor roads, it's a good idea to carry a map. Roads can go by several names and be confusing. Disney World is a particular disaster, since its signage is intentionally incomplete. Don't rely on free maps; laughably, some maps provided by Universal don't acknowledge that Disney exists at all. The **Visit Orlando** (www.visitorlando.com/mapexplorer) has free maps.

SHUTTLES   Universal is easy: You walk, bus, or take a free boat everywhere. At Disney, though, hoofing it is impossible. It's so big as to require a fleet of nearly 300 buses, the **Disney Transportation System (DTS),** which anyone may use for free. Curiously, DTS qualifies as the third-largest bus system in the state, after Miami and Jacksonville's public services. Taking DTS to a theme park eliminates the parking tram rigmarole. However, once you add waiting time, which can be 20 to 45 minutes, plus the commute itself, which can be just as long and require a transfer, you'll find that having a car of your own is often worth the expense.

DTS is particularly overwhelmed during the opening and closing of the theme parks, but dispatchers run extra buses around those times and keep routes rolling for about 2 extra hours before opening and after closing. If you're staying at a Disney resort that offers another kind of transportation—say, the monorail to the Magic Kingdom—then a bus won't be available for the same route. Also, since the system has a hub-and-spoke design centered on the theme parks and Downtown Disney, *you must often transfer if you're going between two second-tier points,* such as two hotels or a hotel and a water park.

On balance, DTS can save you from having to rent a car if you meet both of these criteria: (1) You only plan to go to Disney attractions and nothing else (which would be a shame for you—thumb through the rest of this book); and (2) you're a patient soul who doesn't mind ending a 12-hour day in the parks with a potential hour-plus commute, possibly standing the whole way.

The second shuttle variety is the **hotel theme park shuttles,** which go from independent hotels and are often free (or paid for by resort fees). The upswing is that, yes, you can save money by using them, but there are strong downsides, including wildly inadequate scheduling (you might miss fireworks) and rambling routes. These only go to the park gates, not to restaurants or natural and historic attractions.

A third option is the **I-Ride Trolley** (✆ **407/354-5656;** www.iridetrolley.com; adults over 12 $2 per ride, seniors 25¢, kids 3–9 $1; day pass $5, 3-day pass $7, 5-day pass $9; daily 8am–10:30pm), an excellent shuttle bus with plenty of clearly marked and well-maintained stops, benches to wait on, and genuinely useful routes—except it doesn't go to Disney. Its **Red Line** (every 20 min.) plies International Drive from the shops and restaurants just north of I-4's exit 75 all the way to Orlando Premium Outlets, near Disney; along the way it touches down at SeaWorld and Wet 'n Wild. The second route, the **Green Line** (every 30 min.), takes in Wet 'n Wild and SeaWorld, too, but heads down Universal Boulevard, making it more of an express route, and turns around at Orlando Premium Outlets. It comes within a long block of the entrance to Universal Orlando. Visitors without cars may find it feasible to stay on I-Drive, use this dirt-cheap shuttle to see nearly everything, and then tack on the hated hotel shuttle or a city bus for Disney days.

BY PUBLIC TRANSIT   There's not a lot to love about public transit in Florida. Buses are infrequent (usually one or two an hour), and shelters inadequate (often non-existent), and when the sun's strong, the combination is dangerous. Distances are also fairly great, so journeys can take a while. The Central Florida Regional Transportation Authority runs the **LYNX system** (www.golynx.com), on which one-way fares are $2, day passes cost $4.50, week passes are $16, and transfers between lines are free. Up to three kids 6 and under ride with adults free, and you have to pay with exact change. In downtown Orlando, there's the free **LYMMO** (www.golynx.com; Mon–Thurs 6am–10pm, Fri 6am–midnight, Sat 10am–midnight, Sun 10am–10pm) bus service, which makes a loop between City Hall and the Controlled (including Church Street Station and the Orange County Regional History Center) every 5 to 15 minutes.

For tourists, here are the most convenient routes, many of which stop at Downtown Disney where you can transfer to Disney's free bus system:

- **Route 56** heads down U.S. 192 from the Osceola Square Mall in Kissimmee and straight to the front gates of the Magic Kingdom, where you can catch DTS to the other parks. This makes U.S. 192 east of Disney the only major hotel zone that provides transfer-free bus access to Walt Disney World. Buses run every 30 minutes, but the last one leaves at 10:53pm.
- **Route 8** does most of International Drive, including the Convention Center and SeaWorld. It duplicates the service offered by the I-Ride Trolley (p. 230).
- **Route 50** goes from the central LYNX station in downtown Orlando, down Interstate 4, to Downtown Disney, and to the gates of the Magic Kingdom. It stops at SeaWorld where passengers can connect to I-Drive by on Route 8.
- The lesser Disney areas are served by the 300-series lines. Number **300** goes to Hotel Plaza Boulevard from downtown; **301** to Epcot and Disney's Animal Kingdom from Pine Hills; **302** to the Magic Kingdom from Rosemont; and **303** to Hollywood Studios from the Washington Shores area. Bus **304** is the only one that connects with another tourist zone; it trawls Sand Lake Road, which bisects I-Drive. Once they're off I-4, 301 and 302 pass within a few blocks of Universal Orlando, on Kirkman Road, so if you toss in about 15 minutes of walking, they could technically be used for Universal, too, but it wouldn't be fun.
- **Route 21** goes up Turkey Lake Road from Sand Lake Road to the Universal Orlando park and links with the downtown depot.
- **Route 42** starts at the Convention Center on International Drive, and 75 minutes later, reaches the airport.

In 2014, Orange County added **SunRail** (✆ **855/724-5411;** www.sunrail.com; $2 one-way, $3.75 round-trip), running from DeBary, north of Sanford, to an obscure spot on E. Sand Lake Road near S. Orange Avenue. Tourists only care about the 16-minute jaunt between downtown Orlando and Winter Park, but as most departures are in the morning or evening, targeting commuters, few visitors use it.

BY TAXI   Given so many alternatives, taxis are not a natural choice. You will, however, almost always find a cluster outside of the major theme parks' gates, waiting to take fares to their hotels. If you spend more than $30 a day on taxis (a one-way ride from the Magic Kingdom to the hotel stretch on U.S. 192 east of Disney would cost about $25), smack your forehead, because you could have rented a car for that.

Many companies accept major credit cards, but ask when you summon a ride, because your payment may need to be processed by phone. Companies are not carefully monitored, so only choose a recommended carrier. Call your own:

- **Diamond Cab Company:** ✆ 407/523-3333
- **Transtar:** ✆ 407/857-9999
- **Yellow:** ✆ 407/422-2222

TRAVELING FROM ORLANDO TO OTHER PARTS OF AMERICA

Orlando, while not an important air hub, is well connected to the cities that are, particularly New York, Atlanta, and Chicago. For advice on how to find cheap airfare, see "Getting There," p. 227.

Mouse Clickers: The Best Planning Websites

If you really want to be intense about your planning (for your sanity and relaxation, I don't recommend it), there are obsessive resources online that go into granular detail. You'll find that the official park websites mostly furnish doctored photographs, empty homilies, bandwidth-hogging animation, and a near-total lack of cogent information. Thank goodness, then, for rabid followings.

o **AllEarsNetcom** and **WDWFans.com** offer encyclopedic compendiums of everything Disney, down to the menus, what's under renovation, and which rooms are best.

o **OrlandoInformer.com** comprehensively reports Universal, including deals.

o **WDWmagic.com** and **WDWinfo.com** (and its **DISBoards.com**) host some of the most active message forums for news and Q&As.

o The independently run **PartyThrough TheParks.com** rates drinking and nightlife and **DisneyFoodBlog.com** keeps track of meals.

o **MouseSavers.com, TheMouse ForLess.com,** and **OrlandoCheapo. com** post current Disney deals.

o **Jim Hill Media** (www.jimhillmedia. com)—no one's better at insider gossip.

The **USA Rail Pass** is the American equivalent of the Eurail Pass in Europe—although our national rail system, **Amtrak** (✆ 800/872-7245 or 215/856-7953; www.amtrak.com), hardly compares to the European system. The pass allows travel within the U.S. The cheapest pass is a 15-day pass, which grants eight trips ($449); the most expensive offers 45 days of travel over 18 trips ($879). Those on a grand tour of America may benefit from those rates compared to flying.

From late April to early June, many car renters redistribute inventory by offering **"drive-out"** deals for one-way rentals that originate in Florida and drop off elsewhere in the country. Rates can be as low as $10/day, so look for those.

For bus travel, Orlando is served by **Greyhound** (✆ 800/231-2222; www.greyhound.com) and **Megabus** (✆ 877/462-6342; www.megabus.com). Long-distance bus travel in the United States is a purgatorial experience. Don't.

WHEN TO GO

The main consideration when it comes to selecting a date for your visit is balancing good weather with thin crowds. Crowds keep you from seeing everything. In the peak season (such as spring break or the week after Christmas), the Magic Kingdom's turnstiles spin like propellers. None of the theme parks close on **public holidays.** In fact, they do better business then. In late December, Disney parks sometimes hit capacity and seal gates. But come September, you can do nearly everything in a day.

So when are the **peak seasons?** Put simply: when American kids are out of school. That means midspring, summer, and the holidays. Hotel rates rise then, too. If you want to **save cash,** early January, early May, late August, all of September, and the first half of December are prime. The flipside of low season is that the theme parks trim services when it's quieter. January is a particularly tough month for missing out on rides due to rehabs. And especially in the winter months, you may find it too chilly to enjoy the rides that get you wet, which is a shame since Orlando has some of the best water rides in the world.

The busiest days at all parks are generally Saturday and Sunday. Seven-day guests are often traveling on these days, and weekends are when locals come to play. Beyond that: Tuesday and Thursday see an uptick in the Magic Kingdom; Tuesday and Friday (and evenings) at Epcot; Wednesday is a tad busier Disney's Hollywood Studios; and Monday, Tuesday, and Wednesday can be a zoo (forgive the pun) at the Animal Kingdom. Crowds tend to thin later in the day.

CLIMATE June to September is the heaviest season for rain. It seems like every afternoon, like clockwork, another heavy storm rolls in and shuts rides temporarily. Those storms usually roll out within an hour, just as reliably, but in the meantime, you'll see torrents and lightning. Central Florida suffers more lightning strikes than any other American locale. During those tropical seasons, bring along a cheap poncho from home.

Orlando Average Temperature & Rainfall

	JAN	FEB	MAR	APR	MAY	JUNE	JULY	AUG	SEPT	OCT	NOV	DEC
HI/LOW DAILY TEMPS (°F)	72/49	73/50	78/55	84/60	88/66	91/71	92/73	92/73	90/73	84/65	78/57	73/51
HI/LOW DAILY TEMPS (°C)	22/10	23/10	26/13	29/16	31/19	33/22	33/23	33/23	32/23	29/19	26/14	23/11
INCHES OF PRECIPITATION	2.25	2.82	3.32	2.43	3.30	7.13	7.27	6.88	6.53	3.16	1.98	2.25

Orlando's Calendar of Events

Check the special events pages at the theme park websites to see if any themed weekends or smaller events are in the works. In addition, the events listings at **Visit Orlando** (www.visitorlando.com), **"Orlando Weekly"** (www.orlandoweekly.com), and the **"Orlando Sentinel"** (www.orlandosentinel.com) are comprehensive. You will also find a few listings at **"Orlando" magazine** (www.orlandomagazine.com).

JANUARY

Capital One Bowl. It used to be called the Citrus Bowl—can *anyone* keep track of the square-dancing corporate naming rights anymore? Held New Year's Day at the Florida Citrus Bowl Stadium, it pits the second-ranked teams from the Big Ten and SEC conferences against one another. www.floridacitrussports.com.

ZORA! Festival. The folklorist and writer (1891–1960) was from Eatonville (a 30-min. drive north of Orlando), the country's oldest incorporated African-American town. This weeklong event includes lectures and a 2-day public art fair. ℂ **407/647-3307;** www.zorafestival.org.

FEBRUARY

Winter Park Bach Festival. This annual event at Rollins College began in 1935 and has evolved into one of the country's better choral fests. Although it has stretched to include other composers and guest artists (Handel, P.D.Q. Bach), at least one concert is devoted to Johann. It takes place mid-February to early March, with scattered one-off guest performances throughout the year. ℂ **407/646-2182;** www.bachfestivalflorida.org.

Silver Spurs Rodeo. Lest you doubt Central Florida is far removed from the American Deep South, it hosts the largest rodeo east of the Mississippi (with bareback broncs, racing barrel horses, rodeo clowns, and athletes drawn from the cowboy circuit) over 3 days in mid-February in an indoor arena off U.S. 192. 1875 Silver Spur Lane, Kissimmee. ℂ **407/677-6336;** www.silverspursrodeo.com.

Mardi Gras at Universal Studios. On Saturday nights, Universal books major acts (Bonnie

8

PLANNING YOUR TRIP TO ORLANDO

Orlando's Calendar of Events

Raitt, Hall & Oates, LL Cool J) and mounts a parade complete with stilt-walkers, jazz bands, Louisiana-made floats, and bead tossing—although here, what it takes to win a set of beads is considerably less risqué than it is in the Big Easy. It's included with admission. ✆ **407/224-2691;** www.universalorlando.com/mardigras.

Spring Training. See p. 144 for a rundown of which Major League Baseball teams play where. Mid-February through March.

MARCH

Epcot's International Flower & Garden Festival. This spring event, which lasts from March to May, transforms Epcot with some 30 million flowers, 70 topiaries, a screened-in butterfly garden, presentations by noted horticulturalists, and a lineup of "Flower Power" concerts (Chubby Checker, Petula Clark). It's free with standard entry. ✆ **407/934-7639;** www.disneyworld.com.

Florida Film Festival. This respected event showcases films by Florida artists and has featured past appearances by the likes of Oliver Stone, William H. Macy, Christopher Walken, and Cary Elwes. ✆ **407/644-5625;** www.floridafilmfestival.com.

APRIL

Epcot's International Flower & Garden Festival. See March for full listing, above.

Florida Music Festival. Some 250 bands over 4 days give exposure to up-and-coming musicians—at a pace of 50 per night, all over town. www.floridamusicfestival.com.

MAY

Orlando International Fringe Festival. This theatrical smorgasbord, the longest-running fringe fest in America, spends 14 days mounting some 100 newly written, experimental performances in Loch Haven Park. ✆ **407/648-0077;** www.orlandofringe.org.

Epcot's International Flower & Garden Festival. See March for full listing, above.

JUNE

Gay Days. What started as a single day for gay and lesbian visitors has bloomed into a full week of some 40 events managed by a host of promoters. It's said that attendance goes as high as 135,000, and it's become one of the biggest annual events in Florida. Held around the first Saturday in June, Gay Days are a blowout party with group visits to Disney's parks, an ongoing pool bash at Parliament House (p. 155), concerts (En Vogue, LeAnn Rimes), and several dance events including an all-night, after-hours Rip-Tide dance party at Typhoon Lagoon. Those are sold at www.onemightyweekend.com, and the overview is at www.gaydays.com.

Star Wars Weekends. Hollywood Studios' major annual do, held over 3 weeks in late spring, sees actors from the franchise arrive for signings, parades, and Q&As. It's not uncommon to catch Mark Hamill, Warwick Davis, or Ray Park. The finer points of the Lucas catechism are discussed, and much merchandise is traded at the Darth's Mall market, held in a soundstage. A regular ticket gets you in. www.disneyworld.com/starwars.

SEPTEMBER

Night of Joy. It's actually a long-running pair of nights of outdoor Contemporary Christian concerts—eight or nine acts—spread throughout the Magic Kingdom, which stays open late just for the occasion. Rides run all night, and it's separately ticketed. ✆ **877/648-3569;** www.nightofjoy.com.

Rock the Universe. Universal's festival of top-flight Christian rock bands who perform on stages around Universal Studios. Rides and performances continue past midnight, after regular patrons have gone home. It's separately ticketed. www.rocktheuniverse.com.

OCTOBER

Epcot's International Food & Wine Festival. The World Showcase makes amends with the countries it ignores by installing temporary booths selling tapas-size servings of foods and wines from many nations. That's supplemented with chef demonstrations, seminars, "Eat to the Beat" concerts by known acts (Hanson, the Go-Gos), and tastings by at least 100 wineries. A few of the more extravagant events are charged, but most are free. The festival lasts from late September to mid-November and the hotly awaited details are posted by Disney in the summer. ✆ **407/939-3378;** www.disneyworld.com/foodandwine.

Mickey's Not-So-Scary Halloween Party. The best of the Magic Kingdom's separately ticketed evening events, this one mounts a special parade with fiendishly catchy theme song, a few special shows, a fireworks display that surpasses the usual one, and stations where you can pick up free candy. Kids even show up in costume, although it's not required. The event happens on scattered evenings from mid-September through the end of October. Unfortunately, it's so oversold that you will barely be able to move. Halloween sells out early. Target audience: people who like lollipops. ℂ **407/934-7639;** www.disneyworld.com.

Halloween Horror Nights. Unquestionably Universal's biggest event, HHN is the equivalent of a whole new theme park that's designed for a year but only lasts a month. After dark, the Studios are overtaken by grotesque "scareactors" who terrorize crowds with chain saws, gross-out shows, and eight big, walk-through haunted houses that are made from scratch each year. The mayhem lasts into the wee hours. Wimps need not apply; children are discouraged by the absence of kids' ticket prices. A bawdy revue based on the Bill and Ted movie characters skewers the year in pop culture and draws enthusiastic crowds of tipsy young people. On top of all this, most rides remain open. HHN has legions of fans. Target audience: people who like to poop themselves in fright. (Busch Gardens' Howl-o-Scream event's scariness is somewhere between Universal's and Disney's.) www.halloween horrornights.com.

SeaWorld's Halloween Spooktacular. SeaWorld throws a sweet, toddler-approved weekend Halloween event of its own, with trick-or-treating (kids dress up), a few encounters with sea fairies and bubbles, and show starring Count von Count from "Sesame Street." Target audience: people who have a naptime. It's included in admission.

Orlando Film Festival. Like all festivals worth their salt, this one presents mostly mainstream and independent films in advance of their wider release dates. It lasts only a few days in mid-October or early November, screening at various downtown venues. ℂ **407/843-0801;** www.orlando filmfest.com.

NOVEMBER

ICE! It debuted in 2003 at the Gaylord Palms hotel and has quickly become a holiday perennial. The hotel brings in nearly 2 million pounds of ice, sculpts it into a walk-through city, keeps it chilled to 9°F, and issues winter coats to visitors. Add synchronized light shows and you've got an event that charges $29 for entry—and sells out. ℂ **407/586-0000;** www.gaylordpalms.com.

The Osborne Family Spectacle of Dancing Lights. No, not Ozzy and Sharon, but Jennings, Paul, Mitzi, and Breezy (I swear I'm not making this up), whose preposterously overdone Christmas display at their Little Rock house was deemed so vulgar that neighbors went to the Arkansas Supreme Court to shut it down. Enter Disney's Hollywood Studios. Every 15 minutes, it twitters and "dances" to Christmas carols, all as foam "snow" gently wafts from above. It lasts until the first week of January.

DECEMBER

Mickey's Very Merry Christmas Party. This crowded night, which occurs on various nights starting even before Thanksgiving, is probably Disney's most popular special annual event. It requires a separate ticket from regular admission. What you get is a tree-lighting ceremony, a few special holiday-themed shows, a special fireworks display (very green and red), an appearance by Santa Claus, a special parade, and *huge* crowds. Meanwhile, Disney's warehouse for holiday decorations (it exists) empties out and its hotels deck the halls: The Grand Floridian erects a life-size house made of gingerbread. ℂ **407/934-7639;** www. disneyworld.com.

Holidays Around the World at Epcot. This one features a holiday customs of many nations and a host of costumed storytellers, but its real showpiece is the daily, 40-minute candlelight processional, a retelling of the Christmas Nativity story by a celebrity narrator (recent names have included Sigourney Weaver, Whoopi Goldberg, Trace Adkins, and Neil Patrick Harris) accompanied by a 50-piece orchestra and a full Mass choir. The processional is a WDW tradition going back to its earliest days—Cary Grant did it! www.disneyworld.com.

Grinchmas & The Macy's Holiday Parade. Usual holiday traditions include a musical version of "How the Grinch Stole Christmas" and daily parades by Macy's, which brings some balloons and floats to Universal when Thanksgiving is over. That's included in the ticket price. www.universalorlando.com.

Russell Athletic Bowl. An ACC team battles a Big Ten team, usually a few days before New Year's and always at the Florida Citrus Bowl Stadium. www.russellathleticbowl.com.

New Year's Eve. Yahoo.com reports that Orlando regularly makes its list of top five most-searched New Year's Eve destinations. There's no shortage of places to party. At the parks: **CityWalk** lures top acts such as Cyndi Lauper. Three **Disney parks,** minus Animal Kingdom, stay open until the wee hours. **SeaWorld** brings in big-band music or jazz, plus fireworks.

Getting Attraction Discounts

For a full breakdown of Disney's ticketing system, how it works, and how to ward against overspending, see p. 17.

One of the true discounted programs is the **FlexTicket.** For admission to five parks (Universal's pair, SeaWorld, Aquatica, Wet 'n Wild), you want the Orlando FlexTicket ($320 adults, $300 kids 3–9), which grants unlimited admission to all of the parks for a full 2 weeks. It's sold by those parks. Tack on Busch Gardens for $40 adults or kids. Considering 1-day admission to Busch Gardens alone is twice that, you don't have to get near a calculator to see the savings, but you do have to go to as many parks as possible. Once you've paid for parking at your first theme park ($17 is the going rate), you can keep your ticket and avoid paying it again. Many hotel closed-circuit TV programs promise $10 off, so when you're buying a FlexTicket in person, claim you learned about it from your in-room programming and ask for the deal. FlexTickets are sold online, too (http://tickets.visitorlando.com, the area's official tourism bureau, gives small discounts on it).

Universal and SeaWorld discount the gate price if you book online, and all the parks discount per-day entry if you buy multiple days. SeaWorld and Busch Gardens also offer courtesy admission for members of the military and their families. Check www.herosalute.com to see if you are eligible. **Orlando Magicard** (www.visitorlando.com/magicard) grants discounts to heaps of attractions, meals, home rentals, and hotels. The participants are members of the local tourism bureau. Its discounts aren't much different from what the free coupon circulars promise, but they're still good deals. You will also find coupons through **OrlandoCoupons.com** and the discount circular **HotelCoupons.com.**

A few outfits such sell faintly discounted tickets. **Maple Leaf Tickets** (Ⓒ 800/841-2837; www.mapleleaftickets.com), **the Official Ticket Center** (Ⓒ 877/406-4836; www.officialticketcenter.com), **Undercover Tourist** (Ⓒ 800/846-1302; www.undercovertourist.com), and **Ticket Momma** (Ⓒ 866/996-7508; www.ticketmomma.com) are all accredited by the Better Business Bureau. No Disney deals ever seem deep enough to offset shipping fees or the hassle of picking up your tickets at some third-party office; however, multiple purchases, stays of a week or longer, and third-tier diversions such as dinner shows ($10–$15 off) may work out for you. Tickets are nontransferable. A desk at the Orlando Official Visitor Center (p. 246) furnishes similar discounts on tickets you can trust.

Before Magic Your Way made ticket expiration standard, pretty much every Disney ticket was good forever. That means there are a lot of unused days floating around. It's illegal to sell them, but that doesn't stop people. When you see a sign on the side of U.S. 192 promising discounted tickets, guess what may be for sale? Buying a ticket like this is a gamble, particularly if you don't have the expertise to recognize a fake or a spent ticket. Often, only a Disney laser scan can tell for sure.

Other organizations, such as time-share developers, do offer legit tickets to theme parks and dinner shows, but to get them, you will have to endure heavy-duty sales presentations that last several hours. The requirements for attendance can be tight: Married couples must attend together (gay couples are often excluded—that's legal in Florida), you both must swear your combined annual income is above a certain amount ($50,000, for example, for Westgate branded resorts—yes, run by the timeshare baron in "The Queen of Versailles"), that you are in a given age range (23–65 is common), and that you commit to staying for at least 90 minutes, although being pitched for as long as 4 hours is also common. Even if you're fearless, an entire morning of your hard-earned vacation time is worth a lot more than whatever discount is being provided. After all, how many days of working did it take for you to accrue those 4 or 5 hours? You also may not arrive at the parks until lunchtime, missing (in some cases) a third of the opening hours. Don't be so cheap and discount-obsessed that you throw away your time.

One to be wary of is the **Go Orlando Card** (*©* **866/628-9036;** www.goorlandocard. com), which offers admission to many secondary attractions. The catch is you get an obscenely short time to use it. Rare is the person who can visit enough places to make the price (a 2-day card is $120 for adults) pay off.

[FastFACTS] ORLANDO

Accessible Travel
Hotels and theme parks have their acts together. Nearly everything is accessible. This excellent customer service predates the Americans with Disabilities Act of 1990; as multi-generational attractions, the parks have always worked to be inclusive, and in response, guests with mobility issues have long embraced them in return.

There was a time when guests in **wheelchairs** and **ECVs** were given special treatment and ushered to the front of lines, but now, with so many guests on wheels for reasons including obesity, Disney (with the exception of Make-A-Wish Foundation kids and other special groups, by prior arrangement) feeds everyone into the same attraction queues. You might have to transfer to a manual wheelchair. Once you're near the end, there will usually be a place for you to wait for the special wheelchair-ready ride vehicle to come around.

Often, this translates into longer waits, as special ride vehicles can be in high demand. The park maps carefully indicate which rides will require you to leave your personal vehicle. A very few, pre-ADA attractions, such as Tom Sawyer Island and the Swiss Family Treehouse, require you to be ambulatory. Those are marked, too.

For off-property stays, consider renting a house, which provides much more room; most home-rental companies also comply with ADA requirements.

All the parks have a full range of in-park services for guests of every need. Disney maintains a Special Services hotline to answer all accessibility needs, including full arrangements for the blind and captioning for the hearing-impaired: ☎ 407/824-4321 and TTY ☎ 407/827-5141. Universal Orlando can be reached at ☎ 800/447-0672 [TTY] or 407/224-4233 [voice] (www.universalorlando.com); SeaWorld Orlando's number is ☎ 407/363-2400 (www.seaworld.com); Kennedy Space Center is at ☎ 321/449-4443 (www.kennedyspacecenter.com). Most parks can arrange sign language interpreters with a few weeks' notice; all furnish assisted listening devices or scripts for some, but not all, of the biggest attractions.

Medical Travel, Inc. (☎ 800/308-2503 or 407/438-8010; www.medicaltravel.org) specializes in the rental of mobility equipment, ramp vans, and supplies such as oxygen tanks (be aware that many rides do not allow tanks). Electric scooters and wheelchairs can be delivered to your accommodation through these established companies: **Buena Vista Scooters** (☎ 866/484-4797 or 407/938-0349; www.buenavistascooters.com), **Scootaround** (☎ 888/441-7575; www.scootaround.com), **CARE Medical**

Equipment (☎ 800/741-2282 or 407/856-2273; www.caremedicalequipment.com), and **Walker Medical & Mobility Products** (☎ 888/726-6837 or 407/518-6000; www.walkermobility.com). All the theme parks, except the water parks, rent ECVs for about $50 a day and wheelchairs for about $12 a day. If your own wheelchair is wider than 25 inches, think about switching to the park model, as it is guaranteed to navigate tight squeezes such as hairpin queue turns.

Organizations that offer assistance to travelers with disabilities include the **American Federation for the Blind** (☎ 800/232-5463; www.afb.org) and **Society for Accessible Travel & Hospitality** (☎ 212/447-7284; www.sath.org).

Area Codes The area code for the Orlando area is **407** (if you're dialing locally, a preceding 1 is not necessary, but the 407 is), although you may encounter the less common **321** code, which is also used on the Atlantic Coast. The **863** area code governs the land between Orlando and Tampa, and the Tampa area uses **813** and **727**. The region west of Orlando uses **352**.

ATMs/Banks See "Money," in this section.

Business Hours Offices are generally open weekdays between 9am and 5pm, while banks tend to close at 4pm. Typically, stores open between 9 and 10am and close between

6 and 7pm Monday through Saturday, except malls, which stay open until 9pm. On Sunday, stores generally open at 11am and close by 7pm.

Cellphones See "Mobile Phones," later in this section.

Car Rentals This topic is perhaps the most hotly debated issue in all of Disneydom. But the bottom line is there's only one reason to do without a car: You never intend to leave Disney. If you plan to fan out, such as visiting Harry Potter or the Space Shuttle, get wheels.

Disney guests often justify forgoing a car by saying they can't afford one. This is a fallacy. Disney hotels charge as much as twice what you'll pay to stay at a hotel of similar quality off-site. If you stay at a non-Disney property, you can afford a car and *still* pay less. A large inventory means rentals are cheaper here than in other American cities: $26 a day is common for a compact car.

One caveat is that **parking charges** can add up. Valet is often free in town, but the theme parks charge $17 a day for a space (Universal is $5 after 6pm). If you stay at a Disney resort, it is free. Also, if you pay for parking once at any Disney park, you won't have to pay again for another park on the same day. The bigger hotels now slap on $20-plus nightly fees for parking in their enormous lots. In the rest of Orlando, parking is free, plentiful, and off the street.

Make sure your rental car that locks by remote control fob; those are handy for making your vehicle honk and locating it in those expansive theme park parking lots.

Crime Disney may advertise itself as "the Happiest Place on Earth," but it's still on Earth. That means bad things happen. Never open your hotel room door to a stranger, and never give your personal details or credit card number to anyone who calls your room, even if they claim to work for the hotel. **Pickpockets** are virtually unheard of, but they exist. Be vigilant about bags; you're going to be bumped and jostled many times— one of those bumps could be a nimble-fingered thief.

Customs Rules change. For details regarding current regulations, consult **U.S. Customs and Border Protection** (☎ 202/927-1770; www.cbp.gov).

Doctors There are first-aid centers in all of the theme parks. There's also a 24-hour, toll-free number for the **Poison Control Center** (☎ 800/282-3171). To find a dentist, contact the **Dental Referral Service** (☎ 800/235-4111; www. dentalreferral.com). **Doctors on Call Service** (☎ 407/399-3627) makes house and room calls in most of the Orlando area. **Centra Care** has several walk-in clinics, including ones at 2301 Sand Lake Rd., near Universal (☎ 407/851-6478); at 12500 S. Apopka Vineland Rd., in Lake Buena

Vista, near Disney (☎ **407/934-2273**); and at 8201 W. U.S. 192 (W. Irlo Bronson Hwy.), in the Formosa Gardens center (☎ 407/397-7032). The **Medical Concierge** (☎ **855/326-5252**; www.themedical concierge.com) makes "hotel house calls," arranges dental appointments, and rents equipment.

Drinking Laws The legal drinking age is 21. Proof of age is always requested, even if you look older, so carry photo ID. It's illegal to carry open containers of alcohol in any car or public area that isn't zoned for alcohol consumption (as CityWalk is), and the police may ticket you on the spot.

Driving Rules Americans drive on the right. In Florida, you may turn right on red only after making a full stop unless the signal is an illuminated arrow, in which case you must wait for green. Many intersections are equipped with traffic cameras that will take a photo of your license plate, and rental car companies pass on fines along with hefty fees. If your plans take you outside the Orlando area, some toll roads (in Miami and Tampa, for example) are cashless and can only be paid by a SunPass sensor that must be rented, for an extra daily fee, from your rental agency, otherwise you will incur large penalties. Last, Florida is full of visitors who don't know where they're going. These lost souls will halt, cross three

lanes of traffic, and get in the wrong lane without thinking. Keep a safe distance from the car in front of you.

Electricity The United States uses 110 to 120 volts AC (60 cycles), compared to the 220 to 240 volts AC (50 cycles) that is standard in Europe, Australia, and New Zealand. If your small appliances use 220 to 240 volts, buy an adaptor and voltage converter before you leave home, as these can be difficult to come by in Orlando.

Embassies & Consulates The nearest embassies are located in the nation's capital, Washington, D.C. Some consulates are located in major U.S. cities, and most nations have a mission to the United Nations in New York City. If your country isn't listed below, call for directory information in Washington, D.C. (☎ **202/555-1212**), or log on to **www.embassy. org/embassies**.

The embassy of **Australia** is at 1601 Massachusetts Ave. NW, Washington, DC 20036 (☎ **202/797-3000**; www.usa.embassy.gov.au). There are consulates in New York, Honolulu, Houston, Los Angeles, and San Francisco.

The embassy of **Canada** is at 501 Pennsylvania Ave. NW, Washington, DC 20001 (☎ **202/682-1740**; www. canadianembassy.org). Other Canadian consulates are in Buffalo, Detroit, Los Angeles, New York, and Seattle.

The embassy of **Ireland** is at 2234 Massachusetts Ave. NW, Washington, DC 20008 (📞 202/462-3939; www.embassyofireland.org). Irish consulates are in Boston, Chicago, New York, San Francisco, and other cities.

The embassy of **New Zealand** is at 37 Observatory Circle NW, Washington, DC 20008 (📞 202/328-4800; www.nzembassy.com). New Zealand consulates are in Los Angeles, Salt Lake City, San Francisco, and Seattle.

The embassy of the **United Kingdom** is at 3100 Massachusetts Ave. NW, Washington, DC 20008 (📞 **202/588-7800;** www. gov.uk/government/world/ usa). Other British consulates are in Atlanta, Boston, Chicago, Cleveland, Houston, Los Angeles, New York, San Francisco, and Seattle.

Emergencies Call 📞 **911** for the police, to report a fire, or to get an ambulance. If you have a medical emergency that does not require an ambulance, you should be able to walk into the nearest hospital emergency room (see "Hospitals," below).

Family Travel All parks have a **baby care center** for heating formula, nursing, and so on. But think carefully about whether your child is ready for the theme parks. Too many parents consider an Orlando vacation such a rite of passage that they rush into it too early without considering whether their child will find the experience

overwhelming, or even if they'll *remember* it. I agree with many parenting experts who say that about 3 years old is the minimum age. It's not just that many younger children get wigged out when they see their first costume character, but also because it's no fun for a kid to get turned away from a ride they have their heart set on.

Some experts say kids are not truly ready for the rigors of theme parks until they can walk on their own all day. Whether or not very young children are *advisable,* they are *possible:* Scarier rides have what's called a **child swap.** That provides an area where one adult can wait with a child while their partner rides and then switch off so the other gets a chance. Many rides also have a bypass corridor where chickens can do their chicken-out thing.

Let kids take an active role in planning their vacation. Their excitement will make the going easier. The Walt Disney World website (http://customizedmaps. disney.go.com) provides online maps of its parks, which you can use to highlight a must-see list according to your tastes. With 3 weeks' notice, the resort will print your maps and mail them ahead for free.

Strollers will not be allowed inside most attractions, and they will not be attended in parking sections, so never leave anything valuable in them. Come prepared with a system for

unloading valuables. Also have something that covers the seat; like in parked cars, they get sizzling hot in the Florida sun. Finally, tie some identifying marker (like a white flag, as in "I surrender") to yours so you can identify it amidst the sea of clones.

o **Familiarize yourself with the height restrictions for all rides,** which are posted at the parks' websites and listed on the maps. Universal also keeps physical gauges in front of both its parks. Everything is measured in inches, so if your child is usually measured in centimeters, multiply by 0.393.

o **Bring supplies to kid-proof your hotel room.**

o **Slather your kids in sun lotion.** Florida sun is stronger than you think.

o **Dress kids in bright colors.** You'll spot them faster if you're separated. Some parents even put their phone number on their kids with child safety temporary tattoos (yes, they exist).

o **Dress kids to get wet.** There are water playgrounds, plus frequent rains.

o **Hotels offer "kids eat free" programs**—you pay, they don't. Ask.

- **Theme park strollers are easy, but basic;** they don't recline, and they won't secure kids younger than toddlers. Folding "umbrella" strollers have distinct advantages. They make getting onto trams, monorails, and into other tight spaces easier (not just for you—also for people waiting for you).

- **Bring a picture of your child** or keep one on your mobile phone.

- **Use a walkie-talkie app** such as Voxer or WhatsApp to communicate with your party; the phone carriers are often overwhelmed by the volume at the parks and text messages sometimes arrive with long delays.

Health Your biggest concern is the **sun,** which can burn you even through grey skies on cloudy days. You will be spending a lot more time outdoors than you might suspect—rides take 3 minutes, but some of their lines will have you waiting outside for an hour. Hats are your friends.

Holidays Banks close on the following holidays: January 1 (New Year's), the third Monday in January (Martin Luther King, Jr., Day), the third Monday in February (Presidents' Day), the last Monday in May (Memorial Day), July 4

(Independence Day), the first Monday in September (Labor Day), the second Monday in October (Veterans Day), the fourth Thursday in November (Thanksgiving Day), and December 25. The theme parks are open every day of the year.

Hospitals **Dr. P Phillips Hospital** (9400 Turkey Lake Rd., Orlando; ✆ **407/351-8500**) is a short drive north up Palm Parkway from Lake Buena Vista. To get to **Florida Hospital Celebration Health** (400 Celebration Place, Celebration; ✆ **407/764-4000**), from I-4, take the U.S. 192 exit; then at the first traffic light, turn right onto Celebration Avenue, and at the first stop sign, make another right. Clinics: **Centra Care Walk-In Care** in Lake Buena Vista (12500 Apopka-Vineland Rd., ✆ **407/934-2273;** Mon–Fri 8am–midnight, Sat–Sun 8am–8pm); near the vacation homes south of Disney (7848 W. U.S. 192, Kissimmee; ✆ **407/397-7032;** Mon–Fri 8am–8pm, Sat–Sun 8am–5pm); and by Universal (6001 Vineland Rd.; ✆ **407/351-6682;** Mon–Fri 7am–7pm, Sat–Sun 8am–6pm). In addition, each theme park has its own infirmary capable of handling a range of medical emergencies. If you don't have a car, **EastCoast Medical Network** (✆ **407/648-5252;** www.themedical concierge.com) makes house calls to area resorts for $150 to $275 for most ailments. It's available at all

hours and brings a portable pharmacy, although prescriptions cost more.

Insurance Among many options, you could try **MEDEX** (✆ **800/732-5309;** www.medexassist.com) or **Travel Assistance International** (✆ **800/821-2828;** www.travelassistance.com) for overseas medical insurance cover. **Canadians** should check with their provincial health plan offices or call **Health Canada** (✆ **866/225-0709;** www. hc-sc.gc.ca) to find out the extent of their coverage and what documentation and receipts they must take home.

So what else may you want to insure? You may want special coverage for **apartment stays,** especially if you've plunked down a deposit, and any **valuables,** since airlines are only required to pay up to $2,500 for lost luggage domestically, less for foreign travel.

If you do decide on insurance, compare policies at **InsureMyTrip.com** (✆ 800/487-4722). Or contact one of the following reputable companies: **Allianz** (✆ 866/884-3556; www.allianztravelinsurance. com); **CSA Travel Protection** (✆ 877/243-4135; www.csatravelprotection. com); **MEDEX** (✆ 800/732-5309; www.medexassist. com); **Travel Guard International** (✆ 800/826-4919; www.medexassist.com); **Travelex** (✆ 800/228-9792; www.travelex-insurance.com).

Internet & Wi-Fi Getting online isn't hard. Wi-Fi is now considered an essential amenity, like running water. Most hotels will have free access—sometimes in common areas, sometimes in guest rooms, and sometimes in both places. Walt Disney World's hotels have free Wi-Fi, and so do its theme parks, as do Universal's. (SeaWorld does not yet have free Wi-Fi.) Hotel connections aren't always fast enough to stream movies, but they're usually fast enough for standard uses. Nearly all home rentals come with Internet-connected computers and Wi-Fi.

Language English is the primary tongue, plus some Spanish.

LGBT Travelers Orlando still has a conservative streak, but like most cities, it has come to realize that America welcomes every kind of person. The parks also employ thousands of gay people. As a consequence of all this mainstream visibility, gay visitors to Orlando simply won't need special resources or assistance. Most hotels aren't troubled in the least by gay couples, and gay people can be themselves anyplace. The most intolerant attitudes will come from other guests at the theme parks, who, of course, mostly aren't from Orlando—public displays of affection there are not likely to be attacked, but don't expect a warm reception, either. Sexual affection by

gay people and straight people alike is not celebrated in the parks. Use your intuition—and your common sense.

Mail At press time, domestic postage rates were 34¢ for a postcard and 49¢ for a letter. For international mail, a first-class letter of up to 1 ounce costs $1.15; a first-class international postcard costs the same as a letter. The post office most convenient to Disney and Universal is at 10450 Turkey Lake Rd. (📞 **407/351-2492;** Mon–Fri 9am–7pm, Sat 9am–5pm). A smaller location, closer to Disney, is at 8536 Palm Pkwy., in Lake Buena Vista, just up the road from Hotel Plaza Boulevard (📞 **407/ 238-0223**). If all you need is to buy stamps and mail letters, you can do that at most hotels. For more information, including locations nearest you, go to **www. usps.com** and click on "Calculate a Price." Ask at the theme park Guest Relations desks if mailing your items there will entitle you to a themed postmark.

Medical Requirements No inoculations or vaccinations are required to enter the United States unless you're arriving from an area that is suffering from an epidemic (cholera or yellow fever, in particular). A valid, signed prescription is required for those travelers in need of **syringe-administered medications** or medical treatment that involves **narcotics.** It is extremely important to obtain the

correct documentation in these cases, as your medications could be confiscated; and if you are found to be carrying an illegal substance, officials tend to lock you up first and ask questions later.

Mobile Phones Orlando has the **GSM (Global System for Mobile Communications) wireless network,** which is used by much of the rest of the world. Your phone will probably work in Orlando; it may not work in rural areas. To buy a pay-as-you-go SIM card, ask for a "no-contract" SIM card. Barring those suggestions, phones can be rented from **InTouch USA** (📞 **800/872-7626;** www. intouchusa.com); some car rental outlets do it, too. If you have Web access while traveling, consider a broadband-based telephone service (in technical terms, **Voice over Internet Protocol,** or **VoIP**), such as **Skype** (www.skype.com) or **Vonage** (www.vonage.com), which allows you to make free international calls from your laptop.

The theme parks' new reliance on programming your schedule via apps drains devices quickly. To have enough juice for a 13-hour day, carry a **portable charger,** such as the ones by **Mophie** (www. mophie.com) or **Jackery** (www.jackeryusa.com).

Money This town exists to rake in money. Consequently it places few obstacles between you and the surrender of it. Most ATMs that you'll find are run by third parties, not your bank, which means that you'll be slapped with fees of around $2.50 per withdrawal (around $5 for international visitors). Machines accept pretty much anything you can stick into them. Citibank customers can avoid the usage fee by using the fancy Citibank machines located at most 7-Eleven convenience stores in the area. International visitors should make advance arrangements with their banks to ensure their cards will function in the United States. Also ask your bank if it has reciprocal agreements for free withdrawals anywhere. One institution known to charge international usage fees that are below the industry standard is **Everbank** (✆ **888/882-3837;** www.everbank.com); another is **Charles Schwab** (✆ **866/855-9102;** www.schwab.com), which reimburses ATM fees.

Credit cards are nearly universally accepted. In fact, you *must* have one to rent a car without a hassle. Most places accept the Big Four: American Express, Master-Card, Visa, and Discover. A few places add Diners Club, and some family-owned businesses subtract American Express because of the pain of dealing with it.

Before you leave home, let your issuer know that you're about to go on vacation. Many of them get antsy when they see unexpectedly large charges start appearing so far from your home, and sometimes they

freeze your account in response.

Not only will Orlando clerks almost always neglect to check the purchaser's identification, but also, in the high-volume world of the theme parks, they don't even require signatures for purchases under a certain amount (typically, $25). You just swipe and go. That means you need to be doubly sure to keep your cards safe.

Try not to use credit cards to withdraw cash. You'll be charged interest from the moment your money leaves the slot. *Tip:* There is an exception that the resorts don't sanction, but I certainly do: Instead of using your credit card to draw cash from an ATM, use it to buy Disney Dollars (✆ **407/566-4985,** option 5). They're private scrip (sold at big shops and most guest services desks), valued precisely like U.S. dollars. But they are charged as a purchase, *not* as a cash withdrawal, so there are no additional fees. You can spend them like cash within the respective resorts. Pretty sneaky, sis! Universal sells its own version, Wizarding Bank Notes.

Now that ATMs are common, traveler's checks are nearly dead. Using them, you run the risk of most places declining them. Creditors have come up with **traveler's check cards,** also called **prepaid cards,** which are essentially debit cards loaded with the amount of money you elect

to put on them. They're not coded with your personal information, they work in ATMs, and should you lose one, you can get your cash back in a matter of hours. If you spend all the money on them, you can call a number or visit a website and reload the card using your bank account information.

Travelex Cash Passport (✆ **877/465-0085;** www.cashpassport.com; $3 per ATM transaction) works anywhere MasterCard does; also try **NetSpend** (✆ **866/387-7363;** www.netspend.com; $1 per purchase, $5 per ATM transaction). That one costs $4.

Like traveler's checks, exchanging cash is on the outs, and good riddance, as exchange rates are usurious. Because ATM withdrawals give better deals, old-fashioned exchange desks are few and far between, although you'll still find a few at the airport, at large hotels, at the **Travelex** at Lake Buena Vista Factory Stores (p. 165). If you need to change money, better rates come from banks during regular banking hours (Mon–Fri 9:30am–4pm).

Finding a bank isn't difficult in the "real" world of Orlando around SeaWorld and Universal, but at Walt Disney World, you could use a hand. The nearest bank is the **SunTrust** (1675 Buena Vista Dr., across from Downtown Disney Market-place; ✆ **407/762-4786;** drive-through Mon–Wed, Fri 8am–5pm, until 5:30pm on Thurs).

Newspapers & Magazines Business hotels distribute that shallow McNewspaper, "USA Today," to use as your morning doormat. The local paper, the "Orlando Sentinel" (www.orlandosentinel.com) is less widely available but much better for discovering local happenings. "Orlando Magazine" (www.orlandomagazine.com) is a glossy that covers trends and upscale restaurants. Also see the box on amateur-run websites covering the theme parks on p. 232; those are better for park goings-on.

Packing For the latest rules on how to pack and what you will be permitted to bring as a carry-on, consult your airline or the **Transportation Security Administration** (www.tsa.gov). Also be sure to find out from your airline what your checked-baggage weight limits will be; maximums of around 50 pounds per suitcase are standard. Anything heavier will incur a fee. Paying for the luggage at the airport is often more expensive than online.

If you forget something, there's nothing you can't buy in Orlando. It's hardly Timbuktu. But bring the basics for sunshine (lotion of at least 30 SPF, wide-brimmed hat, bathing suit, sunglasses), for rain (a compact umbrella or a plastic poncho, which costs $8 if you wait until you get into the parks), for walking (good shoes, sandals for wet days), and for memories (camera, storage cards, chargers).

Pets None of the Disney resorts allows animals (except service dogs) to stay on (the only exception being Disney's Fort Wilderness Campground, where you can have your pet at the full-hook-up campsites). The major theme parks offer animal boarding, usually for about $40 per day. Disney offers a single facility, **Best Friends Pet Care,** on the Bonnet Creek Parkway (✆ **407/209-3126;** www.bestfriendspetcare.com). Universal Orlando and SeaWorld will board small pets during the day only.

Universal's three Loews-run resorts allow pets on the property. So do Drury Hotels (p. 220). To find more pet-friendly hotels, two solid resources are **www.petswelcome.com** and **www.dogfriendly.com**.

Stuff You Never Thought to Bring (but Should)

Besides the usual toiletries, recharging cords, and drugs, you might not have thought of these good ideas, too:

- **Earplugs.** Orlando flights are jumping with kids going insane with excitement.
- **Hand purifier.** Turnstiles. Safety bars. Handrails. Furry mice. You're going to be handling a lot of dirty things.
- **Dark-colored clothing.** On almost all flume rides, the seating doubles as a step, so you're bound to stain your butt with a slightly muddy footprint. Also, it's hot and you'll be in lots of photos—and colored shirts show sweat stains.
- **Sandals that fasten.** Water-based rides soak regular shoes and cause pruning. Flip-flops won't always do because they're not hardy and they won't stay on.

- **Skin-tight underwear.** Hot, moist days can cause chafing even in people who rarely experience it. Under Armour or nonpadded bike shorts preempt that.
- **Sunscreen, a hat, and sunglasses.** Okay, so you probably thought of these, but it bears repeating.
- **A mobile phone battery recharger.** Between the My Disney Experience app, Wi-Fi, photos, and social media updating, you'll drain your battery quickly.
- **A superabsorbent shammy.** For lenses and wet children.
- **Pocket-size games.** People talk about rides, but they neglect to mention the hour in line before those exciting 3 minutes. Orlando *is* lines. Bring diversions.

Pharmacies The tourist area hosts mostly national chains. **Walgreens** (7650 W. Sand Lake Rd. at Dr. Phillips Blvd., Orlando; ✆ **407/370-6742**), which has a round-the-clock pharmacy, could, at a stretch, be deemed an outfit with local roots; back in the day, Mr. Walgreen spent the cold months in Winter Park. **Turner Drugs** (12500 Apopka Vineland Rd., Lake Buena Vista; ✆ **407/828-8125**) is not a 24-hour pharmacy, but it delivers prescriptions to most Disney-area accommodations.

Police Call ✆ **911** from any phone in an emergency.

Safety Train kids to approach the nearest park employee in case of **separation.** Never dress kids in clothing that reveals their name, address, or hometown, and unless it's a travel day, remove any luggage tags where this information will be visible. If people can read your address off a tag while you're in line at Jurassic Park, they they'll know you're not at home. Don't leave valuables visible when you park your car. Also, please keep your arms and legs inside the vehicle at all times. Thank you.

Senior Travel Just about every secondary attraction offers a special price for seniors, but the theme parks offer precious little. If you're over 50, you can join **AARP** (601 E. Street NW, Washington, DC 24009; ✆ **888/687-2277**; www.aarp.org) to find out what's being offered in terms of discounts for

hotels, airfare, and car rentals. Before you bite, be sure that the AARP discount you are offered actually undercuts others that are out there. Elderhostel's well-respected **Road Scholar** (✆ **800/454-5768**; www.roadscholar.org) runs classes and programs, both inside the theme parks and around the Orlando area, designed to delve into literature, history, the arts, and music. Packages last from a day to a week and include lodging, tours, and meals. Most are multigenerational; bring the grandkids.

Smoking Smoking is prohibited in public indoor spaces, including offices, restaurants, hotel lobbies, and most shops. Some bars permit it. In general, if you need to smoke, you must go outside into the open air, and in the theme parks there are strictly enforced designated areas.

Taxes A 6.5 to 7 percent sales tax is charged on all goods with the exception of most edible grocery items and medicines. Hotels add another 2 to 5 percent in a resort tax, so the total tax on accommodations can run up to 12 percent. The United States has no VAT, but the custom is to not list prices with tax, so the final amount that you pay will be slightly higher than the posted price.

Telephones Generally, hotel surcharges on long-distance and local calls are astronomical, so you're better off using your **cellphone** or a **public pay telephone.**

Many convenience groceries and packaging services sell **prepaid calling cards** in denominations from $10 to $50; for international visitors these can be the least expensive way to call home. Many public phones at airports now accept American Express, MasterCard, and Visa credit cards. **Local calls** made from public pay phones in most locales cost either 35¢ or 50¢. Pay phones do not accept pennies, and few will take anything larger than a quarter. Make sure you have roaming turned on for your cellphone account.

If you will have high-speed Internet access in your room, save on calls by using **Skype** (www.skype.com) or another Web-based calling program.

For calls within the United States and to Canada, dial 1 followed by the area code and the seven-digit number. **For other international calls,** first dial 011, then the country code, and then proceed with the number, dropping any leading zeroes.

Calls to area codes **800, 888, 877,** and **866** are toll-free. However, calls to area codes **700** and **900** can be very expensive—usually a charge of 95¢ to $3 or more per minute, and they sometimes have minimum charges that can run as high as $15 or more.

For **reversed-charge or collect calls,** and for person-to-person calls, dial the number 0, then the area code and number. If your operator-assisted call is international, ask for the overseas operator.

For **local directory assistance** ("information"), dial ✆ **411;** for long-distance information, dial 1, then the appropriate area code and 555-1212.

Time The continental United States is divided into four time zones: Eastern Standard Time (EST), Central Standard Time (CST), Mountain Standard Time (MST), and Pacific Standard Time (PST). Orlando is on Eastern Standard Time, so when it's noon in Orlando, it's 11am in Chicago (CST), 10am in Denver (MST), and 9am in Los Angeles (PST). Daylight saving moves the clock 1 hour ahead of standard time. Clocks change the second Sunday in March and the first Sunday in November.

Tipping Tips are customary and should be factored into your budget. Waiters should receive 15 to 20 percent of the cost of the meal (depending on the quality of the service), bellhops get $1 per bag, bartenders get $1 per drink, chambermaids get $1 to $2 per day for straightening your room (although many people don't do this), and cab drivers should get 15 percent of the fare. The Disney Dining Plan automatically includes gratuity. Elsewhere, don't be offended if you are reminded about tipping—wait staff are used to dealing with international visitors who don't participate in the custom back home.

Toilets Each theme park has dozens of clean restrooms. Outside of the parks, every fast-food place—and there are hundreds—should have a restroom you can use. Large hotel lobbies also have some.

Visas Citizens of western and central Europe, Australia, New Zealand, and Singapore need only a valid machine-readable passport and a round-trip air ticket or cruise ticket to enter the United States for stays of up to 90 days. Canadian citizens may enter without a visa with proof of residence.

Citizens of all other countries will need to obtain a tourist visa from the U.S. consulate. Depending on your country of origin, there may or may not be a charge attached (and you may or may not have to apply in person). You'll need to complete an application and submit a photo, and your passport must be valid for at least 6 months past the scheduled end of your U.S. visit. If an interview isn't mandated, it's usually possible to obtain a visa within 24 hours, except during holiday periods or the summer rush. Be sure to check with your local U.S. embassy or consulate for the very latest in entry requirements, as these continue to shift. Full information can be found at the **U.S. State Department**'s website, www.travel.state.gov.

Visitor Information Orlando has one of the most responsive and question-friendly visitors'

bureaus in America and it operates a storefront, **Orlando Official Visitor Center** (8723 International Dr.; ✆ **407/363-5872;** www.visitorlando.com; daily 8:30am–6:30pm), in a strip mall on the western side of I-Drive not far north of the Pointe Orlando shopping mall, that's stocked from carpet to rafter with free brochures. Although many, many other places in town (souvenir stands, mostly) claim to offer "official" tourist information, this is the only *truly* official place. Staff is on hand to answer any questions, and its ticket desk has the inside line on discounts.

Kissimmee, the town closest to Walt Disney World, maintains its own tourist office, the **Kissimmee Convention and Visitors Bureau** (1925 E. Irlo Bronson Memorial Hwy./U.S. 192; Kissimmee; ✆ **407/944-2400;** www.floridakiss.com; Mon–Fri 8am–5pm). Its website also lists current discounts. The Kissimmee CVB works with the Orlando bureau, so you won't have to make two trips.

Water Tap water has a distinct mineral taste. Your hotel's pipes are not to blame. Rather, think of Orlando as an island floating over a cushion of water. Most of the city's lakes started, in fact, as sinkholes. The drinking water is drawn from the aquifer, hence the specific flavor and odor. It's safe.

Index

See also Accommodations and Restaurant indexes, below.

General Index

A
Accessible travel, 237–238
Accommodations, 194–226. *See also* Accommodations Index
  best, 4–5
  home rentals, 225–226
  Universal Orlando, 210–211
  Walt Disney World, 196–208
Advance Dining Reservations (ADRs), 24–25
Adventureland, 36–38
Adventurers Outpost, 82
Africa, 82, 85–86
Agent P's World Showcase Adventure, 59
Air travel, 227
A'Lure: The Call of the Ocean, 131
The Amazing Adventures of Spider-Man, 117–118
The American Adventure, 64
American Film Institute Showcase, 77
American Heritage Gallery, 64
Animal Actors on Location!, 112
Animal Kingdom, 81–90
Antarctica, 132
A Pirate's Adventure: Treasures of the Seven Seas, 38
Aquatica, 136
Ariel's Grotto, 44
Artegon Orlando, 167
Asia, 86–87
Astronaut Training Experience, 154
Astro Orbiter, 46
Atlanta Braves, 144
Atlantic Dance Hall, 156

B
Backstage Magic, 97–98
Backstage Safari, 98
The Barnstormer, 45
Baseball spring training, 144
Bead Outpost, 63
Beauty and the Beast—Live on Stage, 75
Beetlejuice's Graveyard Revue, 107
Behind the Seeds, 98
Beluga Interaction Program, 135
Bhaktapur Market, 86
Bibbidi Bobbidi Boutique, 166
Big Thunder Mountain Railroad, 39
Bijutsu-kan Gallery, 65
Blizzard Beach, 91–92
Blue Horizons, 130
Blue Man Group, 157
Blue Spring State Park, 159

Boardwalk Baseball, 138
Bob Marley—A Tribute to Freedom, 158
Boggy Creek Airboat Rides, 161
Bok Tower Gardens, 148
Bruce's Sub House, 60
Busch Gardens Tampa, 139
Bus travel, 230–231
Buzz Lightyear's Space Ranger Spin, 46

C
Calendar of events, 233–236
Campfire sing-along, 52
Camp Jurassic, 119
Canada, 66
Captain EO, 60
Captain Jack Sparrow's Pirate Tutorial, 38
Carkitt Market, 109
Carnival Cruise Lines, 168
Caro-Seuss-el, 123
Car travel and rentals, 228, 238–239
Casey Jr. Splash 'N' Soak Station, 45
Cassadaga, 146
The Cat in the Hat, 124
Center Street (Magic Kingdom), 30
Character meals, 191–193
Characters, Magic Kingdom, 40, 43, 44
Characters in Flight, 94–95
Charles Hosmer Morse Museum of American Art, 147–148
Chase Disney Rewards Visa credit card, 22
Chester & Hester's Dino-Rama, 87
China, 63
Christmas, Florida, 161
Cinderella Castle, 34–36
The Circle of Life, 60
Circus World, 138
City Hall (Magic Kingdom), 31
CityWalk, 157
CityWalk's Rising Star, 158
Climate, 233
Club Cool, 57
Clyde & Seamore, 130
Congo River Adventure Golf, 150
Cornell Fine Arts Museum, 148
Country Bear Jamboree, 40
Cruises (Port Canaveral), 168
Crystal Arts, 30
CSI: The Experience, 140
Curious George Goes to Town, 113

D
Dapper Dans (Magic Kingdom), 30
Das Kaufhaus, 63
A Day in the Park with Barney, 113
Delancey Street Preview Center, 108
De Leon Springs State Park, 159
Der Teddybär, 64
Despicable Me Minion Mayhem, 106

Detroit Tigers, 144
Diagon Alley, 108–109
Dinnertainment, 95
DinoLand U.S.A., 87, 89
DINOSAUR, 87, 89
Dinosaur World, 148
Disabilities, travelers with, 237–238
Disaster!, 107–108
Discounted tickets, 236–237
Discovery Cove, 136–137
Discovery Island, 81–87
Discovery Island Trails, 82
Disney, Roy, 31
Disney Cruise Line, 168
Disney Dining Plan, 22–24
Disney Dollars, 26
Disney Junior—Live on Stage!, 78
DisneyQuest, 93–94
Disney's Animal Kingdom, 81–90
Disney's Contemporary Resort, 149
Disney's Dolphins in Depth, 98
Disney's Fantasia Gardens, 150
Disney's Hollywood Studios, 70–80
Disney's Keys to the Kingdom, 98
Disney's Polynesian Resort, 149
Disney's Winter Summerland, 150
Disney Vacation Club (DVC), 207–208
Disney Water Parks, 91–93
Disney Wilderness Preserve, 160
Dolphin Cove, 131
Dolphin Nursery, 131
Downtown Disney, 94–96, 165–166
Downtown Orlando, 13–14
  accommodations, 224–225
Dr. Doom's Fearfall, 116–117
Dragon Challenge, 122
Dream Along with Mickey, 36
Dudley Do-Right's Ripsaw Falls, 118
Dumbo the Flying Elephant, 43–44

E
The Eighth Voyage of Sindbad Stunt Show, 122–123
The Electrical Boat Parade, 95
Electrical Water Pageant, 52
Eli's Orange World, 167
Emporium, 30
Enchanted Tales with Belle, 43
Enoteca Castello, 64
Enzian, 155
Epcot, 53–70
  best of, 57
  Future World, 54–61
  getting in, 53
  getting the most out of, 54
  history of, 56
  hours, 53
  restaurants, 67–70
  World Showcase, 61–66
  for young children, 59
Epcot DiveQuest, 98

Restaurants

RESTAURANT